x16 - 26
89
118

1 MONTH OF FREE READING

at

www.ForgottenBooks.com

By purchasing this book you are eligible for one month membership to ForgottenBooks.com, giving you unlimited access to our entire collection of over 1,000,000 titles via our web site and mobile apps.

To claim your free month visit:
www.forgottenbooks.com/free626571

* Offer is valid for 45 days from date of purchase. Terms and conditions apply.

ISBN 978-0-267-75469-4
PIBN 10626571

This book is a reproduction of an important historical work. Forgotten Books uses
state-of-the-art technology to digitally reconstruct the work, preserving the original format
whilst repairing imperfections present in the aged copy. In rare cases, an imperfection in
the original, such as a blemish or missing page, may be replicated in our edition. We do,
however, repair the vast majority of imperfections successfully; any imperfections that
remain are intentionally left to preserve the state of such historical works.

Forgotten Books is a registered trademark of FB &c Ltd.
Copyright © 2018 FB &c Ltd.
FB &c Ltd, Dalton House, 60 Windsor Avenue, London, SW19 2RR.
Company number 08720141. Registered in England and Wales.

For support please visit www.forgottenbooks.com

A HISTORY OF OUR RELATIONS

WITH

THE ANDAMANESE.

COMPILED FROM HISTORIES AND TRAVELS, AND FROM THE RECORDS OF THE GOVERNMENT OF INDIA.

BY

M. V. PORTMAN, M.A.I., ETC.,
FELLOW OF THE UNIVERSITY OF CALCUTTA,
OFFICER IN CHARGE OF THE ANDAMANESE.

VOL. II.

CALCUTTA:
OFFICE OF THE SUPERINTENDENT OF GOVERNMENT PRINTING, INDIA.
1899.

UNIV   TO

MAS   NO.:
    930181

CALCUTTA:
GOVERNMENT OF INDIA CENTRAL PRINTING OFFICE,
8, HASTINGS STREET.

DS
491
A5P67
v.2

CONTENTS.

CHAPTER XIV.

PAGE.

Paper by Admiral Sir E. Belcher on notes by Lieutenant St. John—Birth of "Jerry"—Andaman Home moved to Port Mouat—Notes on Port Mouat—Notes on the customs of the Andamanese—Jim is released—Dudhnáth Tewári revisits Port Blair—Notes on the fibres used by the Andamanese—Annual Report for 1866-67—Supposed wreck of a schooner—Mr. Homfray visits the North Andaman—Mr. Homfray's opinion of the Andamanese—Notes and reports—Government letter regarding wrecks on the Andamans—Major N. Davies visits Port Blair—The question of the utility of the Homes raised—Colonel Man succeeds Colonel Ford as Superintendent of Port Blair—His views on the Homes—The Andamanese hospital opened—The Settlement replaced under the Government of India—Wrecks on the Andamans—Colonel Man's report on the Andamanese   513—556

CHAPTER XV.

Captain Anderson takes two Andamanese boys to India—They are transferred to the Burdwán Boys' Orphanage, and die there—Mr. Homfray's notes on the Andamanese—The Andamanese catch runaway convicts—Report on the Andamanese for the year 1869-70—Dr. Day's paper on the Andamanese—Notes on the same—Other papers—Report on the Andamanese for the year 1870-71—General Stewart succeeds Colonel Man as Superintendent of Port Blair—Report on the Andamanese for the year 1871-72—General Stewart's letter on the Andamanese—Mr. Homfray proceeds to the Nicobars—Report on the Andamanese for the year 1872-73—General Stewart visits the distant islands—Employment of the Andamanese—Another visit paid to the distant islands—Mr. Homfray again goes to the Nicobars—Mr. Tuson takes charge of the Andamanese—Review of Mr. Homfray's administration of the Andamanese   .   .   .   .   557—596

CHAPTER XVI.

Mr. Tuson in charge of the Andamanese—Restraint of the Andamanese, and the convict supervision over them, stopped—Syphilis first noticed—Murder of convicts at the Kyd Island Home by the Andamanese—The Andamanese capture runaway convicts—Death of Lípáīa—Mr. Man takes charge of the Andamanese—The Kyd Island murderers arrested and punished—Attempts to civilise the Andamanese—Changes—Capture of runaway convicts by Máīa Bíala—Annual Report for 1875-76—Syphilis—Mr. Man. visits the North and Middle Andaman—Chinamen killed by the Andamanese—Epidemic of ophthalmia—Mr. Man visits the distant islands—Annual Report for 1876-77—Epidemic of measles—Notes on epidemics among the Andamanese—Mr. Man visits the distant islands—Soldiers blown out to sea—Mr. Man visits the distant islands—Syphilis—Notes on the year 1878—Mr. Portman takes charge of the Andamanese—Mr. Man's book on the Andamanese, and comments—Finances of the Andamanese—Mr. Portman attacked by a convict—Visits to the distant islands—Execution of an Andamanese, for murder—Visits to the distant Islands—Annual Report—Hunt after escaped convicts—Visits to the distant islands—Mr. Godwin-Austen takes charge of the Andamanese . 597—646

CHAPTER XVII.

Annual Report for 1880-81—Runaways on the Archipelago Islands—Death of Wologa Jó-la—Ascent of Saddle Peak—Murder of Andamanese on the Archipelago Islands by runaway convicts—Death of Jumboo—Notes on the convict Jemadárs of the Andamanese Department—Report on the year 1881-82—Murder of an Andamanese by convicts—Runaways give trouble—Mr. Godwin-Austen visits the distant islands—Annual Report for 1882-83—Mr. Man takes charge of the Andamanese—Andamanese sent to Calcutta to be modelled—Death of Wói "Tom"—Mr. Portman takes charge of the Andamanese—Survey party arrives—Wreck of the *Scottish Chieftain*—Mr. Portman takes Andamanese to Calcutta—Notes on the year 1883-84—Runaways killed by Andamanese—Islands visited—Annual Report for 1884-85—Burmese convicts escape, and give trouble—Murder of a convict by the Andamanese—Wrecks

CONTENTS. iii

PAGE.

on the coast of the North Andaman—Islands visited—Andamanese taken to Penang and Perák—Annual Report for 1885-86—Islands visited—Mr. Metcalfe takes charge of the Andaman Homes—Mr. Metcalfe visits the distant islands—Value of the Andamanese as pilots for small vessels—Mr. Portman takes charge of the Andamanese—Islands visited—Epidemic of Russian influenza—Case of Tura Né—Islands visited—Trouble with some Andamanese lads—Annual Report for 1890.91—Runaway convicts give trouble—Case of Rang—Cyclone, and report on it—Mr. Portman takes Andamanese to Calcutta—Islands visited—Annual Report for the year 1891-92—Andamanese murder—Wreck on the coast of the Middle Andaman—Andamanese taken to Calcutta—Mr. Bate's account of his treatment by the Andamanese—Ría Badké's case—Mr. Lapicque visits the Andamans—Lókala killed by the Jàrawas—Edible birds' nest collectors' boat blown to Cuddalore from the Andamans in a cyclone—Andamanese operated on—Deaths—Andamanese killed by a crocodile—Andamanese taken to Calcutta—Chípla's case—Chíro's case—Deaths—Cháp's case—Review of our administration of the Andamanese, and the results . . . 647—700

CHAPTER XVIII.

The Jàrawas—Their acquaintance with the people of our Settlement in 1790, *et seq.*—Their numbers—Their relations with the Āka-*Béa*-da—Mr. Corbyn's account—Mr. Homfray's accounts—Wreck of the *Nineveh* on the North Sentinel—Further accounts—General Stewart's account—Further accounts—Expeditions against the Jàrawas—A woman and two children caught, and then released—Further accounts—Mr. Man's notes on the Jàrawas—The North Sentinel expedition—Jàrawas caught and released—Vocabulary of Jàrawa words—Colonel Cadell's note—Jàrawas caught on Rutland Island—Annual Report for 1882-83—Further expeditions—Two Jàrawas caught—Hostility of the Jàrawas—Expedition to Rutland Island—Further expeditions—Further hostility—North Sentinel visited—Further hostility—One Jàrawa caught—Further hostility—Jàrawas killed by Andamanese—Annual Report for 1890-91—Further hostility—Jàrawas move to foreign territory—Murder in Báratán—Expeditions—Jàrawas on Rutland Island—Annual Report for 1893-94—Murder of Andamanese by Jàrawas—Expeditions—Jàrawas caught on Rutland Island—Annual Report for

CHAPTER XIV

Paper by Admiral Sir E. Belcher, on notes by Lt. St John.—Birth of "Jerry"—Andaman Home moved to Port Mouat—Notes on Port Mouat—Notes on the customs of the Andamanese—Jim is released—Dudnáth Tewári revisits Port Blair—Notes on the fibres used by the Andamanese—Annual report for 1866-67—Supposed wreck of a Schooner—Mr Homfray visits the North Andaman—Mr. Homfray's opinion of the Andamanese—Notes and reports—Government letter regarding wrecks on the Andamans—Major N. Davies visits Port Blair—The question of the utility of the Homes raised—Colonel Man succeeds Colonel Ford as Superintendent of Port Blair—His views on the Homes—The Andamanese Hospital opened—The Settlement replaced under the Government of India—Wrecks on the Andamans—Colonel Man's report on the Andamanese.

THE following extracts from a paper published in the "Ethnological Society Transactions, New Series, Vols. 5 and 6," are here given with comments:—

III. Notes on the Andaman Islands. By Admiral Sir Edward Belcher. (From Notes by Lieutenant S. A. St John, Her Majesty's 60th Regiment.)
(Read on January 23rd, 1866.)

In the year 1862 a paper on this subject was read before, and published by the Geographical Society under the title of "A Narrative of an expedition to the Andaman Islands in 1857," by F. J. Mouat, Esq. On that occasion the author of the paper had not himself been in personal or friendly communication with the natives, but obtained his information as to their habits from Dudhnáth Tewári, and another convict, who lived some time with them.

The notes which I have the honour of submitting to you were made by my nephew, Mr. Andrew St. John, Lieutenant in Her Majesty's 60th Regiment, stationed there, and who, from his assiduity in acquiring the Eastern languages, has obtained the post of Assistant Commissioner, at Toungoo, in Burmah, under Colonel Phayre. His Company was stationed at Ross Island, on the South Andaman, from whence he was in the habit of making excursions.

* * * * * *

The Andamanese were chiefly known to navigators from frequent wrecks, as well as for the noted hostile and savage propensities of the natives, defying every effort made to enter into friendly communication.

In 1840 the islands were visited by Dr. Helfer, for scientific purposes, but he was unfortunately murdered by a native immediately on his arrival. By a note in the narrative, we learn that the widow of Dr. Helfer was the niece of Field Marshal Baron Bülow. Accompanied by Madame Helfer he landed, when a savage, concealed behind a bush, transfixed him with a spear: His lady, armed like her husband, drew a pistol from her girdle and shot the murderer on the spot."

* * * * * *

Lieutenant St. John, without preamble, sends me his "Notes on the Andaman Islands, taken during a three days steam trip;" which run thus:—

I. The following notes were taken at the request of the Superintendent of Port Blair (Major Ford, M S.C.) on the occasion of a geological *reconnaissance* made in the Settlement Steamer *Diana* along the Eastern shores of the Andaman Islands, the main object being the search for limestone among the Islands of the Archipelago, and Diligent Straits, (as mentioned by Dr. Mouat), also for pasture and fodder for cattle, and to open communication with a tribe called Bullawadders, said to inhabit the Islands of the Archipelago. To assist in this work a few Burman and Malay convicts were taken with us, also some friendly Andamanese.

II. The expedition started at 11 A.M. on Monday, the 15th of May 1865, and after steaming quietly during the night arrived off the South end of Strait Island (*vide* Lieutenant Blair, and Mouat's chart), about 5 A.M. on the following morning, when we anchored.

III. The very southernmost extreme of this Island is terminated by a light coloured sandstone cliff. It is known to the Malays as the "White Rock" and contains a cave where the noted birds' nests are procured. The boats were lowered and we proceeded to the examination of this cave; but, although the water was sufficiently deep within the cave, we did not care to risk the boats; but, climbing up on the outside, made our way into it on hands and knees over a ledge running along the side of the cave. Inside we found plenty of nests, but in bad condition, as they were full of young birds. The proper time it appears for taking the nests is early in the year when they are beautifully white and hard. We afterwards landed on the beach to the Westward. No traces of Andamanese were observed, though there was a fine stream of water, but doubtless they cross over from the main Island as many traces of pigs were noticed. We examined another cave in an isolated rock, but found it possessed by bats.

(Do these bats prevent the swallows from building or destroy their young? All the caves similarly examined by myself in Burma were never inhabited by both together.—*E. B.*)

IV. Weighed anchor and steamed to the North, making a curve to the Eastward in order to avoid a coral reef which runs out from Strait Island (which from the peculiar growth in patches of some peculiar tree has the appearance of having been cleared). (This has often been remarked upon, and many people insist that a clearing has been made, but such is not the case. The peculiar appearance is due to a cold clay soil on which a special tree grows in patches over the island to the height of about 30 feet only, the remaining jungle rising to over 100 feet.—*M. V. P.*), and passed into the Channel between Guitar and Long Island, when, observing marks placed in the water on both sides (*viz.*, bunches of cane leaves on stakes), dropped the kedge and landed to examine. The two stakes on the Long Island side had evidently been placed to mark a sandy bottom between two reefs of rocks.

(They were mourning garlands placed there by the Andamanese to mark a recent death. Other people have been similarly misled by such stakes in recent times.—*M. V. P.*)

There were no traces of the Malays having been on the shore, but deserted camping spots and an old Andamanese canoe was noticed.

A little to the westward the skeleton of a man bound up in cane leaves was discovered. (This accounts for the mourning garlands.—*M. V. P.*). It was lying on its back on a platform of sticks placed across the forks of a tree about twelve feet above the ground, and had a wooden dish bound over the chest. From the absence of hair and clothes we conclude that he must have been some Andamanese Chief, who was now awaiting until having put off his coat of flesh, he might be restored to the bosom of his tribe. This mode of burial has never been observed in the immediate neighbourhood of Port Blair, as there the bodies are generally concealed in the earth until the bones are fit for use. (Burial in the earth was the most common in use among the Port Blair Sept of the Áka-*Béa*-da.—*M. V. P.*)

Possibly the Andamanese may have changed their custom to avoid European sacrilege. (No.—*M. V. P.*) The skulls, when clean, are painted red and slung round the neck, being used as a box for such small articles as can be put in through the spinal aperture. (Never.— *M. V. P.*). The smaller bones are made into necklaces, and the leg and arm bones are often stuck into the waist belts of the women. (Never.—*M. V. P*).

On steaming further into the channel we observed four Andamanese in a canoe, fishing, but, although both we and our tame Andamanese asserted most loudly that we were Mios (friends) (Māīa meaning merely "Sir") and held out great inducement in the way of "rogo" (pork), they would not approach us, but quietly poled the canoe away into the mangrove swamp. We anchored for the night in a small Bay in the Middle Andaman about three miles North of Long Island.

(*Rongat Harbour.*—This is the first recorded visit to the place. The people at Long Island were of the Kol tribe, and not friendly with the Áka-*Béa*-da Sept of Port Blair, whose language they did not understand.—*M. V. P.*)

V. In the morning we commenced the examination of the southern point of the Bay where a steep and rocky shore seemed to offer promise of limestone; but, much to our disappointment, it proved to be the common igneous rock of former acquaintance, which, from its light colour, probably may have been mistaken by a person who did not land and examine it, for limestone. (The rocks at the South side of Rongat are Serpentine. It is curious that they should have gone so far afield to look for limestone, when the very finest quality of it, in considerable quantity, was to be found close at hand, near South Corbyn's Cove.—*M.V.P.*)

We noticed the fresh footprints of natives in the mud, but were unable to draw them from their cover. An old camp was found, with a broken canoe and fishing net; search was also made for water, but without success. So, weighing anchor, we proceeded to the Northward.

VI. The shore was found to be flat for about two miles, but succeeded by some rounded hills rising to an elevation of about fifteen hundred feet. They lie to the North-West, and though steep, as cliffs, are yet thickly wooded. A little further to the Northward the rocks begin to peep out from the dense foliage, and from an amphitheatre, near the summit of the hill, springs a beautiful limpid stream, which, leaping from rock to rock in its descent, forms, even in the dry season a pretty little cascade. Landing about half a mile to the north, we discovered a large but deserted encampment, with a fine creek running between the hills into the interior. At the foot of the cascade some rocks were found which effervesced with muriatic acid, but Mr. Prince (our engineer), would not pronounce them limestone until he had examined them more satisfactorily.

VII. On awaking next morning I found that we had been under steam for two or three hours and were nearing the Archipelago and South Button, ere reaching which the sharp eyes of our Andamanese discovered smoke to proceed from Outram Island, which they immediately pronounced to indicate the presence of the ferocious Bullawadders; but, as we wished to examine the South Button first, we merely took its bearings, anchoring close to the Button, a mere rock which does not deserve the term of island.

VIII. Here is a bird's nest cave, but it cannot be entered from the sea on account of the smallness of the aperture, (It can be entered from the sea on the south side. The whole island is split up into fissures, which form the caves.—*M. V. P.*), but it is entered from the summit of the island by sliding down the tendrils of a Ficus, and thence by an inclined wedge-shaped rock that seems to threaten to fall on one momently. (This is at present the usual entrance. —*M. V. P.*).

The interior is narrow, but branches out in many directions, the swallow's nests occurring in every nook and cranny. The floor is covered with guano. This Island has long been known to the Malays and Burmese as the "Split Rock." Tamarinds, (?) plantains, and other productions, were found growing.

IX. Quitting the South Button, our course was directed for the spot where the smoke had been noticed on Outram Island. As we neared it, natives were observed on the beach, also a canoe lying off the edge of the coral reef. They did not evince as much alarm as is usual, but reconnoitred us from behind the rocks; and having anchored the steamer, and stored the boat with provisions, we made for the shore. As we neared the shore, they motioned us to keep off, exhibiting by their bows and arrows, no wish to communicate; but upon our making them comprehend that we had food for them, a woman, afterwards found to have visited Ross before, came out from concealment, and desiring the men to lay down their bows and arrows, made signs for us to approach. On our landing they at first exhibited a little shyness, but soon getting more friendly, took us to their encampment, when, as customary, we found most of their valuables and children removed to the bush.

We discovered that they belonged to a race which inhabits the South Andaman, being recognised by our own Andamanese, and also having in their possession an iron pot. We were unable to induce them to accompany us; so, having given them plenty of food, we returned to the steamer and pursued our homeward route along the coast, without discovering any further traces of natives.

(This is the end of Lieutenant St. John's narrative, and Sir Edward Belcher then continues) :—

As these notes were accompanied by short descriptions, and I would not introduce any matters which were not literally derived from personal observation, I wrote to Lieutenant St. John's parents to give me a decided answer before I committed myself. And I am happy to say, that several other very interesting matters were extracted from his correspondence. Indeed, it occurred to me, that, even if they were indirectly the cause of further question, resulting from discussion here, that it might evoke from others who succeed him distinct replies. I say others, because he has now gone to Burmah. He describes the climate of the Andamans as very healthy, although at first relaxing to Europeans.

"The day's march" was merely an expedition of his own, as he states, " he has been the only one to go into the interior, " and he " *saw* the dances performed." These dances were performed when he went on shore with the friendly natives during the steam trip. He observes: "I daresay it would have delighted you to have seen me walking arm in arm on the beach with a savage naked as he was born. These natives are very funny fellows, and clever, but not to be trusted ; their character being exactly that of a spoiled child, so that you must always go about armed." (Very correct.—*M. V. P.*)

NOTES FROM A DAY'S MARCH INTO THE INTERIOR.

The People.—The Andamans are a short, thick-set race (about five feet high) and of a jet-black hue. Their features are generally those of the Negrillo, but vary in a most extraordinary manner, some having almost hooked noses. Their hair when allowed to grow, is short and woolly, but the head is always kept closely shaved (?) ; some few allow a little on the upper lip. (And are very proud of it, when they can grow it.—*M. V. P.*)

They possess no clothing beyond belts and cords made from twisted bark ; (No.—*M. V. P.*) the woman wearing a leaf in front and a bunch of bark behind.—(No.—*M. V. P.*) They paint their persons in patterns with red and white paints ; and when sick, cut the part affected, all over with a sharp shell, (Never with a shell.—*M. V. P.*) or bit of glass.

Very little has been ascertained as to their marriage laws ; but, as far as we have been able to make out, the man only remains with a woman until a child is born and weaned, and then seeks another wife. (Quite incorrect. A statement which has been much quoted since, and has led to error.—*M. V. P.*)

They are excessively quick and clever, delighting in a hoax, so as to enjoy a good laugh over it. In disposition very affectionate, but, like all children, angry when thwarted. They are passionately fond of tobacco, although in their wild state they do not smoke. They are not addicted to drinking spirits.

The South Island is believed to belong to four tribes under separate Chiefs; these have their own districts round which they wander— never remaining long in one place, keeping generally to the sea-shore, and entering the jungle only to cross from one side to the other.

(Correct of the Ár-*yāuto* Septs only.—*M. V. P.*)

Their camps consist of a circle of huts under the trees just above high water mark, and these huts, at the best, consist merely of four upright sticks, two long in front and two short behind, just high enough for a man to sit under, and are slightly thatched with cane leaves.

(The above is a description of the small temporary hunting hut only.—*M. V. P.*)

Their food consists of fish, turtle, dugongs, shell-fish, cuttle-fish, and wild pigs. The latter abound throughout the islands, and are very good eating (?). No larger animals are likely to exist, or their bones would most certainly have been found in their camps.

The Andamanese have always described four races, *viz*:—

The Bullawadders, inhabiting the Archipelago.
The Eari-wadders, inhabiting the Middle Andaman.
The Jerri-wadders, inhabiting the Rutland Island.
The Bojan-ee-jidah, inhabiting the South Island.

The latter always describe the Bullawadders as friendly, but Eari-wadders and Jerri-wadders as hostile, savage, and terrible with the bow.

On a voyage in the steamer round Rutland Island, the only Andaman native we saw belonged to the Bojan-ee-jidah tribe, (the same as our tame Andamanese). We constantly questioned them on the subject, and they remarked whenever a nice position for a camp was noticed, that they attributed it to the Bojan-ee-jidahs, all the bad places to the Jerri-wadders, and from this we concluded that the true meaning of this latter term was as yet obscure, or that they had a tradition of a tribe coming from the Little Andamans or Nicobar Islands.

One of the most peculiar features in the character of the Andamans is their custom of dancing. As yet only two kinds have been observed—the common friendly dance, called Jig-dah-dah, (?), (dah being only the noun termination, the real word is jig), (Jeg-da, "an assemblage" for a dance and feast of a ceremonial nature.--*M. V. P.*), which is generally performed at a meeting between the tribes; and another, (the name of which I have forgotten), which is performed every night.

These dances consist in hopping violently on one foot, and swinging the arms backwards and forwards to the time of a song which is kept up by one man, the women clapping their hands loudly and joining in the chorus. The time is very often beaten on what we call a dancing board; that is, a hollow piece of hard wood in the form of an ancient shield, which being placed on the ground with the hollow downwards, is stamped on by one of the party who keeps it steady by placing the other foot on the pointed end. Places are changed constantly during these performances much after the manner of our country dances.

(The above is not a very good description of the Andamanese dance. —*M. V. P*)

The night dance seems to partake more of a religious character, (No.—*M. V. P.*), and is kept up nearly the whole night, the song being always led by one of the Chiefs or elders. The Chiefs are always young or middle aged men (No.—*M. V. P.*), the old ones apparently retiring from office, and never partaking in the dance. (Incorrect—*M. V. P.*)

On several occasions I have partially seen these dances; but, on one occasion, had the opportunity of witnessing the complete performance.

We were in search of runaway convicts, and had anchored for the night in MacPherson's Straits. On the shore were several fires which indicated the presence of Andamans. These we intended visiting in the morning with the view of inducing them to go with us to Ross.

But we had scarcely made everything secure for the night before

3 x

we heard shouts from the shore, which, as our own Andamanese declared, denoted their wish to come on board. Manning our boat I pulled in the direction of the sound, and soon descried some dim outline in the water at the edge of the mangroves; they were natives, who immediately crowding into the boat, seem delighted to make our acquaintance.

On returning to the vessel, we found that they were all men in a delightful state of nature, not even carrying a bow and arrow.

They were soon engaged tucking into the food we offered them, and when replete, of course went in for a dance, greatly to our disgust, as we were much tired. Next morning we were visited by two of their own canoes, who requested us to visit their camp. I believe the invitation was intended for several days, but as that would have proved too much of a good thing, we merely accepted it for a morning entertainment.

I won their hearts by getting into one of their canoes and paddling about—in all probability the first exhibition they had witnessed of a European so engaged.

(Lieutenant St. John here makes a very common error. He thinks, as many others have thought since, that he was the first to see anything of the Andamanese, forgetting that the Islands had been occupied for seven years, and that friendly relations with some of the Andamanese had existed for three years. He ignores Mr. Corbyn's work with them, and also Mr. Homfray's. Indeed, from the whole of his accounts he would seem to intentionally ignore Mr. Homfray's presence on the *Diana*, and the fact that it was Mr. Homfray with whom the Andamanese were friendly, and whom they had come to see.—*M. V. P.*)

On reaching their camp we were each taken in charge. I was led off by one of the swells to his shed, and made to sit in the bosom of his family. I afterwards presented him with my shirt, then tinted of a lovely red, resulting from their frequent embraces. This red is the only thing one has to fear from them, as they are quite free from parasites, not having a stitch of clothes or a hair on their bodies (?). It is composed of a kind of clay mixed with grease. The dance was soon commenced by the head man of our party of Andamanese, with a bow and arrow in his hand; the others sitting under their huts, myself in the middle, looking on and clapping hands. Our Andaman finished by leading out the women of the other party who carried on the dance, which was finished by Chiefs of the encampment. The dancing finished, two Chiefs standing in the centre—grasped each other by the right hands, and for a few minutes gazed steadily into each other's eyes.

On our arrival no articles whatever could be observed in the camp; but, by means of presents we obtained some bows, arrows, earthen pots, and adzes. Their custom is to hide on the approach of strangers women, children, and effects in the jungle.

* * * * * *

The jungle on the main island is so dense, that it is impenetrable. The natives are not so bad now as formerly, and the clergyman, Mr. Corbyn, has learned a little of their language. They are very ugly, (?) not unlike Hottentots. Major Ford is the Superintendent, and there are about ten different officers. Their houses are first-rate, and the food good: in fact I find it too civilised. There are no ladies at Ross Island, and only one at Viper Island, the wife of the Native Infantry Officer.

I have been in the jungle frequently, but find it hopeless on account of its density and the height of the trees; there are plenty of birds, if you could only shoot them. I go out frequently, pig-hunting, in the jungle, and find it better for one's health than remaining at home: the sport is good, we run them with dogs, and then spear them. It is the only sport we have, and I have the honour to be the only Englishman who has taken to it. Excepting the Burmans, probably no one has seen so much of the interior as myself. It is a curious fact that these savages make beautiful baskets, nets, and earthen pots, though the latter are rare. They are made like the ancient British, but thinner; and I also think it will be found that they are used for burial purposes, though very little, at present, is known of the habits of these people. (The pots are not used for burial purposes.

—*M. V. P.*) I feel convinced that when thoroughly investigated some light will be thrown on the ancient remains in Europe.

Of the animals.—At present a peculiar kind of pig, and rats, are found, although there were some foot-prints supposed to be those of a tapir, observed some years ago. The bones of a recent dugong were found some short time since in an Andaman camp.

An Andaman camp is composed of just two or three little huts perched between two or three trees above high-water mark, and near a water course. On the ground you will find old baskets beautifully made of cane, nautilus shells, skulls of pigs and turtle, a heap of cockle and other marine shells, and perhaps a dancing board, as described. They go quite naked, with the exception of a belt of cord round the loins, and cords also round the wrists and *ankles*, (Never.—*M. V. P.*), frequently or generally a necklace of human bones round the neck.

But they are not cannibals, as formerly supposed.

Arrows are of four kinds, *viz.* :—

I.—Broad iron head, moveable and attached to wooden shaft by a cord; no feathers.

II.—Long bamboo shaft, wooden head, with iron point, barbed; no feathers.

III.—Bamboo shaft, wooden point, no feathers.

IV.—Bamboo shaft, four wooden points, no feathers.

Bows.—Very strong, broad and flat inside, always in the shape of the line of beauty; *i. e.*, the lower part bent backwards (S shape.) (The South Andaman Bow.—*M. V. P.*)

The cord is made of the twisted inner bark of trees.

A cord is worn on the left wrist, to prevent the bow string cutting it, as it snaps very close to the bow.

The arrow is held between the thumb and the second joint of the forefinger. (Sometimes.—*M. V. P.*)

Pot.—Earthern not strong, carried when travelling in a *sling* made of cane. (Wrong, in a cane *basket.*—*M. V. P.*)

Fishing net.—Mesh similar to our landing net.

Fish basket.—Constructed of cane beautifully woven, it is carried over the shoulder, to collect shell-fish.

(It is not a fish-basket only, but is also used for many purposes.—*M. V. P.*)

Adze.—A piece of iron secured into a wooden handle. No iron is found on the islands, except that which may be obtained from wrecks.

Shells are generally used for knives as well as *shaving* purposes. (Never.—*M. V. P.*)

Water vessels.—Large cylinders hollowed out of wood.

Canoes.—Hollowed out of light trees (Sterculiaceæ), propelled in shore by long bamboos; off shore by small roughly made paddles, similar to the sand spades of children at watering places.

These canoes easily upset; but all Andamanese swim like fish; they soon right them again.

The nautilus-pampilius is used for drinking cups, and also for baling the canoes.

(Lieutenant St. John's notes, read by the light of our later and more complete knowledge, show him to have been an intelligent and acute observer, and had he been placed in charge of the Andamanese he would doubtless have done very valuable work.—*M. V. P.*)

During April 1866 the first instance of an Andamanese child being born in the Homes occurred. Moriarty's wife was confined in the Home on Ross Island during the absence of her husband, who was hunting.

Mr. Homfray remarked that all the Andamanese men retired from the hut where the woman was, and the other married women attended to the case, refusing all outside medical aid. The child was first bathed in cold water and then warmed over a fire. He also noticed the practice of naming the unborn child, and of giving it a distinguishing Nickname after its birth, and added that all the elderly women "who retain their milk for a long time help in rearing the child. Few children are born alive, and those that are, seldom live long." He thought it probable that the race would soon become extinct.

The Andamanese now began to assist in recapturing runaway convicts, and were most useful.

In May 1866 Mr. Homfray moved the Andaman Home from Ross Island to Port Mouat, which station he had been directed to open, and went himself to live there. He had some idea of persuading all the people on the Western Coast, to as far north as Interview Island, to come in. Colonel Ford had a high opinion of the strategical value of the occupation of Port Mouat, both from the point of view of establishing friendly relations with the aborigines, and also with the idea of catching the runaway convicts, who used to go across there and put out to sea on rafts.

The first Home was built on the shore a little to the Westward of Mount Augusta, and Mr. Homfray lived for some time in it. The Septs of the Áka-*Béa*-da who inhabited Port Blair did not at all approve of this change, for they were jealous of the Port Mouat Sept, with whom they had had many fights, and feared that the latter would now obtain all the presents.

Mr. Homfray noticed that, as in Port Blair, (and as we have found later, in Stewart's Sound), the Harbour of Port Mouat was inhabited by two Septs, one living on the Northern side of the Harbour, and the other on the Southern side. These latter were hostile when Mr. Corbyn visited the Harbour, and he was attacked there. Pótea, and Bíra were the two Chiefs of this Sept, (the former being the man who kept Dudhnáth in confinement in 1858), and they ranged over the whole of the Labyrinth Islands, and all the country from Port Mouat to the Western end of MacPherson's Straits. They were friendly with the Rutland Islanders, and had their head-quarters on Redskin Island.

The Sept inhabiting the Northern half of the Harbour, to as far as ten miles to the northward along the sea coast, was called Áuto-*Burko*-da, the Chief of which was Máia Wọloga-Jó-la. The people of this Sept were tall and strong and were much feared by the other Áka-*Béa*-da. From their northern limit up to Port Campbell resided another Sept called Eon-la-da. (Yāōla-da, the name of that coast —*M. V. P.*)

Andamanese inhabited the South side of Port Campbell, at Rāō-luntá-bud, the Chief of that place being Māīa Iro-la. The Northern half of Port Campbell was inhabited by yet another Sept. All these Septs kept to their own limits except when invitations were issued for a ceremonial assemblage and dance, called *Jeg*-da. The headquarters of the Āūto-*Burko*-da were at Mount Augusta, then called *Wara-báranga-bárāīj*-da. The Port Blair Septs asked for a separate Home to be built for them at Tytler Ghat, in order to avoid quarrels, and in August 1866 this was built, Mr. Homfray clearing the hill at the back and having a house for himself there.

At this time he practically lived with the Andamanese, and though he never obtained much scientifically accurate information regarding them, and in relating what he saw was apt to arrive at very erroneous conclusions, he certainly knew the people and their ways, had great influence over them, and was much liked.

The murderer "Jim" had kept away until now, but in June 1866 he turned up at the Port Mouat Home, hoping to be forgiven; Mr. Homfray, however, arrested him and sent under a guard to Ross Island, intending to send him to Moulmein to be under the charge of Mr. Redpath, a schoolmaster there, who had formerly been at the Andamans with Colonel Tytler. This gentleman was, however, not willing to receive him, so he was kept on Ross. The other Andamanese interceded for him.

Mr. Homfray remarks during this month that there was much sickness, and that four children had been stillborn. He says that, when in mourning the Andamanese cover themselves with olive ? (grey.—*M. V. P.*) coloured earth, do not put on Kōīób (Red ochre and oil), do not eat pork, and burn, instead of eating, honeycombs. They also shave the head of the corpse, leaving only a small string of hair at the back.

"The Andamanese were not cannibals, and do not eat oysters."

As an instance of Mr. Homfray's misapprehension of their customs I quote the following, which, with other incorrect details about the marriage ceremonies, was for long accepted as correct. He states:—

"Jeedgo" means "a bride," and when a married woman becomes

pregnant, her name is changed from 'Jeedgo' to 'Chana,' meaning "a married woman."

By "Jeedgo" Mr. Homfray may have meant "Jádi-Jog," a spinster, or "Jidga," the Flower Name of some particular spinster. "Chána" is a Honorific applied to elderly women, and to a married woman who has become a mother, however young she may be.

In July 1866 the Port Blair Sept came over to Port Mouat in such large numbers as to alarm the Āūto-*Búrko*-da, there being at one time as many as 100 of the former in the Port Mouat Home. Some parties remained at Aberdeen to try and help Jim whom they knew to be a prisoner on Ross, and they used to wander about that Island, and go off to newly arrived vessels to beg for tobacco and other luxuries.

Mr. Homfray noticed at the change of the Monsoon in October 1866 that, at these changes, the Andamanese Septs move about according to some regular system. "The Port Blair septs go to a place some three miles south of Aberdeen until after the North-East Monsoon has fairly set in; in April, at the end of that Monsoon, they shift again to the North of the Harbour. If a man is absent from his tribe for a lengthened period he seems to know, on his return, exactly where to find them, according to the time of the year."

He again visited, in this month, the Archipelago Islands, and met with several of those people who live in the Northern half of that Group. They were in great distress at having lost their canoes during some stormy weather.

He observes that fifteen births had occurred during the past three months, in the Home, but that not a single child has survived. (The new diet he was introducing was probably the cause of this.—*M.V.P.*)

During November, 1866, four more deaths, in this case of adult Andamanese, occurred. Mr. Homfray remarks :—

"It is curious that the Andamanese seem to know 24 hours before that a person is going to die, by observing the nerves, muscles, and eyes; and if these are weak they at once give up all hopes and begin to collect leaves and cord for the interment."

In three instances he managed to cure the patient after his tribesmen had given up all hope, which surprised them, and gave them confidence in his treatment, though at first he always had to take a portion of the medicine he wanted them to swallow, in order to show them that they were not going to be poisoned. He entertained hopes of their mental and moral improvement, and that they would settle down to an agricultural life, but the wish was father to the thought.

He had heard of a head-quarter camp between Port Campbell and Port Meadows, called Miliatoh-deh, where there was a Lagoon, and high grass and bamboos; also large fine huts. (Māi-li-Tilek was probably meant, where a permanent Éremtága encampment existed.— *M. V. P.*)

During November, Jim having received, as Colonel Ford cousidered, sufficient punishment, was released before a large gathering of the different Septs. These were first collected, with some difficulty, at Port Mouat, and Mr. Homfray then proceeded to Ross and brought Jim, who was marched across by the police and housed for the night in the hulk *Erin-go-bragh*, where the convicts engaged in clearing Port Mouat lived, and where the other Andamanese could not approach him.

They, not understanding what was about to happen, were in a great state of curiosity and excitement, and Mr. Homfray had to precede Jim's party about a mile in order to remove any Andamanese who might be watching, telling them that he had only gone to bring vegetables for them. At 4 P.M. on the following day Mr. Homfray arranged a Durbar of the Chiefs and principal Andamanese, grouping them in a circle with their wives behind them, and leaving a passage by which Jim could be brought in. Mr. Homfray stood in the centre, with armed Convict Police by him, and addressed the Andamanese, requiring them to promise that they would prevent murders in the future. Moriarty acted as interpreter. Jim was then brought in and handed over to his friends, and a great crying ensued, during which the others blamed him for not having escaped before. They said they had been waiting at Aberdeen for several days in the hope of helping him, but he replied that the police guard had watched him too closely. They then smeared him over with red ochre and had a dance.

Human nature among the lower classes seems to be the same whatever the race of people may be. Very similar conversations have ensued on the release of English convicts, between themselves and their "pals," and the entire mental attitude of the Andamanese in this affair is what one looks for among the English.

The Homes seem to have become very popular, once the isolation and restraint of Ross Island was abolished, and the daily average number of Andamanese in them at this period was 100.

In December, 1866, Dudhnáth Tewári, ex-convict No. 276, who had escaped to the jungle in April, 1858, and had lived for a year with the Andamanese, revisited Port Blair while in the service of Major Wraughton, Assistant Commissary General, who stopped there in the *Arracan* while on his way from Calcutta to Rangoon. Mr. Homfray took Dudhnáth to the Andaman Home, and he was at once recognised by the Andamanese, and some of the men appeared glad to see him, though the women abused him for leaving them, and especially for abandoning his wife when she was pregnant.

Mr. Homfray took the opportunity of his presence in the Settlement to test the accuracy of Dudhnáth's statements to Dr. Walker regarding his wanderings, and found them to be fairly accurate. Mr. Homfray says:—

"Dudhnáth was taken by, and lived with the Labyrinth Island Sept, of whom Māia Pótea, a man then of about thirty-five years of age, was, and still is the Chief. (1866.) After Dudhnáth had lived with them for some time a girl named Lipa was given to him in marriage, and she, unfortunately, had a miscarriage; this woman is still alive, stout, and happy, and must be now about 25 years of age. Knowing that her husband Dudhnáth is still alive she yet remains unmolested by any of the Andamanese. (The real reason being that none of them would have anything to do with a woman who had been the wife of a native of India, so much do they dislike them.—*M. V. P.*) Her title is changed to "Módo," signifying "a deserted bride," or woman who has lost her husband while young, and without becoming a mother."

(Módo or Móda was merely her Flower Name, and her retention of it showed that her marriage with Dudhnáth was lightly regarded by the Andamanese. Shakespeare in King Lear, Act III, Scene IV, gives another meaning for Módo, which, in this application, is not more incorrect than Mr. Homfray's.—*M. V. P.*)

" Māia Pótea and Módo Lipa were absent from the Home at the time Dudhnáth visited it. The Andamanese call him " Thoorah Ram-o-ko-lah," meaning the person who is always saying " Thobah Ram," which means in Hindustani " For shame, O God," which he used constantly to be saying to everything he did not approve of."

(I doubted the correctness of this derivation, and on asking the Andamanese, they said the name was Tóra Rámoko-la, pure Andamanese words meaning Tóra, (a common Andamanese name for a man or woman, which they had given to Dudhnáth as a distinguishing name amongst themselves), Rámoko, " a bundle", (because he always carried his property in large bundles, or because he accumulated much property), an Andamanese Nickname given to distinguish him from the other Tóra's.—*M. V. P.*)

" The Andamanese encountered the runaway convicts of Dudhnáth's party in 1858, at MacPherson's Straits, when in pity they spared this man only, perhaps owing to his not having been killed after many wounds, and carried him over to Redskin Island. At different times he visited Rutland and all the Labyrinth Islands, Port Mouat, and even Port Campbell. In the fight at Aberdeen in the year 1859 several Tribes were present, *viz.*, the Port Campbell South Tribe, the Port Mouat North and South Tribes, and the Labyrinth and Rutland Island Tribes, about 250 men in all. Most of the Andamanese that took part in it are yet alive, and are now living peacefully at the Home. They often speak of it. Their object was to get iron in large quantities. None of them were wounded, nor did they fear fire-arms in those days, and they say the shots fell close to, and all around them. The women helped in carrying the loads. The Port Mouat South Tribe led the fight, of whom Māia Ria-lola was the Chief. This is the same Tribe whom Mr. Corbyn met at the south of Port Mouat in 1863, and by whom, but for Topsy, he would have been attacked ; they were then taking the iron out of portions of a wreck which had floated in to the harbour. Mr. Corbyn called the chief " Cassar," and took him to Ross. He has since died, and his tribe has divided and married with others. There were two other runaway convicts, named by the Andamanese Rema-lolah, and Pare-lolah ; the former was Sudloo, who lived awhile with the South Port Blair Tribe, and the latter a Panjabi, who lived with the North Port Blair Tribe."

(With regard to their account of the battle of Aberdeen, I would remark that the Andamanese are great braggarts. They certainly *feared fire-arms* excessively at that and all other times. The names above quoted as given to the two other convicts, pure Andamanese words, support the theory advanced by me to account for my suggested derivation of the name given to Dudnáth.—*M. V. P.*)

In January 1867 the Andamanese began to vacate the Homes for, as usual, as Mr. Homfray remarks, while quite willing to live with us in the rains, when they want shelter, they like the life in the jungle in the dry weather, for then there are no leeches, (though there are ticks in myriads,) they are able to get about quicker, and the pigs are easily caught as they come to the few fresh water streams existing, to drink.

In February, 1867, the Port Blair Sept visited the Port Campbell Sept, and after a short interval the visit was returned. On each occasion much ceremonial was observed, and dances took place. Mr. Homfray observed for the first time that the Andamanese bartered articles with each other, and thought they had learnt this custom from us, whereas in reality it had been an ancient custom of their own. The Āūto-*Búrko*-da were seen bartering rice, tobacco, and dogs, being all presents received from Mr. Homfray, with the Northern Septs who gave them water-buckets and mats in exchange. Whenever visitors came to the Home they always brought honey, when in season, and pork, and then danced, after which they were given turtle and fish. Each Sept reserves a right of *venue* in its own water and ground, and before a stranger can hunt there he must obtain permission or a fight would ensue. Poaching is indeed one of the greatest of crimes among the Andamanese.

In the month of March 1867, during a big meeting between the

Shoal Bay Sept of the Áka-*Béa*-da, and a Sept of the *Puchikwár* Tribe, a quarrel occurred about some trifle which resulted in a serious fight, in which the Chief of Shoal Bay was killed by a *Puchikwár*, and several other people were wounded. Mr. Homfray notes, with truth —

"At the most petty occurrence the Andamanese instantly draw their bows, fire, and then run away to some distant place. They will never stand up to a regular fight."

During this month there was an Agricultural Exhibition on Ross Island, and the Andamanese got a prize for fibres. Mr. Homfray thus describes them :—

Eole-bud-dah.—The bark of a creeper supposed to be the best fibre in the world, with which the men string their bows and make twine.

Pelitah —Also the bark of a creeper which the women collect for making small fish nets, and mats, and twine.

Ahlo-bud-dah.—The bark of a wild *Hibiscus* used by the men for cord rope and large turtle nets. This is commonly used in Burma for making gunny bags and rope."

Of these fibres the first, *Yólba*-da, is fairly good, but will not stand exposure to wet; the second, *Pilita*-da, is a fibre containing a sap which causes it to turn black on exposure to the air, and is very brittle and strengthless; the third *Álaba*-da is the most valuable fibre of the three, and the ropes made from it are strong and serviceable. It is curious that the Andamanese call beer *Yólba*-l'áka-*rais*-da or "the juice of the *Yólba*," from its taste.

They have many peculiar superstitions and customs regarding the use of these fibres.

Mr. Homfray visited the North Sentinel Island during this month, this being the first visit paid to it. He did not land, but saw ten men on the beach who were naked, with long hair, and were shooting fish with bows and arrows. The friendly Andamanese with him said they were Jurrahwallas, who are not friendly to them, owing to an encounter some years ago between that Tribe on Rutland Island, and the Áka-*Béa*-da, in which the Jàrawa Chief was wounded. "They are said to inhabit the Little Andaman and other adjacent islands to the south of the Great Andaman, and to speak a different language."

(Although the Andamanese were wrong in supposing that the people encountered on Rutland Island were from the North Sentinel, yet they rightly assigned them all to one Group of Tribes—*M. V. P.*)

The following is Colonel Ford's Report on the Andamanese for the year 1866-67:—

"Mr. J. N. Homfray, in charge of the Andaman Home, has maintained that influence and control over the Andamanese, which is so satisfactory, (and which has already been reported to Government,) that he has extended his acquaintance and good understanding with other and more distant tribes; and a feeling of confidence in the good will that is demonstrated towards them by the inhabitants of this Settlement, has now extended over the Tribes of the South, and Southern half of Middle Andaman, including Interview Island, where Dr. Mouat's expedition was formerly attacked, as well as those who inhabit the islands of the Eastern Archipelago. The Islanders of the North Andaman, who are said to speak a different language from the Islanders with whom we are acquainted, are still opposed to us, as will be related further on. But, seeing how our good understanding has already spread, no doubt, in course of time, they will hear of the good will that is desired in this Settlement with all aboriginal tribes, and eventually they will, as others have done, come and see, and realise this for themselves. The opportunity of extending our acquaintance with the tribes of the Middle Andaman, more particularly those of its west coast, has been facilitated by the removal of the Andaman Home in May 1866, from Ross Island to the new Settlement of Port Mouat, which place is well suited from its centrality as a Home.

"The Andamanese who originally frequented this Station may be termed the North Port Mouat Tribe called by themselves "O-to-boor-ko-das." Another tribe, which may be named the South Port Mouat Tribe, is called "Ter-moo-goo-das" (Termugu-da). They, too, are associated with the Rutland Islanders, called the "Chow-gullah-the-otto-wallahs" (*Chāōga*-l'ót-*yāūto*-da\). With the Rutlanders are included, for convenience, the inhabitants of such of the Labyrinth Islands as are known to us.

"It appears that until our occupation of Port Mouat, the Port Blair tribes had but little intimacy with those above-named, each keeping strictly to their own side of the hilly ridge that runs longitudinally, and divides the two Ports, which highlands appear to have been always regarded as a boundary line, separating the east and west coasters. Now these tribes freely visit and have a friendly understanding with each other.

"In addition to the above the following tribes have visited the new Home at Port Mouat during the year:—The Port Campbell North and South Tribes. The Port Meadows North and South Tribes. Eastern Archipelago tribe. The South of Middle Andaman tribe called " Ellah-ka-kole" ("*Ér*-l'áka-*kól*-da" "the country of the Kol tribe"—*M. V. P.*)

"Thus a friendly feeling now exists with more than twelve tribes (Septs—*M. V. P.*) or four more than those with whom we were on good terms in the previous year. Our influence, therefore, may be said to extend over the southern half of the Great Andaman, or a space of some 70 miles in length by an average of 15 in width.

" Mr. Homfray states of the races, "there must be at least 600 on whom I could depend, and trust myself, and whose languages are known to us."

" During 1866-67 Mr. Homfray states.—"That their visits to the Home have been frequent, and that the books of the Home show that no less than 25,235 Andamanese received relief in food, which was principally during the monsoon months, when it is difficult for them to provide themselves, and many die of exposure. This shows a number of 1867 souls thus assisted over those of the year 1865-66; this increase being caused by our new acquaintance with the Middle Andamanese. These people, of course, carry back with them to their friends and neighbours the news of our hospitality, and thus it is that the more northern Andamanese may eventually be reached." (Quite correctly surmised.—*M. V. P.*)

" Of life at the Home, Mr. Homfray states, he was a good deal thrown back for the first few months after the removal of the Home, as was to be expected, when he had to establish it at, and, apart from, a new and somewhat remote station. When the new Home (temporary thatched building) was constructed however, matters progressed.

"During the last six months, says Mr. Homfray, "I got them to make canoes, fishing nets, mats, and baskets, and hope this year to get them to help me in building huts (to which work they seem to have no natural aptitude, (!) however, like the inhabitants of Little Andaman) (of whom no one knew anything then—*M. V. P.*) and to cultivation."

"Mr. Homfray's daily intercourse with these people has afforded him the opportunity of making many interesting notes on the character, habits, and customs of this people. He remarks, "naturally the Andamanese have very great fear of strangers, a feeling doubtless much worked upon by their having been formerly kidnapped away and sold as slaves in distant lands. Their fear is greatly augmented by their belief in evil spirits, and they formerly looked upon all foreigners as demons, for they could not comprehend their colour, clothes, or language." Mr. Homfray remarks, "it is now generally understood that they know no Supreme Being;" (wrong.—*M. V. P.*) but he has learnt "that they have some belief in a destroying spirit, and some paradise to which all who die fly to, and rest in." They believe in ghosts, and hence fear to move about in the dark. On the death of one of their tribesmen, they instantly desert the encampment for fear of encountering the ghost of the deceased, returning after a month has elapsed. One of their objects in wearing skulls and bones about their body is as talismans to protect them from any destroying spirit, or any mortal enemy they may be attacked by. They regard the sun and fire, not as objects of worship, but as a comfort to them in keeping their naked bodies warm and free from insects, as also a palliative in sickness from exposure.

"They are quick tempered; this may be attributed to the freedom that they enjoy in their jungles and their savage mode of life. They feel that there they may do as they please; they are untrammelled. At the Home they are not so apt, however, to lose their temper, for they know that some punishment might follow.

"They think nothing of the morrow, and but for the day. By their roving life they can lay by no stores, (they do.—*M. V. P.*) nor have they shelter; (they have.—*M. V. P.*) this state of feeling alters with those who have made any lengthened stay at the Home. They have observed what is done by convicts in hut-making; thus some improvement appears, little though it be, in the construction of their " bodlahs " or sheds, while they would lay by any trifling articles that they become possessed of.

"Constitutionally they are weak, they are very susceptible to fever, and consumption (pneumonia—*M.V.P.*) is a frequent cause of death amongst them.

"They are kind-hearted to one another, sharing what they may be possessed of with each other. All things seem to be in a measure common (no—*M. V. P.*) amongst them, *i.e.*, they all share alike, and alike own everything, though at times some of their principal men may claim the greater right to anything, which some might not wish to share, or part with. Generally, if one express a wish for any article to another, it is given to him.

"They are naturally very cautious in all they do, and wonderfully sly, watching for favourable opportunities. They are very quick-sighted, and able to see long distances, and have a ready perception.

"With but one exception, there has been no active violence, so far as is known, amongst the Andamanese that visit the Home. They have generally behaved well and without offence to any one. The exception was that of a man, known at the Home by the name of Jim, who killed a man of his tribe in a fit of revenge. He was subsequently apprehended, and was confined for six months in the Free Police Guardhouse on Ross Island, (though his imprisonment had been no more than living in the Police Barracks, where he became very fat, lazy, and indifferent). There had formerly been two offers on the part of gentlemen in Burma to take charge of this young man and educate him. As it was not now found possible to induce anyone to take him, it was determined, on a given day, to assemble a chief or elder, and other representatives of each of the tribes, who are friendly with us, and to produce Jim before the assembly, a prisoner, and then to address them (which Mr. Homfray did), informing them of his crime and of the penalty with which by British Law the crime of murder is visited. Mr. Homfray then said, that this would have been the culprit's award, were it not that the Government, in view of the excellent behaviour of the tribes for the past two years, and the peaceful and friendly dispositiou evinced towards the inhabitants of the Settlement, was disposed to be lenient in this instance ; and, therefore, directed the release amongst them of the prisoner who had been punished by imprisonment for his offence ; but that the Government held the tribes answerable for his production at any time, as well as for his good behaviour while at large, and relied on their efforts to suppress similar acts of violence as well towards others as amongst themselves.

"This assemblage took place in November, 1866. Mr. Homfray gave such formality and seriousness to the occasion as he could, and was as earnest in his address to the Chiefs as his knowledge of their language and customs enabled him to be. He discharged this somewhat difficult duty with tact and courage, and in a manner that, from his personal description of the scene, was carefully planned and well carried out. He describes it to have been, as it doubtless was, a duty that caused him considerable anxiety, so as to bring it to a peaceful and successful issue.

"The following is Mr. Homfray's report of the scene :—

"After explaining to the men the reason of the assemblage and the wickedness of " Jim," with the punishment attached, and on their promising that the like would not occur again, I produced the prisoner before them in irons. At first meeting, they all fell on him with loud crying, which lasted 15 minutes, overwhelming him with embraces, and several of them were almost trembling for a while from excitement and joy. For three nights he gave an account of his bygone days of confinement, accompanying the recital with acting and dancing according to their custom. Having grown very fat and lazy from his idle life, it was with great difficulty he managed this, frequently being obliged to drink water and take rest. The usual crying being over, the women set to plastering him all over with red earth and lard, which is always done to those who may be going to recite, and perform in these night dances, to prevent chill from the exposure they may go through while heated in the dance, as also as a charm and marked decoration on the occasion. His muscles has become so weak that at times he was obliged to be supported, and in the day, so that he might complete this ceremony, they fastened leaves and cord round his body, to strengthen the muscles, and keep him from pains and cold. When this was all over, I indulged them with some refreshment, and they then took their leave."

"During the year, Mr. Homfray has visited the islands of the Eastern Archipelago and Port Cornwallis. At the latter place, a collision took place with the Islanders of North Andaman, on the occasion of the despatch of Her Majesty's Steamer *Kwang Tung*, with a party of friendly Andamanese on board, to that place, in search of the wreck of the schooner *Baillie Nicol Jarvie*, and the master and his wife, who were supposed to be in captivity amongst the aborigines of the North Andaman Island. (The report was incorrect.—*M. V. P.*) The party in attempting to land at Port Cornwallis met with an opposition from the aboriginal tribes of that vicinity; one man of the boat's crew, a Native, was slightly wounded by one of a flight of arrows, of which twenty-seven were picked up, that were discharged upon the boats. Lieutenant F. Duncan, R.N.R., commanding the steamer, reports that a few shots were fired from the boats in return, but he imagines without effect, as not a man could be seen.

"It was observed by Mr. Homfray on this occasion that these North Andamaners spoke a different language to that of the aborigines of the South Andaman, who were Mr. Homfray's party, and did not understand the language of those they encountered. The Southerners call these tribes about Port Cornwallis Ea-ra-nud-dabs or North people. (Yerewa-da.)

"Mr. Homfray seems to consider that the race is gradually becoming extinct. Dr. Mouat, in writing about these islands in 1858, considered the population to be 5,000. Mr. Homfray does not reckon them but more than 3,000 in 1865-66, and doubts if there are even so many now.

"During the year, Mr. Homfray reports that there were several births (the average being two monthly,) at the Home, but the infants all died, some of them living only a week, while others existed only for a couple of months. It is difficult, he says, to know what is the cause of this mortality. The mothers have nourishment for their children, but it is a matter of some doubt as to whether they are not in a more naturally healthy condition of body in their savage roving life in their native jungles. Several marriages have taken place. There is little or nothing of ceremony in it, and yet the tie is binding for life. They select wives for themselves, as much as possible from distant tribes. The aged are much respected by the children, who are always with them.

"As a rule, Mr. Homfray thinks that few of the Andamanese live to the age of forty years. (Wrong.—*M. V. P*). Twelve adults died at the Home during the year, the diseases being principally colic diarrhœa which may be attributed partly to the locality selected for their Home being recently cleared, and, therefore, unhealthy land, and to excess in grain diet, their more accustomed food being pig's flesh and fish.

"No progress has been made in inducing these people to barter jungle produce for food, beads, tobacco, etc. It has been before reported that as far as can be ascertained these people have no idea of figures, that is to say, they cannot reckon; the utmost they can do is to count five. These numbers they will repeat, enumerating them on the fingers, but to continue the counting further on the fingers of the other hand is beyond their comprehension. They begin again 1, 2, 3, etc. Where they cannot be made to understand that 5 and 5 are ten, or 10 tens make a hundred, it is almost better, as has already been reported, to refrain from bartering with them, rather than attempt to press it under circumstances so disadvantageous to themselves.

"Indeed Mr. Homfray remarks that he has generally found them dissatisfied after such proceedings, even though to induce them to comprehend the system much that was given in exchange was intentionally largely to their gain."

During the month of April 1867, Colonel Ford received information from the Government of Burma of a report regarding a schooner named the *Baillie Nicol Jarvie*, which was supposed to have been wrecked on the North Andaman Island. The Master, Mr. Cowie, and his wife, were further alleged to be kept prisoners by the aborigines there. Mr. Homfray was sent out in the *Kwang Tung*, and the coasts of the island were carefully searched, but no traces could be found of either the wreck or the missing people. At Port Cornwallis the boat party was fired on by the Andamanese, and one lascar was wounded; shots were fired in return, but it is not known whether any of the aborigines were hit; 27 of their arrows were picked up.

At Interview Island to Mr. Homfray's surprise his party was received in a most friendly manner although this was the first visit paid to these people since Dr. Mouat had a hostile encounter with them, and took away an Andamanese captive to Calcutta in December-January, 1857-58. This man having been well treated while in captivity, and having been returned to his home with many presents, might, Colonel Ford thought, have influenced his fellow-tribesmen favourably, but it is more probable that the good reports of our treatment of the aborigines in the Home at Port Mouat had travelled up the west coast to the Interview Islanders. Our friendly relations with them, established at this time, have never since been disturbed. Further search was made for the *Baillie Nicol Jarvie* on different parts of the Andaman coasts, but no trace of the wreck was ever found. It would appear that she was lost in the Cyclone of November 1864, and the report about her being wrecked on the Andamans, and her Captain and his wife being in captivity there, was a mere traveller's tale, concocted years afterwards.

Mr. Homfray writes of this expedition:—

"Our Andamanese were frightened of going North of Strait Island as they did not know the country or people, and believed there was a great whirlpool which would swallow up the steamer. At Port Cornwallis the people at first accepted our presents, and I met ten of the Islanders armed with bows and arrows, who hid when we landed. None of our friends, who speak a different language and did not understand the Northern people, would go near them. I did all I could to make friends, but without success. The South Andaman Tribes call the people of the North Earawaddahs (Yerewa-da, a possible corruption of the word Jéru, the name of a Tribe in the Southern part of the North Andaman. The Chief of Rutland Island at that time used to speak of all the Northern people with whom he was not acquainted, even of the Kol tribe, who belonged to his own Group of Tribes, as "Yerewas."—*M. V. P.*).

"The savages fired on the boat at Port Cornwallis from the jungle with iron-headed arrows, and one of the boat's crew was wounded in the back.

"At Interview Island the aborigines were friendly and belong to the Middle Andaman tribe called Ellah-ko-kole-wuddahs. (This shows how little Mr. Homfray and his people knew of them. They were, of course, members of the Kédé Tribe. *Ér*-l'áka-*kól*-wa-da is a corrupted compound word, meaning "the people living in the country of the Kol tribe."—*M. V. P.*).

"Our people call themselves Bojen-e-jen-dahs." (*Bójig-ngiji-*da, meaning " our relations "—*M.V.P.*)

"The population of Interview Island is very small; the people have outrigger canoes, and I think aborigines from the Middle and North Andaman come to the Island. They did not seem to know any of our people or to have many words in common with them."

Mr. Homfray at this time thought that the Andamans were peopled by four Tribes, the Yerewas, Kol, Bojig-ngiji, and Jàrawas, and states they are hostile to each other and speak mutually unintelligible languages.

During this month Colonel Ford received a report from Burmah that part of the crew of the Ship *Assam Valley* had been massacred by the aborigines at the Little Andaman Island. A detailed account of the occurrence and our subsequent action thereon will be found in Chapter XIX.

Mr. Homfray was of opinion that the Áka-*Béa*-da Tribe were the most ferocious and treacherous of the Andamanese, and hoped now that friendly relations had been established with them, to tame the other tribes by the medium of their superior rascality. They had been giving him some trouble by stealing pigs from the Government piggery, and he complained that he did not know where to put that establishment, so as to keep the animals secure from the Andamanese.

The pariah dogs having increased so as almost to become a plague in the Settlement, Mr. Homfray ordered several of them to be caught and given to the Andamanese for pig hunting in the jungle. The aborigines, being naturally fond of animals, made pets of the dogs, and found them most useful in the chase, for whereas in former times an Andamanese had to sit and watch for the pig, sometimes losing them, even when wounded, the dogs now both drove them and kept them at bay till they could be killed. So much are dogs valued that at the present time (1895) the Andamanese speak of the days before 1858 when we first occupied the Settlement, as " Bibi *yábá*-len," meaning "in the days when there were no dogs."

Mr. Homfray armed the Parawallahs at the Home with sticks, and also had loaded muskets kept there in readiness for the protection of himself and the convicts in the case of a row. This was a mistake, as it was taken advantage of by the convicts who frightened the Andamanese, and made them pander to their vices, and conceal their misdeeds from Mr. Homfray, for fear of being beaten.

Mr. Homfray's remarks on Andamanese affairs during the year 1867 are given, after which time, though he kept charge of the Andamanese until 1874, he was not able to do much with them, as he was moved from Port Mouat to Ross, and Aberdeen, in January 1868, and though he returned in the following month to Port Mouat for a short period, he had not as much time as before to devote to the aborigines, and only visited the jungle Homes once a week. It should be understood, however, that during the later period of his charge of them, he took as much interest in the Andamanese as ever, having numbers of them living in his house, and expending more than half his pay in providing them with food and luxuries. He had a sort of Andamanese infant school at his house, and did his utmost to teach and civilise the children.

Dr. Day's report on the fisheries in Port Blair contains a chapter on the Andamanese, (quoted in full further on) all the information in which was derived from Mr. Homfray, and may be considered to embody his knowledge of, and views, regarding these people.

Mr. Homfray also mentions in the Monthly Reports during the year 1867 :—

"The Andamanese preserve the seeds of the jack fruit as follows :—

"They rot them first in salt water, and then, when they are sufficiently salted and tasty, bury them in the ground. They are then roasted or boiled and eaten."

(An incorrect account of the Andamanese method of storing jack and other seeds.—*M. V. P.*)

He notes that the slightest change in their drinking water, or in the weather, affects the health of the Andamanese, and states that in July 1867, 6 children were born who all died, and four other children also died from having lived entirely on Jangma-da (a wild fruit) and cockles, also, in August, four men died from over-eating at a feast of larvae ! In this month a dance and assemblage of tribes took place in a village in the Middle Straits to which many people from the South Andaman Septs were asked.

He thought that the greater number of children were in the Port Mouat Tribe who had only been two years tamed, this country being healthier than that of the Port Blair Tribes. Moriarty's wife and another old woman and two young men died in September 1867, from chill and fever, with much pain.

Some of the Port Mouat married people had three children to a family, and the people there were quiet and did not quarrel. Moriarty was much upset by the death of his wife and child.

At the Home it was the custom for all married men to stop on one side, the widowers and bachelors at one end, and the spinsters and widows at the other end.

Moriarty felt his wife's loss as he was not able to live any longer with the married people.

"A wife is a great help to an Andamanese as she does all the home duties, providing the man with shelter, matting, taking care of his food, fetching firewood, water, shellfish, carrying his loads, shaving him, and taking care of him in sickness. The man's duties are, protecting his wife, making canoes, hunting pigs, and spearing fish. Boys will now have to attend to Moriarty's wants."

Two children, a girl aged seven, and the son of Moriarty, a boy of eighteen months of age, named "Jerry" after Mr. Homfray, were brought to him to rear. He notes that the Andamanese kill their children by over fondness, petting, painting, shaving, and always feeding, and nursing them. They look on a corpse, or burial place with fear, strangers keep away from it, and if no relatives are present at the death of an Andamanese, it is the duty of the young men, by the order of the Chief, to convey away the corpse, and either heave it into the sea, or into the jungle at some distant place. This is done for fear that the spirit of the deceased may keep above and hurt anyone straying near. They burn a fire over a grave, or, if the body is suspended on a platform, under that, to keep away the spirit. If they have to pass by it, the elders carry bows and arrows, and the young men a burning brand. " Great pluck is required to extract the skull and bones from the corpse, and these are kept in tokens of friendship, and in remembrance of the deceased, so that when sick, they tie them round the parts that ache, that the spirit of the deceased may be kindly disposed towards them and relieve the pain."

"On account of their dread of evil spirits the Andamanese seldom move about at night, and when they do go, they are well armed and keep watch, throwing balls of fire made of rosin into the air when any of them imagine that they see the spirit nearing. For a distance round the grave burial garlands are suspended, to remind persons that the spirit of some one is there, and that they are not to return to the same spot for some time.

"Jegs," or "assemblages for dances," occur once a quarter.

"The great characteristic of the Andamanese is their fear of strangers. They are learning to control their tempers, but think nothing of the morrow. They are beginning to build improved sheds. They are intellectually quick, constitutionally weak, and are kind hearted to each other, sharing their property. Most things are in common, but the Chief claims some, and what they don't wish to share they hide. They are sly and cunning. They think all strangers are devils.

"They do not know of a God, but believe in a destroying spirit, and a heaven to which all that die fly to and rest. They believe in ghosts.

"They attend to the sun and fire, but these are not objects of worship, being only comforting as warming their bodies and keeping off insects.

"They are forgiving and have good memories, are very intelligent but do not know contentment. The cause of their extinction, which is becoming very apparent, is in the death of all the babies. It is owing to the change of food and mode of living."

Mr. Homfray remarked on the quantity of scurvy among the Andamanese, and appeared to think that it was a complaint recently introduced, but such was not the case. He also noticed that they were unable to bear the cold wind in the open clearings, and gave that among other reasons for their approaching extinction. Many of his remarks above quoted are incorrect, but are again mentioned, though already given in Colonel Ford's Report, because they have been noted as authoritative in recent times, and I wish to show the actual source of the statements.

He further noticed how quickly they "ran down" in illness, (though they pick up again equally quickly), and how soon they die, when ill, a slight ailment carrying them off in a few days, as they seem to lose all heart and become frightened.

He states that they select wives, as far as possible, from different tribes, and thought (a very old and incorrect idea) that they were the descendants of slaves, often ship-wrecked on the Andamans at different periods, which he thought accounted for the different languages spoken. He adds:—

"Now there is no more slavery they cannot get wives and so are dying out. Their numbers must have been greater in Lieutenant Blair's time, as he writes of clumps of coconut palms on the coast which do not exist now, only a few isolated trees being seen, the nuts of which the Andamanese eat, camping near the tree. They will not however trouble to plant the nuts, and uproot and eat any they may see growing."

(Lieutenant Blair does not mention "clumps of coconuts," but Lieutenant Colebrooke saw a few trees which may have marked the site of huts of Malay or Burmese pirates.—*M. V. P.*)

During 1866 there seems to have been some difficulty in keeping the residents of Port Blair away from the Andamanese, and preventing them from bartering. Taking advantage of the ignorance of the savages, the English residents and others used to obtain valuable articles for a few cheroots. Major Ford forbade this and only permitted outsiders to have intercourse with the Andamanese through Mr. Homfray.

In November 1867 the two Chiefs of the Southern Port Mouat Tribe, Pótea and Bira, and the wife of Wologa-Jó-la, Chief of the North Port Mouat Tribe, all died, and received "platform" burial, the corpses being tightly bound in leaves and matting and fastened on a platform in a tree. In the following month the remains were taken down, and the skulls of the deceased were worn as ornaments by the nearest relatives. The Convict Munshi of the Andaman Home, who had acquired some knowledge of the Áka-*Béa*-da dialect, volunteered with several other convicts for service in Borneo under the Raja of Sarawak, and left Port Blair never to return.

In December 1867, 80 members of the Kol tribe came into the Homes for the first time. This tribe has never given any trouble, and is now almost extinct.

In 1867, besides the catastrophe at the Little Andaman Island in connection with the crew of the *Assam Valley*, two wrecks occurred at the Andamans, one of the brig *Nineveh*, which was lost on the North Sentinel Island, and the details regarding which will be given further on in Chapter XVIII; and the wreck of the Ship *Ferozeshah*, which struck on the South Brother Island, on the 10th November 1867. Assistance was given from Port Blair on the news reaching there, and the crew and passengers were all saved.

In commenting on these wrecks the Governor General in Council in Letter No. 46, dated the 20th December 1867, from the Marine Department, to the Chief Commissioner of British Burmah, writes:—

"The Governor General in Council is decidedly of opinion that an expedition should be organized and despatched to those Islands of the Andaman Group that are inhabited by people who thus attack and murder those who land on their coast; provided that the objects of such an expedition can be sufficiently well defined.

"Our object should be to explore the Islands, to seek any means that can be devised of coming into amicable communication with the

Islanders, and to that end, if possible, even where summary punishment has to be inflicted, to capture some of them, in order that they may be afterwards made the instruments of assuring their countrymen of the pacific and friendly intentions of the Government of India towards them; which the alarm and hostility engendered in their minds by the maltreatment in former years at the hands of pirates and slavers, may very probably incline them to doubt.

"That there would be difficulties must be admitted, but the Governor General in Council thinks the thing can be done.

"It appears desirable that the Chief Commissioner of Burma, or the Superintendent of Port Blair—possibly the latter—should have authority promptly to act in such cases, with the view both, as in the case of the *Ferozeshah*, of rescuing any who may be unfortunately left on shore in any of these Islands, and of inflicting summary punishment on the perpetrators of any acts of outrage such as have recently attracted the notice of the Government.

"It is only by prompt retribution that the proper effect can be produced and any hope be entertained that the punishment will fall, not on innocent persons, but on the actual offenders.

"Expense should be considered, and such resistance is not to be anticipated as to require any great amount of force. The means at your disposal may be sufficient if prompt action is taken, but the garrison at Port Blair must not be unduly weakened.

"A Notification has been issued regarding the danger of landing on any of the Andaman or Nicobar Islands, without due precautions against surprise and attack. No. 12, dated 17th December 1867, of the *Gazette of India*."

The Chief Commissioner of Burma replied to the above that it was not possible to take a very decided course of action. The Superintendent of Port Blair had been directed to act promptly in all cases of wrecks on the coast of the Andamans, or of outrages committed by the natives, but to do this it is necessary that he should always have a steamer at the Islands, suitable for work required.

Major H. Nelson Davies, Secretary to the Chief Commissioner of

Burma, was sent by the Chief Commissioner to inspect the Settlement of Port Blair early in 1867, and reported on the Andaman Homes, as follows:—

"No improvement has been made in taming these people. There hardly appears to be any substantial reason for keeping up these Homes, but at the same time it may be politic to do so. Mr. Homfray's knowledge of the Andamanese language is extremely limited."

Major Davies' Report on the Andamans was voluminous and painstaking, but his relations with the Superintendent, Lieutenant-Colonel Ford, were notoriously so strained, and he so uniformly condemned everything in Port Blair, that personal bias was patent, and the Report did not carry much weight. Colonel Ford was, however, asked by the Chief Commissioner of Burma to report upon the utility of the Andaman Homes, as this appeared to be rather doubtful, and to state what he considered to be the advantages supposed to accrue from them. He called upon Mr. Homfray for his opinion, which was given as follows, on the 22nd August 1867:—

"The Homes were started with the object of charity only, and with no idea of usefulness. The Andamanese are the original possessors of the soil, and demand from the usurpers some consideration. We have occupied Port Blair and Port Mouat, where they used to live, restrained their liberty, and annexed their fishing grounds. They have had to retreat before us to avoid fights in which they have been killed, and they have suffered much in health by our advent. The grant of money was given to civilise the Andamanese only, and by the Homes much good has been done, and they have been tamed. They are only expected in return to bring in runaways, not molest the people in the Settlement, and assist the crews of ship-wrecked vessels. They are not willingly subject to us, and to our laws, and we often require their aid. The money is a Government grant in consideration of a treaty of peace with the Andamanese. Were this understanding not in existence the police guards would have to be doubled, it would not be safe for anyone to go to the jungles, and the general safety of the Settlement would be affected. We have taken possession of these Islands to prevent other European Powers from taking them, which matters nothing to the aborigines, and on that very account some sacrifice in money is justice to the original inhabitants of the Andamans whose territory we are now supposed to be ruling."

Colonel Ford agreed with Mr. Homfray, and wrote on the 2nd October 1867, that he thought the Homes were most important and should be maintained. The establishment was originally one of benevolence, and had effected much good by bringing in the Andamanese peacefully, without much cost to Government, whereas they would otherwise have had to be brought in by force at great cost and loss of life. We were also bound to recompense the Andamanese in some way for having annexed their country.

Under any circumstances the Homes should certainly be maintained until the whole of the Andaman Tribes are friendly. They are important as regards the comfort of the Settlement, for without them the Andamanese would loot and fight, we having less control over them, and we should not have the advantage of their services in hunting runaway convicts.

Colonel Ford further showed the good of the Homes by drawing a comparison between our Andamanese and the Öngés of the Little Andaman, with reference to the attack on the people of the *Assam Valley* by the latter, and the saving of the crew of the *Nineveh* by the former people, whom we have tamed.

He added that, if the Andaman Home allowance is withheld, and the Andamanese turned adrift, the Police force must at once be increased.

"Such Homes and such expenditure are still incurred by the Government in Australia, to maintain friendly relations with the Aborigines."

While this matter was under consideration Colonel H. Man was appointed officiating Superintendent of Port Blair, *vice* Lieutenant-Colonel B. Ford proceeding on furlough, on the 19th March 1868. Colonel Man had served for many years in the Straits Settlements, and was acting Governor there at the time when they were transferred from the India to the Colonial Office. He had had much experience with

Indian convicts, and, during the time that he was in the Andamans, he was fully occupied in improving the discipline, and introducing the Straits Settlement Rules. His connection with the Andamans commenced in January, 1858, as he was the officer directed by the Government of India to hoist the British flag at Port Blair, and prepare for the arrival of Dr. Walker with convicts, as related in Chapters VII and VIII.

Such time as he could devote to the question of the Andamanese was spent in establishing an Orphanage for the children, the history of which will be given in a separate Chapter, and in improving and reforming the conditions of the Homes. He decided that these should be established at Mount Augusta, as he found that the cold, bleak air of the clearings in Port Blair affected the Andamanese injuriously, and was one of the causes of their diminishing numbers. (Mr. Homfray added to this that he thought spirits and tobacco had a fatal effect on their health, and that all, including women and children, were addicted to smoking immoderately. He should have prevented them from obtaining the former, and as regards the use of tobacco, I have found that the actual amount smoked by them is not very great.)

A shed 100 feet long by 40 feet wide was erected for them at Mount Augusta, Mr. Homfray observing that, "nothing more permanent is wanted, as they will have to move some day, and such a shed is to the Andamanese a palace." As a matter of fact they dislike living in large and draughty buildings, and prefer their own little huts; when we have erected such sheds for them they have always built their own huts in addition inside.

Colonel Man directed Mr. Homfray to let the Andamanese know that the issue of our stores to them is to be considered as a reward for good conduct, for industrious and peaceful habits, for bringing in runaway convicts safely, etc.; while special presents of value would be awarded for tidings of ship-wrecked vessels, and for helping the mariners.

"The Homes have been of much value to the Settlement as a standing proof of our friendship for the Andamanese, but these people must now understand that a return is expected for our kindness to them, and that misconduct on their part will be followed by a withdrawal of our favours."

Mr. Homfray further wanted a missionary to educate the children, and civilise the adults. A Protestant missionary he thought would be too heavy an expense, as his cost would have to be borne by the voluntary subscriptions of the residents of Port Blair; and though the present residents, he states, are willing to subscribe, yet the community here is always changing, and their successors may hold quite different views.

"An orphanage and school would be the better institution, and might form a means of communicating our ideas to the people in the jungle."

Colonel Man wrote with regard to this proposal —

"I was in hopes of securing the Andaman woman who was brought up and educated at Penang, and who is a particularly well-disposed person of very fair abilities and education; unfortunately my offer to make her matron arrived just after she had accepted service in a family as ayah, or she states she would have come. I have written to the officiating Lieutenant-Governor of Malacca, asking him to see if he could induce her to take the situation, as it would be a rare chance to get one so well adapted for the post."

Colonel Man was of opinion that the distant tribes should be visited and small presents should be given to them, and that our steamers should cruise along the coast establishing friendly relations wherever signs of population are visible. By this means we should gain a knowledge of the country and of the remoter tribes, and perhaps discover wrecks which might escape observation at a further distance from the land.

Mr. Homfray had, in the meantime, established an Andaman Home at Navy Bay, he having been transferred to that station, and Colonel Man wrote to him on the 4th August 1868:—

"With reference to the new Andaman Home at Navy Bay, no labour is to be employed on account of the Andamanese without my sanction. I am unable to see that any advantage is to be gained by introducing these savages into the heart of our Settlement, but it strikes me that it might not improbably lead to quarrels about their women, and so forth.

"If they were being taught industrious habits it would be different, but as our connection with them is restricted to the supply of food, and quarters, to a few of their number, I think it both useless and impolitic to bring them into such close communication with us."

He further wrote on the 8th August 1868:—

"I do not see any reason why the Andaman Home should not have been kept at Port Mouat; and the whole arrangement for the benefit of these savages be made at your weekly inspection.

"The Home appears to me to be simply a house of call, where they are supplied with food, to which they have never been accustomed, and which does not seem to agree with them.

"They appear to be under no subordination: and, though upwards of ten years have elapsed since we came to these shores, little or no progress has been made in gaining a knowledge of their language. Matters must however continue as they are for the present, till I have more time to entertain the question.

"I must acknowledge the very great care, patience, and kindness you have shown towards this people, but I am afraid they are too thoroughly savage in their nature to appreciate it."

On the 9th Feburary 1869, a special Andamanese Hospital was opened at Port Mouat. Colonel Man wished to have a medical missionary in charge there, and was anxious to get the Andamanese away from the vicinity of our stations, where they merely learnt bad habits, were exposed to manifold temptations which they were ill able to resist, and were a constant offence to decency because they would not wear clothing. He thought that they would be healthier at Port Mouat, and would have to work for their food.

The Government of India finally directed on the 17th April 1869 that—

"The site of the Andaman Home is to be on Mount Augusta, and the necessary arrangements for the change be at once made. The establishment of a small hospital for the Andamanese is also approved This should also be at Mount Augusta.

"The Government of India agrees with the Superintendent that the Aborigines should be brought to perceive that some return is expected for the kindness shown to them. The establishment of such an understanding with the tribes is extremely desirable, and with this object Mr. Homfray's proposal to visit the more distant of them, and distribute small presents, is approved. Without, however, implying any doubt of Mr. Homfray, who has shown much zeal and tact in cultivating intercourse with the Aborigines, the Superintendent will strongly impress upon him the necessity of caution in conducting these visits, which otherwise might only widen the gulf which separates us from the Andamanese.

"As far as the adults go, the establishment of friendly and mutually helpful relations is all that can be hoped for. It would be vain to attempt to convert such inveterate nomads into cultivators or artisans. But the establishment of an orphanage or school might do much towards civilising the young, and a moderate expenditure on this head will be sanctioned on a scheme being submitted."

On the 1st January 1869 the penal settlement of Port Blair was again placed directly under the Government of India in the Home Department, and on the 24th February 1869 the Government of India ordered that the Andaman Home Accounts need not to be sent up to them, but that the Finance Department would pass bills for the Andaman Home up to R200 per month.

Colonel Man did not sufficiently appreciate the work which had been done with the Andamanese, nor had he been sufficiently intimate with them to understand the work of civilisation which was slowly progressing.

The Government of India appear to have been alone at this time in knowing what could, and what could not be done with the Andamanese.

The following items of interest occur in the Report on the Andaman Island for the year 1867-68. Colonel Man writes:—

WRECKS.—"The brig *Nineveh* bound from the Madras coast to

Rangoon was stranded on the South-west end of North Sentinel Island in September last; the greatest portion of her crew and passengers were taken off the island by the *Kwang Tung* despatched from here on receipt of the news.

"In November last a boat from the Ship *Ferozeshah* (then lying off the South Brother) brought intelligence that the vessel had been dismasted in a cyclone on her way from Karikal to Penang, with 250 coolies, and a cargo of salt and sundries on board. The Steamer *Kwang Tung* was without delay sent to her assistance, and she was towed into the Harbour. The leaky condition of the vessel rendering it unsafe for her to anchor in deep water, she was towed on to Ranger's Reef, westward of Chatham Island, where she now rests on a soft muddy bottom.

"A vessel, believed to be the barque *Pleiades*, was also sunk in 14 fathoms of water off Landfall Island. Nothing is known of her crew."

Colonel Man notes that Mr. Homfray remains in charge of the Andaman Home, and that friendly relations have been observed with the Andamanese.

"It is desirable that we should continue on amicable terms with these savages, for, though they could effect but little harm to the Settlement, the good treatment they experience here may have a very beneficial effect on their reception of shipwrecked mariners.

"But I am strongly of opinion that some change should be made in the course we adopt with the people. They are certainly not pleasant neighbours, nor sightly, as we cannot induce them to adopt clothing. The effect of our clearances seem to be injurious to their health, and they have decidedly not improved in morals by associating with us. The idle life they lead at the Home, where they have abundance of food, strange to their use, and gained, too, without healthful exercise, is, I think, injurious to them in every way; while their addiction to smoking is also most hurtful. (?)

"Mr. Homfray thinks they are decreasing fast, and mentions that most of their infants die within six months.

"To wean the adult savage from his roaming, desultory life is nearly an impossible task; our only chance of being successful is by turning our attention to the children. I am endeavouring to start an orphanage, and if I can secure as Matron the Andamanese girl, who was carried to Penang, and brought up there, I should have very good hopes of success. She is a well-educated and highly respectable member of society. (As related above, her services were not procured.)

"It has been proposed to establish a mission here; but unless the Roman Catholic system is adopted, of the priest living among the tribes, I should much doubt of his success in the clearings."

Colonel Man mentions that in the rainy season the Andamanese eat preserved jack seeds, which last them three months, and pigs, which are then plentiful and in good condition.

"In August, September, and October they are employed in making lances, (! ?), and in November and December in making nets for trapping turtle which they afterwards spear. (This account is vague and incorrect.—*M. V. P.*)

"Their canoes are simple, made principally from a light wood obtainable in large quantities in these islands, called by them Bahjadahs; the length varies from 20 to 30 feet according to the size or straightness of the log, which is hollowed out by an adze of their own manufacture, the iron of which is obtained from wrecks. Originally their tools were shell and flint. (! ?) These light made canoes can be made to paddle six miles an hour.

"During the year 33,673 Andamanese were fed at the Homes at a total cost of R2,609-3-4.

"There were several marriages and births at the Homes, but unfortunately the greater portion of the infants died.

"The Andamanese are fortunate in the Officer appointed to look after them, for nothing can exceed the kindness, patience, and liberality shown them by Mr. Homfray."

CHAPTER XV.

Captain Anderson takes two Andamanese boys to India—They are transferred to the Burdwan Boys' Orphanage and die there—Mr Homfray's notes on the Andamanese—The Andamanese catch runaway convicts—Report on the Andamanese for the year 1869-70—Dr. Day's paper on the Andamanese—Notes on the same—Other papers—Report on the Andamanese for the year 1870-71—General Stewart succeeds Colonel Man as Superintendent of Port Blair—Report on the Andamanese for the year 1871-72—General Stewart's letter on the Andamanese.—Mr. Homfray proceeds to the Nicobars.—Report on the Andamanese for the year 1872-73—General Stewart visits the distant Islands—Employment of the Andamanese—Another visit paid to the distant Islands—Mr. Homfray again goes to the Nicobars —Mr. Tuson takes charge of the Andamanese—Review of Mr. Homfray's administration of the Andamanese.

In May 1867 Captain F. C. Anderson, [Barrack Master of Fort William, Calcutta, applied to Colonel Ford for an Andamanese boy, whom he said he was willing to adopt and educate.

On the 31st May 1867 Colonel Ford wrote to Mr. Homfray strongly advocating the sending to Captain Anderson of a boy between seven and ten years of age, on the ground that he would be educated and might eventually serve as an interpreter. He asked Mr. Homfray to persuade the elders of the neighbouring tribes to permit some lad to go, and added that if one would not go alone, Captain Anderson would be asked to take two.

By this Colonel Ford showed that he had no idea of allowing Captain Anderson to keep the lads permanently. Mr. Homfray approved of the proposal, but said that not less than two lads should be sent, as one alone would pine, and forget his own language, thus becoming useless for the work of an interpreter. He offered to pay for the entire cost of one boy, if Captain Anderson would take three, but stipulated that they should only be absent for two years, should never be flogged, but should be treated with great kindness, and should not be allowed to forget their own language.

Captain Anderson expressed his willingness to take two boys, but not more, adding that the Medical College were willing to take and educate one. The whole matter was then submitted to the Government of India, and on the 9th September 1867 the Governor General permitted Colonel Ford to send two boys to Captain Anderson, on the understanding that they were not to be taken out of India, were always to be produced, when required, and to be sent back to their homes in the Andamans whenever the Government of India thought fit.

In November, 1867, two Andamanese boys, called "Kiddy Boy" and "Topsy," were accordingly sent to Captain Anderson, and on their arrival he wrote to Colonel Ford acknowledging the receipt of them, stating that they were in good health, and asking for a complete collection of all the articles used by the Andamanese, on the plea that, if the boys were not surrounded by these, they would forget their jungle habits. Mr. Homfray, by Colonel Ford's direction, supplied him with these, and he also wrote to ask for a vocabulary of their language. He stated that he had " exhibited" them in public, and had also taken them to a meeting at the Asiatic Society's rooms, and adds :—

" Do you propose to submit to Government any scheme for their support or clothing, or shall I pay for this ? I am quite willing to do so, if Government refuses, but the terms upon which they have been sent to me are not what I had wished, as I cannot take them to England with me after I have spent time and money on them!"

This, and other correspondence which appears to have passed between Captain Anderson and the Government of India, seems to have caused the Government to look upon what was first represented to them to be a purely philanthropic action, with suspicion, and on the 9th May, 1868, the Governor General in Council reconsidered, on certain letters from Captain Anderson, the question of the disposal of these two boys, and decided that they had reached an age at which Government should procure for them some educational training under persons professionally conversant with teaching.

It was, therefore, decided to place them in the Burdwan Boys Orphanage of the Church Missionary Society. The Revd. Mr. Stern, Superintendent of that establishment, who was in Calcutta at the time, was directed to place himself in communication with Captain Anderson, and to take the boys back with him to Burdwan.

The thanks of the Government were conveyed to Captain Anderson for the care and benevolent interest which he had shown towards these young Andamanese for upwards of four months, and the sum of Rs. 50 per month for each boy was granted to him for the expense he had been put to. Captain Anderson had written to Colonel Man for a third boy, and Colonel Man had received a similar application from another quarter, but this had been refused up to that time, and the wishes of the Government of India were asked for, as he considered it would be better to train up the lads in the Andamans, and when they had become fairly instructed and gained some powers of observation, there would not be the same objection to their leaving their home to see more of the world, as they might afterwards return and be a means of enlightening their fellow-countrymen.

He thought that it was not desirable to hand them over to chance patrons who might turn out to have but a temporary interest in them, and be unable to carry out the plans proposed for their benefit.

His remarks were more than justified years afterwards, as will be shown further on in Chapter XXI.

In the meantime the boys were sent to Mr. Stern, who had kept them for a few months, when Colonel Man, who was in Calcutta on duty, wrote on the 25th March 1869, for them, at the same time thanking Mr. Stern for the care taken of them and the readiness with which all references regarding them had been answered.

Mr. Stern replied in April 1869 that he had sent the boys down to Calcutta in accordance with Colonel Man's request, but that Colonel Man had left before their arrival there. He added that the boys had been with him for a year, and were just beginning to learn Bengali and to know something of English. It would be well, he thought, if they could be left with him for some years longer, as their minds could be developed and trained, and their stay would, he trusted, benefit them. In reply to this Colonel Man wrote, on the 9th June 1869, that, with reference to Mr. Stern's wish to keep the two Andamanese for some years longer, and his proposal to continue their instruction in Bengali and English, he objected to their learning Bengali as it could be of no possible use to them, and they had much better learn English. If they were to pass their lives in Bengal the case would be altered, but they could not be turned to any useful account there, and would merely be considered a sort of wild beast to be stared at and avoided. On the 9th August 1869 Mr. Stern reported to the Government of India that one boy had died a few days before of pulmonary consumption ;—

"Last cold season he was ailing, but was treated by Dr. Martell and appeared to have recovered, but one evening in May last the two boys remained out without our knowledge or permission, and unhappily yielded to the invitation of a neighbouring gentleman to display their diving powers in a tank. When they emerged they were found to be shivering with cold, and the gentleman, to warm them, gave them some liquor, which intoxicated them, and they were discovered by the school servant lying on the damp ground in their wet clothes. Both got inflammation of the lungs. 'Sambo,' (called by Captain Anderson " Kiddy Boy,") recovered and is now strong, but poor "Topsy" died on the 31st July, after much suffering. He was carefully attended by Dr. Martell. Sambo now appears strong and in good health, and there need be no apprehensions regarding him."

From the first Mr. Stern wanted the boys to be placed at an English School in Calcutta, but no such school would receive them. His Orphanage was a Native School where English was not taught, but only Bengali. He thought, however, that unless Colonel Man was able to educate the boy better at Port Blair he might as well leave him where he was.

"Having no Andamanese companion, Sambo will now not talk that language, and will talk nothing but Bengali with the other boys, with whom he is great friends. Let him be kept here for another year. If he improves, continue his education in this country, if not, send him back to the Andamans."

In answer to this, the Governor General allowed the boy Sambo to stop with Mr. Stern for another year, the result being that this boy also died under Mr. Stern's hands, and was never sent back.

Considerable care seems to have been taken of him, but on the 9th February 1870 Mr. Stern writes :—

"Sambo has died from the effects of pulmonary consumption. He was so far recovered at one time that he could be removed to the better climate of Bancoorah, to which the whole Orphanage was transferred for some months. Three doctors tried to save him, but could not."

Mr. Stern now regretted that he had not sent the boy back to his own country when formerly asked to do so.

(The cold mists of the early morning were fatal to the boy, and such a climate was the very worst for a growing Andamanese lad. As soon as he sickened he should have been sent back to the Andamans as the only chance of saving his life.—*M. V. P.*)

Comment on the above incident is scarcely necessary. Captain Anderson's attempt to keep the Andamanese for exhibition, under the cloak of philanthropy, was seen through and thwarted by the Government. Mr. Stern, though no doubt acting for the best, had no knowledge of the habits and manners of the Andamanese, and the deaths of the two boys were exactly what might have been anticipated.

In June 1869 Mr. Homfray remarks :—

"It is in this month that the Andamanese begin to get sick and die. The pigs are in good condition, which excites them to hunt, but again, on the other hand, the severity of the weather soon lays them up with fever, cough, and pneumonia: the married men suffer severely at this period owing to their carelessness in sleeping in the jungles without proper cover. Previous to our coming to the Settlement, and the establishment of the Homes, the Andamanese had better huts than those they construct in these days for their hunting excursions, and also they used to stop longer in one place, which they generally took an interest in, picking the sites, and erecting semi-permanent abodes. This is yet traceable among the distant tribes. The single men are in a better condition, as a rule sticking together and helping each other. In July and August we generally lose a great number of Andamanese."

(In a former report Mr. Homfray has said that he was trying to teach the Andamanese to make huts for themselves, as they had little idea of doing so, and he thought that they had made some improvement in this direction; he now contradicts himself. As a matter of fact the Andamanese had not in any way altered their usual customs or modes of hut-building.—*M. V. P.*)

On the night of the 4th of June 1869 a strong party of convicts attacked the guard of Convict Police at Corbyn's Cove, carrying off their boat and wounding several men. Eleven Andamanese boys, with three Convict Police Peons, were sent after them, and very cleverly arrested fourteen of the runaways six miles south of Ross Island. Colonel Man was much pleased at this, and gave the Andamanese a special reward. He states:—

"The mode of capture was as follows:—While the convict in charge of the party was following up the traces of the runaways, he suddenly came upon the stolen boat concealed in the jungle, and loaded with a quantity of provisions and other stores. He left a guard of Police and Andamanese over the boat, and continued his search, till he came upon the party of convicts, when he directed the Andamanese to surround them and threaten them with their arrows, but not to fire.

"This being done, the convict Petty Officer came up and shouted to the runaways to sit down, which, they being frightened, did, and the whole party were arrested and brought into the Settlement."

Colonel Man thought that a remission of sentence was the best reward that could be given to a convict for such a deed. The Andamanese were rewarded by being given presents, and praised, and made much of before people from other tribes, who came in to visit the Homes.

He notes how amusing it was to see the little Andamanese bringing in their Panjabi prisoners, swaggering, and imitating the capture in pantomime, being evidently very pleased with themselves.

Mr. Homfray again deplores the increase of deceit and falsehood amongst the elder Andamanese owing to their contact with the Natives of India, whose vices, he says, they are ever prone to pick up. He, however, took no decided measures to stop the intercourse, and naïvely admits that he is as cunning as the Andamanese are, and that, " it is by this art that I have succeeded for so long in working so well with them." (Mr. Homfray was a most transparently open-minded and generous man, whose " cunning, " had he attempted any with the sharp Andamanese, would have been seen through at once. He got on so well with them because he was fond of them and treated them well, and they knew this.—*M. V. P.*)

On the 9th October 1869 the Comptroller wrote, in letter No. 3502, that R200 per month had been sanctioned as a grant for the Andaman Home, and was to be kept as an advance by the officer in charge. This amount has, however, always been drawn in arrears.

The following remarks occur in the report on the aborigines for the year 1869-70 :—

" As Mr. Homfray found that the Andamanese were not inclined to remain for a long time in one place, he opened two more Homes for them, at Lekera-Bárnga on the East coast of the South Andaman, about seven miles north of Ross Island, and at Chiriya Tápu, on the South coast, in MacPherson's Straits. The former of these proved to be a very important station, as it was frequented by all the friendly Tribes and Septs from the north.

" The Andamanese were not allowed to visit the Homes whenever they chose without reference to Mr. Homfray, and watch was kept for their canoes, which, when seen to approach without permission, were towed away again. The Port Blair tribe gave the most trouble, the Port Mouat people being obedient and quiet. The reason for this was that the Port Blair people used to row freely about the out-stations, picking up articles by barter, theft, etc., or by begging ; and then exchanged with the other tribes tobacco, dogs, and iron, for baskets, nets, mats, etc., which they had now ceased to make at the Home. This simply made them lazy, quarrelsome, and dishonest, and often ended in a fight. Mr. Homfray thought that they ought to take to agriculture and supply their wants by their own labour." (Unhappily they would prefer going without their luxuries to working for them.—*M. V. P.*)

The Lekera-Bárnga Home was much frequented by new-comers, and Mr. Homfray objected to the dancing night and day, which he called " stupid, unmeaning madness, whereby the Andamanese catch cold, overdo themselves, and are consequently knocked up with severe inflammation of the lungs which carries them off."

He thought the dancing was got up because the Andamanese cannot appreciate the simple enjoyment of a large body of people being collected, and from fear of a disturbance get up a dance to amuse the visitors. (!)

"At a great congress they appear like so many maniacs, frightened out of their wits to know how to get on peaceably, one lot terrified at the other, the guests no doubt being the worst off, being strangers to the country, so they very wisely leave the best part of their belongings behind in the jungle. The hosts get all they can out of them, and keep a careful watch on their arms till friendship is established."

(The Andamanese are subject to bronchial affections, and get chilled during the dances. Mr. Homfray's reason for the dance is ingenious, but not correct. There is always shyness and fear at these meetings, especially at first, and the whole time the people are to a certain extent on their guard, but not so much as Mr. Homfray supposed.)

He objected to the barter among the Andamanese on the ground that the tame Andamanese met with the wild ones from the distant tribes, and, associating with them, were thrown back into their wild state.

(Yet at other times he had tried to encourage this barter, which had really existed from the earliest times. The Andamanese are not so easily changed in disposition, or turned from their own customs, as he imagined.)

At this time he formed Homes at Brigade Creek, and Progress Creek, and found that the Port Blair Southern Sept came to the former place, and to Dhani Khári.

During the year the Andamanese kept in good health, as they had been in the jungle during the heavy rains of the South-West Monsoon, and had not been exposed to chills in the open ; Mr. Homfray also thought that the stopping of their tobacco had improved their health.

Their behaviour in the Homes during the year had been good, and they had assisted in the garden work, and in planting groves of plantains, and Mr. Homfray thought that they valued the gardens for their produce, and appreciated the Homes. He adds :—

"They stick to fire which keeps off headaches, fever, and colds, and which Nature has ordained for man only, and distinguishes him from the animals. They cannot stand breeze, rain, sun, or the malaria caused by new clearings, and when protected from these elements in their own jungles they get on well."

(They are not protected from them in the jungle, and Mr. Homfray forgot the Ár-*yāūto* who are constantly on the water. What were really hurtful were the *continued* cold winds in the clearings, especially at the changes of the Monsoons, from which they got no shelter night or day.—*M. V. P.*)

"While the jungle stands none of these affects them, rain being the only trouble in their wild state; I am, therefore, particular, when clearing new Homes, to only clear a small space, and then to replant it, so as to make it tree-locked, and shut out the breezes, etc."

At this time the aborigines in the Port Mouat Home worked much as they do at present, in catching turtle for sale.

"Strangers from the Middle Andaman and from Interview Island have come into the Homes bringing their own canoes with them, which have outriggers. Several get broken and they are constantly making new ones, which employment they like, and it keeps them out of mischief.

"The Port Mouat people are always at work, while the Port Blair people do nothing but wander about and steal."

(The former had their own country intact, and their own occupations; the latter had lost their country and had nowhere to go, not daring to trespass on the hunting grounds of others.)

Mr. Homfray enumerates the peculiarities of the Andamanese as:—

"Great excitement at meeting, particularly if in large numbers; incessant dancing; roving disposition; fright at evil spirits; wearing of bones; ignorance of medical treatment; absurd music; fear of ghosts; desertion from the place where another Andamanese has lately died; jealousy; and backbiting."

(The Andamanese have certain medical treatments of their own but generally leave the cure to Nature; their music, such as it is, much resembles that of other savages akin to them, and there is nothing "absurd" in it; the fear of ghosts is not peculiar to the Andamanese; I should not consider them to be a jealous people, and they do not backbite. It would have been interesting to obtain Mr. Homfray's enumeration of the "peculiarities" of Europeans.—*M. V. P.*)

He adds:—

"Tattooing is carried on as much as ever. Pigs near the Homes are scarce, and the Andamanese are always straying away from the Homes, hunting, pig being their great food. They prefer living in small numbers according to their clans, as they are better able to agree then, and obtain food more easily."

He hoped that children brought into the Homes at six years of age would be educated and civilised there, and would never return to the jungles, some remaining to farm in the Settlement, and the rest taking service with the residents.

Eight births and 24 deaths occurred at the Homes during the year, the details of these being, six adult males, six adult females, three boys, three girls, and six infants of both sexes. Four marriages occurred; and the deaths were not so numerous as in the preceding years.

Mr. Homfray now stated that, having been in charge of the Homes for six years, and only being able to give an hour once a week to the Andamanese, he wanted a missionary to relieve him of his work.

Being so little with the people he could not show any progress, and if on leave, or taking his term of duty at the Nicobar Islands, (which had been annexed in 1869, placed under the Superintendent of Port Blair, and made an additional Penal Settlement, of which one of the officers from Port Blair was always in charge, they being changed every six months), there was no one capable of looking after the Andamanese, who would, therefore, fall back into their former practices. The mission, if formed, might, he thought, be stationed at Shoal Bay, 18 miles North of the Settlement, where the work would progress peaceably and undisturbed. The Bishop on a recent visit had advocated this, but the Andamanese did not wish to lose Mr. Homfray.

Extract from a report by Surgeon F. Day, F.L.S. and F.Z.S., 1870.

(Dr. Day visited Port Blair in January 1870, in order to enquire into the fisheries there, and, to assist him, Andamanese were placed at his disposal. The following remarks are the result of his observations of them, and of the accounts given him regarding them by Mr. J. N. Homfray, officer in charge of the Andaman Homes.)

"The inhabitants of the Andamans consist of two great elements: the aborigines and the immigrants. The Andamanese deserve more than a casual notice. Owing to the assistance of Mr. Homfray, who has so energetically and successfully worked to promote a good feeling between us and these savages, and has mastered their language, I was able to see them in their haunts, and to enquire into the meaning of what I saw. They worked with us in the jungle amongst the streams, they speared (!) fish in the harbours, shot them with bows and arrows in the sea, exerted themselves to catch the smaller kinds with their hands or nets, and thus enriched my collection by thirty-six species, which I did not otherwise obtain.

"They are computed to be about one thousand in number, whilst the individuals forming the tribes around the Settlement number about four hundred. As a race, those who are living in the vicinity of our Settlement are decreasing in number, few appear to live over forty years of age, scarcely any family number above two living children, and only one has three. From April 1868 to April 1869, 38 deaths were reported, and only 14 births, whilst during the four years only six infants have lived whose parents resided at the Homes; of monthly visitors only 12; of the half-yearly ones some 20; this is somewhat remarkable, with reference to the question of the effects of a fish diet on the production of offspring, and the probable result of civilization on this savage race. (The Andamanese by no means live exclusively on fish.—*M. V. P.*)

"Their language is meagre, remarkably deficient, and the different tribes have distinct dialects, and even the inhabitants of the Little Andaman cannot understand those of the South Andaman. Numerals are entirely absent (11), they do not comprehend their use, whilst the day is divided into three portions—sunrise, mid-day, sunset. In like manner they divide the year into three seasons; first, Dry, *ea ra bodilin*, or northern sun, extending from February to May; secondly, the Rainy, *goo mo lin*, from June to September; and thirdly, *pa pa lin*, or Moderate season, from October to January.

"They are of diminutive stature, scarcely averaging five feet in height, whilst various and contradictory statements have been given as to their probable origin:—at one time feared as cannibals, and even now dreaded by mariners in event of a shipwreck.

"These Islands get a wide berth from vessels not directly interested in proceeding there, as the shipwrecked sailors have hitherto usually met with their deaths from the arrows and spears (1) of the Andamanese, or else the last few survivors have been kept as slaves, and thus probably assisted in continuing this mixed (?) race. Some may be of African origin, their woolly hair, and other signs, apparently afford such a solution, but some again have entirely smooth hair, (None—*M. V. P.*) and but few have very thick blubber lips, or the Hottentots projecting jowl. So long as they are pleased, their features are not exactly unpleasant. They do not like persons to wear hair on their head, or faces, and they shave off all, except one narrow band from the crown to the nape of the neck, which is, however, cut short. (Wrong.—*M. V. P.*) They rarely have eyebrows, beard, or whiskers, and merely a few eyelashes. Formerly, the shaving, which is done generally by old women (No.—*M. V. P.*), was a tiresome process, performed every six months by means of a piece of sharpened flint, but now they use pieces of glass from broken bottles, and undergo the luxury every fortnight. The reason for indulging in this seems to be the impossibility of keeping vermin out of their hair, whilst by thus shaving the appendage no room remains for these parasites to lurk in.

"They consider themselves very handsome, and one of their greatest pieces of abuse is to say, "your nose is ugly," "your mouth is deformed," or such like observations. To them a looking-glass presents great attractions, and, although their mode of attire is primitive, they become exceedingly irritated, should any remarks be passed upon the method in which they paint or adorn themselves. On a casual observation being made, one turned round and angrily demanded " What are you laughing at, you stupid fellow ?"

"Although they joke with one another, and the bachelors chaff the spinsters, so that they generally remain somewhat apart, (?) with strangers they do not like any familiarities in conversation.

"They resemble monkeys, or children, amused with toys, delighted on flying a kite for the first time, pleased at receiving pieces of cloth, which they tie round their heads, or dress themselves with as they perceive others to be clothed, but as soon as it become dirty, tearing it off for their usual adornment.

"They are doubtless very lazy, and receiving tobacco or cheroots seat themselves comfortably in a chair, and direct the servants to bring them a light, which they consider it too much trouble to fetch for themselves. I have seen them cut off large branches of trees to obtain the fruit which they might easily have knocked down by means of a bamboo. In the infancy of the Settlement, they used to root up the young coconut trees, as they considered the tender portion near the root to be good eating.

"The women and children are slaves to their parents; whilst should it suit their views, no untruths are too great to obtain any object they desire. They refuse nothing to one another on its being asked for, and expect everything they demand being given to them in like manner. Their organ of secretiveness appears to be well-developed, but they are comparatively honest with respect to the goods of those they are not well acquainted with, and with whom they never take liberties. They are great backbiters amongst themselves. (No.—*M. V. P.*) In the wilds their tempers are very impatient, and they will let fly an arrow or use a knife at the slightest provocation, but they listen to the aged, and during a quarrel the words of those that are grey-headed at once allays the storm. Should one have fired an arrow at another, he then sits down, all is over : in fact, one moment they may be crying for some loss, the next drying their eyes, when any little incident sets them off laughing.

" They have a great respect for fire-arms, which they look on with considerable awe.

" They are very sharp, and appear to have good memories : thus they soon discovered that they were called by the new comers by names anything but complimentary, and as every race has such epithets at their disposal, which they freely employ, the Andamanese (who are not averse to a joke) recognise each race by the several terms of abuse which they have used in addressing them.

" They have no pets about their homes, except dogs, which they appear to treat well, because they are useful. At first the canine species appear to have great dread of the aborigines, but this they soon get over.

" The painting or adorning of themselves is done by the females. Iron is collected from a mineral spring, this burnt red and mixed with fat is employed as an external application. Dr. Waldie, having been good enough to analyse their red preparation, reports it to be as follows :—

Peroxide of iron	42·7
Quartz in small fragments, and very little of any other rock, or earthy matter	56·4
Water expelled by ignition	·9
	100·0

"When I was at Port Mouat, the Rutland Island Chief was in mourning for his only child, and was daubed all over with olive-coloured (grey—*M. V. P.*) earth,—a process which was daily repeated,—whilst a rather thick coating of mud covered his head. This mourning lasts at least one month. During periods of deep sorrow they are very silent, and entirely refrain from the use of red paint and all decorations, from taking much food, even from eating their favourite pork, whilst honey must not pass their lips, but instead, they have daily to throw honey-comb (No.—*M. V. P.*), if obtainable, into the fire. When the period of mourning has expired, they wash off the olive-coloured earth, and revert to their red paint, with which they are fantastically adorned, serving both as a decoration and a charm. Olive (grey—*M. V. P.*) mud is likewise used as a decoration when painted over the body in an ornamental manner. These colours form the chief, usually the only portion of the clothing of the males, unless they have a string or two round their waist or neck, or round the leg below the knee like a garter, otherwise they are as primitive as man is represented to have been in his primeval condition. As for the women, they adorn their waist strings by twisting pieces of cloth round them, and painting them red, whilst depending in front are a few leaves fresh gathered from the jungles, and behind are some tails of fibre. A string of their ancestors' bones, worn around the neck, completes their attire, unless they have a basket slung over their backs, in which some relatives' skull is carefully carried about, or a broad band over their shoulders, by which they suspend their babies. (The skull is worn suspended by a cord, and is never carried in a basket.—*M. V. P.*) Before marriage, in both males and females, the whole of the body is tattooed, this is done once a fortnight now (No.—*M. V. P.*) (formerly twice a year), a small portion only of the body being operated upon at a time, as a considerable amount of blood is lost in the process. A piece of broken bottle, inserted (Never. It is held in the hand—*M. V. P.*) into the end of a stick, is the instrument employed; formerly pieces of sharpened flint were used. (Flakes of quartz were used.—*M. V. P*). At the age of eight, when they first learn to swim, this commences, and is generally continued up to the adult period of life.

"Destitute of clothing, these aborigines commisserate foreigners going through their jungles; when it rains they say, " you will be wet, your clothes will spoil, whilst our skin soon dries." When the briers tear their garments, these Andamanese laugh and call attention to how much better off they are with nothing to tear.

" Crying signifies with them reconciliation with enemies, or joy at meeting an old friend or acquaintance from whom they have been parted. Should two tribes meet, the new comers have to commence, and women have the priority in weeping; subsequently, the men take it up, whilst it becomes the duty of the hosts to reciprocate in the same manner; first the females weeping and afterwards the males, occasionally the performance cannot be completed in one night, especially, should the parties have been long separated, it may even be continued through several successive days. After the crying has been completed, dancing begins, that of the women a few years since differed from that of the men, they having to clap their hands and sing to the music of the stamping of the men's feet: their songs appear to be a recital of the events which have passed since their separation. The conclusion of the performance was for both parties to join in a grand dance.

" Now, however, the men and women occasionally dance together, the females, who intend dancing, put on a few extra leaves, and they relieve the men in striking the sounding board with their feet. If a person intends dancing all night, he has an extra coating of paint, which is said to be put on in order to act as a preventive against exposure. It is evident they are very fond of dancing: having occasion one day (as we were starting upon a fishing excursion) to go inside one of the convict barracks, the Andamanese set to work to dance on the boarded floor, and it was with the greatest difficulty that we could induce them to desist.

" When one tribe goes into the territory of another, except upon a special invitation, they have to pay homage (No.—*M. V. P.*) by dancing all night before the Chief of the resident tribe, subsequent to which hospitality is extended to them.

" When children are born, the infant is first bathed in cold water, and then warmed over a fire, this being done to harden it and inure it to stand changes of temperature. It is very evident that they do not understand how to rear children, they give them whatever they desire, and over-kindness early consigns the little one to the grave.

"Children are named some months before they are born, after some family or favourite name; consequently, there is no difference between those of the males and of the females; owing to their list of names hardly exceeding twenty, they prefix (No.—They *add* a nickname.—*M. V. P.*) to each, some word expressive of something in their appearance to distinguish one from another, or else according to the locality from whence they come.

"They marry as soon as they are able to support their wives, whilst they are monogamous. It is usual for the young man to eat a peculiar kind of ray fish termed *goom-dah*, which gives him the title to the appellation of *Goo-mo*, signifying "a bachelor desirous of becoming a benedict" (Entirely wrong.—*M. V. P.*), whilst girls when they arrive at the earliest marriageable age, distinguish themselves by the flowers of certain trees.

"Young men, likewise, take a species of oath before marrying (Never—*M. V. P.*) after which they sit still for some days, hardly taking any food. Those who have been pig hunters refrain for one year (commencing in April) from eating pork, using turtle or fish instead, although they do not give up hunting pigs which are required for the food of the tribe; the turtle hunters in like manner use pork during this probationary year, during the whole of which time they must not taste honey. This is apparently done for the purpose of ascertaining whether the individual is able or not to support a family. (Wrong.—*M. V. P.*)

"The marriage ceremony is simple; a man about 16 or 18 is engaged to girl of 13 or 15 belonging to a different family, and with the consent of the girl's guardian, who is generally the Chief of the tribe. At their first meeting, they are seated apart from the others, passing their time in staring at one another; as the shades of the evening darken, the guardian or Chief advances, and taking the hands of the pair, joins them together, they then retire into the jungle to spend their honeymoon. (Incorrect—*M. V. P.*) On their return to the tribe, crying and dancing are kept up with great spirit. After marriage they are not so useful as before for the general welfare of the tribe, as the married woman has now to erect her husband's hut; and look after his welfare, and consequently they are not ordered about by the Chief. As soon as people are married, they object to going into the water, of which they previously had no dread, for, although they never wash, their constant swimming about keeps them clean.

"Sea breezes are considered a cause of sickness, as the Chief of the evil spirits is believed to ride upon them.

"The wife has to perform all the home duties, providing shelter, matting for lying upon, cooking the food, procuring water and shell-fish, carrying loads when changing from place to place, shaving her husband, and taking care of him whilst sick. The husband has to protect his wife, make canoes for fishing, the implements for hunting pigs or turtle, and occasionally spearing fish, whilst he also obtains food, if not provided by the bachelors or spinsters.

"The Chief of the Rutland Islanders appears very like a Madrassee, or as if he were of Madras origin, and is very superior to those of his tribe. He obtained his present position by marrying the widowed queen. (1)

"Widows and widowers have no objection to re-marry. I saw one woman who had done so within the month subsequent to her husband's death, but this was considered rather premature.

"At the "Home" the following is the manner in which they pass the day. At a very early hour they have something to eat, for about 4 A.M. their uncovered bodies become cold, which necessitates their making up their fires, and once up, feeding begins : when residing in the same house there is no rest after this early hour. About 7 A.M. some of the men go out foraging according to the season, it may be pig hunting, fishing, or taking tortoises (1) or turtles. The young men and boys assist in making, paddling, and steering canoes. The women in a body go for shells, shell fish, fruits, and bulbs (1) in which they are assisted by the girls ; whilst the elderly people keep at home, making baskets, nets, bows and arrows, attending the sick, etc. Between 2 and 8 P.M. the foragers return with their spoils; these are, as far as possible, equally divided amongst all.

"The aborigines are a sickly race, suffering much from fever and lung complications, as well as from malaria in newly cleared jungly lands. They have no medicines, their great faith is now in quinine, which they ask for when headache or fever is present; whatever new drug is offered them, they invariably expect the donor to take some of it first, and subsequently they do not object to it. They plaster themselves over with olive (grey—*M. V. P.*) mud for headaches, whilst the same substance rubbed over the body is deemed to be a non-conductor of heat. They cannot stand either strong winds or exposure to the rays of the sun, whilst living as they do almost without shelter, the effects of the climate upon them may be readily imagined. In the month of August the high winds and rain are very inimical to their health.

"Upon the death of an adult the tribe at once desert their encampment, retiring to a distance of eight or ten miles, this is done in fear of the ghost of the departed, which is considered to haunt the spot; they remain away one month. A corpse is viewed with great dread, and almost equal fear is shown on going near a burial place.

"Jacko, Chief of the North tribe, died on July 1st, 1865, and his loss was for several days openly bewailed by his people. He left two married sisters behind, whose husbands had to bury the corpse.

"Death occurred at 6 A. M., and within two hours his remains were rolled up in leaves by the old people, and corded with fibre preparatory to their being consigned to the grave. The latter was merely two feet deep, and only a few feet above high water mark. Here the corpse was placed in a half sitting posture, with the face turned towards the east. Previous to filling in the grave, each took his last farewell of one they had loved so well whilst alive, and one by one in turn gently blew upon his face and forehead. When all was over there did not remain more than six inches of earth above the body, placed there to prevent the ribs from being broken; some stones were now heaped over the grave, subsequently some burning faggots, and mourning garlands were placed on the shore in conspicuous places, to mark a Chief's interment. Before retiring, a cup of water was placed at the head of the grave, in case the spirit of the deceased, during the night, should feel thirsty. Four months subsequently, the nearest of kin went to the grave and brought away the lower jaw which about that time became fleshless; a month afterwards, the shoulder-bone and a rib or clavicle were extracted; and after six months the skull, now freed from impurities. This was slung round the neck of the principal mourner, and subsequently everybody had it in turn to carry about.

"When a stranger dies amongst a foreign tribe, he is entirely neglected, and his funeral rites mostly uncared for; the Chief generally directs some of the young men to carry away the corpse, and throw it into the jungle or sea.

"Should a Chief or great man die, the ceremony is not generally the same as that described for Jacko. They erect a stage, some twenty feet from the ground, and on this the corpse is placed. Thus the spirit of the departed, it is hoped, will keep above, and not injure any one who may incautiously pass near the corpse, whilst a fire is lighted under the stage, for the purpose of disturbing other evil spirits.

"The extraction of the skull and bones, it is considered, requires great skill and courage, whilst keeping them carefully, and wearing them during pain and sickness, it is supposed, will induce the ghost of the departed to be friendly to the wearer.

"In selecting sites for burials they invariably avoid hills, and elevated pieces of ground. (!)

"Should those of other tribes go to condole and sympathise with a widower, the custom is to fall into his lap, embracing and crying for about ten minutes, after which the afflictions are recited.

"It has been stated, and generally admitted, that these people have no knowledge of any religion, and are pure Atheists; but they appear to be more Deists, with very obscure views.

"It is curious to see the state into which the Hindu and Mahomedan convicts are drifting, destitute of religious rites, temples, or priests. Probably, were they left alone on the Andamans, without any fresh importations, their views after a few generations would be much similar to those of the Andamanese, who fear evil spirits have a great (?) dread of witchcraft, and imagine that the spirits of the departed soar away into space, to some place of quietness and haven of rest which they cannot comprehend.

"Being entirely without caste prejudices themselves, they dislike those who indulge in them, and amongst the dark-skinned races prefer the Burmans, who will eat, drink, and smoke with them.

"Formerly, they looked upon all strangers as foes, and their name of an evil spirit was identical with that of a stranger from unknown lands. They strongly object to moving about after dark in dread of meeting ghosts, and at this time no women will go alone, whilst they invariably carry with them a lighted stick, to keep off evil spirits as well as mosquitoes and sand flies. Occasionally, the men turn out, imagine they see a ghost, yell as loudly as possible, and let fly their arrows at where they suppose the spirit is, or they ask that a musket or two may be discharged for the same purpose, after which they are satisfied. At night time, they all huddle together as close as possible, the married people by themselves, and the bachelors and spinsters also in separate places.

"They rub on turtle oil, and wear wreaths of turtle's and fish bones, hoping by this means to enchant the spirit of the victim, and keep away sickness, should they be exposed to wet. Wreaths of turtle and fish bones are also at times suspended at the prows of their canoes, to propitiate good luck to their fishing.

"They cannot be persuaded that the Europeans do not worship fire, asserting if it were not our God, why is it always with us? whilst they have to keep a lighted brand, and did their fire go out, they know no manner of reproducing it. They are surprised at our igniting matches, producing fire by means of a magnifying glass, by rubbing two pieces of bamboo together, by flint and steel, by caps on guns, etc, etc. As respects food, they have never tilled the soil, but have lived entirely upon the products of the jungles or of the waters, and storing up but little for a future day's supply. But one of the first questions asked about this people is, are they cannibals? They scout the idea and ask why, when food abounds, should they devour human beings, a repast on whom they assert would most assuredly cause their deaths. They eat nothing raw, not even fruit (!) In cooking flesh, they either throw it on the embers, turning it over when the under side appears to be sufficiently done, or else cooking the meat of the tortoise (1) and pork in unbaked earthen chatties. Their appetites are large, they appeared able to consume about six pounds of fish at a sitting, and were soon ready to commence again. A large Pinna forms their plate, a Nautilus shell their drinking cup. They have no regular period for their meals, when they are hungry they eat, no matter at what time. As they capture their principal supply of fish and turtle during the low tides, and do not dry or salt any, it follows that they have abundance at that period of the month, whilst they may be comparatively destitute during the intervals. Their chief food at the First or North sun Period is honey, fruits, and turtles; in the Rainy Season they do not wander much about, owing to the difficulty of obtaining shelter; then the jack seeds last them for three months, and in the early part of their Middle Season, pigs, which however soon become scarce, then comes fishing and turtle catching. Pigs begin in September to rove through the jungle, finding their way to the coasts and creeks; during this period many are killed. (The pigs are always roving about, but are not always in good condition.—*M. V. P.*) In the year 1865 they first began to use dogs for pig hunting, which they learnt from some Burmese runaway convicts; previously they had to lie in wait for hours, and sometimes days, even in the hopes of seeing one or two; now the dogs find them almost at once: consequently they are in great request for them. The Andamanese, however, have curious ideas respecting pork as food, and when they are able to please themselves, use it as follows. The children and the weakly persons eat sucklings, the bachelors and spinsters use those of medium size, whilst adults prefer the stronger boar. Beef they consider too coarse for food, neither do they eat birds, as a rule. About the month of January the dugong shows itself in Port Mouat Bay, coming to feed upon a species of seaweed, which is also relished by the turtles. In the month of January honey is generally common, and they bring the combs down from the tree with great dexterity, neither smoking the bees nor being stung themselves. A wild shrub, "jenedah," exists in the jungles, and its juice appears to intoxicate the bees. The aborigines take a piece in their hand, and biting through the bark, they get the pungent white juice into their mouths, this they spit out at the bees which either fly away or become intoxicated. Wax obtained from the honey-comb is much used for their bow strings, also for covering the fibre where the nails or heads are attached to arrows, or stopping leaks in their canoes.

"The Andamanese have no tie to keep them to one place, they wander about for food, or as their fancy dictates; they have no constraint, but that of their Chief or their individual caprice; in short, they love freedom, and they hate control. They have scarcely a want, but as luxuries they esteem tobacco, especially cavendish, and grog. Iron they also require for spears and arrows, and for making adzes to construct canoes; formerly they used to steal the convicts' *dáhs*, pieces of iron, and nails, but latterly they have refrained from helping themselves.

"They do not care for sugar, but are immoderately fond of honey; they eat the cuttle fish, are much addicted to *chitons*, but will not eat raw oysters. Formerly they appear to have consumed almost anything, on wet days, worms, caterpillars, roots, nuts, mangrove seeds, sharks, shell fish, etc., etc., things which they now refuse. (They eat them now.—*M. V. P.*) Amongst fish they prefer the mullet, and one day having placed a quantity of different species before them, they helped themselves in the following order, observing that the first took the best, the last the worst. *Chorinemus*, *Platycephalus*, Horse mackerel or *Caranx*, *Chrysophrys*, *Calamara*, and lastly, *Tetrodon*, or frog fish, which is usually reputed to be poisonous

"They will eat cats, but now dogs are spared, because they are found to be useful. Though nominally fed at the Homes, it is a mistake to suppose that they subsist on the food provided by Government, for they are only allowed Rs. 200 a month to cover all expenses. In the year 1868-69 the following were the earnings of the aborigines: 500 pigs;

150 turtles, and tortoises (1), 20 wild cats, 50 iguanas, and 6 dugongs; whilst the total number of rations given was 48,243, giving a daily average of 132 persons, including women and children, allowing each individual only 9 pies daily, and showing an increase in those fed of 14,575 rations over the previous year, but with a decrease of expenditure of Rs. 209-3-4: thus showing them to be more self-supporting. Since the establishment of these Homes, and at a trifling cost, a great change has commenced, convicts are now unmolested implements of agriculture are not stolen, the fishing stakes are left undisturbed, the gardens are no longer pillaged, runaway convicts have been re-captured, and shipwrecked sailors assisted.

"One of the necessary pieces of property to these people is a canoe, a moderately-sized one being capable of accommodating about 20 persons, and is used for the purpose of obtaining food for about 30. It is scooped out of a tree by men, working with a sort of adze, and who take their turn, during which period they are supplied with food by others. When finished the canoe is a very fragile construction, and rarely lasts above a year, for they are constantly making its sides thinner by ornamenting and scooping out its interior. It is ballasted by stones, and has a prow projecting about two feet, on which the fisherman stands. They are more especially useful for turtle fishing, and the spearing of skates and rays. The bamboo pole by which the native poles about his boat, has a sharp moveable spear which unships at one end, and to this is attached a long line. When the bamboo is thrown (1) and the spear becomes embedded in the prey, it slips away from the bamboo, but being attached to the line the animal is securely held by the fisherman. Their eyes, while slowly and silently moving about, are as sharp as hawks, and the spear is generally thrown with a deadly aim, and should the fish be large, some of the natives dive down under the water, attacking the victim with knives and spears, whilst others endeavour to pass a line over the game. (The " spear" is a harpoon. The Andamanese rarely attack the fish in the water.—*M. V. P.*)

For their small nets they use a fibre as thread, which they neatly work up, employing the fingers as a mesh, gradually enlarging it as required. When turtles are scarce a large net is used, just before the tide begins to ebb, this attached to stakes which encircle the whole of a reef where they resort for food. As the tide recedes they are of course penned in, but they fight most desperately to break through the net. The Andamanese now use spears, (Harpoons.—*M. V. P.*), and but few as a rule escape.

"Their bows and arrows are used principally for shooting fish in shallow water, the upper two-thirds of the arrow is a hollow reed, the lower a piece of heavier wood, armed with a piece of iron or a nail.

"Major Haughton, in 1862, observed in the *Journal* of the Asiatic Society of Bengal upon flint arrow heads having been employed by them for shooting fish, and some such heads are still found in their heaps, (No.—*M. V. P.*) but the aborigines declare they never recollect when such articles were employed, but they do remember their being in use for shaving and tattooing. They throw stones with considerable accuracy, and in this way procured me several sorts of small fishes of the Goby and Blenny families which I should not have otherwise obtained.

"From Port Mouat, as I have observed, I went with Mr. Homfray and the Andamanese to the neighbouring fishing grounds. As their manner of obtaining the finny tribes does not appear to have been recorded, I will give a short description of what I personally witnessed.

"We left the Andamanese encampment at 3 P.M. at low spring tides, taking with us 17 of the aborigines in our boat, their ages varying from about 19 to 10 years. The females and younger children, with three hand or landing nets, remained in the stern of the boats, the bachelors with three bows and arrows and one spear (Harpoon—*M. V. P.*) in the forward part, and as usual the latter were constantly chaffing the former. One youngster took the rudder and we prepared to start for Jolly Boys' Island some two miles distance; scarcely was the anchor raised when a lad in a canoe came with some fish, and likewise handed in a large piece of dead coral, amongst the branches of which numerous beautiful fish, (*Glyphidodons, Apogons,* etc.) were to be seen alive, as well as some lovely little crabs. When I suggested they might have got in there by accident or put there for show, over the side of the boat dashed a young savage, who dived down and came again to the surface with another piece as large as his head, and in it were forty small but living fishes.

"As we were again starting we heard a shout of *Ooch-rah!*, *Ooch-rah* (Fish, Fish), when another canoe arrived, with some splendid specimens obtained by means of bows and arrows. (*Ucha! Ucha!* "There" "There"—*M. V. P.*)

"At last we started, the Andamanese carrying as usual fire with them, and asking for tobacco and pipes, their most constant word being *jay, jay*! (give! give). As a foretaste of what was to come provided they did well, we presented the Chief with a looking-glass, some tobacco, and a box of fusees, and we also gave our fellow passengers another box of fusees, which was entirely emptied before we came to the end of our short pull as they were unable to resist amusing themselves by " making fire."

"We passed shoals of fish, many being of the most brilliant hues; as we neared the shore, the Andamanese pointed out a turtle or tortoise (!) but did not succeed in obtaining a shot at it. On landing they at once found its track, and asserted it had been on shore to deposit its eggs, but I refused to stop to hunt for the nest as the tide was on the turn. Away went the females along the shore, the bachelors with their bows and arrows and spear, as far out upon the reef as they could proceed, whilst the younger children stayed with us to collect shells and small fish. As soon as we commenced wading into the sea, hundreds of fish darted about, either from under one piece of coral to another, or from sea-weed to sea-weed. Now our juvenile companions commenced to give chase: first the little Blennies claimed our attention, and though some escaped into holes in the coral, we took as many as I required.

"Occasionally, whilst feeling under coral or sea-weed for a fish, a crab would lay hold of the hand of the investigator. At one yell rather louder than any which had preceded it, and the assertion that a "sea-devil" had injured a boy, I proceeded to the spot, and saw a beautiful scarlet and banded fish (*Pterois volitans*) swimming off, the lad whom it had wounded refused to touch it. Its fins were expanded, and it was sailing very quietly away, as much as to say " touch me if you dare ?" However, I threw a pocket handkerchief over it, and in this manner procured it. But many fish I had never previously taken darted past us, and the little Andamanese began to warm to their work ; soon larger game rewarded their labours (*Serrani*, several species of *Teuthis*, some mullets, parrot fish, *Hemigymus melanopterus* and *Callyodon viridescens*). Whilst thus employed, we heard a loud shout sea-wards, and on looking perceived a large fish struggling with our archers. It proved to be a Ray, nearly six feet long.

" After an hour's collecting, observing the numerous Sea-slugs, Trepang or *béche de mér*, (*holothuridae*), which are used as food by the Chinese, and obtaining about sixty pounds weight of shells, we went to see how many fish had been procured by means of bows and arrows, and found that in $1\frac{1}{2}$ hours 31 large mullets, averaging about 3 pounds each, had rewarded their labours, and that without the loss of a single arrow. The succeeding day the same individuals killed 56 large mullets by bows and arrows within two hours time. As soon as a fish is viewed all are on the alert; they appear to be at once endowed with a new life, as active as cats, and very acute in their eyesight ; they fire the arrows at objects in the water, which no European unused to the work could perceive. They appear to aim under the fish, and mostly hit it through the bowels : when struck, away darts the unfortunate victim carrying off the floating arrow, but it soon either becomes entangled in sea-weed, or the tired and wounded fish gives in, the arrow floats, the captive's life is nearly over. Had we possessed the means of carrying more fish, a much larger number could have been killed, but the Andamanese suggested they had enough to eat, and declined carrying what was of no use to them.

" As we were about leaving, one of the aborigines brought an *Amphiprion percula*, and on being told that it was approved of, observed that she could get numbers more. She took us to a sea-nettle, *Actinia*, which she pulled off the coral rock by inserting her hand behind the attachment of this polype, and on shaking it into the net two more of these little fishes came out. Subsequently this was repeated to twelve others, and all had two fish inside them, except one which had three. They asserted these fish usually resided within this curious living domicile.

"On returning towards our boat, upwards of one hundred esculent swallows were seen soaring about, and perceiving a cave on our right, it suggested their nests might be there. We sent in the Andamanese, who soon returned with two old ones, and they informed us that the season was passed. We caught some specimens of the birds by knocking them down with our hands as they dashed out of the cave.

"Further on we came across a Chiton, on a rock, which they pointed out as excellent eating, but on being asked whether they eat the Sea-slugs they appeared disgusted at the idea.

"We reached the boat as darkness set in, when the fish were divided, and it was late before we reached their encampment, when the Chief came into our boat to see what he was to get. Having given all the presents, amongst which the spears for dugong hunting seemed to be very acceptable, we left for Port Mouat, where we arrived shortly after midnight."

As will have been noticed, much of the information in the above has already been quoted from Mr. Homfray's reports. Dr. Day's description of the Andamanese mode of catching fish is excellent.

In an amplification of this report, forming a paper read before the Asiatic Society of Bengal in June, 1870, he further states:—

"Their huts, if they deserve the name, are merely palm tree leaves most loosely put together: they try and get shelter under any overhanging trees or rocks. Bones of animals or fish which have been eaten, shells, etc., etc., are all thrown into one heap close by, the smell of which is very offensive. When they can no longer bear it, they move on, returning when they imagine disagreeable odours have disappeared.

(The huts seen were only the temporary fishing huts, and Dr. Day did not see any of the larger encampments.)

"These people, when guests of Europeans, or expecting presents, have moderately good tempers, but a very slight offence rouses them. When in their jungles they are said to be very irritable.

"One evening after we had returned from fishing, the aborigines retired to the Home at Port Mouat, when a lad about 8 years of age ordered a girl, much older than himself, to go and bring him some drinking water; as she did not move at once, he shot an arrow at her which took effect just above the eyebrow. Another day one small boy with a knife cut to pieces a girl's basket for some equally cogent reason.

"When the Andamanese talk of having taken quantities or numbers of anything, it is impossible to have any idea of their meaning, and what still more increases this difficulty is that in framing an answer they often do so from the question, almost repeating the same words. This has perhaps led to their being considered more untruthful than they really are. Thus, being asked if it is true that a wreck has occurred, they will probably say it has, and perhaps it has at some period long past." (The above remarks are very correct, and have not been always correctly observed in later times.—*M. V. P.*)

After this period Dr. Dobson, and other visitors to Port Blair, published papers, or accounts of visits to the Settlement, giving very much the same information regarding the Andamanese, and I have not thought it necessary to reproduce these, as no additional information, except what is incorrect, is to be gained from them, and Mr. Man's Monograph on the Andamanese, published in 1882, supersedes all that has been written before his time, with the exception of Lieutenant Colebrooke's paper.

During the year 1870-71 the only points noted are:—

The Andamanese had been discouraged from visiting our stations in order to prevent any intimacy between them and the convicts, and had been confined to their Jungle Homes, of which six had been constructed for their accommodation in their own haunts. A small garden was attached to each Home, which provided the Andamanese with fruit and vegetables, and on seeing the use it was to them a hope was entertained that they would take an interest in cultivation.

A commencement had been made to teach the people to barter with us, and for the first time, the Shoal Bay and MacPherson's Straits Septs brought honey and turtles, respectively, to the value of R200, for sale in the Settlement.

The Andamanese were now considered by Colonel Man to be a useful body who checked escapes by the recapture of runaway convicts, for which service they received money rewards, which were placed in the Home Fund, they being given pipes, tobacco, looking-glasses, beads, and coloured cloth.

Māia Biala, the Chief of Rutland Island, had especially distinguished himself in catching runaways, and in assisting some fishermen who were in distress, having been blown away in a storm and wrecked on Rutland Island.

Colonel Man left the Settlement on the 16th of March 1871 on furlough to Europe, and, after an interval, during which Major F. L. Playfair held charge as Officiating Superintendent, Major-General D. M. Stewart (now Field Marshal Sir Donald Stewart) was appointed to officiate as Superintendent, being confirmed in that appointment about a year afterwards; during his term of office there, in 1872, the dignity of the appointment was increased to that of Chief Commissioner of the Andaman and Nicobar Islands.

In the Report on the Settlement for the year 1871-72 General Stewart remarks, with regard to the Aborigines :—

"They have been very well-behaved, and have on all occasions given willing assistance in tracking and recapturing runaways.

"Mr. Homfray reports that the tribes in immediate connection with us, are settling down into villages, and seem gradually to be giving up their wandering habits." (He was wrong.—*M. V. P.*)

"They show some interest in the cultivation of fruit and vegetables, and bring honey, wax, shells, and turtles into the Settlement for sale. The care and attention paid to these poor savages seems at last to have been attended with good results, as the mortality rate last year was visibly decreased.

"The children in the Homes on Ross and Viper are thriving, but those who have any recollection of jungle life continue to evince an intense desire to return to it.

"The friendly tribes have now such complete reliance in the disinterestedness of our dealings with them, that steps should be taken to widen the circle of our influence both north and south. With this view it is proposed to depute Mr. Homfray, when the season admits of it, to open communication with some of the more distant tribes who are believed to be more tractable in disposition than some of those who are now on most friendly terms with us."

A certain amount of trouble seems, however, to have been caused by the Aborigines in the Settlement, as, on the 19th December 1871, the Tindal in charge of Perseverance Point reported that the Andamanese came during the day and stole about 200lbs of yams, and also stole about 70lbs. during the night, as well as 16 pieces of sugarcane ; these being taken both from the Government gardens, and from those of the Self-Supporters. This had been going on for some days, and if any one attempted to stop them, they fired on him.

General Stewart wrote to Mr. Homfray on the 1st February 1872, in Letter No. 1908 :—

"You are aware that the Government spends R200 monthly for the "Andaman Home," besides granting rewards for the recapture of runaway convicts at R5 per head.

"As we have already given ample proofs of our goodwill to the aborigines, and as it would be a real hardship to encourage them to rely upon hopes of assistance which could not be permanently kept up, I request you will be good enough to impress upon the Andamanese that the issue of stores at the 'Homes' is not to be made as a matter of course, but as a reward for service done—and that special presents will be awarded for tidings of shipwrecks, and aid to mariners cast on their shores.

"If these men could be induced, on the occasion of their visits to our stations, to bring bamboos and other jungle material for Settlement purposes, they would thus be taught to make themselves useful, and in the course of time to acquire habits of industry which could not fail to improve their present wretched condition, and be the means of ultimately raising them in the scale of humanity."

Mr. Homfray was posted to the charge of the Nicobar Islands from November 1871 to June 1872, during which period Captain Darwood, Harbour-Master of Port Blair, was in charge of the Andamanese.

In January 1872 Captain Darwood persuaded the Andamanese to bring in honey from the jungle for sale in the Settlement. In April 1872 the wife of Māīa Biala of Rutland Island died.

General Stewart, in his report on the Settlement of Port Blair for the year 1872-73, states regarding the Andamanese:—

"The Homes established for the aborigines have now been under Mr. Homfray's charge for nearly nine years, and it must be admitted that his system of management has been attended with the most favourable results. It may be said that the tribes inhabiting Rutland Island, the South Andaman, the Southern half of the Middle Andaman, and the Archipelago Islands, are all on friendly terms with us, with the single exception of the 'Juddahs' or 'Jurrah-wallas,' a small inland tribe about whom next to nothing is really known.

"The Port Blair tribes have behaved well during the year, and have been most useful to the Settlement in many ways; they have cut several forest paths, carried on some cultivation near their Homes, and have been required to do something towards their own support.

"About twenty young men have been trained to use the oar, and now pull remarkably well, although there was a good deal of unwillingness to continue the training after the novelty of the thing had passed away; by a judicious mixture of coaxing and compulsion, Mr. Homfray managed to keep them at the work, and they are now good, useful boatmen.

"The fruit gardens at Port Mouat have been rented by the Andamanese for the current season, and they arrange for the collection of the surplus fruit, bring it to Ross market, and dispose of it without assistance, save from the man who keeps the accounts.

"It was not easy to keep them at this work either, but there has not been a breakdown as yet, and there is every reason to hope that the habits of industry thus introduced will take firm root among this naturally indolent people."

(The abovementioned work was principally done by the convicts attached to the Andaman Homes, and the part the Andamanese took in it was taken under compulsion, and was most distasteful to them, It ceased the moment the compulsion was withdrawn —*M. V. P.*)

"The Andamanese have been very active in arresting runaways in the jungles, and on one occasion intercepted a large fishing gang who had, by the connivance of their Petty Officer, effected their escape from the harbour with a boat; they show great courage in their encounters with runaways, and, though they are sometimes wounded themselves, they generally manage to secure the convicts, whenever they get on their track, without using their arms.

"The Homes are places where food and shelter are provided for those entitled to receive them at our hands. They are, as it were, the headquarters of the different clans, and enable the Officer in charge to exercise a degree of control over them which would be impossible if they were permitted to roam at will about the outskirts of the Settlement.

"The food supplied to the aborigines at the Homes is not intended to keep the recipients in idleness; the object is simply to supplement the scanty fare procurable from the forests and waters, and thus to give us a claim to their gratitude and such services as they can render in return.

"Those who first engaged in taming the savage inhabitants of these Islands, were, no doubt, actuated by higher motives than those here described—motives that have never been lost sight of, but which do not call for remark in a report of this character. Suffice it to say, that by a continuous course of kind treatment, about one half of the inhabitants of the Andaman Islands are now peaceable, well behaved, subjects, and are, in many ways, of the greatest use to our Settlement.

"Although the Andamanese have for many years been characterised as a treacherous, blood-thirsty race of savages, the tribes in intimate intercourse with the Port Blair Settlement have proved themselves to be honest, peaceful, trustworthy, and faithful to their engagements.

"A new Home has been established at Kyd Island, which is connected to Port Blair by a road, cut chiefly by the Andamanese, and which ought in many ways to be advantageous to us.

"The Police Guard at the Home is a check upon runaways, and the Home itself enables us to extend our acquaintance with the more distant tribes towards the north.

"The Homes have, moreover, brought about a better state of feeling among the tribes themselves, as they seldom met in former days without a fight.

"The supply of tobacco to them has been reduced, as they smoke to excess.

"Our connection with the aborigines is influencing their habits and customs in various ways. They have dropped internal quarrels and animosities, are beginning to appreciate the use of clothes, are ceasing to use red mud on their bodies, live more together in communities in settled villages, and take an interest in cultivation.

(As regards these three latter statements, no real change had taken place. General Stewart had been misinformed.—*M. V. P.*)

"It is hoped that, instead of decreasing as was thought, the numbers are increasing. The deaths were twelve and the births twenty during the last year, of whom fifteen are now alive.

"There is a nursery at Viper where the children are well looked after by their convict nurses, but they do not take readily to their own people again."

(This did not last long, as the Andamanese disapproved of it, and the children practically became slaves.—*M. V. P.*)

"The great difficulty is the language, as it would appear that every tribe almost has a dialect of its own, and the difference in these is sometimes so great that the people are quite unable to communicate with each other, except by signs."

During the year 1873, General Stewart visited all the islands of the Andaman Group, and met the North Andaman Tribes at Stewart's Sound and Port Cornwallis in April. He was able to converse with these strangers through the medium of a girl belonging to the Kédé Tribe living at Flat Island on the West coast of the Middle Andaman, who had come in on a visit to the Kyd Island home shortly before he started, and who was taken with him. She was well understood by the people at Stewart's Sound, but only slightly by those at Port Cornwallis. At both places the visits were most successful, as the savages did not evince their usual treachery, seemed pleased with the presents given to them, and expressed a wish that General Stewart should come again and bring dogs and bottles. (The former for pig hunting, and the latter for breaking up to make the glass flakes used for shaving with. These are made from the thick part of the bottle at the "kick," by chipping the glass.)

Mr. Homfray, who accompanied General Stewart with some friendly Andamanese, including a Kédé man named Tóké, conducted the negotiations, and it was due to his personal influence that they were so successful, as even the North Andamanese knew his name.

They had already a few dogs, and seemed to have discovered the usefulness of this animal in pig hunting. Mr. Homfray during the stay of the party in Stewart's Sound went through Austen Strait in a boat, and partly explored that part of the country. The Strait had been supposed to be but a shallow swamp, but was found to be a good boat channel.

From this period dates the commencement of our friendly relations with the North Andaman tribes, and, except at Port Cornwallis, they have never since been disturbed. (At that place, there are two Septs, one Ár-*yaúto*, and the other Éremtága, who were at feud with each other and alarmed at us. We have only, up to now, succeeded in becoming really friendly with the former.)

On the South-west coast of the North Andaman, at Arat, and

especially at Interview Island, the aborigines were most friendly, and some of them visited the vessel.

(There were many reasons for this friendliness on the part of the West coast people, as compared to the timidity of those on the East coast. The Áka-*Béa*-da territory extended once to as far north as Flat Island, and the South Andaman Group of Tribes had always been to a certain extent in touch with the Western Septs of the Kédé Tribe through the Puchikwár and Āūkāū-*Júwōī*. It is quite possible, too, that as there are no harbours on the West coast of the Middle Andaman, the people there had been less harassed by the Malays and other pirates.)

General Stewart adds regarding this visit:—

"Such steps should have been taken long before, and should be continued, but as this is the first time we have met the North Andamanese without a collision, it is evident that the favourable knowledge of us is spreading.

"If they continue friendly, the system of Jungle Homes may be extended; shipwrecked mariners will then be safe all over the Andamans (except on the Little Andaman)."

On this report the Marquess of Salisbury, then Secretary of State for India, remarks on the 4th June 1874:—

"Beneficial results appear to follow from the establishment of Homes for the aborigines."

After leaving Interview Island, as the Tribes to the South were well known, and friendly, General Stewart visited the Little Andaman. The Islanders there were seen in the distance, but kept aloof.

On his return to Port Blair he heard that five of the crew of a Chinese junk, the *Quangoon*, trading between Moulmein and the Straits Settlements, which had touched at the Little Andaman for water on the 5th April, had been massacred at Hut Bay by the aborigines, and he sent down a punitive expedition under the command of Captain Wimberley, the details of which will be related in Chapter XIX.

On a second visit to the Northern Tribes none of them were met with, and General Stewart thought that this might be owing to the fact that, in December 1873, a fight took place at Port Campbell between the Port Mouat tribe, and some Interview Islanders who were down there on a visit, which unfortunately resulted in loss of life.

He thought that the Andamanese were the only real security we had in the Settlement against the escape of the convicts by land, and pointed out that thirty-two runaways had been captured by the Andamanese during the past year.

Forty Andamanese boys were at this time employed as boatmen, but of course much against their will, and only under great compulsion.

Only twelve deaths were known to have occurred during the year 1873—six in the Homes, *viz.*, two men, three women, and a boy; and six in the neighbouring jungle villages. At the Shoal Bay Home a woman gave birth to twins in May 1873, a most unusual occurrence. Both children died shortly afterwards.

A Home had, previous to this time, (about 1870), been built on Viper Island, where Mr. Homfray was now stationed, and remained there as the principal Home until the 28th of May 1882, when it was removed to Haddo station. The Andamanese had a special hospital on Viper, and a piggery, which became such a nuisance that it was moved to Dundas Point in 1880, and shortly afterwards closed.

Andamanese from the Rutland Island Sept had assisted in opening a track to the summit of Ford's Peak on Rutland Island, the height of which was 1,400 feet.

Mr. Homfray recommended the opening of two new Homes at Bluff Island and Long Island respectively, these being at the Western and Eastern entrances to Homfray Strait and suited by their position for advancing our influence with the Northern Tribes; but General Stewart was unable for various reasons to permit stations so far from the Settlement to be opened.

In November 1874, a visit was paid to the Middle Andaman, the Archipelago Islands, Stewart's Sound, and Interview Island. Up to this time Long Island was the farthest point North of Port Blair on the East coast where the aborigines were permanently friendly, but during this year acquaintance was made with the Kédé Tribe on the East coast of the Middle Andaman, who were called by the Southern Andamanese by the generic term "Yerewa-da," and these people soon became both friendly and of considerable use to us as interpreters with the more northerly tribes. On this occasion all the people visited seemed to be friendly, but in the following December the aborigines in Port Cornwallis showed such a determination to oppose the landing of our party that the idea had to be abandoned.

Moriarty, Chief of the Brigade Creek Sept of the Áka-*Béa*-da, died in July 1874, and was succeeded by *Friday* or *Furrutty*, as the Andamanese pronounce the word. The latter had been a captive in Moulmein, and seemed to be intelligent, but was very independent and unsociable in his manner.

At this time there were six Andaman Homes:—Mount Augusta; Rutland Island; Brigade Creek; Kyd Island; Pirij; and *Góp*-l'áka-bąng.

In December 1874 Mr. Homfray was transferred to the Nicobar Islands to take his six months' term of duty there, and was succeeded in the charge of the Andamanese by Mr. Tuson.

Mr. Homfray had, up to this time, been living on Viper Island, but when he returned to the Andamans, in June 1875, he was posted to the charge of Ross Island, and did not again take charge of the Andamanese, though his interest in them continued, for he took three couples with him at this time to the Nicobars, and later on took charge of the Andamanese Orphanage on Ross Island, which charge he held till his death on the 25th February 1883.

He had had charge of the Andamanese for a little over ten years and during that time had done excellent work. When he assumed charge in 1864, we were tolerably well acquainted with the two Septs of the Áka-*Béa*-da tribe who inhabited the North and South sides of the Harbour of Port Blair, and had a slight acquaintance with the

Sept inhabiting the South side of Port Mouat, but with no other of the Andamanese.

With these, even, on account of the murder of three convicts at the North Outpost Home, friendly relations had been broken off, and the task before Mr. Homfray was not an easy one. At their best the Andamanese in those days permitted our presence, and accepting what presents we gave them, stole what they could not otherwise procure.

They were of no assistance to us, were a source of annoyance to the convict villagers, and had no idea of making any return for the kindness shown to them. They were dissatisfied with their treatment in the Home on Ross Island, where they were kept under restraint and compelled to do distasteful work, and great tact was required in the Officer in charge of them to neutralise the effect which had been produced, and to establish really reliable friendly relations.

All this, and more, Mr. Homfray did. When he relinquished the charge, all the Tribes from Rutland Island to Stewart's Sound (with the exception of the Jàrawas), were on friendly terms with us and a commencement of these terms had been made with the people in the North Andaman.

An Orphanage and a Nursery had been established, in which the Andamanese were carefully brought up, trained, and taught; and in the Home on Viper Island forty lads were employed as boatmen, while others, including the elders of the tribes, regularly hunted the run-away convicts for us, bringing them in unhurt when they made no resistance.

Far from being the irreclaimable and ferocious savages they were considered to be in 1864, General Stewart considered that they were of the greatest assistance and value to the Government, and that they were our best safeguard against the escapes of dangerous convicts in large numbers.

To Mr. Homfray is due, almost entirely, the credit for this most satisfactory change, and it should be remembered that, though he was a man without private means, he, for years, supplemented the Government Grant to the amount of half his pay.

It was unfortunate that, owing to his other duties, he was latterly obliged to leave the Andamanese a great deal in the hands, and consequently in the power and under the pernicious influence of, the convicts attached to the Homes. He had also not been able to make any really correct and detailed observations of the habits of the aborigines, and it may be considered that, at the time he made over charge of the Andamanese to Mr. Tuson, such work as he could do with them was done, and well done.

CHAPTER XVI.

Mr. Tuson in charge of the Andamanese—Restraint of the Andamanese, and the convict supervision over them stopped—Syphilis first noticed—Murder of convicts at the Kyd Island Home by the Andamanese—The Andamanese capture runaway convicts—Death of Lípāia—Mr. Man takes charge of the Andamanese—The Kyd Island murderers arrested and punished—Attempts to civilise the Andamanese—Changes—Capture of runaway convicts by Māla Biala—Annual Report for 1875-76—Syphilis—Mr. Man visits the North and Middle Andamans—Chinamen killed by the Andamanese—Epidemic of ophthalmia—Mr. Man visits the distant Islands—Annual Report for 1876-77—Epidemic of measles—Notes on epidemics among the Andamanese—Mr. Man visits the distant Islands—Soldiers blown out to sea—Mr. Man visits the distant Islands—Syphilis—Notes on the year 1878—Mr. Portman takes charge of the Andamanese—Mr. Man's book on the Andamanese, and comments—Finances of the Andamanese—Mr. Portman attacked by a convict—Visits to the distant Islands—Execution of an Andamanese for murder—Visits to the distant Islands—Annual Report—Hunt after escaped convicts—Visits to the distant Islands—Mr. Godwin-Austen takes charge of the Andamanese.

In December 1874 Mr. F. E. Tuson took charge of the Andamanese, and one of his first acts, on finding that over fifty convicts were employed on Viper Island guarding the Andamanese in order to prevent them from leaving it, was, to stop this system of restraint, and relieve the Andamanese of the distasteful work they had been compelled to do by withdrawing the compulsion, doubtless considering, and rightly, that they were not convicts, and should not be treated as such. Far from evil effects attending this action, as some feared would happen, the Andamanese were naturally happier and more contended at being permitted to roam about unrestricted. Of course, so soon as they found that they were not compelled by force to work, all the boatmen and so called cultivators abandoned their labours and reverted to their jungle life.

In January 1875 Mr. Tuson noticed that a woman in the *Góp*-l'áka-*báng* Home was suffering from a bubo and suspected that it might be syphilitic, but no further action was taken in the matter.

On the 12th of February four convicts stationed at the Kyd Island Home were murdered there by the Andamanese. The weekly ration party arrived at Pirij, on the opposite shore, on the 13th, and hoisted the usual signal for a canoe. No notice being taken they made a raft of bamboos and crossed on it to Kyd Island. On arrival there they found the four men lying dead in their hut, killed by arrows, and everything of value, such as the clothes, utensils, rations, etc., removed : in short, the place had been plundered by the murderers The ration men took the canoe, which had not been touched, and went up to *Góp*-l'áka-*báng*, and then on to Viper on the 14th, to report the matter. On the 15th the Deputy Superintendent, the 2nd Medical Officer, and Mr. Tuson went to the spot, and found everything as described. One man had been cooking his food at the time of the attack, and received the first arrow, the Andamanese having torn down the mat wall to get a clear shot. The wounded man had dragged himself into the hut, and had fallen down near the entrance and died there. The other men were in the inner room, and had been shot through holes made in the mat walls. Mr. Tuson had the arrows extracted from the bodies, and brought them into Port Blair in the hope that some of our friendly Andamanese might recognise them. The dead Hindus were burnt, and the Mahomedans buried, and no Andamanese were seen.

On the following day sixteen Andamanese were sent from the Brigade Creek Home to try and find out who had committed the murders, and the reason for their actions. A party from the Port Mouat Home was also sent to the north for the same purpose. The Port Mouat people seemed to fear that they would be held responsible for the murders, but Mr. Tuson re-assured them about this.

He thought that the murders were committed by the Andamanese of the Home on the evening of the 12th. They had left the Home on the 10th to collect pán leaves, etc , and had returned on the 12th, when they cut a quantity of sugarcane. The petty officer in charge, however, seeing that they had brought in no pán leaves, turtle, or shells, as they usually do, took the sugarcane from them and refused to give them any fruit; a foolish act on his part and one tending to rouse their passions. They did not say much at the time but went away at about 5 P.M. They are supposed to have returned after dark, and revenged themselves by killing the men who had offended them.

The convicts at the Pirij and Góp-l'áka-báng Homes were withdrawn to Brigade Creek till some arrangements could be made for their safety. Mr. Tuson very rightly thought that it was necessary to have a party permanently stationed either at Pirij or Kyd Island to facilitate our intercourse with the aborigines and to recapture runaway convicts. Pirij would, he considered, be perhaps the better of the two, if a stockade was built there, and a guard of Free Police provided.

In March the Andamanese sent out to look for the Kyd Island murderers returned, bringing some of the articles stolen from the Home. They reported that the murders had been committed by a party of men from different tribes, and that the reason for them was that the convicts would not allow the Andamanese to take any fruits and would not give them any tobacco or pipes.

(This attack was what we might have expected as the outcome of the repressive policy exercised towards the Andamanese. Mr. Homfray, not being able to visit the more distant Homes, his authority over the Andamanese was delegated to the convicts there, who had the power to make the Andamanese work and to punish them. After this the system was gradually altered, and at present the convicts merely report the Andamanese who give trouble, have no power over them, and have to distribute a certain daily ration to all alike. The Officer in charge personally distributes all rewards, and no one but he can punish. Though Mr. Homfray may have considered it necessary in 1865 that some one other than the Officer in charge should punish the Andamanese, such policy was not necessary in 1875, and it has been found that the best system is the one where the Andamanese look to the Officer in charge of them for everything, and communicate in all matters direct with him, the convicts merely tending the gardens, assisting in runaway hunting, and supplying that care and perseverance in work in which the Andamanese are wanting.)

Mr. Homfray who had returned from the Nicobars for a short time visited the Middle Straits with a party of Andamanese in March and remained there for a week. He did not succeed in capturing the murderers, but obtained their names and also the remainder of the stolen property.

The Andamanese had by this time got over their scare about the murders and flocked into the Homes again, men from the Archipelago bringing in honey, shells, etc.

In the previous month two runaway convicts, who had escaped from Haddo, crossed to Rutland Island on a raft, and having walked to the south end of that island were making another raft on which to put to sea when they were captured by Māīa Bíala and some of his tribe. They offered resistance and were not secured till they had been shot in the legs. Three other convicts had also escaped from the northern stations, and wandered to Lekera Báruga where they found three Andamanese canoes. They took one of these and went in it to Shoal Bay, but met with two Andamanese there who arrested them; only two runaways were however brought back to the Settlement, and these men said that the Andamanese had taken them on shore from the canoe and had given them fish and water. Shortly afterwards the women and children were sent away from the encampment, and two arrows were fired by some one hidden in the jungle, which killed the third convict named Gopal; the others prayed for mercy and were spared on promising to return to their stations. As the truth of this story was doubted, a party of police and Andamanese were sent to the spot and the body of Gopal was found, half-buried. (The truth probably was that Gopal refused to allow himself to be stripped,—the Andamanese always taking everything from every runaway convict they found,—and was therefore killed. The other men had slight scratches on their persons, which were caused, they said, by the arrows of the Andamanese. They probably offered resistance to their capture.)

During this month alone, eleven runaway convicts were caught and brought in by the Andamanese, and R96-8 were realised for the Home Fund by the sale of jungle honey.

In May 1875 an Andamanese man, named Lípāia, was killed by

a huge skate, while fishing. One of his comrades in a canoe harpooned what Lipāia thought was a turtle. Being in shallow water he jumped out of the boat on to it, to secure it in the usual manner, and fell on the spike which is attached to the fish's tail. This entered his breast to a depth of four inches, and, owing to the fish's struggles, a fearful wound was inflicted. The man was taken to the hospital and died there during the night. His body was put on a platform in the neighbouring jungle, and the Andamanese refrained from hunting and fishing in the vicinity for some time, through fear of his spirit, which was supposed to haunt the spot.

Mr. Tuson during this month closed the Andamanese shop on Ross Island, and introduced the present system of house to house sales which yields a larger income than the shop did.

On the 19th of June Mr. Tuson proceeded on duty to the Nicobars, and Mr. E. H. Man took charge of the Andamanese. General Stewart had left the Settlement and was succeeded in the Chief Commissionership by Major-General C. A. Barwell, C.B.

Mr. Man had already interested himself in the Andaman Orphanage, and was anxious to study the Andamanese from a scientific point, and record what was known of this people and their customs before they became extinct.

The three couple of Andamanese who had been with Mr. Homfray at the Nicobars returned with him, and went back to their homes in the jungle, where one of the women died shortly afterwards from the effects of Nicobar fever. Mr. Man at this time mentions a visit of 100 Andamanese from the Archipelago Islands, and 200 from Kyd Island, to the Brigade Creek Home, showing that they were then plentiful.

In July 1875 three of the Andamanese who were concerned in the Kyd Island murders were brought in by other Andamanese, but one of them almost immediately afterwards escaped; three others were brought in in August, also Māia Niáli, Chief of the Archipelago Islands, at whose instigation the murders were committed. The man who had escaped died a few days afterwards in the jungle.

Mr. Homfray, who had been away on privilege leave, returned in

September and assisted in the enquiry into the case, and in October five of the men who were proved to have been directly concerned in the murders were awarded six months' rigorous imprisonment each, and placed in Viper Jail. The sixth man was acquitted. The Homes at Kyd Island, Góp-l'áka-báng, and Pirij had been closed since the murders, and were not re-opened for some years.

Māia Biala and his men caught five Pathan runaway convicts on the 9th August 1875. These men had, four days previous to their capture, been sent in a boat from Aberdeen to Corbyn's Cove to bring *dhani* leaves, under the charge of two armed policemen. They overpowered them, seized their muskets and ammunition, and escaped with the boat to MacPherson's Straits where they were caught.

Mr. Man continued Mr. Homfray's attempts to induce the Andamanese to give up their jungle life and customs, and to settle down to cultivation and a life of industry. He encouraged them to work as carpenters and blacksmiths, to clear and cultivate land, and to bring in bamboos, thatching leaves, etc., rewarding them for their work.

For a time this went on well, and Mr. Man was sanguine as to the results, but was obliged to place convicts in charge of the Andamanese. In November, "Friday," Chief of Brigade Creek, died. He had been a troublesome man, and had tried to dissuade his people from settling down to agricultural pursuits. He was succeeded by Wologa, who, not behaving satisfactorily, was deported to Rutland Island in the following month, and Tura was appointed in his place.

A party of Andamanese from the Kédé Tribe on the West coast of the Middle Andaman visited the Homes during this month.

In December, the Andamanese began to tire of the labour of cultivating, in which it was admitted that they were greatly "assisted" by convicts attached to the Homes, and their work generally fell off. The women who were more accustomed to work, and to be under subjection, were now the principal workers, making thatching leaves, blankets, and sewing clothes. The men reverted to their jungle accomplishments and life.

On the 25th January, 1876, 23 convicts, principally Bhils, escaped from Aberdeen. Nine were shortly afterwards recaptured, but the remaining 14 kept together and contrived to escape into the jungles, having armed themselves with *dahs* and sticks, stolen from the villages.

On the 31st a party of Andamanese fell in with them at Manglután, and thinking they would surrender at once allowed them to approach too close. The result was that they rushed upon the Andamanese and severely injured three of them (two of whom subsequently died from the effects of their wounds), and routed the remainder.

Under these circumstances it became necessary to take very active measures for their apprehension, and no effort was spared in hunting them down with the aid of parties of Police and Andamanese, combined parties of whom tracked them day after day, whilst Police pickets and patrols protected the villages and watched the jungle road in the district. Māīa Biala, being greatly enraged at the death of two of his men, accompanied one of the tracking parties on the 6th of February and found the runaways in a ravine in the jungles, about twelve miles from Aberdeen, where, after a determined resistance, three of them were secured and eight killed.

On being called upon to give themselves up and lay down their weapons, they defiantly replied that they were Rajpoots and would never do so. One man was afterwards found, having died of the wounds received on the 31st, and one was recaptured, wounded, on the 7th, the day after the encounter; he afterwards died; another gave himself up at Port Mouat. This disposed of the whole number, thirteen having been recaptured, and ten having been killed, or died of their wounds.

Māīa Biala, on being asked what reward he would like for his conduct in capturing these runaways, begged for the release of the aborigines who had been imprisoned for the Kyd Island murders, and, with the exception of one old man, who had died in jail, they were released, after having completed two thirds of their sentence.

In the Annual Report for 1875-76 General Barwell writes in the chapter on the Aborigines, para. 10, *et. seq.* :—

" In February 1876 it was discovered that some of the inmates of the Viper Home were suffering from sores, and they were at once transferred to an empty shed on the island, and placed under medical treatment. At first it was thought that the sores were due to a want of cleanliness, but it soon became apparent that the patients were suffering from syphilis. A strict investigation was, therefore, made, and the aborigines of the various Homes were examined, with the result that five men, six women, and four children were found to be more or less affected with the disease; they were accordingly at once placed under medical treatment.

" 11. On making a careful enquiry into the subject, the Officer in charge of the Homes ascertained from the Andamanese that the disease had been known to them during the past three or four years. He also learnt that, though they deem chastity a virtue, it is by no means rare for some of them to form improper connections; but in this they assert that they do not differ from the tribes of the other islands.

" 12. It is thus very apparent that the opinion hitherto prevalent regarding these people, that they are free from any taint of immorality, is entirely unfounded ; and it is fortunate that the facts above recorded have been brought to notice at this comparatively early stage before the disease had spread to a greater extent. Every endeavour is being made to discover any other cases, and all necessary precautions are being observed with a view to prevent the disease affecting those at present free from its taint. Convict Shera, the senior Petty Officer at the Homes, was proved to be the chief, if not sole, offender, and was remanded to section in the labouring ranks. (He subsequently died of syphilis.)

" 13. It is satisfactory that, of those who have been admitted into hospital (numbering about 16), some have been already discharged, and the remainder are progressing favourably; only one woman and one child, who were suffering from the disease in its worst form before being admitted, have as yet died."

Mr. Man did not at this time appreciate the extent to which the disease had spread, through the fact of children being affected with it showed that it must have been of some years' standing. It had probably been introduced at least six years previously, if not more, and subsequent enquiry showed that it had at this time, infected members of distant tribes in the Middle Andaman.

Mr. Man did all in his power to stop the spread of it, and combated it with great energy so long as he remained in charge of the Andamanese, but the mischief had been in existence too long to be checked, and all that could be done was to bring in the sick promptly, give them all the care and attention possible, and improve by suitable diet and preventives the injured constitutions of the children.

With regard to para. 11, Mr. Homfray should have been aware that "free love" was the rule among the unmarried Andamanese, and that even the married women were far from chaste, and were willing to yeld themselves to the convicts for small reward, ands, of course, when threatened.

In March 1876 Mr. Man visited the coasts of the North and Middle Andaman, but only saw the aborigines near Bennet Island, and at Flat Island, where they were quite friendly. At the former place they were only seen in the distance and fled on the approach of the party, and at the letter one family only was seen. Mr. Man, as he always did on these visits, planted at each place where he landed a variety of fruit trees, and left a quantity of presents in all the empty encampments he saw. He deprecated such hurried visits as he had been obliged to make, (he was only absent from Port Blair for four days) as there was not time to stop long enough at any place, and hold a satisfactory interview with the aborigines.

During the year 1875-76, the women at the Viper Home had made 65,000 thatching leaves, and 38 blankets, which, valued at about R350, were given to the Settlement *gratis*. In this Home there were 79 adults and 19 children, representatives of all the Tribes with whom we were on friendly terms.

The ration of rum, which we now learn it had been the custom to issue to the Andamanese, (!) was stopped by Mr. Man as soon as he assumed charge of them, and tea was given in its stead. It is astonishing that, except medicinally, sanction should ever have been accorded to the issue of a ration of liquor to these people. He also insisted on the people in the Homes wearing clothes, not for their own sake, but for that of the European residents in the Settlement.

In April 1876 Mr. Man wished to have the Kyd Island Home re-opened, but this was not permitted.

Further enquiries were made regarding the syphilis among the Andamanese. It was found that a woman from the west coast of the South Andaman had a child aged three years, the father of which was a convict, and the Andamanese admitted that they had been afraid to bring their sufferings to notice because they disliked the restraint they were necessarily subjected to in the hospital, (which of course should have been made comfortable and tempting, not a terror), and because they were prevented from telling by the convicts, who were afraid of being punished.

On the 6th May 1876 a party of Chinamen, who had the monopoly of the collection of edible birds' nests in the Andamans, came into the Settlement bringing two of their men who were dead, and a third who had been wounded by the arrows of the Andamanese.

They stated that they had been living for some days in friendly intercourse with the Andamanese at Oyster Island, when a man of the Puchikwár tribe asked for a *dah* which they refused to give him; he then fired at them, and was only driven off by the blank discharge of a musket.

In June three youths belonging to the Southern Tribe of the Middle Andaman were identified as the murderers of the Chinamen and brought in, coming quite willingly. They said they had been living in camp at Oyster Island with their women, and were friendly with the Chinamen, giving them fish in exchange for food and cheroots. They stole a *dah* during one night in order to barter it back to the Chinamen for food, and the next day the Chinamen fired on their women. These ran to the men for protection, and they decided to give the *dah* back. They paddled to Oyster Island, and hailed two Chinamen who had guns in their hands. They held up the *dah* to show that they had come to restore it, but the Chinamen fired on them, when they crouched down and paddled away.

When they saw the Chinamen had gone to their work they returned in order to punish them for their murderous assault. The three men crept up to the hut in which the Chinamen were taking shelter as it was raining heavily, and fired at them. The Chinese then fired in return. The Andamanese seem to have considered their deeds justified by the action taken by the Chinamen, and Mr. Man accepted their story as substantially correct. They were punished by ten weeks' rigorous imprisonment.

During the month of July an epidemic of ophthalmia broke out among the Andamanese and lasted till the end of the year, and the results were observed for many years afterwards.

In August Mr. Man visited Barren Island, Narcondam, Port Cornwallis, and Stewart's Sound. At the latter place only were aborigines met with, and being very friendly two of them were brought down to Port Blair. After visiting the Settlement and the Homes, and making the acquaintance of the Andamanese of the Southern Tribes, they were taken back to their own country in November. After landing them there Mr. Man visited Port Cornwallis and found the natives there to be friendly, though he could not induce them to come on board the steamer. He then returned to Stewart's Sound and brought away two more of the tribe from there.

Though the aborigines in the North Andaman were still shy, Mr. Man advanced our friendly relations with them by leaving quantities of presents for them in all the huts he visited, and abstained from removing, or otherwise interfering with, any of their property.

Five men of the South Andaman Tribes volunteered to stop at the Sound on the occasion of this second visit, so Mr. Man left them there. About a fortnight afterwards, however, two of them arrived in Port

Blair in an outrigger canoe belonging to the Sound people, and stated that two or three days after they had been left there a party of men from Port Cornwallis came to the village, and at once commenced to plunder all the presents that had been left. A quarrel naturally ensued, and would doubtless have ended in bloodshed had not one of the Sound men had the sense to destroy all the bows and arrows belonging to the Port Cornwallis men, who had left them unprotected whilst plundering. The latter then left the place, but the five men from Port Blair dreaded lest they should return armed and with larger numbers, and having, moreover, managed to offend the Chief of the Sound Tribe by failing to make a sounding board equal to his expectations, they decided to return to the Settlement. They accordingly borrowed two small outrigger canoes on the pretence of fishing, and came south, three remaining at their homes in the jungle, and two arriving, after a seven days journey, in Port Blair. They reported that those people from the Sound, with whom we had made friends, had assisted them, and behaved very well.

Mr. Man was still exerting himself to check the spread of syphilis, and had taken many precautions to segregate and keep clean the patients, also building a special hospital for them. He sent in February 1877 a party to the Middle Straits to look for syphilitic cases there and two men, a woman, and a child were brought in. Hearing from them that there were other cases on the South Andaman, and on the Archipelago Islands, he sent out and had these brought to the hospital. A further party was sent up the west coast to look for cases, and to bring back some convalescents who had left the Home without permission, and gone back to their tribe. Māīa Bíala went with this party and did his utmost to persuade the Andamanese who were diseased to come in for treatment, and to impress upon the others how necessary it was that all cases, when discovered, should be taken to the hospital.

The convalescents were kept apart from the others in a special Home building, but great difficulty was experienced in keeping these people from going back to their jungle villages, where, of course, they would only help to spread the disease.

Mr. Man writes on this subject in his Annual Report on the aborigines for 1876-77 :—

"Para. 33. With regard to the outbreak of syphilis, the existence of which among the aborigines of these parts was only discovered a few months before the preparation of my last Annual Report, I am hopeful that if the present precautionary measures are continued we shall succeed in reducing to a minimum the risk of the spread of this disease to those at present free from its taint.

"Para. 34. These measures consist merely in completely isolating those affected with the disease from the rest of the community. A well ventilated barrack, with concrete flooring so as the better to ensure cleanliness, has been provided for their accommodation at Viper, and they are made to keep their persons clean by frequent bathing. At the same time, in order to mitigate as far as possible the irksomeness of the restraint necessarily entailed by this treatment, and thereby render them in some measure reconciled to their lot,—many of them belong to encampments 30 or 35 miles distant,—every facility is given them for pursuing their customary occupations, and all reasonable wishes expressed by them are gratified. In spite of this, however, two unsuccessful attempts to elude our vigilance and rejoin their friends in the jungle have been made.

"Para. 35. This extreme step of segregating these unfortunate individuals was adopted in January last, and was rendered necessary by the discovery, that although we had succeeded in making them live and eat apart from those unaffected with the disease, the infection was being gradually conveyed to the latter by means of the children still at the breast, it being a common practice with the Andamanese women to suckle each other's infants, and consequently nothing but entire separation proved sufficient to check this source of evil. So far the result has been that not a single fresh case has occurred on the island.

"Para. 36. The only persons afflicted with this malady whom I have hitherto failed in segregating are a few of the Port Mouat tribe, who about nine months ago, on their being cured and discharged from hospital, insisted on returning to their friends. It unfortunately happens that one of them is the brother of the Chief of that part, and is possessed of even more influence than he. The consequence has been, that having heard of the system that I had introduced since their departure, in respect to the discharged syphilitic patients, he and the others have been careful to avoid meeting me on every occasion, and no inducement avails to tempt them to visit Viper Island. All that they will consent to do is to avoid promiscuous living, and to bring to notice any case of one suffering from syphilitic sores.

"Para. 37. I have no doubt that a good deterrent effect has been produced on the many who have witnessed the lamentable suffering and mortality which have occurred among these unfortunate patients, and that such immorality, as is believed to have formerly to some extent prevailed in their midst, has received a wholesome check. (?)

"Para. 38. From the record which has been kept of the progress of this outbreak, I am able to furnish particulars of the admissions, casualties, etc. These figures only refer to the population of about 600 people living within a radius of about 35 miles, beyond which it is believed the disease has not spread.

"The details are:—

"Admissions 54. Deaths 7. Under treatment 5. Discharged 25 (who are isolated at Viper.) Discharged and at large at Port Mouat 7."

The Andamanese were too thoughtless and helpless a race to benefit by the precautions which were taken on their behalf. The disease had, in the first place, spread to a far greater extent than Mr. Man at this time realised, and the Andamanese disliked the restraints of the hospital so much that they preferred remaining in their homes and suffering from the disease, to coming into the Settlement to be cured. Their filthy habits, their custom of sleeping together in a heap, so that the abrasions on the skin of one became inoculated with the syphilitic poison from the open sores of another, and their immorality, all tended to spread the infection, and nothing short of a house-to-house inspection throughout the whole of the Great Andaman, which was impracticable, and the strictest discipline in hospital, would have been of any use. As it was, in spite of

Mr. Man's efforts, the disease spread until now there is scarcely an Andamanese in the Great Andaman who is free from it, or a child who is healthy.

At this time Mr. Man's troubles were many. In addition to his constant steady fight against the syphilis, he had only finished dealing with the epidemic of ophthalmia, which left many of the aborigines entirely or partially blind, (and from which he, himself, owing to his nursing many of the patients in his own house, suffered much), when in March 1877 an epidemic of measles broke out just as he was intending to again visit the North Andaman, and also the Little Andaman and the Sentinel Islands.

It originated on Ross Island, among the native residents, some of whom probably brought it from India. The boys in the Andaman Orphanage on Ross caught it, and passed it on to the people in the Viper Home before Mr. Man was aware of its existence. It, of course, spread like fire amongst a people who had never before suffered from it, and though Mr. Man, as soon as he knew of its existence, did his utmost to prevent it from spreading to the jungle, cases were in a few days brought in from the Port Mouat and Brigade Creek Homes.

The Homes were fumigated, and many of the sick brought into Mr. Man's house to be nursed, but unfortunately, on the very day that the outbreak of measles on Viper Island was discovered, eighty Andamanese from the Middle Andaman arrived at the Brigade Creek Home and mixed freely with the other Andamanese there, three of whom had the disease. Quarantine was attempted, but the Andamanese got frightened and fled from the Settlement to their jungle homes, carrying the infection with them. Before the end of the month 100 cases were in hospital, but their dread of the detention and restraint in the hospital for syphilitic cases prevented others from coming; there were about sixty of these cases segregated in a special building, and kept under some restraint, and when the sufferers at Port Mouat heard of this they fled with all their goods to Port Campbell. Nothing short of a personal visit by Mr. Man in the station steamer would have brought them back, and even then it is more than probable that the sick, at the sight of the steamer, would have guessed Mr. Man's object in coming and hid in the jungle. Māia Biala and a party of An_damanese were out at this time trying to catch some runaways, and it was found on their return that they were then suffering from measles.

Mr. Man reported in April 1877 that, after six weeks of the measles, 51 out of 184 cases in the hospital had died, the greatest number of deaths being among a party of 70 people from the distant villages in the South Andaman, who were on a visit to the Viper Home at the time the epidemic broke out. The syphilitic patients suffered more than any of the others.

The 80 people from the Middle Andaman, who having arrived at Brigade Creek were being kept isolated there, on hearing of the number of deaths that had occurred fled to their homes, many of them suffering from the disease at the time. Some of these soon after returned and reported that after leaving the South Andaman they went to their several homes and all suffered from the disease (thus spreading it throughout the islands).

Māia Bíala, amongst others, died from measles, and Mr. Man writes in the Annual Report on the Aborigines for 1876-77 :—

"Para 31. Among the deaths the most severely felt was that of Māia Biala, the Chief of Rutland Island, which event occurred just after the close of the official year. This man has been deservedly spoken of in high terms by various officers from the early days of this Settlement. It has been greatly due to his influence that we have been able to establish from so early a date the satisfactory relations which subsist between ourselves and these aborigines. He had always been our principal stand-by on the occasion of any more than usually troublesome escape of a party of convicts. The number of runaway convicts whom he has been either directly or indirectly concerned in recapturing must be considerable. He, moreover, contributed largely to the funds of the Andaman Home, by supplying greatly by his own personal exertions most of the turtles which have been sold for the benefit of the Andamanese.

"Para 32. Before leaving the subject of this unfortunate epidemic of measles, I would draw the following inferences from the medical returns:—

"(a) The comparative immunity of the inmates of the Viper Home may be ascribed to the circumstance that the constitutions of these individuals, who have all passed a more or less considerable time with us, have become fairly habituated to the diet and course of treatment to which all the 191 patients were alike subjected on falling sick, while on the other hand,

"(b) the lamentable mortality among the 77 who happened to be visiting their friends at Viper at the time of the outbreak of the epidemic appears to indicate the unsuitableness of our Hospital diet and treatment in the case of savages who have, except on rare occasions, partaken of no other food than what is procurable in the jungles.

"(c) The above inference is confirmed, or at least strengthened, when it is observed how comparatively well it fared with those who suffered from this disease in the jungle where they were deprived of the advantages of professional treatment and had recourse to their own few simple remedies which appear to be prescribed by them for all sorts and conditions of sickness with every faith in their efficacy. This being their first experience of any of the exanthemata, their success in the treatment of the recent epidemic appears all the more surprising.

"(d) The large percentage of deaths among those of the patients who have for some time past been sufferers from syphilis, as compared with that among the other aborigines at the Viper Home, is readily accounted for, and requires no explanation.

"The details of the above are:—

"*At the Viper Home.*—71 Andamanese were attacked and 6 died. Of the syphilitic patients, 43 were attacked and 10 died. Of the visitors in hospital, 77 were attacked and 37 died. Self-treated in the jungle, say, 350 attacked and 56 died."

These remarks, as was found afterwards, considerably under-stated the case. The disease gradually spread throughout the whole of the

Great Andaman, affecting all but the Jàrawa tribes, and was nearly a year in doing so. The actual number of deaths from the measles may not have been more than 15 per cent. of the whole of the population, but the deaths from the *sequelæ* of the disease were many more. Half, if not two-thirds, of the whole of the Andamanese in the Great Andaman died from its effects. All the people inhabiting the west coast of the South Andaman between Port Campbell and the Middle Straits died, as I found on visiting that part of the country three years afterwards. This epidemic was the most serious disaster which has befallen the Andamanese, and owing to the effects of it our treatment of them underwent a change, all attempts to force them to settle down to an agricultural life were abandoned, and our efforts were directed to keeping such of the race alive as we could, and to strengthening the constitutions of the delicate and syphilitic children.

Once the disease had got amongst the Andamanese nothing more could have been done than what Mr. Man did, and with such a race it was futile to hope that the patients could be isolated and the spread of the disease checked. When Mr. Man knew of the existence of it he took prompt action, but he did not know of it until too late. He lived on Viper Island, and the medical authorities on Ross Island, where the measles originated, did not inform him regarding them, nor did the Officer in charge of the Andaman Orphanage, which was on Ross Island, take any precautions. The doctors never seem to have thought about the Andamanese, or the effect of the measles on them, though a recent similar outbreak at Fiji should have warned them, and to their neglect the partial extermination of the race is due. On two occasions since then a similar extraordinary neglect has come to my notice, which I note here :—

Once, about ten years ago, while passing through the Haddo village, about a quarter of a mile from the principal Andaman Home, and a couple of a hundred yards from the house of one of the Junior Medical Officers, I saw a native youth wandering about, covered with small-pox pustules. I spoke to the Junior Medical Officer there who appeared to know of the case, but had not thought it necessary to warn me, or to take any steps to isolate the patients in the Andamanese Hospital which was close to the village. I at once sent all the Andamanese in the Home away to Rutland Island, where they were isolated from the other Andamanese in case infection had already got among them, and where at the same time they were not in communication with the convicts; the Home was disinfected and partly re-built, and on my reporting the matter to the Chief Commissioner, necessary precautions were taken regarding the small-pox case. No evil results followed.

Again, on my return from Calcutta on the 11th February, 1895, with some Andamanese I had taken there, I learnt from Mr. Man, who had taken charge of the Andamanese during my absence, that two cases of measles had occurred in the house next to mine. I closed all the Homes, sent the Andamanese away from the Settlement, and kept them away for more than two months until the rains commenced and all danger of infection had passed away. None of them caught the disease, which may possibly be owing to the fact that many of them had already had it during the epidemic of 1877, but the medical authorities did not communicate with me on the subject until some time afterwards, though the epidemic spread throughout the Settlement, the schools had to be closed, and other precautions taken, which were principally initiated by Mr. Man, who had the advantage of his previous terrible experience, and not by the doctors.

During the year 1876-77 the amount earned by the Andamanese by the sale of jungle and garden produce was Rs.2,167, against R1,204 of the previous year; and 142 blankets and 107,250 thatching leaves were made by them and supplied to the Settlement *gratis*, an estimated value of R678.

Fifteen runaway convicts were recaptured by the Andamanese during the year. Mr. Man found that the most paying work for the Andamanese, as well as the work they were likely to continue at from their natural tastes and habits, was the collection of articles of jungle produce, shells, turtles, honey, etc.

General Barwell remarked in his Annual Report to the Government of India that—

"Mr. Man has been in charge of the aborigines throughout the year, and has taken the greatest interest in them. It is mainly owing to his exertions and tact that such satisfactory progress has been made in our relations with the distant tribes."

In the Resolution on this Report the Government of India remark:—

"The improved relations with the Andamanese appear satisfactory, and Mr. Man's services in this matter deserve special notice."

In May, 1877, Mr. Man made a tour round the Islands in the *Enterprise*. He first visited Port Campbell where he found four measles cases which he took on board; then Flat Island where some people from the Viper Home were landed; then Port Cornwallis where two men were met with, one of whom swam off to the boat. Several other natives were seen there, but were timid, and would not allow Mr. Man's party to approach them, so he gave presents to the two who came off, and left many more in some empty huts. When leaving the harbour he was hailed by a number of aborigines who were on the shore near the entrance, but had no time to stop and interview them.

At Stewart's Sound no one was seen, and he landed the two men from that part who had been staying at the Home. He also visited the Diligent Straits, and the Archipelago Islands, but did not meet with any Andamanese. The measles seem by this time to have spread to as far north as the Middle Straits, but it is questionable whether Mr. Man was not doing more harm than good by thus introducing infected persons among the aborigines of the North Andaman. As the trip was not made with intention of bringing in Andamanese suffering from measles, it would have been better had it been postponed for some months.

A boat containing five European soldiers of the Detachment of the 21st Regiment, in endeavouring to row across from North Bay to

Ross Island in the afternoon of the 18th of June 1877 was carried out to sea during a heavy squall, and owing to the severity of the weather and the thickness of the atmosphere at the time, nothing was known of the occurrence for several hours afterwards. In fact, it was thought, up till the next morning, that the boat had either returned to North Bay or taken shelter elsewhere in the harbour. Owing to the tempest that was raging all that evening and night it was quite impossible to send out a boat to investigate the matter; but at daylight in the morning, on search being made, it was ascertained that the missing boat had certainly been drifted out to sea, and the steamer *Enterprise* was then despatched to examine the Islands of the Archipelago, and Narcondam. After making one trip she was sent out a second time, and when searching Neill and Havelock Islands found on the shore of the former the wreck of a 200 ton country vessel named the *Hawke*, which was embedded in the sand, and from the fact that a number of coconut palms of about three years' growth were springing up around her, it was concluded that she had been laden with coconuts when wrecked.

On the next morning, just as the *Enterprise* was leaving for Port Blair, the search being abandoned as hopeless, some people were seen to be signalling on the coast of the south side of Havelock Island, so a boat was sent off to them. The surf was high, and after some trouble four out of the five missing men were rescued. It appeared that they had been blown away in a squall to Havelock Island, which they had reached in safety, though their boat was dashed to pieces on the rocks shortly after they landed. The fifth man, a Non-Commissioned Officer, was unfortunately drowned while swimming out towards the *Enterprise* on the evening previous to the rescue, in order to give notice regarding the party. The poor fellows who were rescued stated that they had kept themselves alive on the fish they had been able to catch, and on the wild fruits which they had found upon the island.

During this month "Billy," the brother of the chief of Port Mouat, and one of the most influential and best natured men amongst the aborigines, died. He was wounded in the chest by the spike of some fish he had harpooned in the night, mistaking it for a turtle, and only lived for a few hours afterwards.

Mr. Man points out that the greatest number of deaths from the measles have occurred among robust male adults, and the youthful and sickly seem to have suffered less. The Andamanese appear by this time to have seen the folly of keeping the syphilitic cases hidden in the jungle, and began to bring them in for treatment of their own accord, but the disease was spreading rapidly, and though Mr. Man was hopeful that the aborigines would assist him in his work of detecting and bringing in for treatment fresh cases, he regarded them as if they were of a graver and more thoughtful nature than the helpless, thoughtless children they really are.

In September 1877 Chāūr Mio, an Éremtága Kédé from the North-West of the Middle Andaman, came to the Home on a visit. He was the first of his Sept to come to the Settlement.

In November a fight occurred between this Sept and the Ár-*yāūto* Kédés of Interview Island, and four men, two women, and two girls were killed, among whom were the father and step-mother of Chāūr Mio.

In March 1878 Mr. Man made a tour round the Islands in H.M.S. *Rifleman.* At Stewart's Sound two Andamanese came off in a canoe and were very friendly, but it appeared that the people there had suffered much from the measles, and many, including Chánga one of those who had been to Port Blair, had died. At Port Cornwallis the people were still timid, and Chāūr Mio, who was of Mr. Man's party, was useful as an interpreter. After some trouble he induced the aborigines to come to the ship for presents, and Mr. Man then landed amongst them. He found that the measles had been very severe here also.

At Tuft Island he landed Chāūr Mio, and Íra Chápa of the Áka *Béa*-da tribe, who volunteered to go with the former on a visit.

During the year 1877-78 the syphilis had spread steadily, and though Mr. Man thought that there were no cases outside a radius of 25 miles from Port Blair, the infection had really reached to the North Andaman. The patients in hospital were becoming restive under the detention, discipline, and necessarily long course of treatment, and many of them used to run away to their jungle villages while still suffering. Mr. Man thought at this time that the population of the Islands had been reduced by at least one-fourth during the past year, and despaired of stopping the spread of either the measles or the syphilis. Twelve escaped convicts had been captured by the Andamanese during the year; and 139 blankets, and 45,300 thatching leaves were manufactured in the Viper Home.

In May 1878 several aborigines of the Port Mouat Sept, the Chief of which had prevented his people from coming to hospital with syphilis, were found to be infected, and in July a large number of cases were brought in from the Middle Andaman.

Bía Lóla, the son of the Chief of the Port Mouat Sept, killed a girl of that Sept on the 24th of July, and killed another half-breed girl, the daughter of a Hindu convict and an Andamanese woman, on the 31st. The only motives for these murders were that Bía Lóla had been disturbed in his sleep by the children. Mr. Man thought that he was of weak intellect, and in September the Chief Commissioner sentenced him to two years' rigorous imprisonment. He had been educated in the Orphanage, was known to be of a violent and savage disposition, and his subsequent conduct gave me reason to believe that he was a homicidal maniac.

In September Íra Árla, the Chief of the Middle Strait Sept, died from the bite of a tree snake (*Trimeresurus*). He had always been well disposed towards us, and had assisted us in many ways. His successor, Bála Jóbo, had, curiously enough, lost his right hand from the bite of a snake.

In October, Niáli, Chief of the Bálé tribe, died. He was the instigator and ringleader in the murders at Kyd Island in 1875.

During the year 1878 the syphilis steadily increased in spite of all Mr. Man's efforts to stop it.

He was chiefly concerned at this time in attempting to establish friendly relations with the Járawa tribes, the details of which will be described in the Chapter on that subject. Andamanese from all the tribes in the Middle Andaman came in at different times to the Settlement, and our friendly relations with them were established on a firm footing.

One man of the Púchikwár tribe, named Bía *Pag*-da, having been furnished by Mr. Man with tools and seedlings, was said to have made some attempt at clearing jungle, and cultivating, in his village on the shore of Homfray Strait, but little came of it. Several other Andamanese who had been detained for work in the Homes made similar cultivation a pretext for being allowed to return to their own country, as Mr. Man hoped that they would follow Bía *Pag*-da's example. He states :—

"The principal reason why we have hitherto found it difficult to induce those living at the Homes to work continuously at such occupations as cultivation, has been that the jungles provide them with even more than what they regard as the necessaries of life, and because hard work, when unaccompanied with any immediate gain or gratification, as in hunting or turtling, is distasteful to them."

"In the case, however, of men belonging to the distant encampments, who have been for some time located at the Viper Home, these difficulties will be more easily surmounted, for having become accustomed to certain articles of food which are not indigenous, but which can be obtained with little labour, they would, on their return to their homes, feel the necessity for exertion, and with such help as has now been promised them will no doubt succeed in supplying many of their own wants, and at the same time induce their neighbours to assist them. (Subsequent experience has shown that the Andamanese would rather do without the desired articles than work for them, or alter their habits in the slightest degree. —*M.V.P.*)

"With regard to the people of the South Andaman, as they are permanently resident in or near Port Blair, the same results cannot be expected, as they find no difficulty in obtaining all they require by supplying the wants of the residents at the Settlement with turtles, shells, and various other articles which they obtain for sale.

"Most of the convicts who escaped into the jungles during the year were, as usual, captured and brought in by the Andamanese. In estimating the good done by the aborigines in re-capturing runaways, the fact should not be lost sight of that the very circumstance of their being in the harbour and ready at all times to proceed in pursuit of escaped prisoners deters many a convict from making an attempt to abscond, while of those who, after escaping, return of their own accord, many are as much induced to do so by the knowledge that the aborigines are on their tracks, as by the natural obstacles which they have encountered in the jungles.

"The women, and some of the boys in the Viper Home, have been employed in useful occupations, such as making blankets, thatching leaves, and *morahs*. One hundred and thirteen blankets, 10,700 thatching leaves, and 33 *morahs* were manufactured."

Sixty-six fresh cases of syphilis were discovered and placed under treatment during the year.

In June 1879 the clearing made at Tálicháūrat by Bía *Pag*-da was visited by two convict Petty Officers belonging to the Homes, and was said to be about two *bighas* in extent.

On the 10th of July, 1879, Mr. Man made over charge of the Andamanese to Mr. M. V. Portman, and proceeded on duty to the Nicobars.

During the four years that Mr. Man was in charge of the Andamanese his work was made more than usually anxious and difficult owing to the epidemics of ophthalmia and measles, and the ravages of syphilis. To save even a remnant of the race he was obliged to take stringent measures, and enforce restrictions which the Andamanese, blind to their own interests, resented, and endeavoured to escape from. He was also given few facilities for visiting the distant tribes, but such visits as he was able to make, short and hurried as they were, did good, and the establishment of friendly relations with the aborigines in the North Andaman was advanced by him.

In spite, however, of all these difficulties, and of the other official work with which he was burdened, he won for himself a niche in the Temple of Science by his researches into the customs and languages of the Andamanese.

He prepared a Dictionary, and conjointly with Major R. C. Temple a Grammar of the Áka-*Béa*-da dialect, which, however, owing to various reasons, has not yet (1895) been published, and he published a Monograph on "The Andaman Islanders," which gave the public the first detailed and correct account of these people.

This was first issued as a series of papers read before the Anthropological Institute in 1882, and was afterwards published in book form. It would be impossible to quote it in full, and I will, therefore, confine my observations on it to some of those points on which further research has shown Mr. Man's views to be incorrect.

The work, which is an answer to "Notes and Queries on Anthropology," deals almost entirely with the South Andaman Group of Tribes, and often with single Tribes of that Group. Mr. Man's medium of communication with the aborigines was either Hindustani, or the Áka-*Béa*-da dialect of Andamanese, and as many of his advisers were members of other Tribes, some of the mistakes I am about to point out may have been due to their imperfect knowledge of the languages mentioned, or to their having failed to understand the questions put to them. It should also be remembered that Mr. Man had no facilities for living in the jungles and studying the Andamanese in their own haunts.

In the map published with Mr. Man's book, the tribal boundaries are incorrectly marked. The Jàrawas occupied more of the interior of Rutland Island and the South Andaman than is shown; the Púchikwár Tribe inhabited the country North of Homfray Strait; the Bójig-ngíji-da should have been called by their correct name "Áka-*Béa*-da", the Āūkāū-*Júwōī* were an inland Tribe, and did not own so much land as is shown; the Kol Tribe has been shown as inhabiting a large portion of the Kédé territory; and the Jéru occupy more of the interior of the North Andaman than is shown.

Mr. Man uses throughout his work the term "Bójig-ngiji-da" for the South Andaman tribe and dialect, whereas this word simply means "our relations," and "Āka-*Béa*-da" is the word which should have been used.

On the Introduction to the book it is not necessary for me to comment, as all the theories advanced in it, the description of the islands, and the history of the Andamanese, have been dealt with in the present work.

On page 3 Mr. Man accepts the story that the Andamanese from the Little Andaman used in former times to make raids on the Car Nicobarese. This, however, is more than doubtful, and is extremely improbable. The huts of the Öngés do not, except superficially, resemble those of the Nicobarese, and though far larger than the huts of the Great Andaman tribes, are built upon the same plan.

As regards the word "Mincopie" applied to the Andamanese race, an explanation has already been given in Chapter III.

On page 10 Mr. Man refers to the rumours of "long-haired" people on Interview and Rutland Islands. The "long hair" need not necessarily have been "straight," as he assumes, and the rumour probably refers to the Andamanese who allow their hair to grow long. I have seen Interview Islanders with their hair reaching to their shoulders, and some Jàrawas with an immense mop of hair.

On the same page, in para. 9, he states that the Andamanese do not now dye their hair with red ochre, but he was not acquainted with the Öngé Group of Tribes at the time of writing, and the statement he wished to correct probably referred to that Group, who, unlike the other Andamanese, put red ochre on their hair only, and not on their bodies.

On page 11 he understates the age of the Andamanese. Their hair commences to turn grey at about their 50th year, and they are known to live to nearly seventy years of age.

On page 13 the age of a bridegroom should·be given as 24—28 and of a bride as 18—24, and not as stated. Barrenness is by no means rare now, the fault being principally with the men.

The general physiology of the Andamanese has been most carefully studied since Mr. Man wrote, and some of the facts arrived at differ from those recorded by him; as these will be published in another work, it is not necessary to detail them here.

On page 19 Mr. Man remarks "the larvæ of bees found attached to honey-combs is eaten to correct constipation"; but, as the Andaman honey would, without any assistance, "correct" the most obstinate case of constipation, the reason for the Andamanese eating the larvæ is, I think, to be found in their fondness for them only.

The Physiognomy and Motions of the Andamanese, as given by Mr. Man, can only be intelligibly rendered by photography, and the oriental posture of squatting is neither the favourite nor the general sitting position.

Mr. Man, in the note to page 26, gives the Andamanese credit for more modesty than they possess. They laugh at jokes which we should certainly consider "coarse," and their general conversation includes certain topics, and objects and actions are plainly mentioned by name, in a way that might now be considered "Elizabethan."

Again, on the 27th page, Mr. Man states that the Andamanese, when out of temper, never use improper expressions, but this depends a good deal upon what one considers to be "an improper expression."

He here gives a translation as "You long nose." This should be "You hooked nose."

In page 28 the "Oko-paiad" are said to be "invariably of the male sex," but this is incorrect, as women are sometimes "seers."

Mr. Man speaks of Narcondam as containing an extinct volcano, whereas it is merely of volcanic origin; and of Barren Island as being an active volcano, whereas it is quiescent.

In page 31, the name "Puluga-l'áka-báng" is given to Saddle Peak in the Noath Andaman, but incorrectly. The word is Áka-*Béa* da, and that Tribe knew nothing of the North Andaman. The caves in Cuthbert Bay, on the east coast of the Middle Andaman, now bear this name, also other caves in the South Andaman. As the words mean " the mouth of God," they might be applied to caves, but not to mountains. " Kóbunga," means " the deep elbow of a creek," not a " bay." The Áka-*Béa*-da name for Barren Island is now " Tāilichápa," " Stone fuel," or " Burnt stones," and the word given is not now used. Also see page 511.

On pages 32 and 33 the following statement occurs :—

" Beforetheir comparatively recent acquaintance with us, they had not the faintest knowledge of the existence of even the neighbouring coast of Burma, much less of the world at large, and consequently imagined that their islands formed almost the entire terrene area, and that they themselves comprised the bulk of the inhabitants."

I do not think this is correct. They were only too well acquainted with Burmese, Chinese, and Malays, and must have seen many passing vessels, and argued the existence of an outside world from seeing them, and from the pirates and slavers who landed from them on their islands.

On page 33 it is stated that "there a few place-names which are unintelligible to the present inhabitants," and "Turubun" is instanced, but this is a Púchikwár word meaning " the place of Mobwa trees," and the name is perfectly intelligible to the Púchikwár Tribe, though perhaps not to the Áka-*Béa*-da.

On page 36 Mr. Man writes of an Éremtága as being entirely ignorant of fishing, but this is a mistake. What he was ignorant of was the Ár-*yāuto* method of harpooning large fish. All Éremtágas shoot fish in the creeks.

Also, nomadism is not confined to the Ár-*yāutos*, but is common to both classes of Andamanese. The stench, flies, and vermin, in a village long inhabited, necessitates a " move on."

4 L

The camping grounds are actually "on" and not "near" the kitchen-middens.

On page 39, Note 2, Mr. Man thinks that the combining of several small huts into one big one is peculiar to the South Andaman, but this is not the case. Such large huts are to be met with all over the Andamans, and are at their best in the Little Andaman.

Mr. Man, on page 44, thinks that "Lélékanga" is a word recently invented to signify "a drunken man," but this is a mistake. It originally meant "staggering," and was applied to the delirium of fever, the staggering and giddiness of weakness, etc.

I do not think that smoking has had such an evil effect on the Andamanese as Mr. Man asserts. Some of the young men now, who smoked from their earliest years, and whose parents smoked before their birth, have as good constitutions and physique as it is possible for them to have.

Mr. Man, on page 47, states that "swamps are never crossed," but this is incorrect. He also states that "wells are not dug;" but in the dry weather small water holes, corresponding to our wells, *are* dug.

On page 50 Mr. Man states "the Andamanese are, as a rule, very conservative, and prefer to coin from their own resources rather than to borrow from aliens, words expressing ideas or objects which are new to them."

I do not agree with this. The Andamanese adopt Hindustani words, and incorporate them into their own language by adding Andamanese prefixes and suffixes.

On the note to page 54 he states," the belief held by all, or the majority of the tribes of the Great Andaman is, that "Bojig-yáb" is the original language spoken by their remote ancestors, and from which the various other existing dialects have sprung."

This is incorrect. The North Andaman Group of Tribes knew nothing of the Púchikwár Language or Tribe, and some of the Septs of even the South Andaman Group of Tribes were unacquainted with them. It must be remembered that Mr. Man's principal informant, Bía *Pag*-da, was a member of the Eastern Sept of the Púchikwár Tribe, and his views are partly Púchikwár, and partly Kol.

With the statements in para. 9, pages 57 and 58, I disagree almost entirely. Some jests must have been related to Mr. Man, which he accepted as earnest statements of fact.

In the Section, "Initiatory Ceremonies," Mr. Man uses the term "fast" whereas "abstention from certain food only," is meant. On this head much additional information has been obtained since Mr. Man wrote, and his remarks regarding the "Ája Gumul" of females, in para. 14, are incorrect.

With regard to the Section "Marriage," divorce is known, but is very rare after the birth of a child. The women are loose in their conduct before marriage, and fairly good wives afterwards (through fear of their husbands?), but are not "models of constancy"; and the remarks in para. 15, and note 1, on page 70, scarcely agree with those in para. 3, page 67. The rules mentioned in para. 16, page 70 *et seq.*, are by no means strictly adhered to.

In the Section "Superstitions," Mr. Man does not seem to have looked for a practical reason for the customs of the Andamanese, though such can generally be found. Curious mistakes occur in this Section, such as, in para. 7, page 85, it is stated that "Álaba" wood is never used for cooking turtles, whereas the fact is that no other wood but "Álaba" (if it be obtainable, of course) is used.

Also, in para. 9, the words given are said "after," and not "before" the shower, being a sort of spiteful retort.

In paras. 14 and 16 a curious mistake is made. Mr. Man speaks of a "cane bridge," between earth and heaven, whereas "the rainbow" is meant, the error having probably occurred from a mistranslation of the word "*Pídga*," which means both "a cane," and "the rainbow." The latter is said by some not to be the devil's dancing-board, but is the smoke of his cooking pot. Superstitions and legends differ among the different Tribes and Septs. Those given by Mr. Man are of the Eastern Sept of the Púchikwár Tribe.

In page 87, "*Chāi-i-tán*" is translated "Hades," whereas it merely means "the place of the Chāi tree." The rules mentioned in para. 22, regarding the cries of birds, are more honoured in the breach than in the observance, and the same applies to very many of the superstitions.

As regards the Section "Religious Beliefs," Mr. Man speaks of the Creation, Fall, and Deluge. I have to a certain extent dealt with these subjects in Chapter II, but nearly all the facts given in this Section can only be accepted as the opinions of Mr. Man's particular informants. I have collected a large number of legends, etc., from the elders of different tribes, and no two agree. Some of the statements given by Mr. Man are not known to the other Andamanese, and it would appear as if his informants, not quite understanding what was asked, or having no knowledge of the subject, either invented, or answered "Yes" to leading questions.

The same remarks apply to the Section "Mythology."

On page 98, para. 15, a creek called Yára-tig-jig is mentioned. If Yératil-jig is meant, then the word "Kára-dúku" should be translated "crocodile," and not "cachalot." There are many crocodiles in this creek, and one was killed, and the bones brought in to me, in 1895.

Para. 17, page 99, gives facts contrary to all Andamanese ideas, nor can I imagine an Andamanese elder making such a statement in earnest.

In para. 23, page 101, "Chauga-tábanga," simply means "ancestors," and the description of them is a specimen of the boasting, and exaggerated style used by the Andamanese when talking of their own affairs.

In para. 29, page 103, the legend appears to me to be a poetical mode of saying that the people were drowned.

The mythical inscriptions mentioned in para. 30, do not exist, and the rock on which they are said to have been is so exposed to the weather, and of such soft sandstone, that no inscription would remain on it for 100 years. The marks were mere weatherings.

In para 32, page 105, the same curious mistake, regarding the use of the word "Álaba," occurs, that has been noticed above, due evidently to "Álaba" having been written for "Yólba."

In note 6, to para. 3, page 111, Mr. Man states that the arms are generally the first part tattooed, but this is not the case; the stomach from the navel to the pubes is almost invariably the first part tattooed among the South Andaman Group of Tribes, and the back among the North Andaman Group.

In para. 2, page 113, the *only* time the unmarried are not allowed to use paint on their necks is, on their wedding day.

In para. 1, page 114, a mistake occurs. A new born child has its head shaved about six days, not " a few hours, " after its birth, and it is then painted with white clay, not ". red ochre. "

Mr. Man's remarks on page 121 regarding the possibility of the Andamanese settling down to an agricultural life are worth quoting in full. He writes :—

" Notwithstanding the ample opportunities that they have now had of observing the benefits derived from cultivation, and though they undoubtedly prefer such products to the spontaneous vegetation of their jungles, (?—*M. V. P.*), they still consider that the exertion necessary to obtain the former far outweighs every advantage; in short it is their opinion that " le jeu ne vaut pas la chandelle. "

" Further, to quote from Peschel: ' It must be remembered that hunting affords supreme enjoyment, and that agriculture has nothing to offer in compensation for the excitement and delights of the chase.' "

In note 4, page 128, Mr. Man writes : " Their immunity from scurvy, etc. " Far from enjoying an immunity from scurvy, the Andamanese are scorbutic.

With para. 34, page 132, honey *is* made from the flowers of the *rár* tree ; also, some Andamanese say that the best honey is gathered at the full of the moon, and not as stated.

In Section *Tabu*, I have been unable to trace the custom of " Yat tub " described. There is no Tabu, and Mr. Man must mean that the people do not eat what they know does not agree with them. Dugong and porpoise *may* be eaten by *small* children.

In note 4, page 135, the belt mentioned is commonly worn by the Jàrawas, and is not supposed to be a protection in hostile encounters.

In Section, " Hunting and Fishing " several mistakes occur.

In para. 4, Mr. Man states : " No immediate honours are conferred on the successful sportsman." No honours are conferred at any time, and the " successful sportsman " has to be content with the knowledge that he has done well, and provided food for the family.

In para. 5, and note 2, page 137, Mr. Man states that the bows and arrows " are almost identical in form among all the eight Tribes of the Great Andaman, " but this is far from being the case.

There is considerable difference between the Bojig Karama, and the North Andaman Chókio. This difference in the bow is one of the main points by which the Groups of Tribes are distinguished.

Fish bone points are still used in the arrows of the Öngé and North Andaman Tribes; and with regard to the statements in para 12, I have never seen any European who could compete with an Andamanese at shooting *fish* which are stationary, much less in motion.

As regards para 19, I do not know on what data Mr. Man writes of the Jàrawa mode of " release. " Though we are now far better acquainted with these people than we were when he wrote, we yet know very little on this point. The other Great Andaman Tribes have several (not " one ") modes of release, of which six are in common use.

The Jàrawas do not use a " Karama, " which word is only applicable to the bow of the South Andaman Group of Tribes; and the Öngé bow is not nearly so clumsy, or so difficult for a European to use, as the " Bojig Karama. "

To the note to page 141 I would add the correction that, the Jàrawa Tribes were formerly only known to the Tribes of the South Andaman Group.

In para 25, and note 4, on page 142, Mr. Man states that three-pronged barbed arrows are neither made nor used by any of the Great Andaman Tribes, and that Dr. Brander possibly saw the *single* specimen of an arrow answering to this description which was obtained in 1880 from the North Sentinel Island.

I brought in from the North Sentinel Island, in 1880, about two dozen of such arrows, which I showed to Dr. Brander. Two, Three, and Four pronged arrows, with barbed bone tips, are largely used by all the Tribes of the Önge Group, and occasionally by some of the people of the North Andaman.

With regard to the description of turtle-hunting in para. 34, page 144, the turtle are not seen by the phosphorescent light caused by the movements of the canoe. The Andamanese in the canoe are able to see and follow the turtle, because, when moving through the phosphorescent water, it leaves a trail of light by which it can be tracked.

The net mentioned in para. 41 is not used by the Öngés, nor do they harpoon turtle.

One of the reasons for the Andamanese preferring to travel in shallow water, as mentioned in para. 6, page 148, is because they can go much faster by poling in shallow water, than by paddling with their tiny paddles in deep water, where they are influenced more by the tides and currents.

In para. 11, page 149, Mr. Man states that, at the bottom and water level, canoes, though sometimes more, are never less than $1\frac{1}{2}$ to 3 inches thick. $\frac{1}{2}$ to $1\frac{1}{2}$ inches would have been more correct measurement.

He adds, in para. 13 and note 3, that rafts are quite unknown to the Andamanese, but this is not the case, for the Jàrawas use rafts on which they cross the creeks to the present day, and it was of this Tribe that Colebrooke wrote.

Female bamboos, and one kind of wood, are used as shafts for the turtle harpoon, and thorns are occasionally used as a substitute for pins.

In Section "String," page 163; for making "Bétmo," the strips of the inner bark of the "Álaba" are used; they are twisted round, not "tied to," the toes of the maker, and wax is never applied to *Bétmo* rope.

Pilita is a fibre which after being exposed for a few minutes to the air becomes black.

Yólba fibre, even when manufactured into string, would not be brought near a turtle, or taken with them by people who were hunting turtle. The practical reason for this probably is, that, being inferior in strength to *Álaba*, and rotting quickly in water, it is not used in aquatic sport.

Bow-strings are very seldom made from *Pilita* fibre, which has little strength, and the Öngés, and sometimes the other tribes, occasionally use a strip of the inner bark of the *Raō* tree as a bow-string.

The manufacture of *Álaba* rope is quite different from that of *Yólba* rope.

The description of the dance on page 170, though picturesque, is scarcely entirely accurate; that part of the audience who form the orchestra as a rule sit in the open and not in their huts. The singer generally leans on a fish arrow, the point of which is stuck into the broad part of the sounding board, which he "strikes" with the after part of the sole of his foot, (the motion is not "kicking"). The solo is not "recitative," which strictly means "musical declamation," for it is intended to be a song. There are several descriptions of dances amongst the Tribes.

The music given in para. 35, page 172, is entirely incorrect, but for this Mr. Man, as he says, is not responsible.

In note 1, on this page, the chorus is taken up by different people "at different pitches," not "in different keys," which expression does not strictly apply to Andamanese music.

In Appendix F. Mr. Man gives a specimen of the Áka-*Béa*-da dialect, in which I notice that the word " Áwéh " is translated " et-cetera."

It really means "that is all."

It is unfortunate that an Āūkāū-*Júwōi* should have been selected to dictate a specimen of the Áka-*Béa*-da dialect, which was to him a foreign tongue, and with which he was imperfectly acquainted.

At the end of the book Mr. Man re-publishes Mr. A. J. Ellis's

"Report of researches into the language of the South Andaman Island."

On this I would make a few comments.

On page 46 Mr. Ellis states "the Andamanese have scarcely a proper "word for God," but in this he is wrong, as " Puluga " means " God " to the Andamanese mind, and perhaps their conception of the Deity they call *Puluga* is not farther from the truth than the ideas of God entertained by many Christians.

In the alphabet given by Mr. Ellis I observe that, though Áka-*Béa*-da words are used, the Púchikwár and Kol method of pronouncing them is given ; such as " yaba " and " ba ;" pronounced, (as given by Mr. Ellis), " yaba " and " ba " by the Kol, but " yábá " and " bá " by all the Áka-*Béa*-da but one Sept.

" Ngiji " is translated as " friend, " whereas it means " relation," " Áûko-*dubu*-da " meaning " friend. "

" S " is found once ; instance " sissnga-ké " meaning " to hiss."

Page 52. The South Andaman language mentioned is called by the aborigines " Áka-*Béa*-da " and not " Bojig-ngiji-da, " which means " our relations, " or, perhaps, " fellow tribesmen. "

Page 54. The plural is not expressed by the addition of " l'óng-kálak," which merely means "a number " or " few " with reference to the context.

It occurs in a sentence as a word to itself.

Page 55. The negative is formed by adding "bá, " but the instance given is incorrect. "Áb-líga-da " means "a child, " "Áb-liga-bá " means "a small child, " " bá " meaning " small. " The instance is of a diminutive, not of a negative.

I notice that, on page 59, " Pid " is used to mean " hair, " and " ed " to mean " skin. " " Pich " and " áich " are probably the words meant, the final " ch " in each case being pronounced so softly as to be taken for a soft " d " or " t. " " Wāinya " means " scurf, " not " cuticle. "

It is, however, from page 60 onwards that the more serious errors occur. Mr. Ellis states that he looked for some genuine native utterances, not translations, which might illustrate the natural speech of the country. He then proceeds to say that he has found these in certain letters written by Mr. Man, at the dictation of the Andamanese with him at the Nicobar Islands, to the Chief at Bája Jág, "Jambu." These letters were sent to the Officer in charge of the Homes, (myself), who read them to Jambu, and Mr. Ellis gives two of them, which he says, " certainly, if any exist, are genuine specimens of South Andaman literature."

A few lines before Mr. Ellis had written that Mr. Man had to treat the Andamanese quite like children for whom one writes letters, *suggesting subjects*, asking what they would say if they saw Jambu, and so on, and yet he calls these letters " genuine native utterances."

They contain some breaches of Andamanese etiquette which an Andamanese, if left to himself, would not commit; and I may add that they were not fully understood by the Andamanese at the Homes until I translated them into Hindustani and read them out in that language.

With regard to the Note on page 60, Bía *Pag*-da's, two brothers, Íra-tabára and Láūra, were two of the laziest, most untrustworthy, and evil disposed Andamanese in the Islands.

The letters are really from Mr. Man to Jambu, and the diction is English, being quite unlike the manner in which young Andamanese would address their elders.

The first letter commences "Mám Jambu." This is incorrect; " Máia " alone should have been used, (and neither " Jambu, " (a name given to the man by the Naval Brigadesmen), nor " Tura, " his Andamanese name, would have been used) in speaking "to" him. When away from the Settlement the Andamanese never used such nicknames as " Friday, " " Jambu, " etc., when speaking " to " each other, but would use, if any name was used at all, the Andamanese name by which the man was known.

On page 64, para. 19, " tala-tim-re, " is used to mean " tonsured," but " *Jér*-ré, " should have been used, the other word meaning " bald."

In para. 20 " Móda " does not mean " if, " but is a " Flower

Name," and should not have been used, as no woman had two "Flower Names," and Biela was given her correct "Flower Name" of "Ora."

In para. 25, page 65, "Yubur" is translated "govern," but it means "rich." "Ót-*yúbur*-da" is a person with a quantity of property, and in the Andamans, as elsewhere, the rich people often become the governing classes by virtue of their wealth.

In spite of Mr. Man's description of the mode in which the letters were written, Mr. Ellis again, on page 69, calls them "some of the very few expressions of genuine, untutored barbarians which we possess."

They were certainly not untutored in this instance.

I have not thought it worth while to discuss the composition of the sentences in the letter, as the subject is outside the scope of this work, but will merely remark that many of them are not written as Andamanese would speak.

On page 72 Mr. Ellis suggests that the Andamanese language changes very rapidly, and instances the names of places in the neighbourhood of Port Blair which cannot be explained. I have not found that the languages change quickly, and Colebrooke's vocabulary, written a hundred years ago, is still correct so far as I am acquainted with the Jàrawa language. As I have shown, the names which are not understood are names in another dialect not understood by Mr. Man or the Áka-*Béa*-da.

While commenting on some of the errors which occur in Mr. Man's book, it is only right for me to say that, for a first attempt to write a scientifically accurate account of the Andamanese, the number of these errors is remarkably small, and generally unimportant. Mr. Man is to be congratulated, after having been in charge of the Andamanese for four years only, and having had few opportunities of visiting the distant tribes, on having written what is still the standard work on the Andamanese; and what is, I believe, considered to be the first account of a savage race recorded in accordance with the requirements of science. I can state from experience that the existence of his work has much lightened the labour of his successors and has rendered further research into the customs, etc., of the Andamanese, easier than it would otherwise have been.

On taking charge of the Andamanese, one of the first things I had to deal with was the financial question. Mr. Man, just before leaving had stated, " I think it would be feasible to curtail the Government grant by R50 per mensem, " though on what grounds he recommended this I know not, as his average saving per month for the previous year was only R7-0-10. In spite, however, of a vigorous remonstrance on my part, the grant was curtailed as recommended, but after one year the full amount was again given. Every effort had to be made to increase the income, the Andamanese worked harder than usual, and from that time the practice of obtaining the rations for the Andamanese daily from the convict bunniah was abandoned, and the monthly supply was purchased wholesale from the Commissariat Department at a reduced cost.

In August 1879 Jambu was installed as Chief at the Brigade Creek Home, and, with a view to catching the Jàrawas to the south of the Settlement, a track was cut through the jungle from the village of Dhani Khári to Yáratán on the northern shore of MacPherson's Straits, with branches to Chiriya Tápu and Manglután.

In October Bía *Pag*-da was brought into the hospital with syphilis from the effects of which he died after a few months' suffering.

On the 12th December 1879 Lieutenant-General C. A. Barwell proceeded on furlough, and was succeeded in the Chief Commissionership by Major T. Cadell, V. C. I was fortunately thus placed, almost from the first, under an extremely energetic officer, who took the greatest interest in the exploration of the islands and the continuance of friendly relations with the aborigines, and who, during the whole time he was at the Andamans, gave me every facility for visiting the most distant tribes, and for remaining for weeks together in the jungle with the aborigines.

I was first prominently brought before Major Cadell's notice by the following incident which occurred two days after his arrival.

I quote from his report:—

"On the 2ud December 1879, at Viper Island, life convict Tokha, No. 21545, who was working in the chain-gang, without any provocation attempted the life of Mr. M. V. Portman by striking him on the head with a "pátu," while he was passing the gang in a jhampan. Mr. Portman was stationed at Navy Bay at the time, being in charge of the Western Division, and had only come to Viper in order to visit the Andaman Home Before Tokha could repeat the blow he was seized by Ahmed, the convict Jemadar of the Andamanese Department. Mr. Portman received a severe wound which rendered him insensible.

"The convict was tried by the Sessions Court and sentenced to be hanged. The Court, being of opinion that it was essential for the future tranquillity of the Settlement that the sentence should be carried out without delay, directed that the execution should take place at once, and the criminal was hanged on the 12th December 1879.

"These proceedings were subsequently approved by the Governor-General in Council. Ahmed, Jemadar, received a free pardon for his gallant conduct.

"Mr. Portman had never before been brought in contact with his would-be murderer, and the latter said that he ascribes no reason for his crime. He did not by any means present the appearance of a desperate character. He was probably seized with a sudden homicidal impulse, and could not resist the temptation of having an officer within reach of his hoe, just as many boys cannot resist shying a stone at a cat when an opportunity offers."

In January 1880 I visited Port Campbell, where, in one of the most beautiful bays in the islands, was a small camp of Andamanese. The aborigines with me said that nearly all the people on the West coast of the South Andaman had died from the effects of the measles, and the whole coast seemed deserted. I then went on to Interview

Island where the people were very friendly, some coming on board and accompanying me on the voyage. At the village in Port Andaman a young man, named Búluba-la, who had attached himself to me from the first, and has proved to be one of the most intelligent Andamanese in the Islands, tried to make a clean sweep of all the property of the Kédés, but was prevented from doing so by Colonel Cadell, and in spite of his protest that he was only following the usual Andamanese custom, (which was the case), was ordered to return the articles he had stolen. He flung some rope and other things into a high tree in a fit of temper, and his anger was ludicrous when Colonel Cadell waited, insisted on his climbing the tree, procuring all the articles, and returning them to their owners.

At Landfall Island and Port Cornwallis the natives ran away, but at Stewart's Sound they were very friendly, and four strangers accompanied us to Port Blair. Tók, the Chief of North Reef Island, whom I had picked up at Interview Island, made himself very useful in Stewart's Sound in reassuring the timid people there.

Five Andamanese, who had been with Mr. Man at the Nicobars for the past six months, returned at this time to Port Blair.

In February 1880 I heard that Bía Lóla, who had been sentenced in September 1878, by General Barwell, to two years' rigorous imprisonment for taking the life of a little Andamanese girl, because she disturbed his slumbers, and who, when only fourteen months of the sentence had been endured, was pardoned by General Barwell as an act of grace when he was leaving the Settlement, had committed another murder within seven weeks of his release from jail.

He, with a party of Andamanese, had been encamped at Yáratán on the northern bank of MacPherson's Straits, and they were engaged in pig hunting. One day, a large pig having been killed, a youth, named Riala, who was of a pleasant, merry disposition, appropriated the head, which is considered by the Andamanese to be the most dainty part, and ate it. This angered Bía Lóla, and early the following morning, while the others slept, he got up and shot two arrows into Ríala's stomach, killing him immediately.

On hearing of this I went to the outer harbour of Port Mouat where Bía Lóla was encamped, and after some difficulty induced him, with some others who had been with him at the time of the murder, to come into my boat. He was taken to Port Blair, tried by the Sessions Court, and there being no extenuating circumstances connected with the case, was sentenced to death, and this sentence having been confirmed, he was executed on the 19th May 1880. He was hanged at the same time, and on the same gallows, with a Hindu convict, and while the latter behaved in a stolid and unconcerned manner, Bía Lóla trembled and called out to me to save him. This was the first, and up till now (1896), the only instance of the death sentence being inflicted on an Andamanese, but it was rendered necessary as a deterrent, and had a great effect on the others, who all, even Wologa Jó-la, Chief of Port Mouat, who was Bía Lóla's father, agreed that it was merited.

In February Colonel Cadell, Mr. Homfray, and I went through the Middle and Homfray Straits, (this being the first occasion on which the latter place had been visited by any one but Mr. Homfray), and the creeks running inland from Kyd Island. At Tálichaūrat, in Homfray Straits, we visited the clearing said to have been made by Bía *Pag*-da, which had been looked upon as a great step in civilization on the part of the Andamanese. It was a disappointment to find that it was only a patch of ground about 50 feet square which Mr. Homfray had seen much in the same state about six years before. The clearing, such as it was, appeared on enquiry to have been made by the convict Petty Officers, who accompanied the Andamanese to the place. Of cultivation there was not a sign, and the few coconut and papaya trees planted were choked by the undergrowth which the Andamanese had made no attempt to keep down. Colonel Cadell remarked :—

"The sea and forests afford sufficient for the subsistence of the Andamanese, and it is improbable that they will ever take to agriculture."

During this expedition Mr. Homfray was struck with the

diminution in the number of the aborigines, which Colonel Cadell attributed to their contact with civilization, and to the consequent ravages of syphilis and measles among them.

Colebrooke Passage was examined, and Homfray Straits were christened, and laid down on the chart for the first time.

On our return I proceeded for a few days on a visit to Rutland Island, MacPherson's Straits, and the Labyrinth Islands, to see the Andamanese there, and discovered and named Portman Harbour.

At this time I re-opened the Góp-l'áka-báng Home, and had track cut to it from Brigade Creek.

In the Annual Report Colonel Cadell remarked :—

"The Andamanese act as excellent Police in re-capturing runaway convicts. The difficulty of re-capturing the latter is increasing, however, as the number of self-supporting convicts who are allowed to go into the forests is increasing rapidly, and the natives cannot distinguish between them and runaways."

He was also good enough to bring my services with the Andamanese to the favourable notice of the Government of India on more than one point.

In April 1880 I examined the creeks running inland from Kyd Island, in detail. Traces of the Jàrawas were found at Milé-Tilek, and I saw an Andamanese track which connects a point on the Jirka-táng Creek with Port Campbell.

On returning from this duty I proceeded with Colonel Cadell in the *Hugh Rose* to the Archipelago Islands, where we discovered Kwang Tung Strait (though it was not so named till some years afterwards), and found that there were two, and not one Lawrence Island.

We then proceeded north, and at Yól-jig, near Long Island, we found a large circular hut, similar in shape and construction to those built by the Ongés. At Stewart's Sound the aborigines were most friendly, coming off to the ship in large numbers in their canoes ; many of them were suffering from syphilis, and such as could be induced to come were brought with us for treatment in Port Blair. At Port Cornwallis there were no aborigines to be seen, so we explored the creeks at the head of the harbour, and found a shallow passage leading through a most pestilential swamp out to the shore opposite the Table Islands.

These Islands were next examined, many good anchorages being found, and we were much struck with their general beauty. On one of them, now called Temple Island, was a small circular hut similar in shape and construction to those used by the Ongés, but not intended for habitation. It was crowded with hundreds of the skulls of turtles, pigs, etc., neatly tied up, painted with red ochre, and arranged in rows hanging from the roofs and posts, these being trophies of the chase, to preserve which the hut was made.

On rowing round a point in the Table Island Group, we came upon a harbour which, like the other harbours and straits discovered by us, was not marked at all on the chart, and which we christened Cadell Bay. Here, though no one had before visited it, the aborigines swarmed off to the ship in their canoes and were most friendly, having heard of us from the people to the southward. A fat elderly woman of our party, named Chána Cháūrmila, who, being one of the biggest women in the islands had married one of the smallest men, acted as interpreter for us, and behaved very well, laughing and talking to the new aborigines though she had never seen them before, and swimming from canoe to canoe, when at times, owing to her build, her natural and artificial " bustles " were the only parts above water. Here we met with the tallest Andamanese who has been seen, a man named Táī, whose height Colonel Cadell gives as 5 feet, 8 inches. He had a very Negroid appearance, and a coarse good-humoured countenance, but was timid and stupid.

By Northern District Order, No. 266, of the 16th June, 1880, the number of convicts attached to the Andaman Homes was fixed at 13 Petty Officers, and 40 labouring convicts.

On the 11th July, the day before I had intended to start on a visit to Rutland Island, a party of eleven convicts, headed by my manji, Hemráj, and including some of my boatmen, seized my boat (a six-oared whaler) after wounding and throwing into the sea the policeman on guard at Viper Jetty, and taking his rifle and ammunition, and escaped at about 6 P.M. Aided by the darkness and the stormy weather they got away from the harbour, so Colonel Cadell directed me to go north, along the East coast of the Islands, and search for them.

I started the next day in a steam launch, accompanied by Mr. Crawford, Marine Engineer, and in the hopes of heading the runaways went straight to Craggy Island, four miles south of Port Cornwallis, without stopping. The aborigines here, who were living in a large hut built in two-thirds of a circle, were most friendly, and one of them, named "Āina," accompanied me on the launch. After warning them regarding the runaways I looked in at Port Cornwallis, did not stop there on account of the extreme unhealthiness of that harbour, but anchored in Cadell Bay where I remained for some days. There were a great number of aborigines encamped there, who, though almost all strangers to us, were friendly, and during our stay I had excellent opportunities of watching their customs, etc.; the young men played at a variety of games, which had not been previously noted by anyone, and many other novelties of interest were observed.

As nothing was to be seen of the runaways, I went down to Stewart's Sound and anchored in a small mangrove bay near Aves Island. The Andamanese there were very friendly, and I examined some of the creeks which branch inland from the Sound, and went through Austen Strait to the West coast.

During the whole of the trip the weather had been most inclement; high winds and frequent heavy rain squalls prevailing. The steam launch had no awning, but Mr. Crawfurd and I made a sort of tent on the deck, from tarpaulins and logs, which afforded a certain amount of shelter.

On my return from Austen Strait, Mr. Crawfurd informed me that the crown plate of the furnace of the launch was badly cracked and was leaking, and that until it was repaired, which under any circumstances would take some time, and might not be done at all until the launch was brought into Port Blair, we could not proceed. I therefore started on the morning of the 20th July for Port Blair in a large sailing whale boat, in order to procure help, taking with me two police out of the guard of twelve which had been supplied to me, two convicts, and 17 Andamanese. We had very bad weather, and at 4 P.M., seeing the fires of an Andamanese encampment at Ámit-lá-Téd, a point a few miles north of Long Island, I determined to stop there for the night. The people in the village belonged to the Kédé tribe and had never been near the Settlement, yet they came out to welcome us, gave up their huts for our use quite willingly, (it raining hard all the time), and busied themselves in lighting fires and getting food.

During the night the wind shifted and blew very heavily, which, combined with the surf, caused my boat to drag her anchor and drive on shore.

We managed to secure most of the things in her, but on hauling her up found she was so badly damaged that it was scarcely possible for us to proceed. This was an unlooked-for mishap, and the Kédés came to the front by assisting in hauling her up and repairing her. With cloth, dammer, and wax we managed to stop the worst of the leaks, and by 4 P.M., got her afloat and proceeded south, three men bailing her out constantly. By 12 P.M., the leaks had increased so much that I saw it was useless to attempt to go on, and could only put in for the nearest village which was Pich-l'áka-chákkan, in Colebrooke Passage. We arrived there at 2 P.M., on the 22nd, the boat in a sinking condition, and all hands worn out and feeling ill.

On Thursday, the 22nd, we passed the time in the morning by firing off guns and striking some dancing-boards in order to attract the attention of any Andamanese who might be near, and succeeded in bringing two in a small canoe. On obtaining this I wrote a letter to the Chief Commissioner informing him of our condition, and despatched it by four picked Andamanese in the canoe to Port Blair.

We had now three days' food in hand carefully managed, and watched with great anxiety for the Station Steamer. The weather was bad, and the place we were in excessively unhealthy, though having some quinine and opium with me, I managed to keep off fever until the end of the trip.

On Saturday morning, the 24th, the four Andamanese returned

with the letter and boat saying they had never been to Port Blair, and had only been fishing and shooting in the jungle close by. This news considerably alarmed me as our last day's rations were now in hand, but about an hour afterwards some other Andamanese, who had been sent out fishing, returned with the news that the I. G. S. *Hugh Rose* had anchored off Guitar Island. I at once despatched them in the canoe with a letter to Captain Gwyn, and at 2 P.M., on the 25th, Mr. Simpson, the Chief Officer, came to the village and took us all off on board.

We then proceeded to Stewart's Sound, picked up the steam launch and party left there, and returned to Port Blair.

This expedition, though nearly resulting seriously, was of use in showing how far we could trust the Andamanese in that most important part of their duty, the saving of shipwrecked mariners.

The Kédés at Ámit-lá-Téd were most friendly, " Wói, " Mr. Man's Éremtága Aŭkau-*Júwöï*, who was with me, acting as interpreter ; and similar behaviour to theirs we might expect from all the Andamanese of the Great Andaman towards anyone they might meet in the jungle, so long as they were not molested or annoyed. The conduct of the four men sent with the letter is a good example of the careless and thoughtless nature of the Andamanese, which it would seem no amount of training could overcome.

While at Pich-l'áka-Chákkan I had an opportunity of seeing some pottery made, it being from this part of the Andamans where most of the suitable clay is procured.

My Andamanese boatmen who were with me behaved excellently and were hard-working and obedient, though on very short commons.

Ever since I had been in charge of the Andamanese I had filled my house with them, and had trained them to wait at table, row my boat, and do other duties which threw them into daily contact with me, and promoted a great intimacy between us. By being in continued association with them, and having, from the conditions of life in Port Blair, few other associates, I gradually acquired some colloquial knowledge of their different dialects, and of their habits, etiquette, modes of thought, etc. In such a place as a Penal Settlement I found that there were many worse companions than the bright and merry Andamanese.

During the following three months I visited most of the villages in the South Andaman, stopping for a few days in each, and studying the mode of life of the Andamanese and their natures in their own homes.

In November 1880 Colonel Cadell and I visited Port Campbell; Interview, and North Reef Islands, where there were numbers of people who were all most friendly, my former ally, Tók, bringing off a party with five canoes; Casuarina Bay, on the west coast of the North Andaman, this being the first time that part of the island had been visited; Landfall Island which had not previously been landed on, and where the aborigines were very friendly; Port Cornwallis, and Stewart's Sound. The North and South Tribes in the Sound had had a fight about a dog a few days before, and some of the aborigines had been killed, so we stopped there a couple of days while I enquired into the matter and managed to patch up a peace between them. Many cases of syphilis were seen in different parts of the North Andaman, and those who could be induced to come in to Port Blair were brought with us.

From here we proceeded to Barren Island, which, many of the Andamanese on board being from the North Andaman or the West coast, had never heard of. We ascended the cone, and the Andamanese were much astonished with what they saw; as the crater was choked up with a pink mud forming a hard level surface, they commenced their usual dance on this, until the hollow, ringing sound frightened them. The volcano was quiescent, and a little steam was issuing from the sulphur bed near the top of the cone. The outer ring is densely wooded and some of the cliffs have a very imposing appearance; the general view of the island from the north-west is also impressive. The woods are crowded with flying foxes, which the Andamanese discovered, and proceeded to kill and eat.

Some of our party thought that the shortest way to get down the cone was to sit down and slide. They reached the bottom very quickly at the expense of their clothes and persons, as the sharp cinders tore both the cloth and the flesh off, and once started there was no stopping. The boots of those who walked were cut to pieces.

As, owing to the wound I had received in the previous December from convict Tokha, and the fever which I had contracted in the expedition of July, my health had broken down, I made over charge of the Andamanese to Mr. H. Godwin-Austen on the 10th December 1880, and proceeded on sick leave to England.

Owing to the increased facilities granted by Colonel Cadell to the Officer in charge of the Andamanese for visiting all parts of the Islands, I was able to report, before leaving, that, with the exception of the Óngé Group of Tribes, and of a few Éremtágas in the North Andaman, friendly relations were now firmly established with all the aborigines of the Great Andaman, nor have these relations been since interrupted.

CHAPTER XVII.

Annual Report for 1880-81—Runaways on the Archipelago Islands—Death of Wologa Jó-la—Ascent of Saddle Peak—Murder of Andamanese on the Archipelago Islands by runaway convicts—Death of Jumboo—Notes on the convict Jemadars of the Andamanese Department—Report on the year 1881-82—Murder of an Andamanese by convicts—Runaways give trouble—Mr. Godwin-Austen visits the distant Islands—Annual Report for 1882-83—Mr. Man takes charge of the Andamanese—Andamanese sent to Calcutta to be modelled—Death of Wói "Tom"—Mr. Portman takes charge of the Andamanese—Survey party arrives—Wreck of the *Scottish Chieftain*—Mr. Portman takes Andamanese to Calcutta.—Notes on the year 1883-84—Runaways killed by Andamanese—Islands visited—Annual Report for 1884-85—Burmese convicts escape and give trouble—Murder of a convict by the Andamanese—Wrecks on the coast of the North Andaman—Islands visited.

Andamanese taken to Penang and Perák—Annual Report for 1885-86—Islands visited—Mr. Metcalfe takes charge of the Andaman Homes.—Mr. Metcalfe visits the distant Islands—Value of the Andamanese as pilots for small vessels—Mr. Portman takes charge of the Andamanese—Islands visited—Epidemic of Russian Influenza.—Case of Tura Né—Islands visited—Trouble with some Andamanese lads—Annual Report for 1890-91—Runaway convicts give trouble—Case of Rang—Cyclone and report on it—Mr. Portman takes Andamanese to Calcutta—Islands visited—Annual Report for the year 1891-92—Andamanese murder—Wreck on the coast of the Middle Andaman.

Andamanese taken to Calcutta—Mr. Bate's account of his treatment by the Andamanese—Ria Badké's case—M. Lapicque visits the Andamans—Lókala killed by the Jàrawas—Edible birds' nest collectors' boat blown to Cuddalore from the Andamans in a cyclone—Andamanese operated on—Deaths—Andamanese killed by a crocodile.—Andamanese taken to Calcutta—Chípla's case—Chíro's case—Deaths—Cháp's case.—Review of our administration of the Andamanese, and the results.

In February 1881 Mr. Godwin-Austen visited Kyd Island, the Middle and Homfray Straits, and Port Campbell, and thought that the Andamanese were, for some reason, afraid of him, and were unwilling to come to Port Blair. They were probably only anxious not to be kept in the hospital there, for he reports that there was much syphilis in the distant villages.

In April 1881 he proceeded on duty to the Nicobars, when

Mr. O. H. Brookes took charge of the Andamanese. Colonel Cadell, who visited the North Andaman during this month, brought in six men from Port Cornwallis, who were suffering from syphilis. They were returned to their homes, cured, in the following month.

In the Annual Report for 1880-81, Colonel Cadell remarks :—

"The ravages made by syphilis among the inhabitants of the North Andaman are distressing to witness." (It is wonderful, however, how readily most virulent cases of this disease yield to treatment in the hospital, which renders it all the more necessary that every case should be sought out, and brought into the Settlement.— *M. V. P.*)

He notes, with reference to the changes of the Officers in charge of the Andamanese, that "It is curious that any Officer who is placed in charge of this department soon becomes interested in, and attached to, the poor savages, however little he may have cared for them beforehand."

During the year 458 *morahs* had been manufactured by the women in the Viper Home, 7 runaway convicts had been recaptured by the Andamanese, and 21 deaths had occurred at the Homes, the details of these being 5 men, 5 women, and 11 children. There had also been a great increase in the revenue of the Andamanese owing to the work done by them in collecting saleable articles of jungle produce. Mr. Brookes remarks regarding the hunting of runaway convicts :—

"As the Settlement opens out it becomes more and more difficult for the Andamanese to distinguish runaways from other convicts, for the former keep close to the outskirts of the villages, and are consequently mixed up with, and mistaken for, self-supporters, or free people who are collecting jungle materials."

One hundred and thirty-four cases of syphilis were admitted into hospital in the year 1879-80, and 98 in the year 1880-81.

The Government of India remarked on the Annual Report :—

"*Chapter XVI, Aborigines.*—The remarks in this Chapter are interesting, and the Governor General in Council is glad to observe that the friendly relations with the inhabitants of the various Islands, except those of Little Andaman, have been maintained and extended. Mr. Portman's services in this matter deserve special notice"

In July 1881 Mr. Godwin-Austen returned from the Nicobar Islands and resumed charge of the Andamanese.

In August he was told by Punga, the Chief of the Archipelago Islands, that some runaway convicts were on those Islands, so he proceeded there in the *Kwang Tung*, anchoring in, and christening " Kwang Tung " Straits. He then went to Outram Island where he found many traces of the runaways, but was told by the Andamanese in Chárka Júru that the convicts had made a raft and put out to sea.

In September five Burmese convicts escaped and got across to the Archipelago. Mr. Godwin-Austen was informed of this and also that they had murdered some of the Andamanese there, and proceeded to the spot to make enquiries. He found that Punga, the Chief, with some of his people, had captured the runaways, but not watching them carefully, they had risen during the night, murdered Punga, and severely wounded many of the other Andamanese. They then took Punga's canoe, put to sea, and reached the coast of Burma, where some of them were recaptured.

In December 1881 Wologa Jó-la, the Chief of the Port Mouat Sept, died in hospital of fever, and was accorded " platform burial " at Port Mouat by the members of his tribe.

He was one of the most determined and savage of the Andamanese about the Settlement, and was a thorn in the side of the Officer in charge, opposing all orders of which he disapproved, and caring little for us or our presents. He was 5 feet 4 inches in height, with a most forbidding countenance, and was much feared by his fellow tribesmen.

Mr. Godwin-Austen endeavoured at this time to make the Andamanese catch fish for the Settlement, and succeeded in doing so for a short period, but the industry was not continued.

There was much sickness among the Andamanese and many deaths, numbers of syphilitic cases being brought in for treatment too late, and Mr. Godwin-Austen took steps to move the hospital, as the Andamanese are very reluctant to live where deaths have occurred and were also so prejudiced against the hospital that they considered that, when they were admitted for treatment, they were certain to die and their mental attitude of course retarded their cure.

In February 1882 Major M. Protheroe, (who was officiating as Chief Commissioner of the Andamans, during the absence of Colonel Cadell in Europe, on furlough,) and Mr. Godwin-Austen, went on a tour to the North Andaman in the *Kwang Tung*. Stewart's Sound was visited and then the coast opposite Craggy Island, where a party of convicts were landed with orders to cut a track to the summit of Saddle Peak. This was finished in a few days, while Major Protheroe visited the Cocos Islands, and the first ascent of Saddle Peak was then made by him and Mr. Godwin-Austen. They were $4\frac{1}{2}$ hours in climbing to the top; for the first $\frac{1}{2}$ mile from the shore there was flat land, after which they ascended a range of low hills, and then got on to a very steep spur from the main range. The northernmost of the two Peaks was ascended, and owing to the height (2,400 feet), Mr. Godwin-Austen, who climbed a tree on the top, obtained a magnificent view, seeing to as far as Flat Island on the Western coast of the Middle Andaman. Stewart's Sound was then re-visited, and the party returned to Port Blair. On arrival there Mr. Godwin-Austen was informed that some of the Settlement fishermen, who had gone out to the Archipelago Islands to fish and had landed on Havelock Island, had been attacked by the Andamanese there. Three convicts were wounded and one man was missing. Though the spot was visited, and traces of the fight were seen, no one could be found. The attack was evidently due to the murder of the Chief of the Archipelago in October 1881 by runaways, for the Andamanese of his tribe, regarding the fishermen as runaways, and remembering the treatment they had received from the others, shot at all they saw. The missing man had fallen into the water in trying to escape from the Andamanese and was drowned.

In March 1882 Mr. Godwin-Austen visited Interview Island and the West coast of the North Andaman, also Port Cornwallis, at which place he had landed some goats on a former visit. No traces of these were to be found and it was probable that the aborigines had eaten them. All the Andamanese were very friendly, and an old man, with white hair (a rare occurrence among them), was seen in Casuarina Bay.

There were very many cases of syphilis, 5 of which were brought in for treatment. At Craggy Island and Stewart's Sound none of the aborigines were to be seen. A few of the Bálés were met with in Kwang Tung Strait.

In February 1882 I returned from leave, and in April visited Macpherson's Straits and Rutland Island. During this month Jumboo, the Chief of Brigade Creek, died at Tálicháūrat. He was a mild and not very intelligent man, who had given us some trouble in the early days, but who had suffered at our hands, having been unjustly imprisoned by Colonel Tytler on account of the murder of Naval Brigadesman Pratt in 1863. His first wife, "Topsy," had been a most valuable ally to Mr. Corbyn.

Mr. Godwin-Austen during this month began to erect buildings for the Andamanese at Haddo Station, as, owing to the number of deaths there, they had expressed a great dread of, and dislike to living on Viper Island.

During the year 1881-82, 26 runaway convicts had been recaptured by the Andamanese ; only one of them, a man named Gholam Ali, offered any resistance, and he, on raising an axe to strike an Andamanese, was shot dead.

Ahmed, who had been released by the Government of India for having seized the convict who assaulted me in December 1879 had been employed as a Free Overseer in the Andamanese Department until May 1881, when he left the Settlement. This man, with his brother Míran, was convicted at the age of 18 years, for abetment of murder, having been concerned in a riot near Dera Ismail Khan, in which some men were killed, and was sentenced to transportation for life. Both the brothers were men of good character, and they rose very rapidly to Jemadarships, the highest post of trust that can be held by a convict. The Jemadar of the Andamanese Department is practically a free man within the limits of the Andaman Islands, as his duty necessitates his visiting all parts of those Islands without restrictions, and great care is therefore taken to procure the best men for the post. Goodhur, who behaved extremely well during Captain Wimberley's expedition to the Little Andaman in 1874; Ahmed; Dungáhi; both of whom had a considerable colloquial knowledge of the Áka-*Béa*-da dialect, and of the habits of the Andamanese; Nureddin, a very energetic and trustworthy man; and Nágjee; all life convicts; were men of exceptional worth, and obtained their pardons, before the prescribed period, for their exceptionally good conduct during the time they were Jemadars in the Andamanese Department.

Twenty three male Andamanese and 19 females died in hospital during the year; of these, the following were men of importance: Wologa Jó-la (who has been already noticed); Daūra, Chief of Port Campbell, a man of an intelligent nature, who had always been well-disposed towards the Government, but who was violent tempered, and had murdered many other Andamanese. He was a brother of Riala, Chief of Góp-l'áka-báng. Kála, a most intelligent youth, who was murdered by the convicts attached to the Góp-l'áka-báng Home, under circumstances to be described further on; Rima, of the Puchik-wár tribe; and Punga, Chief of the Bálé tribe, who had been murdered by the convicts in the Archipelago. The Government of India remarked upon the Annual Report:—

"It is satisfactory to notice that friendly relations with the aborigines, (with the exception of the Jàrawas and the inhabitants of the Little Andaman) continue to be maintained. The remarks in this chapter are interesting, and great credit is due to Mr. Godwin-Austen for his successful management of the Andaman Homes."

The Orphanage was under the charge of Mr. Homfray at this time and was doing well. A special schoolmaster had been engaged, four of the boys were working as servants, and two were in the Superintendent's Printing Office.

In May 1882 Mr. Godwin-Austen visited the Duratáng Creeks, and with Lieutenant Holland, R.I.M., made a survey of Shoal Bay. On the 28th the Andaman Home was moved from Viper Island to Haddo, where it has since remained. The Andamanese were much pleased at the change.

In June I proceeded on duty to the Nicobars, taking with me some Andamanese, and remained there for three months. While there I learnt, from the Andamanese with me, that in February an Andamanese named Kála had been severely beaten by the convicts of the Góp-l'áka-báng Home, because he threatened to report them for general misconduct, and he died from the effects of the beating. Mr. Godwin-Austen had the case investigated, and though sufficient evidence was not obtained to convict the accused before a Court of Law, yet he was so convinced of their guilt that he removed them from the Home. This was one of many instances of the behaviour of the convicts towards the Andamanese, whom they would always ill-treat when they had a chance.

On the night of the 24th of July 1882 an attempt was made by 17 escaped convicts to take a canoe from the Andaman Home at Tára-cháng.

It was dark, and blowing hard, but the dogs of the Andamanese noticed that strangers were about, and a Párawála, named Puran, went out and found that the runaways had just launched a canoe. He at once raised an alarm and 2nd Tindal Dungáhi, with great promptness, put off in a small canoe with a few Andamanese and prevented the convicts from leaving the harbour. The police were then informed and four of the runaways were caught.

In August 1882 Mr. Godwin-Austen searched the Archipelago Islands for runaway convicts, and reports:—

"Most of the runaways now make for the large creeks which flow into Shoal Bay, where they find without any trouble plenty of good material for raft-making. The roads now also enable them to move about the country much quicker than formerly, so that much time is lost by the Andamanese in searching the jungles, where they had been last reported as seen."

In September a number of Burmese convicts escaped and gave considerable trouble. They were prepared to fight and were seen at Dhani Leaf Creek, when they only dispersed on the Police firing at them. The Andamanese went out and shot two men, wounded a third, and captured the remainder, for which they were suitably rewarded.

In October Mr. Godwin-Austen visited the East coast of the Middle and North Andamans, where the people were friendly, and he found that a runaway convict had been killed at Cháūlbí, near Stewart's Sound. He also visited Narcondam Island, where he noticed the numbers of sea snails, from the shells of which a species of the mother-of-pearl of commerce is obtained; and Havelock Island, where he found two runaway convicts, who had been out for three months.

In November 80 men from the North Andaman came on a visit to the Settlement, the largest number that had yet been in from those parts at one time. "Bála Kunwa", an Andamanese who had stayed with me at the Nicobars in June, died, and Mr. Godwin-Austen writes of him: "he was one of the pluckiest and most useful Andamanese we had, and was specially valuable in hunting runaways and in expeditions among the Jàrawas."

In March and April 1883 Mr. Godwin-Austen *rediscovered* "Port Charlotte" and named it "Kwang Tung Harbour," calling "Canning Island" "Spike Island," which, from its shape, was a more suitable name. Major Protheroe and I visited the harbour in the launch *Port Blair*, and examined and christened "Burton Passage."

In his Annual Report for 1882-83, Mr. Godwin-Austen writes:—

"*Escapes.*—Every year the Settlement is being extended and new roads and tracks opened out through the jungle, so that runaways are able now to be, on the morning after their escape, miles away from the stations from which they escaped the night before, before the Andamanese get on their tracks. Also, during the past year, the Andamanese have been seriously hindered and put off the scent by false information tendered by self-supporting convicts. The Andamanese are unable to keep up a continual search for more than two days unless they are positively on the fresh tracks, and I think that now it is a mistake to send them to the station from which the convicts escaped, but rather, I would recommend that when an escape takes place, they should be got ready to start at once to the place in which runaways were last seen by some reliable person, who, if a convict, should report the matter officially, which should be entered together with the name and number of the convict who made the report, and which might be compared with the statements of the runaways, if they were caught.

"The work after runaways is most trying, and after two or three days the pursuers are hardly able to walk from thorns and bruises, and it is only by the influence of the Convict Petty Officers of the Homes that the Andamanese can be made to move; so that, when it is seen how much depends on the Convict Petty Officers and their tact in dealing with the Andamanese when after runaways, a system of promotions and rewards, or an entry in their character sheet, will recommend itself after a successful expedition."

Nine Andamanese had died in the hospital during the year and 16 runaway convicts had been recaptured by the Andamanese.

On this report Major Protheroe remarked in his Annual Report to the Government of India:—

"Owing to the opening up of tracks and roads through the jungle, the facilities for the escape of convicts are greater than they were, and the Andamanese are often put off the scent by self-supporting convicts giving wrong information regarding runaways.

"On two occasions only had the Andamanese to use force in effecting the capture of escaped convicts; once against a batch of Burmese convicts who had absconded, armed with deadly weapons, stockaded themselves in the jungle and refused to surrender, threatening resistance; and, on the second occasion, an escaped convict who had got as far north as Stewart's Sound, was there killed.

"The gardens at Bája-Jág-da, Góp-l'áka-báng, and Tára-cháng have been surveyed by the Government Amin and handed over to the Andamanese permanently, so that they will not be deprived of them as the Settlement increases. The gardens save the Homes considerable expense, and in some cases yield a slight revenue."

An attempt had been made to persuade the Andamanese to breed fowls and pigs in their jungle encampments, but they were found to incommode them when moving about, no care was taken of them, and they soon all died.

On Mr. Homfray's death, on the 25th of February 1883, I took charge of the Andaman Orphanage which was then on Ross Island.

The Government of India remarked on this Report:—

"*Chapter XVIII, Aborigines.*—The remarks in this chapter are interesting, and the Governor General in Council is glad to observe that friendly relations with the aborigines (with the exception of the Jàrawas and the inhabitants of the Little Andaman), continue to be maintained. Mr. Godwin-Austen's services in this matter deserve special notice."

Mr. Godwin-Austen proceeded on sick leave to Europe in May 1883, and Mr. Man again took charge of the Andamanese.

In June I accompanied Major Protheroe on a tour to the North Andaman, and Stewart's Sound, Port Cornwallis, and Cadell Bay were visited. The aborigines were friendly, but there were many cases of syphilis, and I noticed a diminution in their numbers, as compared with those I saw in 1880. A creek off Cadell Bay, called Pāit-ter-bóliu, was explored, and some of the Éremtágas were seen, but, though not hostile, they were very timid, and would not come to take the presents offered to them.

In July Mr. Man sent four male and two female Andamanese to Calcutta to be modelled for the approaching exhibition; they returned in September, and Mr. Man writes of their visit:—

"They were greatly pleased with all they had seen and with the treatment they had received during their absence. They were shown some of the principal places of public interest in the city, including the Mint, the Government Printing Offices, the Howrah Workshops, the Museum, the Monument (the view from the top of which delighted them greatly), a silk factory, and the Great Eastern Hotel. They were also taken by train to spend a day at Barrackpore, and this, to them, novel mode of travelling, appears to have impressed them more than anything else which they witnessed during their visit to "Wonderland."

The Andamanese evidently excited much general interest among the Calcutta public, from whom they received Rs. 120, or more, in presents at the Zoological Gardens, where the entire party were quartered during their stay.

During July the only Andamanese with a hunchback, a man named Wologa, died.

In August 1883 I was sent round the South Andaman in the *Kwang Tung*, to ascertain, if possible, the origin of a peculiar sound like the firing of guns which had been heard in the Settlement. Nothing to explain the sound was, however, seen or heard. (This matter is further explained in the Annual Report, quoted below.)

In September Wói, one of the best natured and nicest of the Andamanese, died. He was a special favourite with Mr. Man, who writes of him :—

"Wói 'Tom', a youth about 22 (? 28) years, who first came to Port Blair from his home in the heart of the Middle Andaman jungle in November 1875. His death is much regretted, as he was a general favourite. It occurred near Interview Island, and as it is ascribed to 'Juruwin dut-ré' (speared by the evil spirit of the sea), it is probable that Wói succumbed to some lung disease."

In October 1883, owing to the murder of Mr. De Roepstorff, who was in charge at the Nicobars, Mr. Man went down there to take charge, and I resumed the charge of the Andamanese.

At this time a party from the Survey of India, under the charge of Captain J. Hobday, was sent down to the Andamans to make a topographical survey of the Islands, which was not completed until 1887.

Owing to the tact and uniform kindness of Captain Hobday and his surveyors to the aborigines, no collision between them occurred, though the Islands were very thoroughly examined, and if anything was wanting to accustom the more distant tribes to our presence, and to consolidate the friendly relations between us, the survey parties supplied this want.

From this period I devoted myself to the taming of the Öngé

Group of Tribes, and particularly to the people on the Little Andaman Island.

Our relations with the other aborigines of the Great Andaman progressed satisfactorily, and I will only quote such occurrences as are of interest.

In October 1883 I visited Stewart's Sound and the Western coasts of the North and Middle Andaman. When we were off Interview Island I saw many canoes, about two miles out at sea, and proceeding to the southward. On enquiry I was informed that they were going to a wreck on the West coast of the Middle Andaman and that most of the Andamanese from the North Andaman had gone there to loot.

This wreck was that of the British Ship *Scottish Chieftain* which had gone on shore at Bluff Point, about four miles north of Flat Island, some months previously. It appeared that she had sailed from Calcutta, and the 1st mate being ill, an apprentice had to keep his watch. Owing to bad weather no observations had been taken since they left the Sandheads, and they were running by dead reckoning. Their only chart of the Bay of Bengal was dated 1860, and they had no knowledge of the Penal Settlement of Port Blair.

One thick, dark night, the apprentice who was on watch called the Captain and told him that there seemed to be a heavy squall coming up to leeward. Almost as he spoke the ship struck with considerable violence, the main and mizen masts being carried away; and the bow of ship being 'thrown high up on the rocks within a hundred yards off the cliff of Cape Bluff, the loom of which was what the apprentice had mistaken for a squall. The crew got safely away in their boats to the Cocos Islands. They saw the Andamanese who did not molest them, but they were so frightened of them that they would not land on the Island. When I saw the vessel she had broken in two just abaft the deck house, and the after part had sunk in about seven fathoms of water. The bow was in four fathoms and the foremast, with the yards on, and the sails set, was standing; portions of the other masts were floating close by, attached to the hull by the rigging. Everything else movable had been taken away by the Andamanese, who had cut holes in the deck to try and get at the cargo. She had been laden with jute and seed which had swollen and rotted.

Whilst on this trip I made enquiries about the North Andaman Éremtágas seen by the Chief Commissioner and myself at Pāīt-ter-bóliu in July. They are not on friendly terms with the Ár-*yāuto*, with whom we are well acquainted, are said to speak a different dialect, and confine themselves almost entirely to the interior. They appear to be more timid than hostile.

In November, people from Landfall Island and the extreme north of the North Andaman came into the Settlement, and two couples of Andamanese went on a visit to Mr. Man at the Nicobars, where they remained for three and a half months without any ill effects.

In January 1884, I was directed to proceed to Calcutta in charge of 37 Andamanese, including two women, and five Nicobarese, in order to show them the Exhibition held there.

The Andamanese taken by me were selected from the different tribes, and chosen on account of their superior influence, position, and intelligence. In addition to the Exhibition they were shown many things which I thought would be likely to interest them and attracted considerable attention. Perhaps the circus was what they appreciated most, and after that the Zoological Gardens, and the Museum, where they quickly recognised and named specimens of fishes, etc.

They lodged on board the S. S. "*Maharani*" (the Port Blair Mail steamer), and only landed during the day. The Mint was only understood by the more intelligent, and though they did not appreciate a jute factory to which they were taken by the kindness of the Revd. Mr. Judson, who was in charge of some Karens, they *were* impressed there by a free fight which occurred between two tribes of Nágas, who had by mistake been brought together.

On one day Dr. George Watt and I took them with five Angámi Nágas, with whom they had struck up a friendship, round Calcutta on a tramcar, when some of them snatched the turbans off the natives in the bazaars and generally behaved so badly that I have never dared to repeat the experiment.

H. E. the Marquis of Ripon, then Viceroy of India, received them in the gardens of Government House, and gave them a most liberal supply of presents.

During the year 1883-84 a station was established at Kyd Island, and two convicts and six Andamanese were ordered to reside there permanently. This was done with a view to arrest the escape of runaway convicts, who, in the South West Monsoon, are in the habit of making rafts in the Duratáng Creek, and from there endeavouring to proceed to sea.

The number of Andamanese at the villages in the South Andaman had considerably decreased. In this Island, formerly extremely thickly populated, only the following villages remained :—

Taracháng containing about 35 people.

Góp-l'áka-báng with 15.

Duratáng with 15, and

Báráij-Bóroga-da with 4.

Of the Rutland Island Sept, formerly so large and powerful, only two men were then living. The same number existed of the Bája-Jág Sept, whilst of those who used to live in the Harbour of Port Blair none were alive.

Those few, some half dozen, who remain of the Port Campbell Sept, lived at Taracháng, as did those who belonged to Māi Leptu. Of the Brátan Sept none remain. The chief causes of this decrease were, the epidemic of measles which occurred in 1876, and the ravages of syphilis.

On the 26th and 27th of August 1883 a sound as of the firing of guns was heard at intervals. In consequence of this I was sent out in the "*Kwang Tung*" on the night of the 27th to visit Rutland Island, the Labyrinth Islands, and the North Sentinel Island, in search of any ship which might be ashore, and firing signals of distress.

I landed on the North Sentinel and walked some distance into the interior. Several villages were seen, some having as many as

14 huts, whereas formerly I had never seen more than seven. Presents were left in all the huts, but no aborigines were seen. No traces of a ship-wrecked vessel were found, and we returned to Port Blair.

As the firing of guns had continued during my absence, Major Protheroe, the Officiating Chief Commissioner, himself went round the Little Andaman, but with no better success.

On the afternoon of the 26th, one of the Police at Shouldari reported that the water had suddenly left all the streams, even on the hill sides, and had equally quickly returned to them. It was also noticed that the tide in the creeks of the Port Blair Harbour had behaved in a most erratic manner, which was fully corroborated by the recording tide gauge. No particular notice was taken of this at the time, but on the arrival of the mail with the telegrams announcing the terrible explosion at Krakatau, the phenomena we had been witnessing were explained, as similar gun-firing, leading to similar results, had been heard at Rangoon and in the Straits Settlements. What we had heard were probably not the actual Krakatau explosions, but electrical disturbances engendered by them. Many months afterwards I found small pieces of pumice floating in the Southern Harbours, and of course the wonderfully coloured sunsets were seen here as elsewhere.

Two Sindhi convicts of bad character, named Sheikhu and Wádhu, after escaping from Viper Island, committed an attempt to murder at Port Mouat, and a reward of R 50 for each was offered by the Government. They made their way to Port Campbell through the jungle, and were proceeding north, when they met some Andamanese, with whom they camped. During the night they stole their canoe and made off, but abandoned it further to the northward and were seen again by the angry Andamanese, who had pursued them, swimming from Bluff Island to Spike Island.

On arriving on the shore of the latter, the convicts were met by the Andamanese, who had headed them, and, as they would not surrender, were shot to death as they landed. I afterwards saw their bodies among the roots of the trees on the sea shore.

Seven births and 11 deaths had occurred during this year.

Colonel Cadell, in reporting to the Government of India on it, remarked:—

"The friendly tribes of Andamanese are, I regret much to report, rapidly dying out. Great ravages were caused among them by an outbreak of measles in 1876, and syphilis has spread from one end of the Island to the other. Every year shows a decreasing population, the old and middle aged dying, and no children coming up to fill their places. It may safely be predicted that the friendly tribes will be extinct some thirty or fifty years hence. Intoxicating drinks have been successfully kept from them, but it is thought that over indulgence in the use of tobacco has tended to cause a sterility among them."

"Nothing can exceed the kindness with which they have been treated by the successive officers who have had charge of them, namely, Messrs. Corbyn, Homfray, Man, Godwin-Austen, and Portman."

"Hereditary syphilis is beginning to appear among the children, even those from the Middle Andaman having it. It breaks out as hip disease, about their 10th or 11th year, and this would place the date of the introduction of syphilis among the Andamanese, certainly prior to 1873, when it was alleged to have been introduced."

The Government of India remarked in the Resolution on the Annual Report for the year 1883-84:—

"*Chapter XVII, Aborigines.*— "It was found necessary to send expeditions against the Jàrawa tribes, who gave trouble during the year under report, and continued to reject the efforts made to establish friendly relations with them. The Governor General in Council noticed with regret that the friendly tribes of Andamanese are said to be dying out, but the matter appears to be one which is beyond the power of the Government to remedy. The report furnished by the Reverend Mr. Chard, Chaplain of Port Blair, on the Andaman Orphanage, has been read with interest by the Government of India." (This report is alluded to in Chapter XXI; *M. V. P.*)

In April 1884 a party of Malays to whom had been granted the monopoly of the collection of edible birds' nests and Trepang in the Andamans, anchored their Junk in Stewart's Sound, and as they resented the visits of the Andamanese to the vessel, and would not give them any presents, trouble ensued and I had to go up to the Sound to put matters right. I found there many cases of syphilis, which I brought in to Port Blair for treatment.

During this month an Andamanese named Ira Gud was sentenced to one week's simple imprisonment for negligently firing arrows in a village, one of which struck the child of another Andamanese on the head, and killed it.

In April and May I made a complete tour over both coasts of the Andaman Islands and brought in many cases of syphilis.

In October I was sent by Colonel Cadell to examine the reefs on the West coast, and lived for three weeks in the Labyrinth Islands, in camp with the Andamanese. Among other things, a quantity of a coarse variety of sponge was found, numbers of pearl oysters, and some of the large Pinnas containing black pearls.

In December, 234 Andamanese were living in the Homes, and advantage was taken of this to search with them for Jàrawas.

In February the whole of the East coast of the Islands was visited and I spent some days at the Table Islands. All the aborigines were friendly but their numbers were much reduced, and I brought in many cases of syphilis. Some of these poor people were in a shocking condition, being covered all over with sores like small-pox pustules, and the smell from their bodies was so offensive that they could not be allowed on board the steamer, but were towed in a boat some distance astern. Yet many of these cases yielded to treatment, and some surprising cures were effected.

Dr. Gupta, who has been Junior Medical Officer at Haddo for many years, and who, in addition to his other duties is in charge of the Andamanese hospital there, has given much time and care to the aborigines, and by his tact in managing them has gained their confidence, (a most important item with them), and no doubt been the means of saving very many.

Most of my trips about the Islands were made in a large steam launch, of which I took charge, (for I had been a sailor by profession before I joined the Port Blair Commission). I was thus able to visit all the harbours and creeks, and gain a knowledge of the Islands that it would have been impossible to get had I only visited special places in the Station Steamer.

In the Annual Report for 1884-85, I remark that—

"As most of the men in the Haddo Home are recruited from the Middle Andaman and the Archipelago, and as people from these places are either constantly visiting the Settlement, or being visited by parties out collecting shells, etc., numerous visits are not required to be paid to them by me. Eleven births and 28 deaths had occurred at the Homes, and syphilis had been very prevalent during the year."

Colonel Cadell noted in addition—

"Dr. Gupta at Haddo has shown the Andamanese in the hospital every possible attention, and it is entirely owing to his care and tact that the Jàrawa captives were kept alive. The Andamanese also are attached to him, and appreciate their good treatment in the hospital, and not nearly so much difficulty is experienced as formerly in getting even the most distant to come into hospital."

On the 21st of April 1885 a party of Burmese convicts who had escaped, attacked the barrack at North Corbyn's Cove. (They had some time before stolen some rifles and ammunition from the survey camp at Port Meadows.) Some convicts were wounded and even killed, and I was ordered in pursuit. The Burmese had an Andamanese canoe which they had stolen, and on my way up the coast I met two self-supporting convicts, on rafts, who said that the runaways had passed in the canoe a few hours before. I went on to Kyd Island in my steam launch and saw them there just rounding the S. W. corner of the Island. On seeing that they could not escape the launch they ran the canoe on shore on Kyd Island and bolted up the hill into the jungle. The canoe was full of loot they had stolen from Corbyn's Cove Barrack, and from the Kyd Island garden, and they evidently intended to go off to Burma. I went up the hill with the Andamanese, but the Burmese fired on us and then ranaway, and the Andamanese after a long hunt only killed two of them. They were, however, closely pursued, and all of them were eventually either killed or captured, the heads of the last remaining being brought in on the 24th of May after a fight in the jungle on the slopes of Mount Harriett.

I went, on leaving Kyd Island, to the North Andaman, where I joined Colonel Cadell. At Stewart's Sound I learnt that a party of Sindhi convicts, who had escaped from the Settlement some time before, had been captured by the Éremtágas of the Jéru Tribe, living to the North of the Sound, in the interior of the North Andaman; and, as they offered resistance, they had been killed and their bodies burnt. Three syphilitic cases were brought in, and I heard that Total, the Chief of Long Island, and Burko, the Chief of Chāūlbi, had died.

On the 7th October 1885 Petty Officer Habib, No. 25399, was murdered by some Andamanese on the East coast of the South Andaman, near Lekera Báruga. A party of Andamanese had been camped there while engaged in cutting a canoe; when this was finished, and they tried to launch it, the canoe smashed, and they were so enraged at the loss of their labour that they decided to go away to their own country in the sulks.

Habib attempted to prevent them from doing this, so in a fit of rage they set on him and shot him to death.

News was brought to me of the occurrence by some other Andamanese, who had witnessed but had not taken part in it, and the next month I proceeded to Mount Kunu, arrested the guilty parties, and the two ringleaders, Rima and Bira, were sentenced by the Chief Commissioner to five years' rigorous imprisonment each.

In October a cyclone passed over the North Andaman, and the British Ship *Helen Pembroke*, which had been to Port Blair with a cargo of coal, and had only left a few days before the storm; the *Fazel Kureem*; and another native craft, were all wrecked on the North-West coast. The crews of the two former vessels only were saved, having got away in their boats to the Coco Islands, and it was satisfactory to learn that, though they met with the Andamanese, no collision occurred, and they were even well-treated by them. Of course the savages were unable to resist plundering the wrecks, and when some of them came into the Settlement some weeks afterwards, it was ludicrous to see them swaggering about in the clothes of the shipwrecked men; one would have on a pair of sea-boots; another, an elaborately adorned cap, formerly the property of the wife of the Captain of the *Helen Pembroke*; while a third would have a shirt hanging over his back and tied round his neck by the sleeves. Some wore stockings on their arms, with slits in the soles for the hands to come through; and it must be remembered that these articles were all the attire they had.

In November 1885 I was directed by the Chief Commissioner to undertake the collection of edible birds' nests on the part of the Government, as the Malay contractors had failed to pay the amount due, and had left the Settlement. I accordingly went round the Islands visiting all the caves in which the birds build, and arranging for the collection of the nests. At " Árāinj-l'áka-pónga," on the eastern mouth of Homfray Strait, I found that the Andamanese living there had sheltered the others who had murdered Habib, and had refused to give them up when I sent men up for them, so I burnt down the village as a punishment.

At Interview Island I found many syphilitic cases which I brought in, and when passing through the Labyrinth Islands I saw a small raft hidden in a mangrove swamp, and some smoke issuing from the adjacent jungle. I landed with a party of Andamanese and found three runaway convicts whom I brought in. One of them, on our approach, tried to hang himself to a tree by his loin-cloth.

In December 1885 I took 13 Andamanese to Penang and the Nicobar Islands, having been directed to visit the former place in order to make enquiries about the sale of edible birds' nests there.

In Penang the Andamanese were so mobbed by the people that it was impossible to take them about and show them the place, nor could I obtain any protection or assistance from officials.

From the name "Handumán" which the Malays give to the Andamanese, and from the fact that these Islands are caled by the Malays, who are the oldest and most constant visitors to them, "Pulọ

Handumán", it was suggested by the Hon'ble Mr. Maxwell that the word Andaman is merely a corruption of the Malay "Handumán" which is the manner in which the Malays pronounce the words Hanumán of the Rámáyana. This appears to me to be a more satisfactory and probable derivation for the name of these Islands than those given by Colonel Yule.

From Penang I went down to Thaipeng in the state of Perák. Here the Andamanese were treated very kindly. Mr. Swettenham, the Acting Resident, gave them the old Residency to live in and took precautions that they should not be molested. They were, therefore, able to go about and see a good deal of the country, and enjoyed their visit there very much. The train from Port Weld to Thaipeng, by which they travelled, and the Malay knives with which they were presented, seemed to impress them most, (after, perhaps, a number of very fat Chinese pigs they saw in some crates on a truck in the station, and from which I could scarcely tear them away).

In my Annual Report for 1885-86, I state:—

"As the Andamanese are so rapidly becoming extinct, the number of people at the Haddo Home has diminished, and it is now very difficult to obtain sufficient for the requirements of the Government and for the support of the Home. Nearly all of the sale work of the Home is done by Andamanese from the northern half of the Middle Andaman and from the North Andaman.

"Many visits were paid to the Middle and North Andaman during the year, but nothing of any importance occurred.

"It has been noticed this year that syphilis is raging throughout the whole North Island, scarcely a person being free from it, and the number of aborigines appear to be reduced. As it is difficult to bring patients from such a distance, it appears to me that the only means of effectually combating the disease is, to treat the patients in their own homes, a work which would surely be appropriate to the people of the Andaman Mission.

"The North Andamanese now come occasionally to Haddo and constant communication is kept up. In all cases of wrecks, or where the aborigines have met with the Survey parties, they appear to have behaved very well.

"Only six runaway convicts were brought in by the Andamanese during the year. The work of runaway hunting, always hard and distasteful to them, is now becoming more difficult than ever. Owing to the size of the Settlement and the fact that the self-supporting convicts and free people go out into the adjacent jungles for produce, the Andamanese are often at a loss to know whether any person they may meet, in, or on the confines of, the Settlement, is a runaway or not. Further, as nearly all the men of the South Andaman Tribes are dead, there is no one to lead the parties of searchers, as it is of no use sending men from the North Andaman to search in the South Andaman jungles, and as mere trackers the Andamanese are poor, not comparing with the Australian black, or the Punjab tracker.

"Excepting the great increase of syphilis, the health of the Andamanese has been better than usual. The number o f deaths are however, far in advance of the number of births, and the race is fast dying out. I always send the women to the jungle to be confined, as the very small babies seem to thrive better there.

"During the year there were seven births in the Homes, against 23 deaths. Among the latter may be noticed that of "Bála Jóbo," Chief of Mount Kunu, who had succeeded "Ira Árla," as Chief there, in September 1878."

The Government of India, in the Resolution on the Annual Report for 1885-86, Chapter XVI, Aborigines, state:—

"The remarks in this chapter are very interesting, and the Governor General in Council is glad to observe that the efforts which the Superintendent and Mr. Portman have been making for several years to establish friendly relations with the inhabitants of the Little Andaman have at last been rewarded with success. His Excellency in Council, however, notices with regret that the aborigines are throughout the Islands reported to be suffering severely from syphilis. The Andamanese Orphanage does not appear to have been successfully managed during the year; but now the Chaplain of the Station has taken charge of it, it is to be hoped that an improvement in the management will take place."

In April 1886 I visited the East coast of the Islands, and in May no less than 94 cases of syphilis were brought in from the North Andaman for treatment; specially trained Andamanese were sent out for this purpose and did their work on the whole fairly well.

I established a Trepang fishery at this time, which is worked by the Andamanese and the convicts attached to the Homes, and yields a fair income. The money was badly wanted, as, while the number of Andamanese in the Homes and Hospital had increased, the Government had ceased to issue medicines to the latter, and the cost of maintaining them was very heavy.

In June I paid another visit to the East coast of the Islands. In August an epidemic of mumps attacked the Andamanese very severely, with all possible complications, and ran through the Islands. No deaths occurred from it.

In September I made some investigations as to the possibility of a pearl fishery being established, and a few small but good black pearls were found.

In October, as the Chief Commissioner was anxious that the coast line, at least, of the Little Andaman should be correctly laid down by the survey party which was now concluding its work, I proceeded on special duty to the Little Andaman with the view of taming the aborigines there, and Mr. T. J. Metcalfe took charge of the Andamanese.

On my return from the Little Andaman in February, I visited the West coast of the Islands with Colonel Wimberley, the officiating Chief Commissioner, and then proceeded on a year's furlough to Europe in March.

During the year 1886-87 most of the work with the aborigines was done at the Little Andaman, and will be described separately, the visits to the different parts of the Great Andaman being made principally with the view of detecting and bringing in the cases of syphilis.

Thirteen deaths and two births occurred in the Homes during the year, and the number of syphilitic cases treated was greater than that in any previous year.

In the Resolution on the Annual Report for 1886-87, Chapter XVII, Aborigines, the Government of India remark:—

"The Governor General in Council notices with regret that the numbers of the friendly tribes of the Andamanese are said to be becoming less and less year by year, and that it is probable before long the race will cease to exist, except in the Little Andaman, which is said to be more thickly populated than the other Islands. Mr. Portman's report of his two visits to the Little Andaman has been read with interest by the Government of India. The Reverend Mr. Chard's report shows that the Andaman Orphanage appears to have been successfully managed during the year."

During the time that Mr. Metcalfe was in charge of the Andamanese, most of the work lay at the Little Andaman, but in September 1887 he paid a visit to the East coast of the Islands; a similar visit was paid in November. In December he visited the West coast, and in February he made a long and very thorough tour of inspection round the whole of the Great Andaman. He noticed a very old man with white hair on the West coast of the North Andaman, and appears to have met with a good number of Andamanese wherever he stopped. They were all friendly, and he distributed presents, and brought in the sick as usual.

In 1886 a very good sea-going steam launch had been supplied to the Settlement, in which most of the tours were made, and Mr. Metcalfe noticed how well the Andamanese seemed to understand handling and piloting her. They had had pretty considerable practice by that time, and were really very smart. On one occasion I was going by night to the West coast of the North Andaman, and leaving Port Blair in the evening, was off Kyd Island at about 10 P.M. The night was thick and squally, and I was tired and ill, so lay down to sleep for a short time, leaving the Launch under the charge of our best pilot "Búluba-la," commonly known as the "The Cat." Without waking me he took the vessel through the Middle Straits, and only roused me at 2 A. M., when it was time to drop the anchor off the north end of Spike Island.

The Andamanese in piloting a vessel judge by two things; the look of the water, and the reefs, which are generally visible; and knowing, by going about in their own canoes, where they are unable to pole because of the depth of water, they take the vessel in the deep water, and are able to say with confidence that at least 18 feet will be found at low water, that being the average length of a poling bamboo.

Mr. Metcalfe was much attached to the Andamanese, and was very kind to them, and they understood this and were fond of him in return.

On the 22nd of March 1888 I returned from England and resumed the charge of the Andamanese.

The only matters commented upon during the year, besides Little Andaman and Jàrawa affairs, were, the rapidly approaching extinction of the race, and the continuance of syphilis. Several runaway convicts were caught by the Andamanese, and five deaths occurred at the Homes.

In April 1888 I visited the principal places in the South Andaman, and in September I visited the North and Middle Andaman, bringing in several cases of syphilis. In January the Middle and North Andaman were again visited, and Colonel Tucker, Officiating Chief Commissioner, also visited Barren Island, and left a number of goats there, which have since thriven, and multiplied considerably.

Sixteen runaway convicts were caught by the Andamanese during the year 1888-89, and much work was done in connection with the Jàrawa tribes.

There was a great deal of sickness among the Andamanese during the year and many cases of syphilis were brought in. Thirty-three Andamanese died at the Homes, and no births occurred. One man named "Bía Juru," a famous turtle catcher, was seized with cramp and drowned one night when out after turtle, and the Andamanese said of him that "The spirit of the sea had killed him at last because he had killed so many turtles".

In April 1889 I again went round the South Andaman visiting the different harbours and villages, but the whole of that year is merely a record of sickness and deaths.

In June, as there was sufficient money in hand, I engaged a self-supporter Compounder to look after the Andamanese sick, and I note in the monthly report :—

"He has done extremely good work already in visiting the distant jungle stations and bringing in the sick. By his care and attention also the numbers in Haddo Hospital have been reduced from 26 to 8 at the end of the month. It was this man to whose attention the cure of Tálai the Jàrawa was owing in March 1884. He is liked by the Andamanese and strongly recommended by Dr. Gupta."

Visits were paid to the Little Andaman and expeditions were sent against the Jàrawa tribes, but the only occurrence of note in the year among the tribes of the Great Andaman was, that in February 1890, a fight occurred between members of the Cháriár and Jéru tribes on the West coast of the North Andaman, in which two men were killed, and Kàūnmu, the Chief of the Cháriárs, was wounded in the leg. The Jérus, being Éremtágas, retreated into the jungle in the interior of the Island and were not seen again.

Shortly after this I visited the North Andaman in the *Ross* and found all quiet, and Kàūnmu's wound healed.

In addition to the above, two instances of Andamanese losing their temper over trivial matters, and at once firing arrows about the place indiscriminately, (as is their custom when put out), occurred in the Settlement during the month of February. In each case wounds were inflicted on entirely innocent outsiders, and in each case I punished the delinquents with a very severe flogging.

Eleven runaway convicts were captured by the Andamanese during the year. Of these, three had got to sea on a raft of Bamboos, and were aimlessly drifting about not more than a mile from land, with nothing to eat and drink, when they were found by me as I happened to pass in the *Ross*.

Twenty deaths occurred at the Homes and no births.

During the year 1890-91 the principal event was an outbreak of Russian Influenza which spread rapidly throughout the Islands, and the Andamanese, with their constitutions already weakened by syphilis, had no strength to fight the disease, but died in large numbers. It broke out in April 1890; in May I went round the Islands in the *Ross* and found many cases, and in this month 11 deaths occurred from it, one being that of Punga, the Chief of Port Mouat; in June 27 deaths occurred, one being that of Punga "Karl," the last representative of the Rutland Island Sept. All work at the Homes was stopped on account of the disease and special food, tonics, and wine were given to the Andamanese in the hope of keeping them alive.

In July a party of Andamanese, with a convict Petty Officer, was sent to the Archipelago Islands, and returned with the news that two men and a woman had died there of Russian influenza. On the 29th ten men and six women came in from Long Island and reported that, with the exception of a few people at Mount Kunu, Juruchàng, and the Archipelago Islands, they were the only survivors of the tribes between Port Blair and Rongat.

"There appears to have been considerable mortality from the disease in the jungles, and at present, with the exception of the people in the Homes at Haddo, Táracháng, Góp-l'áka-báng, and Duratáng, who are collected from all parts of the Great Andaman, the total number of survivors of the tribes from Rutland Island to a line drawn across the Middle Andaman from Rongat to Bár-l'áka-Bil would seem to be about 20 men and 12 women. How great the mortality has been north of this line I am unable to say at present.

"From the fact that, though they all suffered from it, none of the Andamanese in the Home at my house died of Russian Influenza, it would seem that my system of keeping them under my direct care is the only one which is likely to keep the remainder of the race alive.

Steps were therefore taken to bring more Andamanese into this Home, where they receive a special training."

In August 1890 I received information that an Andamanese of Homfray Strait, named Tura Né, had, about three months previously, killed an old woman in a fit of passion, because she had accidentally burnt his bow. I was directed by the Chief Commissioner to enquire into the matter, and on the 31st August I arrested Tura Né at Mount Kunu, and brought him, and a witness to the crime, to Port Blair.

He was tried by the Court of Sessions, found guilty of culpable homicide not amounting to murder, and sentenced to two years. rigorous imprisonment.

It appeared that he, with some other Andamanese, including the old woman, were moving from one village to another in a canoe, in the early morning. The Andamanese always carry, on a heap of sand on the bottom of the canoe, a small fire, and the old woman had raked this fire together and was crouching over it, warming herself as she found the morning mist chilly. She did not notice that a bow which Tura Né had lately made, and thought a good deal of, had fallen on the smouldering part of a log and was becoming charred. Tura Né, seeing his bow near the fire, picked it up and found that it was burnt. He flew into a rage, abused the old woman for her carelessness, and snatching up an arrow and another bow fired at her and killed her. This is a good instance of the manners of the Andamanese, and if they would act thus when they know that they are certain to be punished, it is easy to realise the state of their existence before our arrival, and how timid they were when they met, and how careful not to offend each other.

Colonel Cadell and I visited the East coast of the Islands in August 1890. The influenza was still raging and many deaths had occurred. At Stewart's Sound, where, in 1880, 14 canoe loads of people came off to me when I visited it, only about 14 people remained alive. I paid another visit to the Sound in October. The influenza seemed then to have abated, and on going farther North to the Table Islands, Cadell Bay, and Landfall Island,

I did not find any cases. I brought in for treatment six people who were suffering from syphilis.

In December Colonel Cadell and I visited the Archipelago Islands and the coasts of the South Andaman, but few aborigines were seen.

In March 1891 I went out in the *Ross* to collect edible birds nests, and took with me a boat, a canoe, and a number of Andamanese. One night while we were at anchor at Spike Island, three Andamanese stole the canoe with all the torches, tridents, and other implements used in the collection of the nests, and bolted. On enquiry from the Andamanese at Lekera-Luntá I learnt that the runaways had gone up the Yéretil Creek so went up after them in my boat. On arrival at Yéretil village I found a large party encamped, with several canoes, amongst which was mine, and the three missing Andamanese were in the huts. On seeing me two of them fired at me, and the three then ran away into the jungle. One of them was brought back by some men of my own party who had gone in pursuit, and he, on finding that he had to go back in the canoe, attacked me, biting one of my fingers to the bone, and, being much stronger than I, got me down on the ground with his foot on my chest and tried to cut my throat. Some of the others hauled him off, and he was tied up and put into the boat. I waited in the village for some time to see if the other two would return, but, as they did not do so, I took some photographs of the scene, and then burnt the village down, and returned to the *Ross*, bringing with me all the canoes and other property of the people in the village, whom I told that these articles would be returned to them when the missing men were brought to me. I then steamed through Homfray Straits to the Archipelago Islands, and went on with the birds' nest collection. Two days afterwards, while at anchor at Strait Island, a party of Andamanese came up in a canoe. They had captured and brought in the other two men, so I returned all their property to them.

The boys who had given all the trouble resumed their usual duties and appeared to think that they had had their spree out, and that it was now time to turn to work again, not showing the slightest shame, or indeed any change in their manner towards me. An Andamanese is always so comic a creature that it is impossible to preserve a grave demeanour towards him for long.

In my Annual Report for the year 1890-91, I remark :—

"*Paragraph 8.*—All the people on Rutland Island and Port Campbell are dead, and very few remain in the South Andaman and the Archipelago. The children do not survive in the very few births which do occur, and the present generation may be considered as the last of the aborigines of the Great Andaman. Even these have their constitutions to a great extent undermined by hereditary syphilis, and are unable to endure much exposure.

"I am endeavouring to keep the race alive as long as possible, and am collecting all the children at my house, where they are well fed and looked after, and are taught to pull in my boat, wait at table, and make themselves generally useful. I have also provided a gymnasium for them. I have now 36 boys with me.

"The man 'Joseph,' mentioned in the Report for last year, (quoted in Chapter XXI), who had returned to Port Blair after spending ten years in India and Burma, and who was made over to me by the Chaplain as a quite incorrigible blackguard, has now married and settled down in the Middle Andaman. He is very intelligent and obedient to my orders, and I find him of great use. During the last season he has supervised the Trepang fishery at Mount Kunu.

"54 men, 5 women, and one female child have died during the year, which, owing to the influenza, has been one of the most unhealthy years we have had.

"Eleven runaway convicts were recaptured by the Andamanese during the year."

The Government of India, in the Resolution on the Annual Report for 1890-91, remark :—

"*Paragraph 11.*—The Government of India notice with approval the endeavours which are being made by Mr. Portman to prolong the existence of the race."

In July 1891 some convicts were trying to escape on a raft from the Western coast, when a party of Andamanese, who were searching for them, came up. The runaways were headed by an elderly Brahmin, who was serving a second sentence in Port Blair, and had a mania for attempting to escape. When they saw the Andamanese they pushed off on the raft, but stuck in the shallow water. The Andamanese called to them to surrender and waded out towards them, when the men threatened them with an imitation gun, made from a bamboo. This they pointed at the Andamanese, made a noise with their mouths as if to imitate the firing of a gun, and then threw some slugs at them. The Andamanese, though taken aback at first, as soon as they found that the gun was not real, fired on the runaways, killing one and wounding two others, who were then brought in.

A case among the Andamanese also occurred during this month.

A lad named " Rang," living at Bája Jág-da, had taken a small basket belonging to a woman there for his tobacco. She objected to this, and the other women of the village joined her in rebuking the man, who got angry, and, snatching up his bow and a pig arrow, went outside the hut and fired into it, hitting another man, who happened to be standing up, in the chest, and inflicting a severe wound. Rang was at once arrested and brought to me. I tried him under Section 324, Indian Penal Code, and sentenced him to six months' rigorous imprisonment.

" Kápo, " the wounded man, recovered.

The above is a good instance of the childish anger and behaviour of the Andamanese. Rang had no quarrel with Kápo, but in their rage they seem blinded to all except the idea of inflicting some injury on some person or thing. Such instances were common in the villages in former times.

On the night of the 1st of November 1891 a cyclone passed over the Settlement of Port Blair and the South Andaman, destroying numbers of buildings, in the falling of which several convicts were killed or wounded.

The R. I. M. S. *Enterprise* was driven on shore on the South Point Reef, and, with the exception of six natives who, washed into the surf, were pulled on shore and saved by the women in the Female Jail there, all hands were lost. The trees were either felled or badly injured, and the roads were blocked with fallen branches. In the jungle the debris was so thick and matted that even the Andamanese were unable to make their way along their accustomed paths. All the buildings at the Homes were levelled, the falling of the Barrack at Bája Jág-da killing an Andamanese girl. The Andamanese hospital at Haddo fell, killing an old blind man, and injuring another man.

A few days afterwards, when the sea was sufficiently calm to permit of the *Ross* being sent out, Colonel Cadell directed me to go round the Islands and ascertain what damage had been done. The following was my report on the tour—

" *Paragraph 2.*—In accordance with your instructions I left Port Blair on the morning of the 8th November 1891 in the *Ross* accompanied by Mr. P. Cadell, I. C. S., and proceeded north, keeping as close to the coast as possible. From Port Blair to Kyd Island all the trees were stripped of their leaves and smaller branches, and after passing Borua-Táng, 11 miles north of Ross Island, we noticed that many of the larger trees had been blown down. At Kyd Island, 18 miles north of Port Blair, the wind had reached its greatest violence, and many of the trees were down.

" A mile out at sea the water was black and thick with mangrove mud, and the stench peculiar to mangrove swamps was very powerful. This may be due to the mangrove trees having been torn up by the storm, and the black mud, which accumulates round their roots, being set free and washed away by the tide. At Rógo-lo-chong, 30 miles north of Port Blair, the jungle no longer appeared stripped of its leaves and branches, and at Strait Island, 34 miles north of Port Blair, I learnt that, though heavy rain had fallen, no storm of importance had passed.

" Just south of Strait Island I met five canoes full of Andamanese.

" They had been at a village near Rógo-lo-chong, 28 miles north of Port Blair during the storm, and stated that, during the night of the 1st, they were so frightened by the falling branches that they went into the sea until the storm had passed. I proceeded through Colebrooke Passage, 33 miles north of Port Blair, where the jungle was in its usual beauty, not a branch being broken or a leaf blown off, and passed through Homfray Strait to Lekera-luntá, anchoring for the night between Bluff Island and the south end of Spike Island. Here, 34 miles north of Port Blair, I found a storm had passed, breaking many of the smaller branches of the trees in the jungle, but not of sufficient violence to give the jungle the stripped appearance it has near Port Blair.

"In Homfray Strait a few branches were blown about, but the leaves were not off the trees. I learnt, partly by observation and partly from the Andamanese I met near Strait Island, that the cyclone had passed over the Archipelago Island, stripping the trees south of Tádma-Juru (a Strait 24 miles north of Port Blair), doing considerable damage between that place and Nicholson Island, 28 miles north of Port Blair, and apparently leaving Wilson Island, 30 miles north of Port Blair, untouched.

"I have sent two parties to look along the coast of the Archipelago Island for any wrecks which may have occurred.

"On the 9th we steamed down the West coast of the South Andaman. At Breakfast Bay, 28 miles north of Port Blair, the trees again appeared stripped of their branches and leaves, and many trees had fallen.

"At Port Campbell, 18 miles north of Port Blair, and in the same latitude as Kyd Island, the wind had evidently been of great violence. Montgomery and Petrie Island, at the entrance of the harbour, had the majority of their trees down, and the cliff at the south side of the harbour, formerly having a crest of lofty trees, was bare. Portions of the cliff, which is of soft sandstone, had fallen into the sea.

"From here to Ép-luntá, 5 miles north of Port Blair, the jungle had the appearance of a forest in England in winter. About five miles south of Port Campbell I saw some Jàrawas on the beach. They have of course experienced a great fright, as the jungle in their country is so damaged, and have very probably received injuries from falling trees. Had I been able to do so, I would have left food and presents for them on the beach, but the heavy sea on the reef prevented my landing.

"At Port Mouat the damage was not so great as at Port Blair, and further south the wind had perceptibly less force. Termugli Island was not injured, and all the trees on Grub Island were standing with their leaves on, though they were stripped of leaves and branches on the mainland, a mile off. The jungle in the Labyrinth Islands had not suffered much.

"The trees on the Yáratán Hills and at Biriwil-lá-loichera, the south-west corner of the South Andaman, had been stripped of their leaves and branches. I anchored in Portman Harbour for the night.

"The jungle on Rutland Island had not suffered much and the leaves were not off the trees.

"On the 10th we proceeded to the Little Andaman. The jungle on the Cinque, Passage, and Brother Islands showed no signs of a cyclone having passed. We anchored in Bumila Creek at 11 A.M., and were received by a quantity of Öngés, both men and women, who had collected on either bank. Some of them swam off on board, and I learnt that no storm of special violence had passed, and that Kógio Kāī, Tómiti, and all the Támbe Ébui people were turtling on the South Brother Island, which they would not be doing had they just experienced a cyclone.

"On the 11th we returned to Port Blair as the weather looked stormy. On the way up I noticed that the zone of greatest violence of wind commenced at about 11 miles south of Port Blair.

"3.—From the above observations I draw the following conclusions:

"The greatest violence of the wind was in Latitude 11° 58' North.

"The zone of violence of wind sufficient to strip the trees of their leaves and branches, and to fell several, was from Latitude 11° 2' North to Latitude 12 °8' North on the East coast of the Island. This zone only extended to Latitude 12° 4' North in the Archipelago Islands, which are about 15 miles east of Port Blair.

"On the West coast of the Islands this zone extended from 11° 5' North Latitude to 12° 8' North Latitude.

"The whole storm, including the above, and those parts of the Island where the wind had sufficient force to break the branches off the trees, extended on the East coast from 10° 58' North Latitude to 12° 14' North Latitude, and on the West coast from 11° 0' North Latitude to 12° 18' North Latitude. Outside of this zone rain and dirty weather undoubtedly occurred, but there was no storm of any exceptional violence.

" 4. Near the Southern and Northern edges of the zone of great violence the wind seemed to have been capricious; often levelling the trees in one place, and not even blowing the leaves off exposed clumps of trees half a mile away."

In February 1892 seven aborigines of the Great Andaman and four Ȯngés from the Little Andaman accompanied me on a visit to Calcutta. This was the first occasion on which the Ȯngés had visited any country outside the Andaman Islands, and when they were brought away from their own land I was not able to explain what was going to happen to them. They seemed nervous on the voyage up, and during the first few days in Calcutta, but kind treatment and the assurance that they would soon return home, reconciled them to the visit in a short time.

On board the *Shahjehan* (the Andaman Mail Steamer) great care was taken of them, and special arrangements were made for their comfort by Captain Edge and by Mr. Sandilands, the Chief Officer.

In Calcutta they lived at Spence's Hotel, where a room for them had been previously engaged, and their privacy and security from annoyance ensured.

They were received in the Government House Gardens by His Excellency the Viceroy, (the Marquis of Lansdowne) on the 5th, when they danced, showed their skill in shooting with bows and arrows, and did gymnastic exercises. His Excellency expressed his pleasure at having seen them, and completely won their hearts by the large quantity of really valuable presents he gave them.

They were taken through the town to the Howrah Bridge, up the Ochterlony Monument, to the Museum, and to the Zoological Gardens.

They were also shown through the principal shops, where they were uniformly treated with great courtesy by the proprietors, who put themselves to considerable trouble to show the Andamanese mechanical figures, toys, arms, etc., which they thought would amuse and interest them.

The presents they chose naturally consisted of knives, axes, and other similar weapons; also pipes and tobacco; but I added two English footballs (to which game, since their return, they have taken a liking), and some English bows and arrows, which they admit are far superior to their own.

They were also taken to the Botanical Gardens, the Viceroy kindly lending his Launch for the purpose, and seemed to examine the trees and plants with great interest. They were delighted with the piece of Andaman jungle which Dr. Prain pointed out to them, and which they at once recognised. While there, His Excellency the Viceroy, and the Bishop of Calcutta, who happened to be visiting the Gardens, stopped and spoke to them.

Of course they excited considerable interest in Calcutta, and frequent visits were paid to the Hotel by both residents and travellers anxious to see them.

The visit was naturally not such a surprise to the aborigines of the Great Andaman as to the Öngés, (two of the former indeed had been to Calcutta before), but the whole of them were interested and pleased, and there can be no doubt that such visits do great good and indirectly influence the savages in their treatment of people who may be shipwrecked on their coasts.

In March 1892 I made a long tour round the Islands in the *Ross*. At Barren Island I found the goats were doing very well, and in Stewart's Sound was a timber ship, upside down, which had been capsized at sea, and then floated in with all sails set. I was unable to tow her back to Port Blair, and she eventually became water-logged and sank in the Sound.

In my Annual Report for the year 1891-92 I remark :—

"The Andamanese at the Homes have been continually employed during the year in hunting runaway convicts. There are now so few aborigines of the South Andaman left (and these are naturally the only people acquainted with the jungle near the Settlement and competent to direct the hunters) that very much work has been thrown on to them, and they have in consequence grumbled loudly that they never have any time for their own pleasures and pursuits, even at last threatening to do no more work. As these people are not slaves, and can only be persuaded, not compelled, to work for us in this manner, and as no presents or luxuries we can give them will compensate them for the pleasures of their jungle life, I have been obliged to arrange the runaway hunting on a different footing.

"The majority of the convicts who escape keep on the confines of the Settlement, and, if they meet Andamanese, easily delude them by passing themselves off as free men or self-supporters collecting jungle produce. To send Andamanese to hunt such runaways is a waste of time and energy, and it has been settled that this work should fall upon the police, parties of labouring convicts, and the inhabitants of adjacent villages. The Andamanese would only be sent out when the whereabouts of the convicts is positively known. They would thus, ordinarily, only pursue those convicts who are known to have gone away to the distant jungles, or to be attempting to put out to sea on rafts.

"Twenty-six runaway convicts were re-caught during the year by the Andamanese. Two were Burmese, caught near Interview Island by the Trepang collectors; three were putting to sea on a raft from the Labyrinth Islands; nine were found at Rutland Island, where they had crossed on a raft; four others were putting to sea on a raft from the Labyrinth Islands; and three were found on a raft near Kyd Island.

"These last had only one pound of rice and no water, and would, of course, have perished miserably in a few days had I not chanced to pass in the " *Ross* " and capture them.

"I fancy the majority of the runaways who are unaccounted for, either lose their way in the jungle and die of starvation, are shot by the Jàrawas, or else put off to sea on rafts and die of hunger and thirst.

"The general health of the Andamanese was good during the year. Two births and 13 deaths occurred at the Homes."

The Government of India, in their Resolution on the Annual Report for 1891-92, state :—

"*Para. 10.*—The Government of India have observed with satisfaction the interest which Mr. Portman continues to take in the Andamanese."

In May 1892 a party of Andamanese came into the Settlement and brought two Andamanese who had committed an attempt to murder in the Middle Andaman. One of them, (they were both bachelors) had an intrigue with the wife of a man living in the same village, and used to frequent this woman's hut when her husband was absent. One day the husband returned earlier than usual and caught the lover and his wife, but, contrary to all the customs of other countries, it was the lover, and not the injured husband, who took umbrage, and the former, assisted by a comrade, fired two arrows into the village, wounding the husband and a child who was in the way, and then went off to the jungle with the other bachelors of the village. The wounds inflicted were slight, but as the comrade had already been concerned in the murder of Orderly Habib, in October, 1885, I detained the two men at my house and kept them at hard work for some years, as I consider this, and flogging, to be a better mode of punishing the Andamanese than sending them to Viper Jail, where they would associate entirely with Indian convicts and learn nothing but evil. I also insisted on both of them marrying, in order that they might be able to appreciate matters from the husband's point of view.

In July there was a good deal of gonorrhœa among the Andamanese in the Haddo Home, and in order to cure the diseased persons I found it necessary to separate the husbands and wives, keeping the former at my house under treatment while the latter were being cured in Haddo Hospital. A good deal of trouble was given by the husbands, who objected to this arrangement, not understanding the necessity for it, but my orders were enforced, with the result that, at the end of the month, only two cases remained in Hospital.

On the 8th of January 1893 I received a report from Lokala, my Andamanese Agent in the Middle Andaman, that a wreck was ashore at Jéder-lá-kuk, on the east coast of the Middle Andaman, about 62 miles from Port Blair. I at once reported the matter to the Superintendent and the R. I. M. S. *Nancowry* was despatched to the place on the morning of the 9th. She returned on the 12th, bringing five Burmese sailors. It appears that these men had been driven away in their ship from Burmah, owing to bad weather, had struck on the Andamans early in December, 1892, and had been there ever since. Owing to their fear of the Andamanese they seem to have made no attempt to come down to Port Blair.

In February I again took a party of Andamanese to Calcutta, where they enjoyed themselves and kept in good health in spite of unusually cold weather. Nothing of importance occurred, and the visit was a replica of the one paid in the previous year.

The following incident occurred in March, 1893, and is illustrative of the present attitude of the aborigines in the Middle Andaman towards strangers. It will be found of interest when compared with their conduct 30 years before.

Mr. Bate, Officer in charge of No. 99 cargo sailing boat, the property of a Rangoon merchant, brought his vessel to Port Blair in February, 1893. He addressed a letter to me after his arrival, thanking me for the kindness he had received from the Andamanese and stating—

"On the 29th January I sailed from Rangoon in charge of cargo boat No. 99, bound for the Cocos, but owing to bad weather, and the vessel having no keel, she drifted helplessly to the southward, and as I sailed from Rangoon with 8 days' provisions on board, I naturally fell short, and on the 11th February I put into Cuthbert Bay, or very close thereto, in hopes of being able to get some water, and scarcely had my anchor been down before two Andamanese came off in a small canoe followed by three others in a large canoe, and on learning what I wanted they immediately set off ashore and returned in their largest canoe and took off two of my breakers, two buckets, and a baler, which they filled up and brought back in the evening; they also insisted upon my going ashore to visit their huts, and they also caught me a lot of fresh fish, in exchange for which, before sailing, I gave them a few cheroots and a little rice.

"On the 15th, owing to the vessel being perfectly helpless to beat up against the wind, I put into a place about 10 miles to the southward of my former position, and was again treated with similar kindness, and again on the 18th, finding myself in the same predicament, and about the same distance to leeward of my second landing place, I put into the land, for more water and hopes of fish, with the same result of hospitality. After this I made up my mind to put into Port Blair, where I arrived on the 22nd February. In conclusion I might add that the hospitality received from these Andamanese was the more a surprise and welcomed, as my chart (one of the latest) bears a remark that the inhabitants are few and treacherous."

This behaviour on the part of the Kédé and Kol Tribes was most satisfactory, and is the best testimonial that could be obtained in evidence of the good results of our establishment of friendly relations with the aborigines.

At the beginning of the month of March a report was made to me that a man of the Puchikwár Tribe, named Ría Badké, had shot a woman of the Kédé tribe, named Jéru, in the Middle Andaman. By order of the Superintendent I proceeded in the R. I. M. S. *Nancowry* to Lekera-Luntá on the 4th, and there arrested Ría Badké, returning with him, the witnesses in the case, and Lokala, the Government Agent for the Middle Andaman, to Port Blair on the 5th March.

It appeared that in the previous January Ría Badké was living with several other Andamanese in an inland village on the east side of the Middle Andaman. A man there named Bira had taken his dogs without permission, and had not returned them, or given Ría Badké anything in exchange. The latter brooded over this, and one evening, when the Andamanese were sitting in their huts, shot at Bíra who was sitting with his wife. Their hut was surrounded with leaves but the couple were known to be inside. Through not being able to see them the arrow missed Bíra but hit his wife in the right side, killing her. Ría Badké pleaded guilty to the crime, and gave himself up willingly. He was tried by the Court of Sessions, found guilty of culpable homicide not amounting to murder, Section 304, I. P. C., and nominally sentenced to three months' rigorous imprisonment, to be remitted on a flogging of thirty stripes being inflicted.

Men were collected from the different tribes, and the flogging was inflicted, with some ceremony, in their presence.

It is noteworthy that the deceased woman Jéru was the one about whom the fraças between the lover and jealous husband, mentioned above, occurred.

In March 1893 Mr. Lapicque of the Paris University came to the Andamans in Madame Lebaudy's Yacht, the *Semiramis*, to study the Andamanese. The expedition was sent out at the instance of Mr. Dieulafoy, with the intention of studying the pure and hybrid Negrito races in all parts of the world, but owing to the lawsuit between Madame Lebaudy and her son Max Lebaudy having been decided in favour of the latter, the yacht was recalled after having been absent a few months. Mr. Lapicque made many observations in Port Blair, and was taken in the *Ross* to the Little Andaman and round the South Andaman. He left at the end of March for Mergui.

"Lokala" was shot by the Jàrawas on the 15th of September 1893. This man was the Government Agent for the Middle Andaman, and lived at Lekera-Luntá, where all the Andamanese from the North call on their way to Port Blair.

He used to collect and forward to me news of wrecks, runaways, etc., has often arranged quarrels among the Northern Tribes, and has reported and arrested Andamanese offenders. With all this he remained a great favourite with his own people, and no other

Andamanese was capable of filling his place. He was first taught by me in 1879, when he lived for a year with me as a boatman.

In October 1893 a remarkable adventure was met with by the party who were visiting the edible birds' nest caves in order to clean them. This party, consisting of Free Moung Yu, the collector, 11 convicts, and 6 Andamanese, left on the 28th of September in a sailing cutter to visit the different caves. They had finished their work of cleaning and had arrived at Ranguchâng, seven miles south of Port Blair, on the evening of the 26th of October.

The weather was then very stormy, and Moung Yu, who had been away longer than usual, sent up one convict and some Andamanese to inform me of his whereabouts and safety. I supposed that he would remain at Ranguchâng till assistance came, and on the 27th the steamer *Ross* was sent down there to tow the boat in. No traces of it, however, could be found, and the whole party, which then comprised Moung Yu, 10 convicts, and four Andamarese, were given up for lost. A cyclone was blowing, and we supposed the boat had been driven out to sea and sunk, as it had been seen at 2 P.M. off Brookesabad, five miles south of Port Blair, heading in a north-easterly direction, and then a heavy squall came down and it had not been seen afterwards.

Search was made by parties of Andamanese, and by the R. I. M. S. *Nancowry*, on the Archipelago Islands, the East coast of the South Andaman, on Narcondam and Barren Islands, and on the open sea to as far south as the Invisible Bank, without success.

On the 24th of November the S. S. *Shahjehan* arrived with the mails from Madras, bringing the whole party.

It appeared that on the morning of the 27th of October, finding the anchorage at Ranguchâng bad, Moung Yu had put to sea and endeavoured to reach Port Blair. He had actually got as far as the Sesostris Buoy, two miles south of Ross Island, when a heavy squall came down and blew the boat out to sea.

Owing to the heavy wind and sea the boat was unmanageable, and it was only after they had been drifting for two days that the storm moderated and the sail was hoisted. There was very little food in the boat, and the party had to depend on the rain for drinking water.

On the 1st of November they had got into muddy water with branches and leaves floating in it (doubtless the mouths of the Irrawaddy), and, had they kept on the same course, would have landed in a few hours.

The wind, however, changed suddenly, and with some force, to the north-east, and the boat was blown through the Preparis Channel in a south-westerly direction. On the 2ud of November they met with a sailing ship manned by Europeans, who on their approach ordered them away and would give them no assistance. Less rain fell from this date, and in addition to the want of food the party suffered much from thirst.

The helm was taken by the manji of the boat, Convict Babaji, No. 8247 B, relieved by Moung Yu, and to these two men the others owe their escape from death, as the rest of the crew lay at the bottom of the boat in a despairing stupor, and could hardly be roused to bale her out when necessary.

On the 12th of November at 4 P.M. land was seen, and at 8 P.M. Moung Yu anchored the boat in order to stop any attempt on the part of the convicts to escape.

On the 13th of November at 8 A. M. they followed a steamer up the Cuddalore River (which they discovered to be the place at which they had arrived), and anchored opposite the police thana, after having been eighteen days at sea.

The party was landed, kept for three days at Cuddalore, and then sent on to Madras for shipment to Port Blair.

The Andamanese, who were described in the papers as the African Guards of the convicts, were not particularly impressed by what they saw, or by their extraordinary voyage, although one of them had never before left the North Andaman As usual they were well treated by all with whom they came in contact.

The above account shows what can be done with a good sailing boat, properly handled; also, how much exposure and starvation can be endured by the native convicts. The latter point is of interest with regard to those who escape and put to sea on rafts.

It is to be hoped that the crew of the European sailing vessel who refused aid to the boatmen, may never find themselves in a similar predicament, or be similarly refused aid in their turn.

In November 1893 an Andamanese, whose foot had gangrened, was operated on by Dr. Gupta in the presence of myself and a number of Andamanese. The foot was removed under chloroform, and the sight of the man peacefully sleeping through the operation has given the Andamanese much more confidence in the treatment they receive in hospital.

On the 26th of February, 1894, Riala, the Chief of the Áka-*Béa*-da Tribe, died of fever, at about 57 years of age. He was the oldest man in the South Andaman, and was one of the few remaining Andamanese who remembered Port Blair, and the life of the savages, before our occupation in 1858, as also the events following that occupation. He had always been well disposed toward us, was of a mild, even temper, and a great favourite with his tribesmen, being one of the few Andamanese who had never committed a murder. He had passed nearly the whole of the year previous to his death at my house, when he had told me the old legends of his people and the traditions of his race.

In March I visited both coasts of the Islands, but very few Andamanese were seen. The cyclone which had carried the edible birds' nest collectors to Madras in October 1893 had evidently passed over the North Andaman with great violence, as the jungle was torn and felled, and the aborigines were burning what they could of the undergrowth in order to clear paths for themselves.

"Mébul-pé-lá-pich" died of peritonitis on the 11th of March 1894, having only succeeded Riala as Chief of the Áka-*Béa*-da tribe on the 27th of the preceding month.

He was the last of the South Andaman Éremtágas, and was a man of peculiar disposition; keeping very much to himself unlike the other Andamanese. He was unmarried and was averse to coming into the Settlement, or mixing with the convicts. Though quiet and amiable, the other Andamanese seemed to be in some awe of him, possibly owing to his unusual height and breadth, and the abnormal amount of hair on his face. (His nickname Pé-lá-pich means "moustache.")

He had always been attached to me and we had made many expeditions together against the Jàrawas, he being, on account of his pluck and knowledge of the jungles, the best hunter I had.

An Andamanese man and his wife were fishing on the coast at Ranguchàng one day in March, and as the woman turned over a large stone with her hands in order to look for prawns in the pool underneath, a sea snake coiled under the stone, which she had not seen, bit her on the arm.

The bite of these snakes (Hydrophis sp) is deadly, and the woman expired about twenty minutes afterwards. The poor husband, who was much affected, carried the dead body of his wife to the Haddo Home, about nine miles distant, on his back.

Seven runaway convicts were caught by the Andamanese during the year 1893-94, one of whom had put to sea on a raft, and fought and gave much trouble before he could be captured.

The year was a sickly one, and 22 deaths occurred at the Homes, while there were no births. From May to November, 1893, I was obliged to stop all work at the Homes, and let the Andamanese do as they would, giving them tonics and nourishing food.

On the 11th of May 1894 some North Andamanese were out hunting pig in the jungle north-west of Port Mouat, and while swimming across a creek called Wilima-Jig, one of their number, an elderly man named Jurul, was seized by a crocodile and taken under the water. He was not seen again, and the others, in a great fright, came in to report to me. Of course nothing could be done.

Such occurrences, though rare, are not unknown, and the Andamanese mentioned two cases during the last 30 years of men being killed by crocodiles, one occurring in Port Blair Harbour, and the other on the west coast of the North Andaman. The crocodile frequents the salt water creeks, and its name in Áka-*Béa*-da "Kára

Duku" (Duku being the name for the big water lizard of the reefs) shows that the Andamanese identify it.

In July there was much sickness among the Andamanese. Work was stopped, and large rations of milk were given to them. At this time the Homes on the South Andaman contained : Haddo (including the hospital), 127 Andamanese ; Mr. Portman's house, 75 ; Táracháng, 33 ; Duratáng, 7 ; and Góp-láka-bàng, 3. Many of these, in fact a large majority, were people from the North and Middle Andamans and outside these Homes there were no aborigines on the South Andaman, except Jàrawas.

During this month Póiàla, the Chief of the Bálé Tribe, died suddenly of heart disease, while out hunting in the jungle near Rangucháng. His death was much felt by the Andamanese, as he was a great favourite, and they recognised how few of them were left, and how much even one man was missed from among them.

He had done good work for the Government in the past, by catching runaway convicts who had got over to the Archipelago Islands ; and always had an influence for good over his Tribe.

In August I took a party of Andamanese to Rangoon for a couple of days. They enjoyed the visit there, but nothing of importance occurred. The great Pagoda impressed them more than anything else.

On the 24th of January 1895 I proceeded to Calcutta on leave, taking with me 15 Andamanese, including four Öugés from the Little Andaman. The whole party were lodged in Spence's Hotel as in former years, and during their stay in Calcutta were taken round the principal shops, and shown things of interest.

Owing to small-pox being very prevalent in the town they could not be taken to the Native quarter, nor to any places where there was a chance of their catching infection, but they were shown the Museum and the Zoological Gardens.

His Excellency the Viceroy (the Earl of Elgin) received them at Government House, Barrackpore, on the 3rd of February, having sent the Launch *Lytton* to Calcutta to bring them up the river. They enjoyed this trip more than anything in their visit, as they got a good view of the railways, buildings, and bridges, as well as of the native fishing craft, etc.

His Excellency most kindly directed that they should be allowed to purchase a quantity of presents, selected by themselves, at his expense, and to these were added others purchased from the Home Funds, as it was considered advisable, particularly in the case of the Öngés, that they should impress their countrymen by the presents they brought back, and by their account of their reception and treatment in Calcutta.

They were also received by Mr. Hewett, the Home Secretary, in his garden, and were exhibited to a large number of people. On these occasions the Andamanese say little at the time, and it is not till some months after, during casual conversations, that one learns how every incident has been noted by them, and the impression the visit has made upon them.

With the exception of two men, who had a few days of ordinary fever, they kept in good health in Calcutta, and have not suffered from illness since their return.

On my arrival in Port Blair on the 11th of February I learnt from the Deputy Superintendent, Mr. Man, that two cases of measles had occurred at Aberdeen, and he further informed me on the 19th that one of the children of his Head Clerk, also living at Aberdeen, had measles of a virulent type, so I at once closed all the Homes in Port Blair, including the Home for boys at my house, and sent the Andamanese to the jungle until all danger of infection was past.

They were kept there until the following June, and no case of measles occurred among them, which may be partly owing to the fact that some of them had had the disease during the previous epidemic. It will be observed that, as on the former occasion, the medical authorities took no steps on behalf of the Andamanese, nor did they communicate with me on the subject until after Mr. Man and I had done all that was necessary.

Two cases of murder occurred during the year 1894-95, both being murders of Andamanese by their fellow tribesmen.

The details are as follows :—

1st.—Hearing a report of a murder in Stewart's Sound in October 1894, I sent up Tindal Jáfar to enquire. He returned on the 4th November, bringing a small and wild boy, named Chipla, of the Jéru tribe, who had shot another boy Jérako dead, because the latter stole his pork. This occurred in Stewart's Sound where Chipla's parents reside, and they, fearing the anger of Jérako's relations, fled with Chipla into the interior of the North Andaman, north of Port Cornwallis. The matter was reported to the Chief Commissioner, who directed that, as Chipla was a small boy who had never been in the Settlement or accustomed to any sort of discipline, and knew nothing beyond his own savage customs, he would be suitably punished by a flogging of 24 stripes, and also that he was to be kept till grown up in the Home of boys at my House, in order to be taught.

Tindal Jáfar, who acted with tact and ability in arresting the accused in the interior of the North Andaman, at great personal risk, and without coming into any collision with the Andamanese, was rewarded by a year's remission of sentence.

2nd.—While investigating Chipla's case, Jáfar heard of another murder on the North-west coast of the North Andaman, and I sent a party of experienced Andamanese to investigate it.

They returned on the 10th of December, bringing in a man named Chiro, and stating—

Some weeks before a party of four Andamanese with their wives were encamped in the village of Tórop-tót-chettu on the north-west of the North Andaman. One morning one of the men, named Pāūro, took the dogs belonging to two other men named Chiro and Kāūpo, without asking their leave, and went out hunting. The two owners of the dogs told a lad named Tāūp, who was present, to go and bring them back. This Tāūp refused to do, so Chiro shot at and killed him.

Chiro made no resistance to his arrest and pleaded guilty to the above. The matter was reported to the Chief Commissioner, who ordered that, in consideration of the fact that Chiro was a savage who had never left his own country before, knew nothing of any language or people but his own, and was not fully aware of the nature of his crime, and also that, if he were imprisoned, he would merely pine away and die without any good being effected, he should receive a flogging of thirty stripes and be detained at hard work at the Andaman Home for a period of five years. He died in June 1895.

Twenty-eight deaths occurred at the Homes during the year and only two births. Fifty-eight Andamanese were vaccinated.

In addition to the death of Póiàla, the following Andamanese of importance died:—

Chána Punga, wife of Lípāia, Chief of the Puchikwár tribe. She was a very capable woman, and had great influence over the Andamanese, by whom she was much respected. At the time of her death, in November 1894, she had been a grandmother for some years.

Wóloga Jerra Bud, who was killed by the Jàrawas at Port Campbell in August 1894. He was merry and a gentle man, a good sportsman, and an universal favourite. He had worked well and willingly for us in the Homes and on expeditions for over 18 years.

In June 1895 there was a very high sick and death rate; among those who died were—

"Tótal," an Andamanese man, generally known as "Toby," who had been educated in the Orphanage, was for some time in the Superintendent's Printing Office, and had been for the last seven years of his life in the Home at my house. Though passionate and bad-tempered, he had considerable authority among the Andamanese, on many occasions had been of use to me, and was very intelligent. He was sufficiently educated to be able to write down for me, in an intelligible manner, the songs and legends of his people, in his own language, but in the English character.

"Kót," a very intelligent man from Stewart's Sound, who had been for six years with me.

"Kāich," the widow of Jurul, who had been eaten by a crocodile on the 11th May 1894.

On the 10th of July news was brought to me from the Middle Andaman that, several weeks before, a party of Andamanese from the North Andaman and Interview Island had been encamped on the West coast of the Middle Andaman. One of the men, named Cháp, who had gone up to his country from the Home at my house a short time before, asked the women to give him some firewood. They refused to do so, and he, after the manner of the Andamanese, flew into a violent passion, seized his bow and arrows, and fired off several at random, hitting no one. Having exhausted his stock of arrows he ran down to the canoes on the shore, took up a heavy spear from one, and returning with it stabbed Kép, the Chief of Interview Island, on the back of the right shoulder. The wound was a very severe one, and after lingering in great pain for several days Kép died from the effects of it. Only one man, named Bui, who had been formerly trained in Port Blair, made any attempt to seize Cháp, and he took away his spear, but being much smaller than Cháp, was unable to arrest him as he wished to do. The remainder of the Andamanese ran into the jungle and hid, making no attempt to arrest or punish Cháp, nor, though they had bows and arrows with them, did they fire a single shot at him.

The Andamanese custom, indeed, in a row of this kind is, that whoever draws first blood is the winner, and the other side run away; nor is it Andamanese etiquette to interfere with a man who goes "Berserk," as he may have right on his side. These people seem to become helpless with terror when a man runs "amok" in this manner. They are great cowards, and in a fight one man never attempts to assist or defend another in want of help. The camp of Andamanese dispersed after the row, and Cháp, after burning down my big Trepang-drying shed, which had taken nearly a month to erect, went into the interior of the North Andaman.

Kép was an elderly man, of mild and peaceable disposition, and had always been most friendly with us since I first made his acquaintance at Interview Island in January 1880.

Cháp, too, had always appeared to be well behaved, though somewhat stupid and deaf, and was for some months at my house. He was one of the Andamanese who accompanied me to Calcutta in

February 1895, and was presented to His Excellency the Viceroy in Barrackpore Park.

When I heard the above related story I made arrangements to arrest Cháp, and as soon as the weather was sufficiently calm for me to send a party up the West coast, I despatched Jemadar Jáfar, and a number of trained Andamanese from the Haddo Home, to make enquiries.

They returned on the 1st of September with the information that Cháp had gone to Tāō Két, a village on the South-west coast of the North Andaman, and gathering about a dozen of his fellow tribesmen round him, had threatened to kill any members of the other tribes who came near. I sent the party back to Tāō Két to arrest Cháp. A number of Andamanese from the North Andaman and from Interview Island had previously come in, through fear of Cháp and his people, to live at Lekera-Luntá, and these men, with three canoes, Jáfar took with him. They had very stormy weather after leaving Lekera Luntá, and their progress was hindered.

On nearing Tāō Két Jáfar sent one of the canoes, containing some of the principal men of the North Andaman, about a quarter of a mile ahead of him. These people, on coming to the village, found about 12 male Andamanese there, (among whom was Cháp), who fired three arrows at the approaching canoe, hitting no one. On seeing Jáfar come up the villagers ceased firing and sat down quietly in their huts, while Cháp ran away into the jungle.

This occurred at mid-day, and Jáfar took all the people of the village, and all their property and canoes, away to an outlying Island, leaving a man of the same tribe, named Bállo, whom he had brought with him from Port Blair, in the village to watch for Cháp.

According to the Andamanese custom, the latter, who had been watching Jáfar's movements from the jungle, when he saw him go off to the Island, returned to Tāō Két during the night. Bállo, as previously arranged with Jáfar, lighted a fire on the shore as soon as Cháp arrived, and Jáfar seeing this sent across a canoe with some friendly Andamanese from the South Andaman Tribes, who arrested Cháp and brought him away to the Island. He made little resistance and did not attempt to escape on his way down to Port Blair, where he arrived on the 23rd. I at once held an enquiry into the case and found that the facts differed considerably from the one-sided version of the story I had been given in the previous July by the Interview Islanders.

Cháp, after leaving my house in April, had been living with the Interview Islanders, and had formed an illicit connexion with a widow of that tribe. To this the other members of the tribe objected, and Kép, the Chief of Interview Island, on several occasions reproached Cháp for his conduct.

In May the party were encamped on the West coast of the Middle Andaman, and a further quarrel on the same subject between Kép and Cháp occurred. The latter got very angry, fired off several arrows indiscriminately among the collected Andamanese, careless of whom he wounded, and then, having hit no one, ran down to the canoes on the shore, snatched a spear from one of them and hurled it at Kép, inflicting a severe flesh wound on the back of his right shoulder.

Some slight skirmish seems then to have taken place, in which Cháp was wounded by an arrow in the right eye.

All the Andamanese then, with the exception of Bui, who got the spear from Cháp and tried to arrest him but failed, ran away into the jungle, and Cháp, after setting fire to the big Trepang-curing shed, which was at the encampment, went off to his own country.

Some weeks afterwards Kép died from the effects of the neglected wound, which might have been healed had he been brought in at once to hospital, and his friends were anxious to kill Cháp in revenge. He, however, had gathered a few of his own tribesmen together at Tāō Két, and they announced that they would kill anyone who came near them. The matter was then reported to me.

On the above facts being reported to the Chief Commissioner he was pleased to direct that, as Kép had been only wounded by Cháp, and had died from the effects of the *neglected* wound; as Cháp had been wounded himself in the row, and had since then only stood on his defence against the Interview Islanders who wished to kill him and his friends; and, as no hostility had been shown towards the Government, and Cháp readily surrendered to Jáfar and came into Port Blair without attempting to escape or giving any trouble, he would be sufficiently punished by a flogging of 30 stripes and five years' detention in the Settlement, during which period he would have to work daily at the Homes. The flogging was accordingly inflicted in the presence of Andamanese from the North Andaman, Interview Island, and the Southern tribes, on the 27th of September 1895, and Cháp has since been detained at work in the Homes.

This last episode brings us up to the present time.

From the above account it will have been seen how swift the disastrous effects of our relations with the Andamanese have been to them.

From 1858 to 1862 they were in great numbers round the Harbour of Port Blair, were thoroughly hostile to us, and were of the two the more powerful party, and much hampered our development of the infant Settlement. As we grew stronger their hostility changed to a more cunning and treacherous policy, merging into timidity.

When friendly relations were established the Andamanese were at first independent and insubordinate, but under Mr. Homfray's rule became more disciplined. Syphilis was then introduced, the epidemics of ophthalmia and measles followed, to be succeeded later by Russian influenza; and we have now a sickly remnant of the race entirely subordinate to us, and to a great extent dependent on us.

With the attacks of the epidemics all idea of training them to agriculture and altering their mode of life was abandoned, and our one effort has been to keep alive such as remain, and prevent, if possible, the entire extinction of the race.

The Chief Commissioner wrote in 1891 :—

"The decrease in the number of the Andamanese is very apparent.

"All the people of Rutland Island and Port Campbell are dead, and very few remain in the South Andaman and the Archipelago. The children do not survive in the very few births which occur, and the present generation may be considered the last of the aborigines of the Great Andaman."

Twenty years ago the Andamanese resented living in the Homes for long, and preferred the free sporting life in their jungle encampments. Now the only encampments of the Andamanese in the South Andaman are the Homes, which contain nearly 250 Andamanese, against under 100 of 20 years ago.

Though the numbers in the Homes have nearly trebled since the grant of R200 per mensem was awarded, that grant has not been increased. The income of the Andamanese is derived from this grant, the sale of the produce of their gardens, of the jungle materials they collect, and of their curiosities; also by the manufacture of Trepang, an industry I have lately started; and the total income for a year is from R6,000 to R7,000. The total expenditure for a year is from R7,000 to R9,000, for whereas formerly medicines for the hospital,* and other articles, were obtained from the Settlement authorities gratis, everything has now to be paid for by the Andamanese, and the Funds have to be assisted yearly from the private purse of the Officer in charge with a grant of from R2,000 to R3,000.

The Andamanese who remain still work for the Government by hunting runaway convicts, and acting as guards and assistants to the edible birds' nest collectors.

---

* NOTE.—These have since been allowed to the Andamanese *gratis*.—M. V. P.

CHAPTER XVIII.

The Jàrawas—Their acquaintance with the people of our Settlement in 1790 *et seq.*—Their numbers—Their relations with the Áka-*Béa*-da—Mr. Corbyn's account—Mr. Homfray's accounts—Wreck of the *Nineveh* on the North Sentinel—Further accounts—General Stewart's account—Further accounts—Expeditions against the Jàrawas—A woman and two children caught, and released—Further accounts—Mr. Man's notes on the Jàrawas—The North Sentinel expedition—Jàrawas caught, and released—Vocabulary of Jàrawa words—Colonel Cadell's note—Jàrawas caught on Rutland Island—Annual Report for 1882-83—Further expeditions—Two Jàrawas caught—Hostility of the Jàrawas—Expedition to Rutland Island—Further expeditions—Further hostility—North Sentinel visited—Further hostility—One Jàrawa caught—Further hostility—Jàrawas killed by Andamanese—Annual Report for 1890-91—Further hostility—Jàrawas moved to foreign territory—Murder in Bárátán—Expeditions—Jàrawas on Rutland Island—Annual Report for 1893-94—Murder of Andamanese by Jàrawas—Expeditions—Jàrawas caught on Rutland Island—Annual Report for 1894-95—Further trouble—Visit to the North Sentinel—Summary, and future policy.

WE have now to consider a Group of Tribes with whom we are only partially acquainted, though some of them inhabit the jungles in the vicinity of Port Blair.

The headquarters of this Group is undoubtedly the Little Andaman Island, and I have therefore called it the Òngé Group of Tribes, as the aborigines of the Little Andaman call themselves Òngés.

Besides the aborigines on the Little Andaman, there is a tribe on the North Sentinel Island, about which very little is known, though it is suspected to be quite a recent offshoot from the Little Andaman people, if indeed all communication between the two islands has actually ceased. The people on the North Sentinel, judging from their ornaments, weapons, &c., appear to be in every way similar to the Öngés, but Tómiti assures me that the dialects are different.

On Rutland Island a small tribe exists, called by the Andamanese Jàrawas, or " Jangil."

On the South Andaman another and larger tribe of these Jàrawas, (or " Mincopie," as Lieutenant Colebrooke says that they call themselves) inhabits part of the interior, and they may be connected with the Rutland Island tribe.

The bow of the South Andaman Jàrawa is different from that of any of the other Tribes on the Andamans, while the Rutland Island Jàrawa bow sometimes resembles it, and sometimes more nearly approaches the appearance of the bow of the North Sentinel and Little Andaman Tribes. With the Öugés of the Little Andaman I will deal in another Chapter, and I now propose to record all we know of the Jàrawas in the interior of the South Andaman, on Rutland Island, and on the North Sentinel Island.

On reading Lieutenant Colebrooke's account, quoted in Chapter III., it became evident to me that the aborigines with whom the people in Lieutenant Blair's Settlement on the South Andaman in 1790 *et seq*, were friendly, and whom they took to the Car Nicobar and to Calcutta, were members of the South Andaman Jàrawa tribe. The description of their habits, weapons, and utensils, and the vocabulary given, leaves no room for doubt on this point.

From the Áka-*Béa*-da I have learnt that in former times the Jàrawas were more numerous and powerful than they are now, and they inhabited the Southern part of the Harbour of Port Blair, the Western part, and much of the neighbouring interior. Many "Kitchen-Middens" on the shores of the Harbour have been pointed out to me as the sites of Jàrawa villages, and the Áka-*Béa*-da further prove their contention by showing that these shell-heaps contain the refuse of articles which the Jàrawas eat, but which the Áka-*Béa*-da will not touch.

It appears to me quite possible that some disease was introduced among the Jàrawas by the people of Lieutenant Blair's Settlement which reduced this tribe considerably in numbers, and thus enabled the Áka-*Béa*-da to obtain the upper hand. The greatest hostility exists between the tribes, though individual friendships between Jàrawa and Áka-*Béa*-da have been known, and the languages are entirely distinct. It would appear as if the Öngé Group of Tribes had at one time inhabited as one body the whole of the country from the Little Andaman to Port Blair, and had passed from one island to another freely; the people on Rutland Island would make excursions in their canoes during the calm weather to the North Sentinel and form a small colony there, as that Island has fine, open, and easily traversed forest, with plenty of pig, and sheltered lagoons in which fish and turtle could be caught.

As the South Andaman Group of Tribes spread to the southward and occupied the coasts of the South Andaman, the Labyrinth Islands, and Rutland Island, the Öngés retreated to the Little Andaman, not often venturing farther north than the Cinque Islands on account of the hostile encounters with the Áka-*Béa*-da they met with, (for, whatever they may be now after years of hostility, I hold that the Öngé Group are the mildest, most timid, and inoffensive of all the Andamanese).

The Ár-*yaūto* Sept of Öngés naturally abandoned the South Andaman, but the Éremtága Sept remained in the interior of that Island, and on Rutland Island, and, not having canoes, only moved by land, or occasionally crossed the creeks on bamboo rafts, as Lieutenant Colebrooke describes, and as I have seen them do now both in the Great and Little Andaman.

The people on the North Sentinel also did not dare to visit Rutland Island any longer, and the various Septs of the Group thus drifted apart and became inimical; their bows, &c., altering more or less, but their languages remaining allied though so altered as to be mutually unintelligible.

In this state they were found by Lieutenant Blair who established friendly relations with a few of them, and considered them to be more timid than hostile. He had less difficulty with them than with the savage Áka-*Béa*-da, with whom his friendly overtures were never successful.

The Jàrawas then occupied all the coast at Haddo, Navy Bay, and the creeks running inland south of Viper Island, and appear to have been fairly numerous and to have held their own against the Áka-*Béa*-da. Of course the fact of Lieutenant Blair being on good terms with the former would make the latter even more hostile than they would otherwise have been.

Of what took place between 1794 and 1858 we have no knowledge, but when we re-occupied the Andamans in the latter year, the

Áka-*Béa*-da were by far the stronger and more numerous tribe, and had occupied the whole of the land round the Harbour of Port Blair, driving the Jàrawas into the interior of the island, and fighting with them when they met.

Cases are however known, (as was only to be expected), of individual Áka-*Béa*-da becoming friendly with the Jàrawas, and so late as 1860 a man of the former tribe, named Méba Mót, used to frequent the Jàrawa camps, sometimes stopping in them for three or four days, and taking with him his infant son Kála.

As we became on friendly terms with the Áka-*Béa*-da they prejudiced us against the Jàrawas, whom they described in the blackest terms, and the latter, seeing us allied with the Áka-*Béa*-da against them, resented or distrusted our friendly overtures, from timidity at first, and finally from downright hostility.

When the present Settlement was first opened we were not aware that there were different tribes of Andamanese speaking different languages, nor did we know of the divisions of the race into Ar-*yāuto* and Éremtága; Lieutenant Colebrooke's account of the Jàrawas, and his vocabulary, was supposed to apply to all parts of the islands, and Dr. Mouat merely notes, when the Andamanese at Craggy Island failed to understand the word "Padoo" given by Lieutenant Colebrooke as the equivalent for "friend," that, "there may be different tribes and dialects."

When all the Andamanese were equally hostile to us it mattered little whether they quarrelled amongst themselves, and notice was not taken of one Sept more than of another.

As our acquaintance with the A'ka-*Béa*-da increased and a few of them became on friendly terms with us it was observed that more than one tribe of Andamanese existed, and Mr. Corbyn, during a visit of exploration he made into the interior to the south-west of Viper Island, was told by his Andamanese friends of another tribe residing there, the members of which were hostile, and of whom his friends stood in great dread. These were of course the Jàrawas, and Mr. Corbyn's description of his tour, which is excellently given, is here quoted.

"It has long been the Superintendent's desire to find some passage through the interior to the opposite coast; and it was supposed, from the formation of the land on the other side of Viper, that one of the many creeks which penetrate into the interior towards Port Mouat might afford such a passage, or at least conduce far enough to diminish very considerably the extent of jungle to be cleared; and it was to examine one of these creeks that I went with Lieutenant Carr, on the 20th of July, 1863, taking a party of Burmese and nine men of the 9th Madras Native Infantry, and as guides two Andamanese, Topsy and Jacko.

"We had three boats, each of which carried a guard of sepoys, one our baggage and provisions. The latter, which was the heaviest, gave some trouble and retarded our progress, till we came to difficult passes of the creek, where the first boats had to stop to remove impediments, and thus allowed time for the slower one to overtake them.

"The creek which we selected for exploration is a mile to the south of Viper, and runs mainly south-west, (Dhani Leaf Creek—*M. V. P.*) and has already been partly explored by Colonel Haughton, who was able, with the Settlement gun boat and a light Burmese canoe, to go and return some twelve or fifteen miles in one day.

"We started for two days and provisioned ourselves accordingly, but the Sepoys, mistaking Lieutenant Carr's order to supply themselves with two days' provisions, took only two meals, which compelled us to return sooner than we otherwise should have done; though fortunately we had, in some measure, anticipated such a dilemma by taking a superfluous bag of rice to make up any accidental deficiencies. The Burmese were as scantily provided with food as the Sepoys, for their whole stock was only a little rice; but if they had not brought a morsel with them they would have fared, at least to their own taste, as sumptuously as any of us. In the first place their knowledge of the vegetation, much of which exists nowhere else but in their own country, and for which the botany of no other country but theirs supplies a nomenclature; the knowledge of the properties of herbs, plants, and fruit, and forest trees, would have enabled them to find sustenance where a Bengal or Madras Native would not have thought of seeking for it. As soon as we halted for the day three or four of them would sally forth into the jungle with a pack of common pariah dogs, which they had trained to pig-hunting, and in a few minutes we would hear yelps, crashing of branches, and encouraging exclamations of Ho! Ho! to which the Burmese with us would respond with grunts of satisfaction; and then, in a few minutes more, back they would come with all the dogs jumping and yelping after them, dragging a huge-tusked hog, or, as it sometimes happened, a sow and some of her litter. They also found beds of cockles in deep waters of the stream, where we should not have known that they existed; they brought these to the surface with their feet, and soon collected as many as would have served for a meal. But their ingenuity was exerted in other ways, besides satisfying their appetites. Their overseer, with some others, as soon as we halted for the night, felled bamboo branches, stitched together wild plantain and palm leaves, and in an hour or two built huts and *matchans* enough for all our party. Altogether, their contrivance, activity, and good temper, contrasted favourably with the fastidiousness and helplessness of the Sepoys, who proved an incumbrance to us, rather than of any service. They would have acted differently under ordinary circumstances; but, of course, they felt all the inconveniences of such rough campaigning, and complained that they had neither tents nor an adequate supply of food, and their caste scruples added to the difficulty; for most of them declined all food except rice which we offered them.

(The above is an Andaman experience which has not been confined to the Reverend Mr. Corbyn—*M. V. P.*)

"On the first day we stopped at a place ten or twelve miles from the mouth of the creek where some Burmese had been a few weeks before cutting bamboos, and had left thatched huts which we occupied during the night. We used every precaution to guard ourselves against attack, took up our oars and placed them under a guard, and lashed the boats to the bank to prevent the convict boatmen escaping with them, which we suspected they had a design of doing, and we set Sentries, and lighted a large fire which illuminated the forest and enabled them to watch every movement; the Natives and Burmese also lighted fires opposite their huts, and for want of more solid fuel, piled upon them dry and green bamboos, the crackling of which, bursting and blazing in all directions, sounded like the explosion of so many guns, and often startled us during the night, when we suddenly woke up with the sound of a loud volley, and before recollecting ourselves imagined that it was a real discharge of musketry, and that the savages were attacking us. At first we were all in high glee and good humour; the Burmese regaled to their heart's content on roast pig, rice, and cockles, puffed their huge cheroots and bandied fun with Topsy and Jacko; the Sepoys collected round the poor Mussulman and rallied him on the subject of his religious scruples and aversion to pig's flesh. Topsy and Jacko went about the camp levying contributions, and amusing everyone with their merry pranks and eccentricities; altogether our camp presented a lively and diverting spectacle. But our mirth was soon damped metaphorically and literally by the deluge of heavy rain which descended upon us at midnight. Great was our anxiety to know whether our roofs would bear it. But in a few minutes down came the drizzle, drop by drop, on our coverlets; the sluices in the thatch widened; the winds splashed the rain in upon us from the open sides, and we were soon as much exposed as if we had been lying on the bare and uncovered ground. But there was no retreat from the rain and tempest,—the jungle was impenetrable, and it would have been like a retreat from Scylla into Charybdis to seek shelter in the bamboo grove, for the ground was covered with leeches. Fortunately, soon after daybreak the rain ceased, and a bright and unclouded sky gave promise of at least a brief interval of fair weather. We re-lighted our fires, dried our clothes, and in less than two hours had made preparations to embark again on our voyage of discovery. But we had now to encounter many obstacles to our progress: the stream in many places was almost impassable with logs and branches which had floated down the current and accumulated in narrow channels, and formed bars which we had to cut and clear, or with much labour and difficulty drag our boats over.

"Large trees too had fallen right across the stream, and formed bridges so close to the water that our boats had to be weighed down almost to their full depths to allow of their passing under. We had frequently again to drag our boats across shallow bars in the stream, which varied in depth from less than a foot to more than fifteen feet. The banks on each side were densely wooded, and showed no signs of foot-tracks; there were no huts nor any traces of aborigines, though they must at some time have been there,—for Topsy and Jacko knew every turn of the creek, and shewed us a short passage where two branches of the stream met, which they could not have known unless they had examined both passages as we did, and thus found which was the shortest.

"Nothing could adequately describe the luxuriance of the vegetation, and the wild beauty of the scenery as it appeared to us under all the favourable effects of fine weather, and the sensations excited by its novelty and freshness. Creepers, rising to the full height of the forest and overspreading its surface, decked with their bright leaves and lovely flowers the whole of the sloping landscape.

"The trees rose to almost incredible height, and each supported a little forest of its own of ferns and flowering orchids, and countless varieties of creeping plants which covered their stems and branches, and struggled upwards to the surface. Wild palm and plantain trees, and prickly cane, spread their branches over the stream, and bunches of little plantains hung down tantalizingly. Sometimes we passed under almost perpendicular heights, as densely planted with trees of prodigious size, towering into the air from their lofty summits. Every turn of the stream presented a new feature of rare loveliness and grandeur. (A description of Andaman jungle by an enthusiast who saw it for the first time.—*M.V.P.*)

"In some places the stream widened into the breadth of a large river; its course, as it penetrated further, became more rambling and irregular, winding by turns in almost opposite directions. We had proceeded many miles without seeing any place on the banks where we could have effected a lodgment, for the jungle was so thick that would have been a work of some hours to clear enough ground for encampment. But about 3 P.M. we came to a large bamboo grove on a high embankment, a most inviting situation, which would have afforded natural shelter if we had not preferred to cut down the bamboo trees and make huts out of the branches. This was soon done, though half the grove was felled in the operation; and the Burmese, who had wisely collected palm and plantain leaves during the day, completely thatched two huts before night; the other huts were partly sheltered by the bamboo trees which still remained, but not enough to save their occupants from a complete drenching when the rain fell, as it did very heavily during the night. The Burmese succeeded in catching two large pigs which they liberally shared with Topsy and Jacko.

"These two were very much alarmed when they found it was our intention to proceed further the next day, and did their utmost to dissuade us. They made me understand that we should encounter an unfriendly tribe of aborigines of whom they themselves seemed to be in great dread.

"Jacko pointed to my heart and represented the act of a savage aiming at me with his bow and arrow, of the arrow piercing my heart and of my falling wounded, closing my eyes, and expiring. Topsy also pathetically enacted the death scene, and both waved their hands deprecatingly in the direction disapproved of, and entreated me not to proceed further but to return to the "Burra Chab," and said that there were none of their tribe in the other direction. (They were evidently alluding to the Jàrawas.—*M.V.P.*)

"When we were about to start in the morning they again seemed alarmed, and Jacko made the sound of the twang of a bow and the same signs that the savages would attack us, but we pointed to our weapons and discharged some shots to show him that we were prepared and able to defend ourselves, and he at last appeared to forget the danger, real or imaginary, in the prospect of getting more pigs and of returning the same day to Ross, which we promised him he should do. We had thought, as the stream was gradually becoming narrower and more shallow, we might find some indication of its source in the course of the day, but after proceeding ten miles, the stream again widened and became deeper; we were indeed effectually stopped by a bar of some length, but if we could have drawn our boats across it, we might still have continued our journey for many miles further; and perhaps at length have found an outlet in the sea with which, from the direction in which the stream flowed, it seemed likely that it communicated. (No.—*M.V.P.*) It was the opinion of those of our party most competent to judge, that, in this expedition up the creek, we traversed altogether a distance of about thirty miles (No.—*M.V.P.*), but of course such calculations are very uncertain, for it would be impossible to judge by mere eyesight of distances over unknown tracts of country, especially by water.

"Before we returned, a Burman climbed to the top of one of the highest trees on the bank where he was likely to have an extensive view, for the country on both sides of the stream was flat, and no hills or elevations of land were visible. He looked in the direction in which we supposed we heard the sound of waves beating against the shore, and said that he saw a vast blank space which he believed was the sea, but could not positively say whether it was the sea, or a cloud, or only empty space. We returned to the Settlement on the evening of the 22nd of July."

On the 3rd of January, 1865, Major Ford, when writing about the road he was making to Port Mouat, notes that the aborigines inland on the south side were the most troublesome; and Mr. Homfray when searching for some runaway Burmese convicts at Port Mouat in February, 1865, was told that a hostile tribe of Andamanese existed on Rutland Island.

In March, 1867, Mr. Homfray writes:—

"I had occasion, in pursuit of runaways, to visit the North Sentinel Island, a distance of about 25 miles to the westward of Port Mouat, with some Andamanese accompanying me We saw some ten men on the beach, naked, long haired, and with bows and arrows, shooting fish. My friends told me that they were 'Jurrahwallahs,' who were not friendly to them, having some years past encountered some of that tribe on Rutland Island in which their Chief was wounded. They inhabit the Little Andaman and other adjacent islands round about to the south of the Great Andaman, and speak a different language. There being a surf, I anchored the boat clear of it, not thinking it advisable as I could not induce them to approach the boat for presents, we did not land. The men were black and sturdy-looking, and used to conceal themselves on our boat approaching nearer. The Andamanese were very frightened of them, and advised me not to have anything to say to them as they show no mercy. Being in a single open boat a distance at sea with convicts, I did not think it prudent to run any risk."

The Jàrawas seem to be very much what we have made them. They were much less timid at the time of this visit than they are now, and were merely given a bad name by our Andamanese because the latter were at enmity with them, and ignorant regarding them.

It is remarkable that the Andamanese have all along recognised all the Jàrawas as belonging to one Group of Tribes, and have accurately described their territory. Probably, in the past, there have been several cases of friendship between individuals of the different tribes.

In April, 1867, Mr. Homfray took with him Andamanese from the Port Blair, Port Mouat, and Rutland Island Septs, and proceeded on an expedition to the Little Andaman. On his way down the coast the Rutland Islanders named all the small islands, and told him stories of their adventures on them; they claimed that the Cinque Islands and Passage Island belonged to them, and stated that they frequently went there to get turtle and large fish. They had at times encountered people from the Little Andaman there, whom they called "Jurrahwallahs," and of whom they were much frightened, but they generally succeeded in driving them back across Duncan Passage to the Brothers Islands, which appeared to be their limit.

Mr. Homfray thought that these Little Andamanese inhabited the North and South Sentinel (the latter island is very small and is uninhabited; Mr. Homfray had not visited it.—*M.V.P.*); and had tried to conquer the Rutland Island Sept, which he thought might account for that island being so thinly populated. The Rutland Islanders had shown him at different times, at the Homes, baskets and ornaments they had taken from the Jàrawas they had killed, and similar articles were seen at the Little Andaman.

Early in October, 1867, the steamer *Defiance* came to Port Blair from Burmah with the news that the brig *Nineveh* had been wrecked on the North Sentinel Island, so Major Ford sent the *Kwang Tung*, under the command of Lieutenant Duncan, R.N.R., with a detachment of troops and Marine Service men, to search for the crew and passengers. Eighty-four of these were rescued, but seven had left on a raft in the hope of getting across to the mainland for help, and were still missing.

Both the *Defiance* and the *Arracan* were sent in search of them, and the North Sentinel Island was examined, also the whole of the west coast of the Great Andaman. The missing men were at length found by the Andamanese, who were most useful and behaved very well, on the west coast of the South Andaman, and were brought into Port Mouat in a very exhausted condition.

There was a very heavy surf at the North Sentinel, and Captain Duncan and his party did excellent work in rescuing all the people.

Nothing was seen of the aborigines, and no collision between them and the shipwrecked people seems to have taken place.

In June, 1869, Mr. Homfray writes:—

"The Little Andaman people, called 'Jurrahwallah,' are gradually advancing towards us. They have reached Rutland Island, and are beginning to settle down there. They have built a large shed, as in their own country, on the East side of the Island, and have got to it *viâ* the Cinque Islands. Myo Bealolah, the Chief of Rutland, gets on very well with them, and I have asked him to try and coax them into the Home, which I hope will be done."

"Formerly, these Jurrahwallahs were kept away from the South Andaman by the Port Mouat and Southern Tribes, but now, as the numbers of the latter are decreasing, the Jurrahwallahs advance unmolested. The Port Blair Tribe sometimes encounter them on the highlands north of MacPherson's Straits, and fight, repulsing them. They have been blown on these shores during the south-west monsoon, and have not been able to get back to their own country."

The above paragraph contains as many incorrect statements as are possible in its size.

The Jàrawas were not "gradually advancing," but were stationary on Rutland Island, and were gradually retreating before us on the South Andaman. The former, who had, "built a large shed on the east side of the island," had been resident there for many centuries.

Mãīa Bíala did not get on at all well with them, and there were constant fights, but the Jàrawas being the weaker tried to keep out of his way.

Mr. Homfray mentions in April, 1867, that a Jàrawa child had been captured about 30 years before by the Rutland Islanders on the Cinque Islands, and had been brought up by them, becoming entirely of the Áka-*Béa*-da tribe, and not knowing his own tongue. His name was "Mãīa Ira Jàrawa."

He died on the 4th March, 1876, leaving a wife. Although he had lived for so many years on intimate terms with the Áka-*Béa*-da, they treated him as a stranger at his death, and threw his body into the sea instead of giving it "platform burial."

Lieutenant Colebrooke's account shows that the latter half of Mr. Homfray's paragraph is entirely incorrect: the Port Blair Tribe had advanced, and the Jàrawas had retreated, during the past 60 years.

When Mr. Homfray recorded what he *saw*, he gave most valuable and correct information, but his speculations and statements, based on what he was told, were unhappy.

At this time gangs of convicts who were clearing jungle to the south of Port Blair Harbour used to meet with the Jàrawas, and some of them have since told me that these people were not nearly so hostile as the other aborigines, but merely took the weapons and utensils the convicts had and then dismissed them without harming them.

It would then have been possible, had we had the information we possess now, to have made friends with the Jàrawas easily, through the intervention of Méba Mót and such others of the Áka-*Béa*-da as associated with them.

General Stewart, when writing on the 9th of August, 1873, to the Government of India about the Jàrawas, remarks :—

"They are never (?) found on the coast of the mainland, and they are not on friendly terms with the tribes we know.

"They are said by our Andamanese to be the same as the people of the Little Andaman, and at one time they occupied the whole of the South Andaman. We have not been able to establish friendly relations with them, or find out anything about them.

"During the last twelve months the convicts employed in cutting roads to MacPherson's Straits and the fishing gang employed there have more than once met, and been robbed of their clothes and tools by, the Jàrawas, but as the latter have never attempted to hurt any of the convicts it is an indication that they are milder in disposition than any other section of the Andamanese whom we know, and compare favourably with the Little Andaman people, who never meet strangers without attacking them.

"I am very anxious to secure a means of communication with the aborigines of the Little Andaman, and I cannot help thinking that, if my recent visit had preceded the attack on the Burmese vessel (in April, 1873), I might have had some measure of success, as the Little Andamanese must have been watching our movements about their villages, and did not attempt to molest us, and no doubt the appearance of the *Undaunted* so soon after the attack had the effect of making the aborigines reserved and timid, though we showed no appearance of hostility."

(For details of this visit, see the next Chapter. In the above conclusions, General Stewart was mistaken. The Öngés were at their usual tricks of letting the people get on shore and wander away from their boat in supposed security, in order that, when they got far enough away, the boat could be broken up, and then the visitors could have been easily massacred.—*M. V. P.*)

"After Captain Wimberley's capture of the Little Andamanese, I urged Mr. Homfray to try and catch one of the Jàrawas, to ascertain if their language was the same as that of the Little Andamanese; but before the Jàrawas were brought in the Little Andaman boy died,

"The two Jàrawas were cleverly caught by Goodur, the convict jemadar of the Homes. He took out a volunteer party of convicts from Viper, with three days provisions, proceeded to the Jàrawa country, and came upon a party of about fifty of these people dancing. Goodur concealed his men in the jungle and told them not to move till he called out, and then walked in among the Jàrawas, holding up a pair of looking-glasses. The Jàrawas bolted, one man stopping for an instant to examine the glasses and thus being caught. He called to his friends to help him, and after some hesitation these turned and threatened battle, but seeing so many convicts, whom Goodur had now called up, they all bolted without drawing a bow. One unlucky little woman who could not run, being big with child, was also caught. These people were kept for a fortnight, treated with the greatest kindness, and let go where they were caught with a quantity of presents."

(They were much more well-disposed towards us then than they are now, and it is a pity that the matter was not pushed on with then, and friendly relations established.)

General Stewart in his Annual Report for 1872-73 also writes:—

"The Homes established for the aborigines have now been under Mr. Homfray's charge for nearly nine years, and it must be admitted that his system of management has been attended with the most favourable results. It may be said that the tribes inhabiting Rutland Island, the South Andaman, the southern half of the Middle Andaman, and the Archipelago, are all on friendly terms with us, with the single exception of the "Juddahs," or "Jurrah-wallahs," a small inland tribe about whom next to nothing is really known.

"During the last year the parties employed in cutting pathways from Port Blair to MacPherson's Straits have met these Juddahs on several occasions, and have been more than once robbed of their clothes and tools by them. Strange to say, however, the members of this particular tribe have never attempted to kill or maim any of the convicts, though it is doubtful what their action would have been if the convicts had offered any strenous resistance."

(They generally went down on their knees to the Jàrawas and

prayed to be let go, and the Jàrawas laughed and jeered at them, took their property and sent them away.—*M.V.P.*)

"The savages have as yet encountered only small parties of convicts, who were easily overpowered and plundered, but it is probable that these parties might have successfully defended themselves if they had made the attempt, as a man who was taking a small sum of money to pay the convicts stationed at MacPherson's Straits succeeded in saving the coin, although he was stripped of everything else.

"Two of the tribe (a man and a woman mentioned in the previously quoted letter) were captured in May last, and kept in Port Blair for some weeks. They were very kindly treated and taken to see the Andamanese children at the Orphanage. They visited some of the nearest Homes and ought to have been convinced that we treat the islanders who do not molest us with much consideration and kindness.

"Whether there is any connection between this inland tribe and the inhabitants of the Little Andaman, who are also called 'Juddahs,' by the Port Blair tribes, is not known, as the prisoner taken at the Little Andaman in March last died a few days before the two Juddahs above referred to were captured.

"There is, however, one very marked difference in their respective characters, for the Juddahs on South Andaman seem to be peaceably disposed, whereas the Little Andaman Islanders habitually kill, or attempt to kill, everyone that lands on their shores."

The Government of India hoped that fuller information might be obtained regarding these Jàrawas, and directed that, if possible, researches should be made regarding the dialects of Andamanese spoken by them.

I also find the following note regarding the Jàrawas:—

"Two Jarrawuddahs from Dhani Leaf Creek were brought to the Homes in May 1873, and after remaining a fortnight were returned to their own locality with presents of cloth, looking-glasses, cocoanuts, yams, bows and arrows, etc. Though similar in appearance to the Port Blair tribes, they differ from them in their language, habits, and customs,

"The women of the Jarrawuddahs do not wear any covering, and the males do not tattoo their bodies like the aborigines round the Settlement."

(The women *do* wear a tassel of fibre instead of the fig leaf worn by the women of the Great Andaman Tribes, and neither male nor female Jàrawas tattoo themselves.—*M. V. P.*).

I have noticed that there is a typical shape of head among the Öngé Group of Tribes, and their faces have more pointed chins, and not the square shape common to the other Andamanese.

From this time more interest was taken in this people, and mention of them is made in the Reports.

In 1874, they were seen three times during the year; two runaway convicts on Rutland Island were wounded by them, and six of them were seen on the east coast of the South Andaman just north of the edible birds' nest caves at Chiriya Tápu. It must be remembered that at this time it was thought that the Jàrawas on the South Andaman, and those on Rutland Island, were one tribe.

In December, 1875, six convicts were seized by a party of Jàrawas at Brigade Creek, and five of them returned to Port Blair after having been kept in captivity by the Jàrawas for 19 days. (This was their report, but I do not believe it. They made the excuse of a long captivity among the Jàrawas in order to escape the punishment due to them for escaping.—*M. V. P.*).

This story unsettled our friendly Andamanese in the Home at Brigade Creek, and they moved to another part of the country.

On the 24th, a party of Andamanese and convicts was sent into the jungle to look for these Jàrawas, of whom between 30 and 40 were seen, and fled as soon as they met our people; the latter being equally frightened, turned tail also.

In January, 1876, two expeditions were sent to search for the Jàrawas, and one party visited four villages, in which they left quantities of unsuitable presents, and brought back specimens of the Jàrawas' weapons, and utensils. It was unfortunate that, at the outset, the Jàrawas' huts should have been looted thus, and the presents left, being such things as matches, pipes, tobacco, and looking-glasses, the uses of which were unknown to these savages, were useless to them, and by no means compensated them for the articles taken away.

In March, 1876, another expedition was sent out but was unsuccessful. Mr. Man was informed that the Jàrawas who ordinarily lived to the southward of the harbour of Port Blair had left that part of the country. It was thought at this time that these people, and the tribe of Jàrawas who lived in the jungle north-west of Port Blair, were two different tribes, though Mr. Man considered that they might be allied, and that they originally came from the Little Andaman, (which they undoubtedly did, though at some very remote date.— *M. V. P.*).

They were really one tribe, which, though slightly separated by our clearing between Port Blair and Port Mouat, was not prevented from occasionally crossing it, and had never divided into two distinct tribes, though, like the other Andamanese, small groups of families formed distinct communities, and wandered about independently of each other.

In April, a bow and a bucket were brought in by the Chief of Góp-l'áka-báng, who had found them with a Jàrawa he had captured while up a tree getting honey, but who broke his bonds and escaped during the night, while our Andamanese were asleep, so was never brought into the Settlement.

In July, 1876, another expedition was sent against the Jàrawas, which was unsuccessful.

Mr. Man hoped by catching and taming the Jàrawas to establish through their influence, friendly relations with the aborigines of the Little Andaman, not knowing that the two tribes spoke different and mutually unintelligible dialects.

He notes that our Andamanese are very afraid of the Jàrawas, and is unable to understand this, as he considered that the latter were very quiet and inoffensive, never molesting or annoying us, and only desirous of keeping away from us, while we were constantly annoying them. (This view was correct, as the hostilities were commenced by us and our Andamanese, and after some years of this we so aggravated the Jàrawas that they began to attack us in revenge.—*M. V. P.*).

Mr. Man thought that all communication between the North and South Jàrawa Tribes had ceased owing to our opening out Port Mouat, and supposed (incorrectly) that they did not dare to cross the strip of cleared land. He frequently left presents in their huts, and endeavoured to prevent our Andamanese from molesting them, or stealing their things.

He thought that the North Sentinel people were distinct, but that the Öngés of the Little Andaman, and the Jàrawas, were once one tribe, and inhabited all the intermediate islands between the Great and Little Andamans, also the North Sentinel.

In June, 1877, another expedition found a Jàrawa hut, 42 feet long by 46 feet wide, in which the savages were living. None of them were, however, captured.

In September, four Jàrawas were seen in the jungle south of the Settlement; they ran away on the approach of our Andamanese, and presents of looking-glasses, coloured cloths, necklaces, and Nicobar coconut shells were left for them, Mr. Man being of the opinion that these *much valued* presents would more than compensate the Jàrawas for the loss of their own property, which the Andamanese on this occasion stole. Unfortunately, all the above-mentioned articles are of no use to the Jàrawas, and are not in the least valued by them, as subsequent experience at the Little Andaman has taught us.

In February, 1878, a further expedition into the same country was fruitless.

In March, Mr. Man steamed round, but did not land on, the North Sentinel Island.

In April, 1878, an expedition was sent into the jungle north-west of Brigade Creek, and returned with three Jàrawas, a woman, and two small children.

Mr. Man remarks that the woman wore no leaf covering, and was not tattooed. He hoped to keep these people long enough to become friendly with them, but 24 hours after their capture the Brigade

Creek Home was attacked by the Jàrawas, and our Andamanese there becoming much alarmed, Mr. Man released the woman and children with a quantity of presents. (Having gone so far, it would perhaps have been better in the end had he fought the Jàrawas who attacked the Home, and endeavoured to capture some young men who might have been tamed and used as go-betweens.)

In October, 1878, two Jàrawa canoes (always easily identified, as they are unlike the canoes of the other tribes) were found on the beach in MacPherson's Straits, and presents were left in them.

Now the Jàrawas of the Great Andaman have not got canoes, (though this was not known at that time), and there can be little doubt that these were the property of a party of Òngés who had come up from the Little Andaman to the Ciṇque Islands, and were then living on them.

It is the custom of the Òugés living at the north of the Little Andaman to come up for turtle, etc., to as far as the Cinque Islands, every third or fourth year, during the break of calm weather which occurs at the change of the monsoons in October; and to return to their homes in the following February or March.

In January, an Áka-*Béa*-da who was cutting a canoe near the Brigade Creek Home was fired at by a Jàrawa, who missed him and ran away. Nothing further was done in the matter.

In February, 1879, another Jàrawa canoe was actually found on the Cinque Islands; presents were left in it, and several Jàrawas were seen, but no collision occurred between them and our party.

It was thought that they were members of the Rutland Island Tribe, whereas, in reality they were Öngés; had they been caught and tamed then, (as was done under similar circumstances six years afterwards), the establishment of friendly relations with the aborigines of the Little Andaman would have been accomplished years earlier.

It is noteworthy that, on this occasion, the Òngés visited Rutland Island and MacPherson's Straits, for in 1885 Kógio Kāī told me that they were afraid to come farther north than the Cinque Islands on account of some men with long hair who fought with them. These "men with long hair" may have been convicts, but it is more probable that the A'ka-*Béa*-da are meant, as they allow their hair to grow to a considerable length, while the Öugés keep theirs close cropped.

(I have had occasion to point out, with reference to similar stories about long haired men being seen among the Jàrawas, which some officials have thought to mean convicts living among them, that " long hair" does not necessarily mean "straight hair ").

In March, 1879, the Cinque Islands were again visited and presents were left there, but the Öngés had by that time gone back to the Little Andaman.

In May, 1879, another similar visit was paid to the Islands, and presents were again left.

In his Annual Report on the Andamanese for the year 1878-79, Mr. Man makes the following remarks about the Jàrawas:—

" As the little that is known about the Jàrawas is confined to a few persons, and has never been placed on record, it may not be out of place to mention in this, my last report, what I have been able to ascertain regarding these savages who have hitherto so persistently kept aloof from us.

" The punishment inflicted by us on the natives of the Little Andaman within the past fifteen years for the murder, first, of the crew of the " Assam Valley ", and second of some Burmese who had landed on the coast for water, and the subsequent fatal encounters which have taken place on our visiting the Island, with the object of communicating with the inhabitants, have no doubt been the cause of our continued failure to become acquainted with those members of the same tribe (?) who frequent the islands near the southernmost borders of the Settlement. (Quite incorrect, there being no communication between the two tribes.—*M. V. P.*) The additional circumstance of our being on friendly terms with their traditional enemies, the Bójig-ngijis, doubtless contributes to their avoidance of our friendly overtures. (This is more probable.—*M. V. P.*)

" From the statements of the aborigines of our acquaintance, and from the fact of there being Jàrawa ' Kitchen-middings ' in or near this Harbour, it is evident that the Jàrawas were for a considerable period permanently resident on a great portion of the South Andaman, and that they have been gradually driven to their present haunts in this island, not so much by the Bójig-ngijis, as by ourselves while engaged in establishing this Settlement, for our intercourse with the aborigines from the early days of our Settlement having been limited to the latter tribe, they have by degrees been enabled to visit and occupy those parts in the vicinity of this Harbour, into which they never formerly ventured without risking an encounter with the Jàrawas.

"That the Jàrawas were originally of the same tribe as the people inhabiting Little Andaman, there appears to be no reason whatever to doubt, for, while in the construction of their huts, bows (No. —*M. V. P.*), arrows, pails, baskets, and cooking pots, etc., they exactly or very closely resemble the Little Andamanese, they differ more or less markedly in this respect from the rest of the aborigines of the Great Andaman.

"The Jàrawas (Sometimes.—*M. V. P.*) build large circular huts, capable of accommodating often over 100 persons (The Ongés do.— *M. V. P.*), the eaves of which are within two feet or so of the ground, and they have separate huts for cooking purposes, thereby keeping their dwellings in a more cleanly state than is possible with the ill-ordered ménage of the Bójig-ngijis, and the other Great Andaman Tribes, who live, cook, and sleep for the most part in miserable lean-to's, even the surroundings of which they make no effort to keep clean. (The women sweep round the huts daily, and the more permanent huts of the Great Andaman Tribes are somewhat better than "miserable lean-to's.—*M. V. P.*)

"Unlike the Bójig-ngijis, and the aborigines of the North and Middle Andaman, the Jàrawas do not shave (they cut their hair short —*M. V. P.*), or tattoo themselves, nor have they ever been seen smeared with either the red earth (yes, on their heads.—*M. V. P.*), or white clay (they use a yellowish-white clay.—*M. V. P.*), which is so constantly in use with the rest of the aborigines of the Great Andaman. In fact, except, perhaps, in dialect, there is reason to believe, as already remarked, that the Jàrawas and the inhabitants of the Little Andaman are of the same tribe. ("Of the same Group of Tribes," would have been more correct.—*M. V. P.*)

" The assumption is that those living south of this Harbour, in Rutland Island, and the Cinque Islands, are in communication with the natives of the Little Andaman, and therefore in their case it is not improbable that they speak the same dialect as the latter, but in the case of the isolated party of Jàrawas occupying the jungle north-west of this Harbour, as they have had their means of communication with their friends in the south cut off for the past fifteen years or so, owing to our occupation during that period of the narrow neck of land separating Port Mouat from this Harbour, they may very possibly at some future time be found to differ from their former fellow-tribesmen in their dialect, for it is well established that savage dialects are subject to variations arising from defects of hearing, memory, and other causes, from which the arts are exempt.

"Evidence of this is afforded in the fact of the striking resemblance between the weapons and implements of the Bójig-ngijis and those of the natives of the North and Middle-Andamans, although their dialects have, in lapse of time, so changed that a man of one tribe is almost unintelligible to one of another."

(Far from there being a "striking resemblance," I think there is a striking difference between many of the weapons and implements of the North and South Andaman Groups of Tribes; moreover, an examination of Lieutenant Colebrooke's vocabulary, and a comparison of the words in it with those we know of the Jàrawa tribes, shows that the Andamanese dialects do not change very rapidly.

Mr. Man's assumption regarding the connection between the different tribes of Jàrawas was incorrect.

The people on the Cinque Islands *were* the Öugés of the Little Andaman, the Rutland Island Jàrawas are entirely separated from the others, and the supposed two tribes in the jungles of the South Andaman are one and the same tribe, and have not been separated at all, as I shall presently show.—*M. V. P.*)

" With reference to the Jàrawas living between Port Campbell and this Harbour, it is a curious fact that the very existence of this inland tribe has not only been called in question, but ridiculed (*vide* page 145 of Proceedings of the Asiatic Society of Bengal, 1876).

The author of the remarks therein published (Mr. F. A. De Roepstorff —*M. V. P.*), had, however, based his views on convictions formed on erroneous data. Had he enjoyed the same opportunities as myself he would soon have ascertained that it is an undoubted fact, not only that this off-shoot tribe of Jàrawas is distinctly an inland tribe, in that its members subsist entirely on the produce of the jungle (No, they come to the coast for fish, etc.—*M. V. P.*), but that similar (?) communities exist in the heart of the Middle Andaman, and very probably also in the North Andaman."

(This is beside the point. The existence of the Jàrawas, not of Éremtága tribes, was called in question.—*M. V. P.*)

"It has been customary to believe that, 'the Andamanese live quite close to the sea, and wended their way along the shore, getting their subsistence in shell-fish from the coral reefs, and in fish from the sea, and that pig hunting is quite subsidiary.' It is true that there are Andamanese who could be thus described, but they are the 'Ár-*yāutos*' or 'coast people', whereas the 'Éremtága' or 'jungle dwellers,' are distinct in their mode of living, and it is simply because the knowledge of most of the residents here concerning the aborigines is confined to the little they see and hear, that they imagine that all the Andamanese are a coast-living race, or at least are mainly dependent on the sea for their supplies of food. This idea is however entirely erroneous. (Not entirely.—*M. V. P.*) From my intimate acquaintance with the Andamanese during the past four years, I can state as a positive fact that their jungles contain, as far as their requirements are concerned, such an abundant supply of food at all seasons of the year, that many times the present numbers of inhabitants, (both Ár-*Yāutos* and Éremtágas) could find ample provision for all their wants without resorting to the coast at all. Similar Negrito tribes are found far from the coast in the interior of New Guinea (?), Borneo (?), the Philippines, and the Malayan Peninsula."

"On this subject Mr. Blanford has said, 'It is very difficult for a civilised human being to understand how savages live, or even to conceive what a marvellous variety of animal and vegetable productions on which savage man, at any rate, can subsist, are to be found in the forests of all tropical regions.' He added his belief that, 'man could certainly find food wherever monkeys could exist.'"

(An unfortunate argument to adduce, as there are no monkeys in the Andamans.—*M. V. P.*)

"While on the subject of the Jàrawas I would mention the inhabitants of the North Sentinel, an island of only some 12 (20.—*M. V. P.*) square miles, and situated about 20 miles to the west of Port Mouat. Regarding these people, whom the Bójig-ngijis also call Jàrawas, scarcely anything is known. They have evidently had no communication with any of their neighbours for a considerable period (on the contrary, they are the one tribe of Jàrawas which is supposed to be in recent, if not present, communication with the Önges; see below.—*M. V. P.*), and have been in fact for a long time a distinctly separate community. No canoes have ever been seen on or near their coasts. (They have several canoes.—*M. V. P.*) In March, 1867, when approaching their Island in search of some escaped convicts, a few of the inhabitants were observed on the coast by Mr. Homfray. No attempt at landing was made, as the Bójig-ngijis who accompanied him apprehended a hostile reception. As far as could be judged, their general appearance accorded with that of the rest of the aborigines of these islands. It was observed that they wore their hair long. This is peculiar to the inhabitants of Little Andaman, and to the Jàrawa tribes living in our vicinity. (Quite wrong. The Önges wear their hair cropped close, and many of the people on the Great Andaman wear very long hair.—*M. V. P.*)

"For a period of exactly eleven years, *viz.*, in March, 1878, no other visit was paid to the Island from this Settlement. (Mr. Man forgets the wreck of the *Nineveh* and the visits paid on that occasion in October 1867.—*M. V. P.*) In that month I passed close along the east coast of the Island in H. M. S. "Rifleman," when I observed two small sheds of recent and substantial manufacture. They were about two miles apart, and were situated on the border of the jungle. None of the inhabitants could, however, be seen.

"It would be particularly interesting to make the acquaintance of this isolated tribe, and also of the people above referred to as living between this Harbour and Port Campbell. It is a subject of much regret to me that the numerous attempts I have made to become acquainted with the latter tribe have been so unsuccessful. The only way of opening up communication with the North Sentinel people will be by means of the Station Steamer or Schooner, as the Andamanese are not in the habit of venturing out so far to sea in their canoes."

The above was written by Mr. Man on insufficient and incorrect data, but serves to show the prevailing ideas regarding the Öngé Group of Tribes so late as 1879.

In August, 1879, a month after I had taken charge of the Andamanese, I sent a party of convicts to cut a track through the jungle south of the Settlement, from Dhani Khári station to Yáratán on the north coast of MacPherson's Straits, and joined this with other tracks to Manglután on the west coast, and Chiriya Tápu on the south coast. Expeditions in search of Jàrawas were able to move rapidly along these tracks with rations, etc., and thus I established headquarter stations in the Jàrawa country, and saved much time and toil by not working through the thick jungle.

In November, 1879, the tracks being finished, I sent a party to look for the Jàrawas; they saw three men who ran away, and brought in a marble-wood bow and some other articles.

Early in January, 1880, I paid a visit to the North Sentinel Island with Colonel Cadell. We saw tracks, and villages, but none of the aborigines. On the 26th of the same month, I went again to the Island in the I. G. S. "Constance" and stopped there for a fortnight. Captain Allen, and Lieutenant Hooper of the "Constance," and Lieutenant H. H. Dobbie of the European Detachment in Port Blair, accompanied me in making a very thorough search throughout the interior of the Island. The villages, weapons, and utensils of the North Sentinel people I have since learnt are exactly the same as those of the Öngés, and, so far as I could tell, their customs seem to be the same.

One day, while marching through the jungle, we came upon a camp of Jàrawas, and captured a woman and four small children unhurt. These were kept for a few days on board the *Constance,* and the woman and one child were then released with a quantity of presents. The *Constance,* a sailing schooner, went back to Port Mouat for a day, during which time Lieutenant Hooper and I camped on a small islet off the north-western coast of the Sentinel. During the night a bonfire, which we had lighted as a beacon for the *Constance* to steer by, attracted a very large number of sea snakes (Hydrophis *sp.*), which crept round us on the sand, and, as their bite was certain death, effectually banished sleep.

A few days later, while crossing the island from the south-east to the western coast, Lieutenant Hooper and I met, on a track in the middle of the forest, an old man with his wife and child.

Our party were spread out in crescent form, and the Jàrawas came to the centre where Lieutenant Hooper and I were. The old man had drawn his bow and was about to fire at Lieutenant Hooper's head when my convict orderly, a Pathan, named Amirullah, who had been stationed at the right point of the crescent, and had got behind the Jàrawas, jumped on his back and spoilt his aim. We caught the three unhurt and brought them on board. The next day we took the six Jàrawas in to Port Blair, where I kept them at my house for some days. They sickened rapidly, and the old man and his wife died, so the four children were sent back to their home with quantities of presents.

This expedition was not a success, for, misled by Mr. Homfray's statements regarding the numbers and ferocity of the aborigines, they were met in a less conciliatory manner than was desirable, and we cannot be said to have done anything more than increase their general terror of, and hostility to, all comers. It would have been better to have left the Islanders alone, until the Öngés of the Little Andaman were tamed, and then to have approached them with the assistance of the latter. The facts which justify this view were not, however, known at that time.

In many features the North Sentinel differs from the other Islands of the Andaman Group. It is chiefly composed of coral and lime stone, and large boulders of dead coral are to be found on the surface all over the island, the sharp edges of which make walking difficult and painful. The soil is light and admirably suited for the growth of coconut palms, the surface drainage being excellent. The jungle is in many places open and park like and there are very beautiful groves of bullet-wood trees. Magnificent specimens of the *Bombax Malabaricum* are to be found; the buttressed root of one was measured by Colonel Cadell and found to be 27 feet long and 15 feet high where it left the trunk. The aborigines are few in number and painfully timid; they resemble the Öuges, but of their language nothing is known; their food, like that of the other Andamanese, consists of roots, fruit, fish, pig, and turtle, etc., and their methods of cooking and preparing their food resemble those of the Öngés, not those of the aborigines of the Great Andaman. They dig small water-holes in the dry weather, and build lean-to huts, like those of the Jàrawas in the South Andaman, and of the Öngés, but do not make the large bee-hive shaped huts seen as permanent villages in the Little Andaman.

Sometimes they camp temporarily in the buttressed roots of trees. I have noticed exactly similar huts on the North Sentinel, the South Andaman, Rutland Island, the Cinque Islands, and the South Brother Island.

The North Sentinel Islanders smear themselves over with yellowish clay as do the other Jàrawa tribes, but I have not seen them use red earth on their heads, possibly because this pigment is not found on the Island. This Group of Tribes do not wear the skulls of their deceased relatives, but I have found both on the North Sentinel, and on the Little Andaman, the lower jawbones of men, ornamented with a fringe of twisted fibre, and evidently intended to be worn; in the former island I also saw a skeleton (of an old man, I think) placed in a large bucket, in a sitting posture, and hidden in the buttressed roots of a big tree. In one place there, close to a village, was an immense heap of pigs' skulls, which delighted our Andamanese, as the tusks had not been taken from them, and my people spent an afternoon in collecting these. The Öngé Group of Tribes do not seem to use the pig's tusk as a plane or spokeshave, in the manner the Great Andaman Tribes do, probably because this tool is only used for smoothening the bow, and the Önge bow is rough and coarse.

In features the North Sentinelese most closely resemble the Jàrawas on Rutland Island, and there is a peculiarly idiotic expression of countenance, and manner of behaving, common to both.

In March, 1880, I visited Rutland Island and the Cinque Islands, in the hope of finding Jàrawas, but did not meet any.

In my report for the year 1879-80, I express an opinion, which subsequently proved to be correct, that the clearing between Tytler's Ghat, and Homfray's Ghat had not separated the Jàrawas, or divided them into two tribes, but that they crossed this land whenever they chose.

In April, 1880, while exploring the creeks running inland from Shoal Bay, I found a small Jàrawa village at Milé Tilek, and accordingly commenced to cut a track to that place from the Brigade Creek Home, in order to use it as a headquarter station from which the Jàrawas could be searched for.

On the 13th of May, Daūra, the Chief of Port Campbell, reported to me that some members of the western tribe of Jàrawas had attacked his people, killing one man, and wounding another. I sent my Jemadar, Ahmed, up to the Middle Andaman to bring in Andamanese, and as my track to Milé Tilek was ready, went out there on the 20th with 30 convicts, and 140 Andamanese, camping at the foot of Mount Chulnga for four days. On the third day one of our searching parties found a very old but lively woman, with white hair, and brought her into my camp. She did not appear to be particularly alarmed, and made herself completely at home, elbowing the men away from the fire, sleeping with the elders in their hut unconcernedly, and occasionally bursting out into what were, no doubt, torrents of abuse.

We let her go on the following day with as many presents as she could carry.

On the 29th, I went round to Constance Bay in a steam barge, taking 30 convicts, and 120 Andamanese. We camped in huts at Kōīób-lá-tinga, and remained there till the 11th of June. The weather was most inclement, being one continued storm of wind and rain, (the burst of the south-west monsoon in fact). Three search parties were sent up to as far as Port Campbell, one travelling along the coast, one going from Bája-luntá-jig to Pártám-jig, and one going along the Chulnga range of hills. They returned on the 8th of June completely worn out, and much dispirited at having seen nothing. I reported the result of the expedition to Colonel Cadell, who ordered me to return to Port Blair and to try again when the weather improved. On the morning of the 10th, 1st Tindal Nureddin suggested that he should take a few Andamanese and look in the hills close to my camp for a few hours, as the Andamanese who had been hunting there on the previous day had seen some footmarks.

He went, and returned by midday bringing one old man, three women, and six children. These people had apparently been encamped with some others, within a mile of us, for several days, without our knowing it, which shows how difficult it is to find the Jàrawas in the thick jungle, and how close one may be to them and yet miss them.

They were unhurt, and it speaks well for convict Nureddin, who had a loaded rifle in his hand, that, when he came to their village and they fired at him, and hit him with one arrow in the knee, he did not fire back at them but merely shot in the air in order to frighten them.

I brought these Jàrawas into Port Blair, and kept them with me on Viper Island for several days. They sickened and had to be released after about a fortnight, during which time I managed to get on fairly good terms with them. The man was too old to be tamed; with Andamanese women by themselves nothing can be done, for even if friendly relations were established with them they would have no influence, on their return, with the male members of their tribe, would rather indeed be looked upon doubtfully or even with hatred unless the relations were so far advanced that they could act as interpreters and come and go with presents, which few of them are either brave or intelligent enough to do; and the children, with the exception of one boy, were too young to be influenced.

It was noticed that they were unable to swim, and that when sick they had a custom known to the other Andamanese of crumbling the leaves of a shrub and rubbing their bodies over with the fragments.

The yellow clay which they smear on their bodies they keep moulded into balls, about the size of a man's head, and these clay balls are generally found in baskets in their huts; knives of tortoiseshell with serrated edges are used by them; and among their ornaments are wreaths of plaited fibre with locks of human (Andamanese) hair attached as tassels. As with the other Tribes of this Group, the yellow roasted bark of a species of Dendrobe is plaited into their ornaments and gives them a very pretty appearance. The tail feathers of the king crow stuck into a band of this plaited bark are sometimes worn as a head-dress.

They are not nearly as good shots with their huge and unwieldy bows as are the Áka-*Béa*-da with theirs.

As a rule, when a Jàrawa village was entered by us, we found afterwards that the Jàrawas destroyed it, and did not again build on that site, as if they were afraid of our knowing where they lived.

I attach some of the words I was able to obtain from these people, and give a comparison between them and the words given by Lieutenant Colebrooke, in Chapter III; also the corresponding Öngé words.

The pronunciation is intensely nasal—

English.	Jàrawa.	Öngé.
Arrow	Bártoi	Bártoi.
Colebrooke	Buttohie.	
Axe	Doi-i	Doi-i.
Bamboo, a	Otálé	Āūdálé.
Colebrooke	Otallie.	
Bow, a	Á-ai-i	A-āī.
Colebrooke	Tongie.	
Bucket, a	Uhu	Ukui.
Crab, a	Kágāī	Kágāī-á.
Drink, to	Ínjowá	Ínjóbé.

English.	Jàrawa.	Öngé.
Colebrooke	Meengohee.	
Eye, the	Íjammá.	Unijéböī.
Colebrooke	Jabay.	
Fire	Tuháwé.	Tuké.
Colebrooke	Mone.	
Foot, the	Mongé.	Mugé.
Colebrooke	Gookee.	
Hair, the	Enōīdé.	Māūdé.
Colebrooke	Ottee.	
Hand, the	Mómé.	Mómé.
Colebrooke	Monie.	
Iron	Tánhi.	Doi-i. (An iron adze.)
Colebrooke	Dohie.	
Leaf, a	Bébé.	Bébé.
Colebrooke	Tongolie.	
Nautilus shell, a	Gá-āī.	Gá-āī.
Navel, the	Inkwá.	Önikwálé.
Net, a	Bórtai.	Chiqué.
Colebrooke	Bototee.	
Nose, the	Inámá.	Uninyaiböī.
Colebrooke	Mellee.	
Road, a	Ischélé.	Ichélé.
Colebrooke	Echollee.	
Run, to	Áhá-bélábé.	Akwé-bélábé.
Colebrooke	Gohabela.	

English.	Jàrawa.	Öngé.
Sea, the	Étálé	Passage Island. (A small islet in the sea). Détálé.
Sit down, to	Átáun	Unán-tököbé.
Colebrooke	Gongtohee.	
Sky, the	Baīngabá	Béng-nouge.
Colebrooke	Madamo.	
Sleep, to	Ómóhán	Ómokábé.
Colebrooke	Comoha.	
String	Étai	Ébé.
Stone, a	Uli	Tāīyi.
Colebrooke	Woolay.	
Tooth, a	Ánwāī	Mákué.
Colebrooke	Mahoy.	
Water	Énulé	Ingé.
Colebrooke	Migway.	

Colonel Cadell remarked in his monthly report for June, 1880, on the above-mentioned expeditions:—

"Mr. Portman deserves much credit for his conduct of the expedition against the Jàrawas undertaken in most inclement weather. The circumstances which led to the attack by the Jàrawas on our Andamanese near Port Campbell, reported last month, are not known. The attack created great alarm among the aborigines who are on friendly terms with us, and they flocked into the Andaman Home on Viper Island. It being considered necessary to reassure them, and to take some notice of the attack, the expedition mentioned in last month's report was sent out. It failed to catch any Jàrawas, except one old woman, who was very rightly allowed to go at once, and the expedition mentioned in this month's report was then sent round to the West coast from which operations were commenced. It consisted, like the previous one, of about 120 Andamanese and a few convicts and Petty Officers, and was under the direction of Mr. Portman, who remained in a temporary hut on the sea shore and sent parties into the jungles. It was known that the Jàrawas are very few in number, and our parties were made so strong as to prevent any likelihood of resistance. Our party, as narrated by Mr. Portman, effected the capture of an old man, and nine women and children, who were brought into Port Blair, and after being treated with great kindness for a few days, were allowed to return to their homes. It was intended to retain an intelligent boy of about 13 years of age in the hope that he might act as a go-between, but he seemed to be sickening and it was therefore resolved to send him back."

In September, 1880, I went to Portman Bay, on the east coast of Rutland Island, and sent a party of Andamanese and convicts ashore there to look for Jàrawas. There were signs of a blow from the S. E., so the Commander of the I. G. S. *Hugh Rose*, moved up to MacPherson's Straits, returning to Portman Bay the next day.

In the meantime, a woman and two children had been captured, but as the *Hugh Rose* had left and the Andamanese feared that they would be attacked by the other Jàrawas, they released them giving them a quantity of presents.

In November, I sent parties of convicts and Andamanese into the jungle south of Port Blair, and to Rutland Island, to search for Jàrawas, but none were seen. I visited the North Sentinel Island at this time, but did not see any of the aborigines.

Nothing more was heard of the Jàrawas until March, 1882, when the tracks of some were seen in the southern jungle, and it is probable that they had recently moved down there from the north-west jungle.

The Andamanese had at this time abandoned Port Campbell on account of their dread of the Jàrawas, and those who formerly lived there had moved to Port Mouat.

Our Andamanese also reported that Jàrawas' tracks had been seen near Góp-l'áka-báng, and Kōiób-lá-tinga; they usually come down to these parts during the dry season.

In April, 1882, the Jàrawas attacked a party of convicts who were cutting a track from Ranguchàng to Chiriya Tápu, in the jungle south of Port Blair. Major Protheroe, the Officiating Chief Commissioner, sent me down to enquire into the matter. Two convicts had been killed, and I found and burnt their bodies, and one was wounded. A party of Jàrawas out pig hunting had come upon them, and had fired a volley of wooden-headed arrows with such force that, in one instance, the arrow had passed through a sapling four inches thick, and the point protruded about 6 inches on the other side.

Nothing more was seen of these Jàrawas, though the jungles were searched.

In June, 1882, a search was made in the jungle near Kōiób-lá-tinga for Jàrawas, but without success.

In his Annual Report for 1882-83, Mr. Godwin-Austen remarks:—

"The Jàrawas have given more trouble during the past year than hitherto, which I am able to account for only in one way. During the past year much has been in the way of opening out tracks through their country, *i.e.*, that lying between the south of the Settlement and MacPherson's Straits, which they probably took to be a move on our part to hem them in and so capture them on their first appearance. At Ranguchàng, in April, 1882, they surprised a working party cutting a track through the jungle, or very probably came upon the party suddenly, and fired, but the place was well chosen for an attack to be made. On the second occasion, in December, 1882, a party of convicts, pig hunting, ventured too far into the jungle towards Mang-lután, where they came upon some Jàrawas, and two of them were shot. Parties of our Andamanese have on two or three occasions been out after them; the first expedition was to Kōiób-lá-tinga where they remained searching the jungles for a week, but only found some deserted huts.

"The northern Jàrawas have evidently shifted their quarters to Port Meadows. (Some few did so, or rather to the jungle near there, and opposite to Shoal Bay.—*M. V. P.*)

"The searches made towards the south have never(?) been successful; huts have been seen, but always empty and old.

"The only way to ensure success would be to organise three or four large search parties, composed of Police, Andamanese, and convicts; in each party about forty men, and thoroughly scour all the country to the south of the Settlement."

(Success in expeditions after Jàrawas can never be "ensured." The finding of these people is purely a matter of chance.—*M. V. P.*)

"Their head-quarters might be Dhani Leaf Creek, Ali Masjid, and MacPherson's Straits, or they might work together. Andamanese by themselves would never be thoroughly successful, they would probably meet, fire a shot or two, and then retreat."

In August, 1883, Mr. Man sent a party to search for the Jàrawas on Rutland Island, but none were seen.

In September, the Island was again visited, and presents were left in some deserted Jàrawa huts.

In November a party was sent into the southern jungle to search for Jàrawas, and returned after a few days with a middle aged woman. I kept her at my house for four days, gave her a large quantity of presents, which she was allowed to select for herself, and then sent her back to her own coun[t]ry, releasing her on the spot where she had been captured. She had not been wounded or ill-treated in any way, and did not seem to be alarmed.

In January, 1884, I went to Rutland Island to look for Jàrawas, and found a small new village on the shore at the north side of Portman Bay, but nothing was seen of the savages.

In February, I sent out a party to search for Jàrawas in the southern jungles, but no trace of them was found.

On the 4th of March a party of Malays (birds' nest collectors), returning from Chiriya Tápu to Ross, had anchored their boat on the coast three miles below Ranguchàng in the afternoon, when they were surprised by a party of about ten Jàrawas, who came out on the shore and fired on them, missing the men, but hitting the boat. The Malays at once came in to Port Blair.

On this being reported to me I went down to Ranguchâng on the 6th, with a large party of Andamanese and convicts who proceeded to beat through the jungle. These parties all returned to my camp on the 9th, having caught two women, who by my orders were at once released. Many huts, new and old, were seen, and their baskets, buckets, ornaments, etc., were brought in as a punishment to them.

Another expedition was made on the 12th to the same country, but was not successful.

As the Jàrawas living in the jungle south of Port Blair probably did not exceed thirty in number, search after them was extremely difficult. On the 20th, I received a report that a Policeman, attached as a guard to the Survey party who were cutting a track near Mile Tilek, had been wounded in the shoulder by a party of Jàrawas of the western tribe. In communication with the Chief Commissioner it was arranged to send out an expedition into the country west of Port Blair, and on Sunday, the 23rd, a large party of Andamanese, convicts, and Police was sent to Port Mouat with orders to search through the jungle to Port Campbell. I proceeded in a steam barge to Kyd Island, and landed a similar party at Já-táng, directing them to search through the northern jungle to Port Campbell, and then went on, through the Middle Straits, to that place (where the engines of the steam barge, which were out of repair, broke down entirely), and waited for the arrival of the search parties. Two of these arrived on the evening of the 26th having seen many old huts, and the party from Port Mouat having come across a village of eleven huts (with every trace of recent habitation) on the hills above Tóra Két.

Giving them rations I sent both parties off to Port Mouat.

I had sent two Andamanese with a letter to the Chief Commissioner, informing him that the steam barge had broken down, and on the morning of the 28th the *Nancowry* arrived and towed her back to Port Blair. In the meantime, an expedition, accompanied by the Chief Commissioner as far as Milé Tilek, had left, and sleeping at Milé Tilek on the night of the 24th, entered the jungle on the morning of the 25th.

After going a short distance they saw a village, and a little way further met with the Jàrawas who were collecting honey. A fight ensued, in which one Jàrawa was killed with two arrow wounds, one was wounded in the leg with an arrow and captured, and one child was caught unhurt. This party then returned to Port Blair bringing with them the wounded man and the child. Everything was done for their comfort, and the wounded man was most carefully tended in the Haddo Hospital.

The party which left Port Campbell for Port Mouat on the 26th arrived in Port Blair on the 31st. In the hills above Tóra Két they had met with six Jàrawas, who, after a few shots had been exchanged, ran away. No one was hit.

On the 23rd of May, four self-supporting convicts who had gone up the Rangucháng creek to collect canes and thatching leaves were attacked by the Jàrawas. One convict was killed on the spot, and two others were wounded, one of whom afterwards died from the effects of his wounds.

On the 6th of June an expedition was sent into the southern jungles and returned after two days having caught two Jàrawa women near Pole Bay. One of them was the same woman who had been caught in the previous November, and both were unhurt and did not seem to be frightened.

I kept them till the 18th, and they lived with Tálai, the man who had been captured in the previous month; I found that they spoke the same language and that the elder of the women appeared from her manner to be related to him. This led me to suppose, what has since been shown to be correct, that there is only one tribe of Jàrawas on the mainland of the South Andaman.

Tálai begged me by signs to let the women go, and they were escorted back to the place where they were caught by a party of our Andamanese, who released them and gave them a quantity of presents.

Tálai, who had been wounded in the right thigh, an arrow having gone through the fleshy part of it, recovered after about a month, and was soon on the best of terms with us. I kept him in my house after his discharge from the hospital, and he was most friendly, accompanying me wherever I went, and fraternising with the Andamanese.

He was a young and well-made man, with a merry face, and was always full of fun. The little boy who was caught with him, and whose name was A'pi, was too young to understand much, and merely played about with the other Andamanese children.

On the 23rd of June, I went down to Rutland Island with 70 Andamanese and 30 convicts to search for Jàrawas, one party examining the jungle between Port Blair and MacPherson's Straits, and the other searching on Rutland Island. I took Tálai and A'pi with me, in the hope that I might learn something from them regarding the whereabouts and mode of life of the Jàrawas. Huts and recent traces of Jàrawas were seen, but none of the people were met with, and whilst the search was being conducted, Tálai, who was not kept under any restraint, wandered away from the two Andamanese boys with whom he was shooting fish on the coast and left us. He was tracked to the northern end of Rutland Island where it was found he had made a small raft and crossed MacPherson's Straits into his own country.

As he was very friendly with us, and had never been ill-treated since his capture, I was in hopes that he would have given a good account of us to his fellow-tribesmen and have induced them to become cn more friendly terms, but subsequent events showed, either that he did not do so, or that the other Jàrawas paid no attention to what he said.

From the 1st to the 14th of July parties were kept on Rutland Island searching for the Jàrawas in very inclement weather, and on the 14th I proceeded in the *Kwang Tung* to Portman Bay and there found that one of them had just caught a male Jàrawa of the Rutland Island tribe, aged about 30. He was brought up to Port Blair where it was found that he could not speak the same language as the tribe of Jàrawas on the mainland, and that he was an Ár-*yaüto*, and not an Éremtága, as they are. I could, however, distinguish a connection between the two languages, and at some former period they were undoubtedly the same.

This man, whose name I believe to be "Hálía", was unwounded

and was well treated, being kept in my house and given quantities of presents. He seemed to be friendly but half-witted, and as he sickened he was returned on the 30th with his presents to the place where he was caught. Nothing has been heard of him since.

On the 28th, I tried to send the child A'pi back to his own tribe. My party wandered about with him from village to village, but when he was left in any of them with his presents he refused to stop there, and accordingly was, after a week, brought back to the Settlement to which he appeared delighted to return.

On the 18th of August, 1884, I sent two parties, each consisting of nine Andamanese and three convicts, to Ranguchángo, and Bumlitán, respectively, with orders to search for Jàrawas, as some self supporting convicts of Bumlitán village had seen them close to that place, and were much alarmed. A large village of 14 huts was found in the adjacent jungle, and was visited by Colonel Protheroe and myself. The search parties also found a large hut in which were hatchet heads, weapons, and various ornaments and utensils of the Jàrawas, thus showing signs of actual occupation. Had these parties done their duty, the Jàrawas should have been caught, as on the same evening about 20 of them were met with at the hut. Each party fired, no one was hurt, and our people ran away.

In November, a party was sent to look for Jàrawas on Rutland Island, but could not find any. Smoke was seen on the Cinque Islands, evidently from a camp of Öngés, but, unfortunately, the weather was so bad that it was impossible to cross over there in canoes, the only means of transit available.

Traces of Jàrawas were also seen in the southern jungle in this month. In December, parties searched in the southern and western jungles for Jàrawas without success.

In January, 1885, Colonel Cadell and I visited the North Sentinel and searched through the jungle without seeing any of the aborigines, who were as timid as ever. Presents were left for them, and their property was not molested.

On the 26th of March, two convicts who were hunting for pigs in the jungle near Ógra Báráij were murdered by the western tribe of Jàrawas. On the 29th, two large parties of Andamanese, convicts, and Police, were sent into the jungle from Milé Tilek, and Ógra Báraij, respectively, to search for the Jàrawas; and, accompanied by a third party, I proceeded with the *Port Blair* and the *Locust* to Kōīób-lá-tinga on the 30th.

On the arrival of the parties at my camp it was supposed, from their reports, that the Jàrawas had gone into the Tóra Két jungle, and I sent a large party to search that place.

This party returned to Kōīób-lá-tinga on the 7th of April with two Jàrawa women, whom they had caught in the Tóra Két hills. These women were elderly, and as I did not consider it of any use to bring them in to the Settlement I released them that evening. I sent Ápi, the little Jàrawa boy, back with them, but he only remained two days, and then came back to my camp, stating that, in his own country, he got nothing to eat.

He was very young, accustomed to our ways and food, and had almost forgotten his own language.

These women, like the others formerly caught in the southern jungle, did not seem to be alarmed, and were, if anything, exacting and quarrelsome. One of them, to his horror, took a great fancy to one of my Andamanese boys named " Mark," (who had his hair trimmed *à la* Jàrawa), and tried to persuade him to accompany her back to her home. I seconded her efforts, but nothing would induce Mark to stir.

They did not seem to recognise Ápi or to care about him, and made no effort to detain him with them.

They had pinched and ill-tempered faces, unlike the jolly round features generally seen among the Andamanese.

On the afternoon of the 31st of December, 1885, a party of Andamanese men and women who were returning to Duratáng after a pig hunt on the mainland were attacked by the Jàrawas at Játáng, and one woman was wounded in the side by an arrow. Our Andamanese ran away, dropping in their flight the pigs they had killed, and the Jàrawas took these and went back into the jungle.

The North Sentinel Island was surveyed by Captain Hobday and his party in March, 1886. None of the aborigines were seen.

In the heavy surf on the reef encircling the island a boat was upset and a Police constable of the guard was drowned.

In April I left the Jàrawa boy Ápi on the Little Andaman with Kógio Kāī, one of the Öngés, who seemed attached to him, but he did not thrive, and died there a few months afterwards of bronchitis. While in my house with the Öngé captives he had struck up a childish friendship with Eketi, an Ongé of about his own age, and I had hoped this might lead to good.

In January, 1887, I took a party of Öngés to the North Sentinel Island, which they seemed to know, and gave a name to. We searched for Jàrawas, the Ongés going alone, as I hoped they might recognise them or be able to speak to them, but Tómiti told me that he had come close to them and had heard them speak, but did not understand what they said, and thought they were not the same people as his tribe.

In December, 1887, a party of Andamanese were pig-hunting at Māī-i-leptu on the North-Western corner of the South Andaman.

One of their number, having fever, stopped to look after the canoe while the others were in the jungle. The sick man was wandering about on the shore when some Jàrawas came out and fired at him, hitting him with one arrow in the back. He fell on the sand and the Jàrawas ran up and hit him on the head with a piece of wood; he got up and ran away and was again shot at, being hit this time in the arm, and he would no doubt have been killed had not the other Andamanese come up most opportunely and driven off the Jàrawas. The wounded man eventually recovered after many months treatment in hospital. On the 7th of March, 1888, two self-supporting convicts of Mitha Khári village who had been cutting bamboos and hunting pigs in the jungle beyond Tusonabad, and were returning with a dead pig, were met by a party of Jàrawas. One convict had the sense to hide in the jungle, and saw the other run away pursued by the savages; he then came in to the Settlement and reported the occurrence. Nothing more was seen of the missing man or of the

Jàrawas, and an expedition which was at once sent in pursuit was unsuccessful.

In May two convicts who had escaped into the western jungle were caught near Milé Tilek and said that they had met with the Jàrawas, who had fired on them, wounding one of them in the foot, and killing a third convict who was with them. A party was sent to search for these Jàrawas, but after hunting from the Middle Straits to Port Campbell, and from there on to Milé Tilek, they returned, having seen several huts but none of the aborigines.

On the 13th of June at 6 A.M., a self-supporting convict, while looking at some vegetables in his garden in the village of Mutthra was shot at and killed. From an examination of the arrows it appeared that this murder had been committed by the Western Jàrawa tribe, and an expedition started into their country on the 15th. After searching in the jungle in very inclement weather, when owing to the heavy rain and the water lying on the ground tracking became nearly impossible, the party returned on the 24th having only seen the tracks of the Jàrawas, and not having been able to come up with them.

On the 29th of June a report was received by me that a convict watchman at Tytler's Ghat had heard a noise in the coconut trees there, and, on calling out, was wounded in the foot by an arrow, and saw some Andamanese running away. On the 30th a party was sent out to investigate the matter and it was found that the assault had been committed by a party of Jàrawas who had come up from the south.

On the 1st July an expedition was sent into the southern jungle to search for them, while I went in the *Ross* to the north end of Alexandra Island and searched along the coast.

On the 3rd the search parties joined me, those who came from Yáratán, on the north coast of MacPherson's Straits, having met with the Jàrawas and captured, while he was shooting fish on the shore at Biriwil-lá-lōīchera, at the south-west corner of the South Andaman, a full grown man, who was unhurt. I returned with him to Port Blair on the 4th, and a further search was made for the Jàrawas without success.

The captive appeared to me to talk a language akin to that spoken by the Öngés, so on the 7th an attempt was made to get him down to the Little Andaman. Owing to the very bad weather this was unsuccessful, but I took him down there on the 19th, and met several of the Öngés. As he seemed to get on with them I brought a few back to Port Blair with me, and the Jàrawa attached himself very much to these people, and particularly to Kógio Kāi, but, though they conversed all day long they did not seem to understand each other very well. Kógio Kāi admitted to me that the Jàrawa is an Öngé like himself, and not one of our Andamanese, but though most of the nouns and many of the verbs are the same in both their languages, yet there is a great difference of dialect, much the same indeed as that which exists between the Kédé and Cháriár Tribes.

All this would tend to prove that the Jàrawa tribe near Port Blair is an offshoot of the Öngés of the Little Andaman, but that the members of it have had no communication with the Öngés for some considerable period. The captive appears to have come with his tribe from the jungle west of the Settlement, crossed our clearings at Tytler's Ghat between the turtle tank and the coconut plantation, and entered the southern jungle on the hills south of Tytler's Ghat. From this, it would seem that the supposed two tribes of Jàrawas have never been separated even since the Settlement was opened, and would corroborate my remarks on this subject in my report for the year 1884-85, *viz.*, that there is only one tribe of Jàrawas who wander over both the western and the southern jungles.

On the 26th of July I took the Jàrawa and the Öngés in the *Ross* round the coast of the former's country, but he declined to give us any information regarding it. (He may not have known its appearance like this as he had never seen it from the sea.)

We remained out till the 28th, when, seeing that he would not or could not, tell me what I wanted to know, I returned to Port Blair.

Iké, as we had discovered his name to be, after living with me on good terms, and in good health, and having learnt a little Hindustani, was released on the 2nd of September, 1888. Accompanied by three Andamanese with whom he was accustomed to associate here, and was on friendly terms he was taken to Dhani Leaf Creek, from there on through the jungle to Manglután, and, as he evinced no desire to stop at either of these places, on to Táracháng. Here he was feasted by the Andamanese and given presents, and was then taken to Kōīób-lá-tinga. He did not seem to care for the northern jungles, so was brought back to Tytler's Ghat: here he recognised the coconut trees where he and his party fired on the watchman, and, leading the way, went south to the hills above Biriwil-lá-lōīchera. On arrival there he told the Andamanese with him to put down all his presents and to go away, and that he would look after himself, on which they left him.

He was in good health and spirits during the latter part of his captivity, had learnt a little Hindustani, understood something of our ways, was on very friendly terms with all our Andamanese, and on his departure was given everything he fancied, and we hoped that he would turn up again and that the kindness he had received had produced an impression on him.

Note.—Since writing the above he has been met in a Jàrawa camp, during a fight between the Jàrawas and our Andamanese; he stole all he could carry from our camp, and abused us in the Hindustani he had learned.—M. V. P.

Nothing more has ever been seen of him, and though presents were left in the same place in the following month at intervals, they were not taken, and there were no traces of Jàrawas in the southern jungle. It is probable they had crossed over into the western country.

Iké, though merry and very comical in his ways, was not intelligent, and like all the Éremtágas was cunning and timid without the pluck or ferocity of the Ár-*yaūtos*.

On one occasion, while at my house, he went out for a walk through the Aberdeen Bazaar and along the coast towards the Female Jail, through the coconut plantation, by himself, and without telling anyone that he was going. The Convict Petty Officer and the Andamanese in charge of him thought that he had run away and a great search and fuss was made. While this was going on he returned quietly and without their knowledge, and coming upstairs to me in my house, told me with great glee how everyone had been running about looking for him, and calling out "bhága," "bhága."

His hair was worn in a mop, no part of it being shaved or clipped, and the length showed that it could not have been cut for many months. He is the first Jàrawa I have seen with such long hair.

Although nothing further was seen of him after his release, the District Superintendent of Police informed me in November, 1888, that the Police Guard at Poi-Cháng-Jig, a forest station near Shoal Bay, had seen the Jàrawas there and had fired on them unprovokedly.

It is possible that Íké may have been with this party and may have been intending to come in with friendly overtures which this action on our part repelled. Under any circumstances the action of the Police is to be regretted, as it is of little use attempting to establish friendly relations with these people if they are fired on whenever they make their appearance in the Settlement.

On this occasion, had they been approached judiciously, it is quite possible that a friendly meeting might have been held, which would have led to subsequent friendly intercourse.

On the 10th of September, 1889, at about 6 A.M., a party of Jàrawas attacked some of the Port Mouat Andamanese, who had gone out to hunt turtle with a Convict Petty Officer, and having been up all night, were asleep in camp on the shore at Lekera about ten miles north of the outer harbour of Port Mouat.

The Jàrawas were first seen by one of our Andamanese, who instinctively took up his bow and arrows; on this the former fired, hitting an Andamanese man named Ira Terra in the thigh as he was lying down, the arrow completely penetrating the thigh and entering the stomach. A general fight seems to have ensued, both parties retiring in the end. There appears to have been no other motive for this attack than the mutual dislike and dread these tribes have for each other.

On the following day another party, consisting of two men and four boys of the same tribe of Jàrawas came upon a Burman pig hunter of the Northern District at Milé Tilek. They shot one of his dogs, stole the two pigs he had killed, and threatened to kill him, but he escaped. I sent out two parties to search for the Jàrawas, but they returned after ten days' absence in very inclement weather, without having seen any traces of them.

Ira Terra recovered from his wounds.

On or about the 10th of February, 1890, a party of Andamanese while proceeding up the west coast from Port Mouat to Port Campbell were attacked by Jàrawas near Tóra Két. An Andamanese man called "Joseph" was shot in the leg by them.

It appeared that the Jàrawas had been living on the west coast, having possibly been annoyed in their inland homes by a "must" elephant ("Napier"), whose tracks had been seen lately close by Jàrawa villages in the interior.

I sent out an expedition against these people, and meeting with them in the jungle near Port Campbell a fight ensued. A Jàrawa man was wounded, and by an accident a child was killed, an arrow, which was aimed at the man carrying it, striking it. A female child of about three years of age and unhurt was brought to the Settlement. I at once sent the parties back to try and capture some woman or man of the tribe in order that I might return this child to them but after a search of ten days they returned without having caught any one. The child remained in the Settlement and was adopted by an Andamanese woman, but after some months it sickened and died in hospital in August 1891.

A further expedition was sent to look for the Jàrawas in May 1890, but was unsuccessful.

On the 10th of August, 1890, I heard that some self-supporting convicts who were out pig hunting in the jungle, north-west of the Settlement, had been attacked by Jàrawas. One man had come in wounded and two others were missing.

On the 11th I sent a party of convicts and Andamanese to search the jungle from Anikhét to Port Campbell and from that harbour to Port Mouat, going round myself in the *Ross* on the 13th to meet them at Kōiób-lá-tinga. They returned on the 15th having found the body of a convict near Port Campbell riddled with arrows, but no traces of the Jàrawas, whom they believed had gone to the north.

The other missing man had returned to Port Blair in the meanwhile.

I further received information from the Andamanese that a party of them, when returning from Port Blair to Mount Kunu in July, had been fired on by the Jàrawas in the Middle Straits and that the latter had crossed the straits on a raft and were living in the jungle between the Middle and Homfray Straits.

I sent a party of convicts and Andamanese to examine the Báratán country for traces of Jàrawas; they saw an old hut and some footmarks but nothing recent, and thought they must have re-crossed the Middle Straits, so I landed the party at Páp-luntá-jig, on the south side of the Straits, with orders to search the Jàrawa hills from there to Port Blair. They returned after a few days having seen nothing.

It appeared that our extended clearings had driven the Jàrawas to the northern half of the South Andaman, and to the Báratán country, where, so far as we know, they had formerly never been, although there is a tradition of their once having lived there. Another party of Jàrawas reside permanently in the jungle between Port Campbell and Port Mouat, and the tribe would thus seem to have divided.

On the 10th of November, 1890, three self-supporting convicts of Kádaka-Cháng village were murdered by the Jàrawas in the jungle near their village. A party of Andamanese and convicts were sent in pursuit.

On the following morning three convict pig hunters of the Northern District were attacked by Jàrawas in the jungle near Anikhét, two being killed and one wounded. The tracks of three Jàrawas were found, and a large party of convicts and Andamanese were sent out after them. They traced them up to Port Campbell, where they were obliged to wait for more rations: they then crossed that harbour, and on the sand found the tracks of three men. When following these up three Jàrawas appeared on the sand in rear of them and fired: a fight ensued, in which one Andamanese, (Íra Jódo), who had most pluckily run in ahead of the others, was badly wounded, and two Jàrawas were killed: a third was wounded but made his escape into the jungle.

In the waistbelt of one of the dead men was found a dáh which was afterwards identified as the property of one of the pig hunters, who was murdered at Anikbét, and in all probability the Jàrawas killed were the murderers.

I think it likely that they had joined the remainder of their tribe who are believed to live in the hills north of Port Campbell, and a number of whom had camped near the Settlement at the time of the murders, and, if this is the case, the fact of their having committed these murders, and their subsequent death, would become known to the tribe from whom, it was hoped, we should not receive any further aggression, at least for a long time.

In December, 1890, I visited the North Sentinel Island, saw a few Jàrawas in the distance on the shore, and found some villages composed of new huts. The Sentinelese were, however, as timid as ever, and fled into the interior on our approach. Quantities of suitable presents were left in their huts and nothing of theirs was injured.

On the 7th of January, 1891, I received a report from the Northern Divisional Officer that a number of Jàrawas had shot at, and wounded in the mouth, a convict on the road near Bindrabun village.

I collected a party of Andamanese and convicts and despatched them on the 8th in search of the Jàrawas. They were absent till the 21st, having crossed to Port Campbell and from there worked through the jungle to Port Mouat. The footmarks of sixteen Jàrawas were seen near the Settlement, but these separated, and though on the banks of creeks traces of two or three were occasionally seen, none were met with or captured.

Some people in a canoe, taking rations for the party to Port Campbell, saw two Jàrawas in the distance on the shore near Tóra Bi, and the search party found in the adjacent jungle a large hut over forty feet in length.

In my Annual Report for 1890-91, I remark, with regard to the Jàrawas :—

"Were I able to get amongst these people, as I did at the Little Andaman, I have no doubt that in time friendly relations could be established with them, but it is hopeless to try and tame people whom one cannot even see. Few in number, they roam over a large tract of thick jungle, occasionally appearing on the coasts, or visiting the confines of the Settlement and murdering any convicts they may meet. When pursued, the tribe separates into parties of two or three, moving with great rapidity; and on the few occasions we have met with them the meeting has been accidental.

"The man "Íké" has never been seen since his return to his tribe, and though I was apparently on good terms with him, and he was well treated, the pleasures of civilisation have not proved sufficient to induce him either to return, or presumably to give any good report of us.

"The few Jàrawas we have caught in the last ten years, treated well, and returned to their tribe, have not had any effect on our relations with the others. The Jàrawa baby caught last year is still with us, though sickly, and has forgotten the little she ever knew of her own language. (She died in August 1891.)

"At the same time the present state of affairs is not without its advantages, and though I fear that the Jàrawas will continue for some time to be a source of annoyance to the Settlement, yet they will certainly shoot any runaway convict they may meet, and the knowledge of this acts, I think, as a deterrent to convicts who think of escaping.

"The Jàrawas appear to be retreating to the north as the Settlement is opened out, and are gradually occupying jungle which belonged to Septs of the Áka-*Béa*-da which are now extinct."

In November, 1891, when visiting the Islands after the cyclone, I saw a few Jàrawas on the beach at Tóra Bi. Owing to the heavy surf I was unable to approach or leave presents for them, and I fear these people must have suffered much during the storm, which passed over their country, destroying the jungle and rendering the forest impassable for many months afterwards.

On the 12th of November, 1892, a party of eight Andamanese went to Rutland Island to catch turtle. While there, two of their number came across a couple of Jàrawas in the jungle, who shot at, and slightly wounded, their dog, whereupon one man, named "Owen," fired an arrow in their direction which frightened them away. Nothing more was seen of them.

On the 1st of February, 1893, an Andamanese girl named "Bira," one of a party of eleven women living in the Brigade Creek Home, and engaged in collecting *pán* leaves in the adjacent jungle, got separated from the others, and in the evening was missed. A search was made for her, and on the 2ud, at about 11 A.M. her body transfixed by a Jàrawa arrow was found a few hundred yards from the Home.

Another similar arrow was sticking in a tree close to the body.

A party of Andamanese was sent on the evening of the 2nd in search of the Jàrawas, but after remaining seven days in the jungle, and having tracked the Jàrawas up the centre of the South Andaman to a point between Kyd Island and Port Campbell, they returned without having seen them. They stated that the jungle, since the cyclone, was almost impassable, and several of them were wounded by thorns, etc., in the search.

There appears to have been no reason for this murder. The Jàrawas thus come at intervals on the outskirts of the Settlement, murder in this manner any one they meet, and then retreat into their own jungle, where it is almost impossible to find them.

On the 16th of August, 1893, "Ríma," an Andamanese man from Homfray Strait, brought in the news to me that, about a month before, while four other Andamanese were pig-hunting in the jungle south of the eastern entrance to the Strait, two Jàrawas were seen, who had been attracted by the noise of the dogs.

These Jàrawas at once fired on our people, killing an old man named "Lípāīa," and wounding another man of the same name in the back (who subsequently died from the effects of the wound). Ríma fired one arrow in return, wounding a Jàrawa in the left shoulder, and then our people ran away. The dead men were buried on a small island at the entrance to the Strait.

On the 25th, an Andamanese man, named "Ría Chána," reported to me that, as he was coming through the Middle Straits in his canoe four days before, a single Jàrawa, who was shooting fish on the west bank opposite Rétin, fired at him, missing him. Ría Chána fired three arrows in return, missing the Jàrawa, who then decamped.

I had been aware for some time that, owing to the cyclone of November, 1891, having destroyed the jungle between Port Blair and the Middle Straits, that country had been rendered almost impassable; and that the Jàrawas, being driven out of their own country, had crossed the Straits at Rétin and were living on Báratán Island. An Andamanese of Lekera-luntá reported to me at this time that he had seen a Jàrawa village of seven huts on the hill near Ámit-lá-bōicho, and it would appear that these people have occupied both banks of the Middle Straits. Up to this time they had kept quiet, but now these attacks deterred our people from passing through the Straits or hunting in what is their own country. They further reported that, judging from the footmarks, there were a large number of Jàrawas: a village of seven huts would ordinarily accommodate seven married couples only, though on a pinch I have known about forty people live in the same number of huts.

On the 15th of September, 1893, while Lokala and Tótal, two Andamanese men, were out pig hunting near Ámit-lá-bōicho in Báratán Island, they came upon a party of Jàrawas who fired on them. Tótal escaped, but was so frightened that he lost his way in the jungle, and it was two days before he returned to his village of Lekera-luntá, bringing with him Lokala, who had been badly wounded in the right shoulder and in the lower part of the spine. They then came in to report to me, and Lokala was treated in Haddo Hospital by Dr. Gupta. He died on the 26th from his wounds.

The large iron head of one arrow was stuck in three of his vertebræ, and considerable force had to be used before it could be extracted. He was a great favourite with the Andamanese, who were much incensed at his murder; he has been further mentioned in the preceding Chapter as being the Government Agent in the Middle Andaman, and a most useful man to us.

It was considered necessary, therefore, on this occasion to make some sort of demonstration to overawe the Jàrawas and drive them out of a country to which they had no right, and in which they seemed unable to live at peace with the rightful owners.

On the 28th, I proceeded with a party of Police armed with rifles and buckshot cartridges, convicts, and 97 Andamanese, in the R.I.M.S. *Nancowry*, to Lekera-luntá, where 1 picked up 30 additional Andamanese. On my way there, in the Middle Straits, I left a party of Andamanese with a canoe, who were instructed to watch the Straits till my return in case any Jàrawas tried to cross.

On the 29th, parties, each about 30 strong, composed of Police, convicts, and Andamanese, were landed at the following places: the western mouth of Homfray Strait; Ópilémi, about half-way through that Strait; Géreng-tót-kāīcha, at the eastern mouth of the Strait (the place near which Lípāīa was killed about two months before, as noted above); at the southern end of Colebrooke Passage, and at Rógo-ló-cháng.

At the latter place I saw a fire on the beach, so left a party of Andamanese in a canoe to make enquiries and come on after me, while I proceeded in the *Nancowry* to Āūrol-kāīcha in the Middle Straits. All the parties had orders to return in three days to the Middle Straits, between Āūrol-kāīcha, and Rétin.

On the 30th I sent a party of Police, convicts, and Andamanese, to search the western shore of the Middle Straits, while I proceeded in the *Nancowry* to Ámit-lá-bōīcho. This party returned in the evening to Rétin, having only seen old footmarks of Jàrawas.

On the 1st of October a similar party made a search on the Eastern bank of the Strait, also without success. Four of the five parties returned that evening, only one of them, that which started from Géreng-tót-kāīcha, having seen the Jàrawas.

They stated that at 3 P. M. on the 30th, when near the head of Luru-jig, they came upon a large Jàrawa hut in which were about six people, dancing. A woman gave the alarm, the Jàrawas fired on our Andamanese just missing Tura Né, who fired back, the Police then fired in the air to frighten the Jàrawas and prevent a general fight, as they had been instructed to do, and the Jàrawas then ran away at such a pace as to preclude all chance of our people, who were tired with their long tramp, from catching them.

The Andamanese said they wounded two of the Jàrawas with their arrows, but the Police said they did not see any wounds inflicted.

In the hut were found Lokala's bow, arrows, and knife, and the sight of these enraged the Andamanese so much that they burnt the huts down. Some sort of punishment was thus inflicted on those Jàrawas, who were probably to blame, and they would be frightened and more careful for a month or two. I expected that they would recross the Middle Straits, and return to their own country, but as a precautionary measure I warned the Andamanese to hunt on Báratán Island in large parties only.

In the hut was also found a brass *karrahie*, probably formerly the property of some runaway convict whom the Jàrawas had shot. The number on it was illegible.

On the 2nd of October the remaining party from Rógo-ló-cháng returned. They had seen the remains of a Jàrawa camp on the shore with a fire and the bones of a pig, but though they had followed up the tracks for three days they saw no one.

On the 3rd I returned to Port Blair. The weather during the whole time had been very inclement, with continued and heavy rain but the Police and convicts worked well and without a grumble, beating through the country carefully, though the cooked rations they took were sodden and uneatable the first day, they had no shelter from the rain at night and got little sleep, and the leeches were unusually numerous, most of the men coming in with their feet badly bitten and swollen.

On the 15th of October a further party of 22 Andamanese and eight convicts was sent to Báratán. They were joined by 50 more Andamanese at Mount Kunu, and searched through the country for Jàrawas till the end of the month but without success.

It appeared that, as I anticipated, the Jàrawas were so frightened at the expedition sent against them after Lokala's death that they recrossed the Middle Straits on a raft, which was found and broken up, and returned to their old haunts in the hills north of Port Campbell.

In November, a search was made for them in the whole of the country between Port Mouat and Cape Bluff, but no traces of them were seen.

On the 24th of February, 1894, I proceeded to Portman Bay in a lighter, as I was anxious to find out more about the Jàrawa tribe on Rutland Island. These people have no canoes, live in the interior, and, in former times were said to be numerous. I found several of their villages, some containing as many as sixteen huts, and from their tracks am of opinion that they do not live altogether, but go about in parties of from eight to ten in number.

On the 3rd of March, a boy of my party was collecting honey in the jungle near my camp when he came upon two adult male Jàrawas sitting by a fire. One of them was armed with a dáh, probably obtained from some runaway convict, whom he had shot. The Jàrawas rose to attack the boy, who fired an arrow at them in self-defence, wounding one in the shoulder. They then made off.

On the same day I came upon a party of eight Jàrawas of both sexes while I was going up a creek. My party showed no hostility but the Jàrawas ran away, and, as they were running through a mangrove swamp, I could not get up to them.

On the 4th a party of Andamanese met four adult male Jàrawas fully armed, near my camp. Neither side showed any hostility, and after a few minutes the Jàrawas ran away.

My object was, by moving parties of Andamanese about in the Jàrawa country with strict orders not to show any hostility to the Jàrawas, to accustom the latter to our presence. Eatables, and such articles as they are likely to value, were left in their villages, and none of their property was touched; by such means I am in hopes that friendly relations may be established, as they will learn that we do not molest them, and our advent means to them a supply of the articles they most require.

This policy has since been continued on Rutland Island, but so far without any effect. It is one, however, from which satisfactory results can only be expected after it has been in force for several years. I received news during this month that some of the Jàrawas had crossed Homfray Strait and were living in the interior of the Middle Andaman near Yéretil. We were aware that they had crossed the Middle Straits and had occupied Báratán, which is otherwise almost uninhabited, but this new move on their part into the most frequented portion of the Middle Andaman will be certain to lead sooner or later to a collision between them, and the Āūkāū-Jūwöi and Puchik-wár Tribes, to whom the country belongs.

I endeavoured to impress upon the Andamanese there that the Jàrawas should not be fired on except in actual self-defence, and that, if possible, youths of the tribe should be caught and brought to me, when I might have some chance of influencing them.

In March, two Jàrawas were seen by a party of Andamanese on the shore at Port Campbell, but no fight occurred.

During this month, I visited the North Sentinel Island and left presents in their huts for the aborigines, but did not see any of them.

In my Annual Report for 1893-94, I remark:—

"Our only chance of becoming acquainted with the Jàrawas, who at present appear to be hopelessly hostile, is by capturing some of the young men, as was done with the Öngés of the Little Andaman, and keeping them apart until they are really friendly. At present any meeting between them and the other Andamanese ends in a fight, and I have, therefore, instructed the latter in the Middle Andaman to capture such Jàrawas as they may meet, if possible without wounding them, and to bring them in to me.

"Every effort will be made during the current year to become better acquainted with them, but it is very difficult to capture them, even when they are seen, which is seldom; to hunt for them without any certain clue to their whereabouts is useless."

During April, 1894, a party of Andamanese were kept on Rutland Island, but none of the Jàrawas were met with.

In May, some Jàrawas were seen on the western coast of the Middle Andaman near Flat Island, and some others came out on the southern side of the eastern entrance to the Middle Straits. These two places are about thirty miles apart, and it would appear that the Jàrawas have divided into at least three parties, the third living in the jungle south of Port Campbell. They were as timid and hostile as ever, and efforts made by the Andamanese to approach them were unsuccessful. Andamanese again searched Rutland Island for Jàrawas, but found none.

On the 22nd of August, 1894, I received a report from a party of Andamanese who had been turtle hunting on the west coast, that on the 19th they were in camp in Port Campbell, and while they were cooking a pig in their hut just inside the jungle on the sea-coast, one of their number, Wóloga Jerra-bud, had gone out on the beach to pluck some leaves, when he met a single adult male Jàrawa, who at once shot him through the right lung with a pig-arrow. Wóloga screamed, staggered back to the hut, and fell dead. The Jàrawa ran away, and nothing more has been seen of him or his tribe.

This murder was entirely unprovoked, as Wóloga was unarmed at the time, and it can only be attributed to the inveterate hostility of the Jàrawas to all strangers, a hostility caused by ignorance and timidity. On the 24th I sent a party of 16 convicts and 38 Andamanese with instructions to follow the Jàrawa tracks, and, if possible, catch some. They tracked from the place where Wóloga was murdered, and on the side of a hill in the interior found a large hut resembling those in the Little Andaman.

Two women were seen who ran away at the approach of the party, and in the hut was found an axe evidently procured from some runaway convict whom the Jàrawas had murdered. Nothing else was seen, and worn out by the bad weather the party returned. More Andamanese were sent to Rutland Island in pursuance of my policy of accustoming the Jàrawas to their presence there, but none of the latter were seen.

On the 16th of October, 1894, I sent a party of convicts and Andamanese to hunt for the Jàrawas in the western jungle. A village was found north of Port Campbell, and one male Jàrawa was seen, who fired on our party and ran away. None of our Andamanese, who were very tired, could catch him.

On the 5th of November, I sent a party to look for Jàrawas in the northern part of the South Andaman. They were absent for a fortnight, and on their return reported that they had seen a single male Jàrawa on the shore at Breakfast Bay. He bolted into the jungle, and gave the alarm to the others who made off. Our people pursued them for a week, but did not come up with them.

Three new villages and two old ones were seen, and the Jàrawas are believed to have crossed the Middle Straits again, and gone to live in Báratán.

A party of them has been again seen on the shore near Flat Island, on the west coast of the Middle Andaman.

On the 17th of this month, Moung Yu, the collector of edible birds' nests, was passing in his boat under the cliff on the south-east corner of Rutland Island when he was hailed by the Jàrawas from the top.

They appeared to be more friendly, but waved him away when he turned his boat towards the shore. He had the sense not to land or annoy them in any way.

I have known for some years that the Jàrawas have a village on the top of this cliff, and have often left presents in it. There is a beautiful view from it, and the Jàrawas are able to see what the Öngés are doing when they visit the Cinque Islands, which are opposite and only two miles distant; they can also see the Port Blair Mail Steamer, and other vessels which pass through Manners Straits, at which they must be mightily puzzled and astonished.

A few days after Moung Yu passed I visited the village, which consisted of eight huts, and had apparently been abandoned about four days before I came. Nothing in it was disturbed, and a large quantity of eatables and other suitable presents was left.

During February, March, April, and May, parties of Andamanese were kept on Rutland Island.

The North Sentinel Island was visited on the 15th of February, 1895, and I took some Öngés over there from the Cinque Islands, as I had learnt at their camp there that one of them was a Sentinelese, who had, some years before, left the North Sentinel in a canoe and come across, *viâ* Rutland Island, to the Cinque Islands and the Little Andaman.

After a search on the 15th and 16th on the coasts of the Island, some of the inhabitants were seen near the north-west point in a canoe; though called to by the Öngés, and by their own countryman, whom we had brought with us, they showed the usual signs of fright and hostility, and as we did not wish to provoke an encounter, the search party returned without getting close to them.

From my very slight knowledge of the Öngé language, it is quite likely that I misunderstood the supposed Sentinelese, and he may either have been driven away from the Sentinel in a storm, possibly as a child, and have been adopted by the Öngés when he reached them on the Cinque Islands, (the adults with him being killed), or there may really be occasional intercourse either between the Sentinel Jàrawas and those on Rutland Island, or between the former and the Öngés.

It was interesting to note that, unlike their behaviour when in the jungles of the Great Andaman, the Öngés on each occasion that they have been to the North Sentinel, have taken the lead in searching the forest for Jàrawas, and seemed to have no fear of them.

On the 15th of March three Burmese self-supporting convicts of Cadellganj village, who were in the jungle pig hunting about two miles north-west of that village, were surprised by Jàrawas. One who was carrying a dead pig was wounded in the wrist by an arrow, and dropping the pig turned and saw two Jàrawas, when he ran in at once to the Settlement. On a search being made on the two following days the dead bodies of the two other convicts were found riddled with arrows.

From the fact that the body of the pig was also found, I imagine that the Jàrawas fled back to their camp immediately after the murder.

Nothing has been heard of them since.

Owing to the Andamanese having been sent away from the Settlement on account of an epidemic of measles having broken out, I was not able to send any on the tracks of these Jàrawas for some days, and those who did go on the 18th did not find anything. News of the occurrence was, however, at once sent to the distant stations where the Andamanese were, and search was then made; numbers of Jàrawa tracks were seen, but none of the people were met with.

At this time of the year water is scarce, and our Andamanese, who are not acquainted with the Jàrawa country, are not able to go out for long on account of the want of water.

The Chief Commissioner and I went to Port Campbell and saw the Andamanese there on the 22nd. We impressed on them the necessity of really searching for the Jàrawas, and threatened to stop their supplies if they did not do this work. They however did very little, and I stopped their supplies till the commencement of the rains.

On the 27th, a party of Andamanese whom as we passed we had seen coming off towards the steamer from the south end of Rutland Island, as if wishing to speak to us (though we did not stop), arrived from that Island.

In the morning they tried to hail us they had caught in a village in the interior two elderly Jàrawas, a man and a woman. These two were the only Jàrawas in the village, and were caught without a fight, and unwounded.

This is the first time any of the Rutland Island Jàrawas have been caught since July, 1884, at which period we were not friendly with the Ongés. I was anxious, therefore, to take our two captives to the Little Andaman at once, in the hope that the Ongés, who are certainly the most nearly allied tribe to the Jàrawas, might be able to converse with them and thus establish friendly relations. A vessel was not however available, and as the Jàrawas, particularly the old man, began to pine and sicken, both developing a nasty cough, and as there was a fear that they would catch the measles, I was obliged to send them back with a quantity of presents to their own home, on the 31st.

Though we were not able to do much with them, yet they had been well treated since their capture, had not been wounded in any way, and had been given many presents; so I hope the account they gave of us to their fellow-tribesmen may not have been a very bad one.

While in my house the man, who was surly and evil-tempered, kept begging my Andamanese to kill him by throttling him or cutting his throat, and rejected all overtures of friendship. His wife appeared, to be more friendly, and was pleasant looking, but when she was willing to make friends with us her husband abused and beat her, and once tried to kill her when she went away for a short distance with an Andamanese woman, being only prevented from doing so by his guards.

Both in personal appearance, and in their weapons and ornaments, they resembled the Ongés. They talked rapidly and indistinctly to each other, and I did not recognise any of the words they used.

On being taken down to be released they tried to escape at Chiriya Tápu, as if they knew the place (or hoped to cross to Rutland Island from there); they evinced the greatest delight when they arrived in Portman Bay, singing and talking, and pointing out the different places where their huts were. They were taken to the hut where they had been caught and left in it, surrounded by presents of eatables and weapons. On their way to it they pointed out the road to the Andamanese who were escorting them, danced and sang, and seemed to be quite pleased and friendly.

It must be remembered that these Jàrawas hailed Moung Yu in a friendly way in November, 1894, and were not interfered with in any way.

In my Annual Report for the year 1894-95, I remark :—

" I am of opinion that the only way to catch the Jàrawas will be by sending out armed parties of Police and convicts, as was done on former occasions when they have been caught, and using our Andamanese merely as trackers, as they are too afraid of the Jàrawas to make any real effort to catch them when alone and unsupported by firearms. There are very few Andamanese now alive who are acquainted with the Jàrawa country, and those few are old. The jungle, too, has, since the cyclone of 1891, been almost impassable, and in any attempt to capture them, the Jàrawas have in every way the advantage of us, nor do I think that, except by some lucky chance, any capture will be made.

" A party of armed Burmese or other convicts, who are accustomed to living in the jungle, assisted by good Andamanese, and well supplied with rations, might, by getting on the track of the Jàrawas and keeping them continually on the move, wear them out; as whereas our party would be fed, the Jàrawas would not have leisure to provide food for themselves, and, as they store nothing, must soon be worn out by hunger."

In April, 1895, the Andamanese at Port Campbell made several short expeditions into the Jàrawa country without success. They stated that they had seen a big Jàrawa man, who was living away from his tribe with only his wife and children in the jungle near Tóra Bi.

In May, 1895, a party of 24 Andamanese, with Police, and selected Burmese convicts (as recommended above) was accordingly sent out to search for Jàrawas.

They were divided into two parties, one of which entered the jungle at Constance Bay, and the other on the west coast opposite Butáng. They both searched up to Port Campbell, where a supply of rations had been sent for them, and then by different routes came back to Port Mouat. The Jàrawas were seen, but managed to get away before the party could come up to them.

They stated that the jungle was still much broken and matted with rubbish, and the march was a very trying one; many of the Andamanese who went, including the leaders of both parties, were in hospital for some weeks after their return.

Major Temple, the Chief Commissioner, decided, on this, to have broad tracks cut in different directions through the Jàrawa country, so that a body of men with their rations could march swiftly and without inconvenience into the very heart of the forest, and form depôts there from which they could search in every direction.

In March, 1896, three Jàrawas fired at some convicts of the Forest Department who were working in the jungle near Milé Tilek, wounded one man and killed another. Three parties were sent in search of them, and they were tracked to a small new village of three huts on the side of Mount Chulnga, after which all trace of them was lost.

The parties found many old huts (which the Jàrawas are said to inhabit during the rainy season) on the coast between Port Campbell and Port Mouat, and none of these huts have been touched, as I am anxious that the Andamanese should learn where the Jàrawas reside, in order that, instead of aimlessly tracking them, they can go round from village to village till they find one which shows signs of habitation, and then track from there; this plan will save much unnecessary labour and keep the men fresher for their work.

On the 30th of March, 1896, the North Sentinel Island was again visited, and the corpse of a Hindu was found at the water's edge near the southern landing place, pierced in several places by arrows, and with its throat cut. On a further search being made, bundles of bamboos tied together with cane, which had evidently formed part of a bamboo raft, where seen stuck in the bushes on the shore, and some clothing bearing the numbers of three convicts was in the sea.

Enquiry showed that three convicts had escaped from Bája-Jágda on the 18th of March, and having made a bamboo raft, probably in Constance Bay, had drifted across to the North Sentinel, arriving there probably on the 27th of March. The raft had been smashed in the heavy surf that beats on the fringing reef, and it is likely that two of the convicts were then drowned; the third, after reaching the shore, had been killed by the Sentinelese.

A new village of eight huts was found by my search party on the east coast, and near the southern landing place were two temporary encampments, not of huts but of leaf beds merely, one on the beach containing ten beds, the same number of glowing fires, and the marks where four canoes had been hauled up; and one on the hill to the west containing four beds. The aborigines had been living there when the *Elphinstone* arrived, and, on seeing her anchor, had fled to the northward. None of them were found, but presents were left in different places. It is evident from the above that the crew of a small native craft wrecked on the Sentinel would be murdered by the savages, and even in the case of a wreck with many people, any stragglers who might go into the forest to search for water, etc., would be cut off and killed. Firearms are the only useful defence against them, and with these a small party could easily protect themselves.

This occurrence, the corpse of the Hindu having been seen by convicts of our party, will give the convicts in Port Blair to understand that there is a tribe of hostile savages on the Island who will murder all who land there, and the knowledge of this may deter those who wish to escape from doing so, in that direction at least.

Having summarised all that has occurred between the Jàrawas and ourselves, we have now to consider how these people are to be brought on friendly terms with us, or, if this cannot be done, in what manner they should be treated.

As regards the Jàrawas on the North Sentinel Island, if the Government decide to convert the whole Island into a coconut plantation, for which it is admirably adapted by nature; or if, for scientific or other reasons, it is considered that the aborigines should be tamed, then the Officer in charge of the Andamanese should take a steam launch, a lighter with water tanks, a sailing cutter, and some Andamanese canoes over there in the month of February, anchor them in the lagoon on the south side of the Island, and remain there for about two months. He should take with him Andamanese, convicts, Police, and a good number of Öngés, including the man mentioned above who is supposed to be a Sentinelese, whose name is Dàūwacho-chégálé-bāī, and who lives at Támbe-Ébui.

Search parties should go through the jungle and catch some of the male Jàrawas unhurt, and should keep them in the camp, taking them out turtle catching, and feeding them on turtle, yams, and such food only as they are accustomed to in their own homes. They should be given presents, and half the number caught should, after a few days, be allowed to return to their villages; if the Öngés could accompany them, so much the better.

If others do not come in willingly with the Öngés, they must be captured, and this procedure must be persevered in until the majority of the people on the island have spent some days in the camp, are accustomed to us, and find they are well fed and not injured. No attempt should be made to take them away from the Island. In this way we might get on a friendly footing with some of them, and the Island should thereafter be visited whenever possible, presents of turtles, and such other articles as they value (iron, arrows, yams, plantains, files, knives, and Andamanese adzes), being left in their huts. In the dry weather these people generally live on the edge of a marsh in the north-west corner of the island.

A similar policy might be pursued with regard to the Jàrawas on Rutland Island, who have not been much molested by us.

In this case it would be as well to facilitate the transport of rations, etc., if a broad track was cut through the jungle from Portman Bay to Wood-Mason Bay, and from the middle of this track another should be cut down the centre of the island to the south coast.

The Jàrawas chiefly inhabit the southern half of Rutland Island, and have villages in the jungle of the south-eastern and south-western hills.

With the Jàrawas of the Great Andaman circumstances are different. In the case of the North Sentinel and Rutland Island, we have a somewhat open jungle, and Islands which the Jàrawas will not leave, and where, after a time, they can be found; but on the Great Andaman there is nothing to prevent their going from Mac-Pherson's Straits to Port Cornwallis, and no doubt, as the other aborigines become extinct, and our Settlement and Forest operations spread, they will move farther and farther to the north.

When the Settlement was first opened in 1858, the Jàrawas occupied the interior of the South Andaman to perhaps as far north as Port Campbell, and it would then have been comparatively easy, with the assistance of such men as Méba Mót, who were on good terms with them, and accustomed to go to their villages, to establish friendly relations with them, for they were less hostile and ferocious than the Áka-*Béa*-da, and were only timid. Now their timidity has grown into bitter enmity and hostility against all comers, and they shoot every stranger they see whatever his colour may be.

At the time of their murder of the convicts of the Forest Department in March, 1896, persons who were unacquainted with the nature of the Andaman jungles, or the habits of the savages, talked about exterminating them, (a step directly in opposition to the declared policy of the Government of India, as before shown in this work), and of driving them out of the Island, or of capturing them by means of parties of Police and convicts, or even of Gurkha soldiers, as was suggested!

I consulted Brigadier-General Cummins, who was in the Settlement at the time, as the capture of Chin rebels and Burmese dacoits was instanced in favour of the above proposals, and he was of opinion that they were absurd, and could not possibly be carried out successfully.

Andamanese have no baggage, have no paths through the jungle, which is very dense and matted, can cross mangrove swamps faster than any other people can follow them, and can go by night as well as by day, swimming the broad creeks and leaving no trail. They travel, also, at a speed which no other person can hope to compete with, at least for long. In order to tame them, they must be caught, and it is this catching which is so difficult. Tracks are being cut through the Jàrawa country, and friendly Andamanese will move about there, visiting the different villages and endeavouring to meet with them, though such meeting will only take place by chance, and will then catch them if they can, as they have done in the past.

Once caught, they might be kept with the Officer in charge of the Andamanese until they are to a certain extent tamed, and learn a little Hindustani; they might also be taught to smoke, thus establishing a craving which intercourse with us can alone satisfy; and when the Öngés come up to the Cinque Islands, they might, accompanied by a party of our Andamanese, be sent there to live amongst them for weeks or even months. Their languages being allied, and their weapons, ornaments, etc., being in many instances the same, more is to be hoped for from the Öngés' influence than from anything else.

Possibly, after this treatment, some of them, if returned to their own homes, might be the means of inducing the others to become more friendly. The principal difficulty, after they have been caught, in carrying out the above policy, is, that in captivity, the Jàrawas sicken and die.

Until this is effected, if it ever is, we must be prepared for attacks on the convicts working in the jungles, and also on our friendly Andamanese, who, no matter what they may be told, will always fire on a Jàrawa when they meet him, from fear.

The only partial protection which can be afforded to gangs of convicts working in the jungle is for them to be accompanied by Police, who should at intervals of a quarter of an hour fire two shots, one half a minute after the other. A single shot might attract attention, but be disregarded when no further sound was heard, the second shot would warn the Jàrawas (who would of course be on the alert and listening when they heard the first), that we were about, and they would flee.

Very little is known of the customs of the Jàrawas, and an investigation of these would, from a scientific point of view, be most valuable. Their isolation in small bodies in the interior, or on such a small island as the North Sentinel, would lend additional interest to the research, and it is evident from what little we do know, that the Ár-*yaüto* and Éremtága grouping exists among them, for the Sentinelese and the Öngés have canoes and catch turtle, whereas the Jàrawas of the Great Andaman cannot even swim, and neither they, nor the Rutland Island people have canoes, so far as we know at present.

CHAPTER XIX.

The Little Andaman—The *Assam Valley* expedition—Telegrams—Instructions—H. M. S. *Sylvia's* visit—Visit of the *Kwang Tung*—Lieutenant Duncan's report—Mr. Homfray's report—Further expedition ordered—Major Dakeyne's orders—Lieutenant Much's despatch—Additional papers—Dr. Douglas's report—Wilson's report—Orders of the Government—General Stewart's visits, and reports—Captain Wimberley's report on his expedition—Orders of the Government—Remarks by General Stewart—Further visit, and remarks—Further visits—Hostility—Visit to Hut Bay—Treachery of the Öngés—Mr. Godwin-Austen's visit, and report—Mr. Man's visit, and report—Another visit, less hostility shown—Öngés on the Cinque Islands—Fight at Jackson Creek—Öngé captured—Eight Öngés on the Cinque Islands—Öngés captured—Öngé captives who survived were tamed—Found to be from the Little Andaman, and released there.

OUR attention was first drawn, after our present occupation of the Andamans, to the Little Andaman Island, in 1867. Dr. Mouat did not visit it in 1857, during his tour round the Andamans in search of a suitable spot for a Penal Settlement, as he was aware that no harbour existed there, and after the founding of the Settlement nothing had occurred to call for a visit to it.

In April, 1867, Major Nelson Davies, Secretary to the Chief Commissioner of British Burma, was at the Andamans on a visit of inspection, when the following telegrams which had passed between the Firms of Messrs. Bulloch Brothers at Akyab, and Rangoon, were delivered to him on the 6th of April, by post, per S. S. *Arracan* which had been sent from Rangoon to bring him back there.

(It should be remembered that there neither was then, nor is now, telegraphic communication with the Andamans, and all such messages are despatched to those Islands by post from the last telegraph station, at Rangoon, Calcutta, or Madras.)

      Telegram, dated 5th April, 1867.
  From—Messrs. Bulloch Brothers, Akyab,
  To—Messrs. Bulloch Brothers, Rangoon.

Assam Valley arrived under charge of Chief Officer on 21st, at noon. Captain and seven of the crew went ashore on the south end of Little Andaman Island to cut a spar, were seen to land and haul up the boat; an hour afterwards a crowd of natives were seen on the beach dancing. No Europeans were seen afterwards. The ship hovered about till Saturday evening, 23rd, and came on here. Report to authorities."

Telegram, dated 6th April, 1867.

From—Messrs. Bulloch Brothers, Akyab,
To—Messrs. Bulloch Brothers, Rangoon.

"The bearings of the spot where the Captain and crew of the *Assam Valley* landed are on the south end of Little Andaman Island, south-east point bearing east half north, south-west point bearing west by north; a sandy beach, quite bold, with a large rock close to the water's edge. Mate has a Master's certificate."

Major Davies forwarded these telegrams to Major B. Ford, the Superintendent of Port Blair, with a remark that it was probable that the whole party of Europeans had been murdered by the Andamanese, but if any had escaped they must be very badly off for provisions.

He directed that the Station Steamer, *Kwang Tung*, should be at once despatched to the spot indicated in the telegram, and that Mr. Homfray, with such Andamanese as he might think useful to him, should accompany the Commander, also that an armed force of such strength as the Superintendent might deem sufficient, should be sent.

Major Davies added :—

"The first object will be to endeavour to recover the missing men, or trace what has become of them, and every caution should be taken by the exploring party to guard against a surprise by the natives. No vengeance should be taken on the aborigines unless proof of the murder of some of the Europeans be clearly established."

At the time of the receipt of these tidings the *Kwang Tung* was absent at the North Andaman with Mr. Homfray, who was looking for the wreck of the *Baillie Nicol Jarvie*, which was supposed to have been lost on the Andamans during a cyclone, and regarding which there was a rumour, that the captain and his wife were being kept in captivity by the Andamanese.

H. M. S. *Sylvia*, (a surveying vessel) however, happened to be in Port Blair, Commander Brooker having called for coals and provisions on his way from England, *viá* Trincomali, to the Corea, on particular service. Twelve hours after the receipt of the news regarding the *Assam Valley* on the night of the 16th, Commander Brooker went down to the Little Andaman. He found that it was impossible to land at the spot mentioned in the telegram on account of the heavy surf; but saw from the boat a coil of rope and a sailor's blue cap lying on the beach. He fired three rockets over the island, and coasted up the eastern side in the hope of obtaining a landing, but without success. Nothing was seen of the missing men, and only a few Andamanese huts, the aborigines from which came out on the shore after the boat was withdrawn. The *Sylvia* returned to Port Blair on the evening of the 18th.

On the 18th the *Kwang Tung* returned to Port Blair, and was at once despatched to the Little Andaman, which she reached on the 19th. Mr. Homfray had been directed to endeavour to get into communication with the aborigines in a conciliatory manner, but was told that if he took any presents for them he was to defer the distribution of these until some result had been obtained from the search. If he found that any violence had been offered to the Europeans, then, of course, no presents were to be given.

No prisoners were to be taken unless hostility was shown, nor were any to be detained or brought away, unless sufficient evidence of violence to, or the murder of, the people of the *Assam Valley* was found. Mr. Homfray states that he took with him Andamanese from the Rutland Island, the Port Blair, and the Port Mouat Septs, and on his way down to the Little Andaman they named all the Islands to him and told him stories of their adventures on them. The Rutland Islanders claimed that the Cinque and Passage Islands belonged to them, and stated that they frequently went there to catch turtle. At times they encountered the people from the Little Andaman there, but generally succeeded in driving them back to the

Brothers Islands, which appeared to be their legal northern limit. They gave Mr. Homfray a most terrifying account of these people, whom they called "Jurrah-wallahs."

(For convenience sake, when writing of them, they will be called by their own name for themselves, "Ongés," although this name was not known until 1886; otherwise they may be confused with the Jàrawas mentioned in the previous Chapter.)

On arriving at the rock mentioned in the telegram, the Commander of the *Kwang Tung* (Lieutenant Duncan, R. N. R.,) despatched two cutters under the command of the Second Officer, with Mr. Homfray and some Andamanese. This party failed to effect a landing on account of the surf, the very Andamanese not being able to swim on shore. Several aborigines were seen on the beach, but none came to where the boats were. The weather looked threatening, so the boats were recalled and the *Kwang Tung* stood to sea for the night.

On the morning of the 20th she again steamed to the same spot, and three boats were despatched to the shore, but, owing to the heavy south-west swell, landing was found to be impossible. Some of the Andamanese again attempted to swim through the surf, and nearly lost their lives in doing so.

Lieutenant Duncan then steamed round the south-east end of the island, and anchored in a bay six miles to the northward. Seeing three large huts on the beach, and there being but little surf, a landing was attempted. On Sunday morning (the 21st) three boats were despatched from the ship; the party effected a landing, and the boats were backed into deep water, but no sooner were the party separated from their boats than numbers of aborigines were seen to be collecting with the intention of cutting them off. On seeing this the ship's party retreated towards the boats, but, before they could embark, a shower of arrows was fired at them wounding two of the Settlement Naval Brigade men. The ship's party fired to cover the retreat; the savages followed the men to the beach, and while they were wading through the water to reach the boats, the natives knelt on the water's edge and fired until dispersed by a volley from the boats.

Lieutenant Duncan reported that Petty Officer Cooper behaved very well in this skirmish. He considered the Öngés to be most hostile, and thought that the missing men from the *Assam Valley* were probably dead. The *Kwang Tung* returned to Port Blair on the 21st.

Mr. Homfray's account of the Little Andamanese is as follows :—

In the South Bay of the Little Andaman he saw four encampments at distances of two miles apart, with crowds of men round them, and thick smoke issuing from their huts. He went to the shore in a boat with some Andamanese who insisted on taking their bows and arrows. They hid them in the bottom of the boat and advised him to be very careful, as they said the Öngés were very treacherous, and would show no mercy to any one they caught.

Mr. Homfray adds that they spoke a different language from our friendly Andamanese, that no one could communicate with them, and that the only thing to do was to land with a very strong force of soldiers and conquer them, as an attack from them could not be avoided.

On approaching the shore the Öngés hid themselves, and owing to the heavy surf his party could not land. For an hour they hailed the Öngés, showing presents, and then Lieutenant Duncan recalled the boats. The next day they made another attempt to land, which also failed owing to the surf. Three Andamanese swam ashore with a line to which was attached two life buoys, and two more swam alone. They took their bows and arrows and fired shots in the air as they swam. (Was this Mr. Homfray's idea of approaching the aborigines in a conciliatory manner ?) The Öngés hid in the jungle. The surf knocked our five men about and stunned one by a blow on a rock ; the others saved him from being drowned and returned to the boats, and the party then went round to Hut Bay and landed opposite an encampment. There were a large number of savages moving about there whom they hailed, and presents were held up. The Öngés, however, seemed to want to trap our party into the jungle and then cut them off. After an hour they disappeared, and the beach was searched for traces of the missing men of the *Assam Valley*.

Again some Öngés appeared at the encampment and Mr. Homfray went towards them. The majority hid as he approached and only two came out, enticing him into the jungle as he advanced. A creek was between them, and Mr. Homfray was on the point of crossing it when he saw eight men in his rear creeping up with bows and arrows in their hands. Three Marine Service men, two stokers, and Māia Biala, the Chief of Rutland Island, were with him at the time. They all retreated to the boats; the Öngés followed and were within ten yards of Mr. Homfray when he reached the sea. He hailed them and made signs that he would give them presents, but they advanced, levelling their bows, and after several discharges of arrows by which two Marine Service men were wounded, one in the calf and the other in the finger, the party got into the boats, firing into the jungle and thus frightening the Öngés away. The Andamanese who were with our party had first swum off to the boat, got their bows and arrows, and two of them fired on the Öngés and checked them.

Mr. Homfray states that he took some Andamanese women and children with him in order to make friends with the Öngés, and adds that "he had them all naked in order that there might be no mistake about who they were."

He thought that the Öngés showed traces of intercourse with the Nicobarese from the shape of their huts, thus continuing an old fiction from the same point of view as that from which it originated, as when closely examined the huts of the Öngés are found to have only a superficial resemblance to those of the Nicobarese.

Mr. Homfray noticed that the bows of the Öngés were inferior to those of the Áka-*Béa*-da, and that the former were very bad shots He adds in his report a variety of speculations regarding them which are of no value and need not be recorded here, being entirely incorrect.

Major Davies, not considering that the result of the above expedition was satisfactory, and wishing that a more decided opinion should be arrived at regarding the fate of the crew of the *Assam Valley*, and that the Öngés should, if necessary, be punished, addressed Major

Ford on the subject. The latter directed that the I. G. S. *Arracan*, which had come to take away Major Davies, should be sent to the Little Andaman. Captain Barrow was in command of this vessel, and her officers were Mr. Dunn and Mr. Eastwood. Mr. Homfray was sent with some Andamanese, and a small Military force was also despatched, composed of Lieutenant W. L. Much, of the Second Battalion of the 24th Regiment, in command, ten men of that regiment, seven Naval Brigadesmen, and eight Madras Sappers. Dr. Douglas was in medical charge of the party, and Lieutenant Glassford a young officer of the 9th B. N. I., who had only arrived in the Settlement a few days before the expedition started, volunteered to come as a passenger. He had come to Port Blair in command of the company of his regiment which was acting as a guard over the convicts in the ship *Mandalay* from Bombay.

Captain W. J. Dakeyne, commanding the troops in Port Blair, issued the following instructions to the party:—

"Supposing the surf admits of a landing being made;

"The officer must distribute his men in three parties, two for landing and attack, the third remaining in the boats to give support if needed to those on shore. The two parties on shore should keep together, or if extended at short intervals, give support one to the other, no two men being unloaded at the same time.

"Should the surf permit of a landing, but the aborigines oppose the party effecting the same, then certain men previously told off should be directed to open fire, wounding only, if possible, but not killing those opposed to them, and a rush then made to capture the wounded and those making off.

"In this way, the object in view, *viz.*, that of obtaining information, may probably be attained.

"Should decided hostility be shown, then each man will of necessity be compelled to make his fire as telling as possible.

"Should the aborigines on the other hand come forward in an apparently friendly way, (every precaution being taken to guard against surprise) then the services of the interpreter and the Andamanese accompanying him will be brought into play.

"The Officer Commanding will not under any circumstances move inland further than there is any necessity for, certainly not more than say a mile or two, the strength of the party under his command nor yet the equipment of the force allowing of it."

The *Arracan* proceeded to the Little Andaman with the party on the 6th of May, and with regard to the subsequent proceedings the following extract from Lieutenant Much's despatch is given :—

" We anchored in the East Bay (Hut Bay.—*M. V. P.*) of the Little Andaman at 4-15 P. M. on the 6th, and went round the following morning to a place about a mile and a half from the spot where the boat's crew of the *Assam Valley* are supposed to have been captured.

" At about 8-30 A.M. I left the ship in the second cutter with a Petty Officer and six Naval Brigadesmen, and a Jemadar (Mootien), and four privates of the Sappers, and made for the rock which indicated the spot where the massacre is supposed to have occurred.

" The second gig containing Mr. Homfray, some Andamanese, and a Havildar and two privates of the Sappers followed.

" The first cutter containing one sergeant, one corporal, and eight privates of H. M.'s 2-24th Regiment, with orders to act as coverers to the parties when on shore, followed next.

" About 150 yards to the west of this rock the surf appeared to admit of a landing being effected, and Mr. Dunn, Officer in charge of the boats, ran the boat in stern-on, and on a hint from that officer we all jumped out wading to the shore in about from four and a half to five feet of water, rifles in hand and the ammunition slung round our necks, part of which from the swell on was unavoidably wetted. Being thus landed the second cutter moved off outside the surf. The first thing done on landing was to dry the ammunition.

" The Havildar and two privates of the Sappers, who according to orders should have landed with us, were unable to do so, **Mr.** Homfray not bringing his boat in close enough to give a chance; nor yet landing himself any part of the day, which undoubtedly was a great drawback to the success of the expedition, as regards obtaining information as might have been done regarding the fate of those we had come in search of from the wounded aborigines. (Not at all, Mr. Homfray and his Andamanese could have done nothing, not being able to talk to the Öngés.—*M. V. P.*) The party under my command, (the powder being then dry,) moved along the shore in an easterly direction towards the rock, the base of which the water at high tide reached. At about 50 yards' distance from this rock, high and dry on the sand, we found the skull of an European (so pronounced by Dr. Douglas), and a little further on an ankle boot, such as is worn by sailors; and beyond, nearer still to the rock, the knees and planking of a boat that was painted white, and inside lead colour. Here too, closer into the jungle, the ground had evidently been cleared for the purpose of cooking.

"Proceeding on, past the rock, at a point about 100 yards distant, we noticed a party of aborigines who showed themselves from time to time, as they rose apparently to have a peep behind the bushes skirting the jungle, and who discharged their arrows at us as we approached. Noticing that many were retiring, and as I thought, probably with the intention of surrounding us, I threw back the left flank of our party and again moved on. On arrival at the point, so to call it, finding that the ammunition was running short, my own in part damaged, and the rest expended, 1 signalled to the second cutter to come to shore and take us off. I must here mention that the surf since our landing in the morning had increased considerably and was running some fifteen to twenty feet high.

"Mr. Dunn in reply to my signal backed the cutter in, but in so doing unfortunately the boat was upset—all hands being washed out of her—some gaining *terra firma*, others being dragged out from the surf, Mr. Dunn amongst them much exhausted, and one officer, Lieutenant Glassford of the 9th Bengal Native Infantry, a passenger per steamer *Arracan* from Port Blair, drowned. This occurred at about 11 A.M.

"Seeing the fate of this boat I marched the party on towards East Bay in the hope of meeting with a spot from whence to re-embark. The first cutter containing 2-24th men coasting along as we advanced, and firing on the natives who were not visible to us.

"About 300 yards on we came across the bodies of four men, the heads of whom, mere skulls in appearance, protruded from the ground the rest of the bodies being partially covered with sand, but to these bodies I could not give more than a cursory glance, my whole attention being given to the critical position in which we were placed from the want of ammunition, the apparent little chance of boats ever reaching us, and the knowledge that in our state with the enemy down upon us in any number, our case was hopeless.

"Naval Brigadesman Watson picked up a seaman's blue cotton jacket much torn and rotten, which he brought home.

"Between 1 and 2 P.M., finding that the boat with the 2-24th men on board, as also the other boats, did not follow us, but on the contrary were signalling to us to return, we retraced our steps nearly to the place where we had landed in the morning. Here it was that the first cutter sent a raft; Mr. Dunn, one Naval Brigadesman, one lascar and I got on to it. The raft remained fully five minutes exposed to the violence of surf, from which we were very slowly hauled out. We proceeded, holding on the best way we could, for about 300 yards from the beach, when a surf larger than usual swept Mr. Dunn and myself off. We then struck out for the shore, which we all but reached utterly exhausted, and were dragged out luckily by those standing there. About 30 rounds of ammunition, which had been sent from the ship on the raft, reached us all right. This was a great boon, as we were then reduced to two rounds in all. A fresh attempt to send the raft ashore was made, but without success. About an hour later in the day Dr. Douglas, 2-24th Regiment, and Privates Thomas Murphy, James Cooper, David Bell, and William Griffith, gallantly manning the second gig with its secunnie (a man named Toke —*M. V. P.*) made their way through the surf almost to the shore, but finding their boat was half filled with water they retired.

"We also, seeing their approach, attempted to meet them part way, but failed to do so, losing in our endeavours the greater number of our arms, and spoiling what little ammunition we had left.

"A second attempt made by Dr. Douglas and party proved successful—five of us being safely passed through the surf to the boats outside. A third and last trip got the whole of the party left on the shore safe to the boats, when we all proceeded on board the steamer, which we reached about half past 5 P.M., much exhausted and with little clothing, having had to strip to gain the boats.

"Saving Lieutenant Glassford drowned, there were no casualties.

"We sailed the following morning (the 8th), reaching Port Blair in the afternoon.

"From what I saw myself I should say that there were about 30 aborigines killed. The jemadar, who went into the jungle a short distance, says there were fully 100 killed. (!)"

"I cannot speak too highly of the manner in which all the party who proceeded on shore behaved, both officers and men of both services. To commence with Dr. Douglas, who at the risk of his own life gallantly made three trips through the surf to the shore with his soldier crew. This was accomplished by no ordinary exertion. He stood in the bows of the boat and worked her in an intrepid and seamanlike manner, cool to a degree, as if what he was then doing was an ordinary act of every day life. Privates Murphy, Cooper, Bell, and Griffiths, his four gallant volunteers, behaved equally cool and collectedly, rowing through the roughest surf when the slightest hesitation or want of pluck on the part of any one of them would have been attended with the gravest results, not only to themselves, but also to the party on shore they were attempting to rescue. I can only express for myself and for those who were with me on shore the deep sense of gratitude felt by all for the services rendered on this occasion by Dr. Douglas.

"I trust that no opportunity will be lost in bringing to the notice of Government the name of one who to save the lives of others, risked his own."

Lieutenant Much also commended the remainder of the members of his force.

It appears from additional papers, that Dr. Douglas and Lieutenant Glassford were with Mr. Homfray in the gig in the morning, and after Lieutenant Much had landed, Lieutenant Glassford changed into the second cutter.

Mr. Eastwood was in the first cutter with the covering party, Mr. Dunn in the second cutter, and Mr. Homfray (who had formerly been an officer in the Government Marine Service) was in charge of the gig. When Mr. Dunn was trying to back his boat in to get Lieutenant Much off, his steering oar was broken, and the boat turning broadside on to the surf was upset in the next roller. Lieutenant Glassford sank at once. Mr. Dunn died almost immediately after this expedition. Captain Barrow reported that when landing Lieutenant Much in the first instance, at 9·30 A.M., the rudder of the second cutter was broken, and an oar had to be used to steer her. At 11-30 A.M. Lieutenant Much signalled for the cutter, and she was then upset and Lieutenant Glassford was drowned.

Captain Barrow then ordered Mr. Lindsay (one of his officers) to make a raft to assist the shore party who were being attacked by the aborigines. Mr. Lindsay went on shore with a line and a life buoy, and made a raft and sent ammunition on shore, but Lieutenant Much who tried to get off, and all his party, but three lascars, were washed away and had to swim on shore again.

Dr. Douglas had been on shore with Lieutenant Much, but had swum off to the boats.

The Andamanese came down in considerable force soon after the party landed, sending some well directed showers of arrows among them. On this our party fired into them, and though they very seldom showed themselves openly after that, a considerable number of them were killed and wounded.

Dr. Douglas remarks about the skull found near the rock:—
" It was rather a large skull, and from its shape, and from some of the brains remaining on it, must have belonged to a European. One of its sides (I think the right) had been beaten in as if with a club or axe, and the interior of the skull contained putrefied brains and hair. The hairs were short and brown and there was only a small tuft near the fracture.

" About ten minutes after the second cutter was swamped, when going to the assistance of Mr. Dunn, First Officer, I observed a body in white clothing in the middle of a roll of surf about 100 yards from the shore, which must have been that of Lieutenant Glassford. I only saw it for a few moments, it then disappeared and was not washed up while I was on the beach, although I looked out for it."

Alexander Wilson, Petty Officer of the Naval Brigade, stated that he found the bodies of four Europeans buried in a line close together on the shore with their faces upwards and their feet towards the sea. The bodies were lying at full length, there was no flesh on the skulls, nor yet hair, and they were much decomposed. He counted 57 Andamanese killed. About 200 natives came out while Lieutenant Much and Mr. Dunn were getting off on the raft and attacked Wilson and the party on shore. They retired when fired on, and Wilson's party advanced about 15 yards up the beach, where he saw in the jungle at least 100 pits with bows and arrows lying alongside them.

In this expedition six of the seamen lost their clothing, consisting of frocks, trousers, boots, hats, and black silk handkerchiefs.

On a report of the result of the expedition being submitted to the Government of India through the Chief Commissioner of British Burma, the latter wrote on the 9th of September, 1867, forwarding a copy of a letter from the Secretary to the Government of India in the Military-Marine Department, expressing the very high satisfaction with which the Right Hon'ble the Governor General in Council had received the report of the excellent conduct of the expedition which went in search of the missing crew of the *Assam Valley*.

A copy of the letter had been furnished to the Major-General Commanding the Division, with a request that he would communicate the contents in such manner as he may deem fit to the officers and men of the 2nd Battalion, 24th Regiment, mentioned in the Despatch, as also furnish the information required regarding Jemadar Mootien of the Madras Sappers and Miners; but to the other officer and men (including Jemadar Mootien), whose services were made mention of, and who were at Port Blair, the Superintendent was requested to be so good as to communicate himself the manner in which their conduct has been viewed by the Viceroy. It was further ordered that, on receiving a detailed list of the private property lost by them, they should be compensated in full.

Extract from Letter No. 86.

From—The Secretary to the Government of India, in the Military-Marine Department.
To—The Chief Commissioner of British Burma.
(Referred to in the proceeding letter).

" Having laid before Government your Secretary's letters Nos. 117.C, and 160 of the 10th of April, and the 30th of May, 1867, regarding the expedition which went in search of the missing crew of the *Assam Valley*, I am directed to state that the Right Hon'ble the Governor General in Council has received with the highest satisfaction the report of the excellent conduct of all engaged in the search : of the manner in which the third expedition in the *Arracan* was conducted; and particularly of the gallant behaviour of Assistant-Surgeon Douglas and the four men (Murphy, Cooper, Bell, and Griffiths, Privates of the 24th Regiment), of the 2nd Battalion, 24th Regiment, who volunteered to assist him in bringing off the party left on shore by the swamping of one of the boats.

" 2. The conduct of Doctor Douglas and these men, as well as that of Lieutenant Much, of the same regiment, who behaved so creditably, will be brought to the notice of Her Majesty's Government.

" 3. The Governor General in Council will admit Jemadar Mootien of the Madras Sappers and Miners to the Order of Merit, for the excellent services rendered by him on the occasion, on intimation being received in this Department (Military-Marine), that he is not already a member of that order, an early reply on which point is requested.

" 4. I am directed to request that you will be so good as to convey to the Commander of Her Majesty's Ship *Sylvia*, the acknowledgement of the Government of India for the promptitude with which he complied with the request of the Superintendent of Port Blair, to proceed in search of the commander and crew of the *Assam Valley*."

" 5. His Excellency in Council sanctions the grant of compensation in full for private property lost by the officers and men who accompanied the expedition from the *Arracan*.

" 6. Petty Officer A. Wilson of the Naval Brigade, and Toke Secunnie, will be suitably rewarded for the part taken by them in the hazardous service.

" 7. I am further to add that the question of sending another expedition at a suitable season is under consideration."

SD. H. K. BURNE,

Officiating Military Secretary,
Government of India, Military-Marine Department.

The 28th August, 1867.

With reference to the above, Dr. Douglas and the four Privates mentioned, were each given the decoration of the Victoria Cross.

Toke, the Secunnie, was given a donation of two months' pay; and Petty Officer Wilson was awarded a silver watch and chain which were sent to Port Blair to be delivered to him. Before they reached there Wilson had left, so they were kept for him by the Superintendent. Though he afterwards passed through Rangoon in a ship (having left the Government Service and entered the Merchant Navy) notice of this was not given to the Superintendent who finally sent the articles to the India Office in London. Wilson was last heard of in Bremen, and was advertised for, but never found. He, therefore, never received the articles.

No further expeditions were undertaken to the Little Andaman with reference to the *Assam Valley* affair, and the Island was not again visited until the 6th of April, 1873, when General Stewart paid a short visit to it.

Great caution was observed, as General Stewart was of opinion that the Little Andamanese were notoriously the most hostile and treacherous of the Andamanese. He was surprised to find that they lived in carefully constructed huts of considerable size, showing by their habits that they were far in advance (he thought) of the tribes with whom we had hitherto come into contact. Their houses were all fitted with bamboo platforms for sleeping purposes, and some of them had bed accommodation of this description for from 50 to 100 persons.

The property found in their houses was left untouched, and, as the aborigines kept themselves out of sight, General Stewart left some presents in their huts and canoes.

On his return to Port Blair he learnt that five of the crew of a junk trading between Moulmein and the Straits Settlements had been murdered by the aborigines of the Little Andaman three days previously, and he despatched a punitive expedition under the command of Captain R. J. Wimberley to the island.

General Stewart's report on the matter to the Government of India is as follows:—

    Extract from Letter No. 58, dated 15th April, 1873.
    From—The Chief Commissioner of the Andaman Islands,
    To—The Government of India.

" On my return to Port Blair on the night of the 8th of April 1873, I learned that five of a crew of a junk (the *Quangoon*) trading between Moulmein and the Straits had been murdered by the natives of the Little Andaman, where they had been landed in search of water three days previously.

" 2. It would appear that the vessel had been blown away from the coast of Burma by strong easterly gales and lost all reckoning till the Little Andaman was sighted.

" 3. Taking the Island to be the Car Nicobar, a boat, containing seven men, was sent on shore on the evening of the 5th instant.

" 4. On reaching the beach five of the crew went into the bush in search of water, leaving two of their comrades in the boat.

" 5. They had not gone very far when they found themselves surrounded by a number of the Islanders, who fired arrows at them, and proceeded at once to lay violent hands on those nearest to them.

" 6. Three of the five sailors managed to evade their pursuers, but one (a Chinaman) was so severely wounded that he could not be induced to leave the shelter of the jungle as he knew that his wounds were mortal.

" 7. The two unwounded men, providing themselves with pieces of wood, swam off to the junk, which they reached about 9 P. M. These men, when passing the spot where they had left their boat, found traces of blood about the place, and that the boat itself had been broken up.

" 8. On learning the fate of the missing men, the junk at once proceeded to sea, and made its way to Port Blair, where it arrived on the morning of the 8th instant.

" 9. An expeditionary party was at once organised for the purpose of rescuing the captive sailors, if alive, and punishing the guilty Islanders.

" 10. This party consisting of Sepoys and friendly Andamanese was placed under the command of Captain Wimberley, Officiating Deputy Superintendent, and left Port Blair on the 10th instant.

" 11. Captain Wimberley was instructed to confine his operations to the villages in the immediate vicinity of the spot where the outrage was committed.

" 12. Captain Wimberley's report, (a copy of which is attached) shows how effectively he carried out his instructions.

" 13. He was specially directed to make some of the Islanders prisoners, as we can never hope to come to terms with these savages until we have the means of communicating with them in their own language.

" 14. Although the affair was petty enough it is due to Captain Wimberley to acknowledge that it was carefully and thoroughly well managed from first to last.

" 15. The Islanders are contemptible as an enemy in open country but it is easy to compromise troops when dealing with them in their impenetrable jungles ; and, on this account, the proceedings of the latter party are all the more creditable to those concerned."

Captain Wimberley submitted the following report regarding the expedition to General Stewart:—

"2. At 10 P. M. on the 10th of April, 1873, the expedition left Port Blair in the I. M. S. *Undaunted*, arriving the following morning at Hut Bay on the east coast of the Little Andaman, and anchoring at 9 A.M. off the spot indicated by the two Burman sailors who had escaped from the savages as the place where they had, when in the junk *Quangoon*, been attacked by the aborigines.

"3. The force was as follows:—

"One Jemadar and 22 rank and file of the 27th M. N. I.

"One convict Petty Officer in charge of 20 Andamanese from the southern tribes. One native dresser.

"Assistant Surgeon Duzer was in medical charge.

"Captain Beresford, of I. M. S. *Undaunted* kindly placed at my disposal three of his officers and the four Quartermasters of the vessel.

"4. With the exception of eight Andamanese for whom there was not room in the boats, the force embarked in the ship's boats at 11 A.M. and were pulled ashore.

"The Quartermasters were ordered to remain, each in his own boat, and Mr. Litchfield, second officer of the *Undaunted*, was requested to take charge of the four boats and follow up the land party, keeping as close to the shore as possible.

"Four Sepoys and a Naick were left in one of the boats to act as a covering party, if required. Mr. Fenn, Chief Officer, and Mr. Jones, 3rd Officer of the *Undaunted*, accompanied me.

"5. We first proceeded along the beach in a southerly direction and finding the surf there very heavy, I was compelled to request Mr Litchfield to take the boats back to the place where we had effected a landing.

"6. After proceeding some distance we were shown by the sailors of the *Quangoon* the rope by which their canoe had been fastened, and a few yards further on we found the canoe itself, which had been hacked to pieces by some sharp cutting instrument.

"7. Being thoroughly satisfied that the tale told by the *Quangoon* men was in all respects true, we commenced a search in the jungle adjoining the sea shore for any traces of the bodies of the unfortunate victims.

"We succeeded in finding three articles of their clothing, some of which were blood-stained and had been pierced by arrows, but we could find no traces of the five missing men, and fear that there is no doubt that they fled into the heavy jungle where they were caught and destroyed by the Islanders.

"8. We continued our march in a southerly direction along the outskirts of the jungle for some two miles, and finding no trace of these men and seeing no sign of the enemy I decided to burn their houses, which consisted of four huts, each distant from the other about half a mile, and in each of which about 40 men could be accommodated, and one enormous hut about 60 feet in diameter, and which was capable of holding at the least some 150 men. (This was at Töi Bàlöwé —*M. V. P.*) In this hut were hung up their canoes.

"9. While burning hut No. 2 we were attacked by a large force of the enemy who were concealed in the jungle, and whose tactics evidently were to cut us off from our boat.

"They let fly their arrows in all directions and a sharp fight, lasting about ten minutes, ensued, which, however, as might have been expected, ended in favour of the Enfields and Sniders, and the savages ultimately took to flight, leaving nearly the whole of their bows and arrows in our hands.

"We were fortunate enough to take one of their number a prisoner uninjured. This was accomplished by Havildar Shaik Dadoo, 27th M. N. I., and Convict Petty Officer Goodur, who behaved excellently throughout the affair.

"10. On our side Private Mahomed Mucktoor was wounded by arrows in two places, once in his right wrist and secondly in the left breast. The second arrow fortunately was partially stopped by the leather cross belt which it pierced through, or otherwise it would have gone through his lung.

"This man behaved remarkably well, and though bleeding profusely from the wound in his wrist, he begged hard to be allowed to remain with the force.

"Private Anunt Rao was also rather severely wounded in the right thigh, and was at once despatched on board the steamer.

"11. As the fight occurred in low brushwood jungle, and every man that fell was dragged into the dense jungle by his comrades, where I considered it unsafe to follow, it is impossible to say how many of the enemy fell, but from my own observations, and from the blood scattered about, I should put down their loss at 10 or 12 men at the lowest. One of the savages, who from his appearance and war paint (?) was undoubtedly a Chief, stood deliberately and fired three arrows at our men, and in spite of numerous shots fired at him escaped into the interior in a most marvellous manner, apparently unhurt.

"12. We then proceeded to burn the remaining huts, and while so employed the enemy again showed in considerable force on the open beach at a distance of some 2,000 yards. Mr. Litchfield, who from the boats was nearer them than we were, computed their number at about 200 men.

"It appeared as if they could not make up their minds whether to risk attacking us again or not, but on our attempting to follow them up, they retreated sullenly and we lost sight of them in the jungle. This conduct on their part was, I have no doubt, due to their having lost so large a number of their weapons.

"13. As by this time the surf had increased to a very great extent, and as I had carried out my orders, and taught these Andamanese a lesson which they will remember for some time, I gave the order to re-embark in the boats.

"14. This was effected with great difficulty as the surf was very high and the troops had to hold their pouch belts and rifles above their heads, while they waded up to their waists in water.

"15. Eventually, the embarkation was safely concluded and we returned to the *Undaunted* without any accident, having been more than four hours on shore; and reached Port Blair on the morning of the 12th with our prisoner."

On the above reports, the Government of India, in Letter No. 92 of 26th May, 1873, to General Stewart, state :—

"Your action in the matter is approved, and I am to request that the thanks of the Governor General in Council may be conveyed to Captain Wimberley for the manner in which he performed the duty entrusted to him. Private Mahomed Mucktoor's conduct has been brought to the notice of the Military Department.

" I am to enquire whether you would recommend the remission of any part of convict Goodur's sentence in consideration of his good conduct while attached to the expedition."

Jemadar Goodur eventually obtained a free pardon as a reward for this and subsequent instances of good conduct.

The captive Öngé was put under the charge of Mr. DeRoepstorff, by his request, and was kept on Mount Harriett where he died shortly afterwards. Many attempts were made to learn his language, and the greatest kindness was shown him, but having one day seen his face in a looking-glass he seemed to recognise something, (possibly, as he might think, the ghost of one of his own countrymen, or something else equally " uncanny "), and pined away. He used often to sit and watch the North Sentinel Island which is visible from the summit of the mountain, as if he knew it, or perhaps fancied it to be the Little Andaman. General Stewart, as related in the previous Chapter, directed Mr. Homfray to bring in some Járawas from the neighbouring jungle in the hope that they might be able to communicate with the Öngé, but he had died before the man and woman, who were caught, could be brought to him.

As these two Járawas allowed themselves to be captured and brought in without very much resistance, some people imagined, (erroneously) that they were the parents of the Öngé, who had come up to Port Blair to search for him.

General Stewart remarked :—

" The captive died before anything could be made of his language, and we are thus still without the means of communicating with the inhabitants of the Little Andaman, save by signs. Strenuous efforts will be made next season to bring about a better understanding with them, as it is impossible to tolerate their barbarous propensities any onger.

"They are probably not more cruel than the tribes in this neighbourhood were, before the latter were brought under the influence of our rule, and it is hard to believe that similar methods of treatment will fail in this instance to produce like results."

In pursuance of the above policy, General Stewart, accompanied by Mr. Homfray and some friendly Andamanese, again visited the Little Andaman on the 20th of April, 1874.

He explored the creeks and noticed big patches of dead and rotten mangrove trees, as if the swamp had been cleared. He thought that the Island was rising in the centre.

Presents were left in some canoes found on the shore of Jackson Creek. On the 21st, as these presents had not been touched, Mr. Homfray sent some Andamanese into the neighbouring jungle to look for traces of the Öngés. The latter, who had been lying in ambush, then appeared on all sides and attacked our Andamanese, who retreated into the sea without returning their fire.

Convict Jemadar Goodur, who was with four Andamanese, had to fire in self-defence, and wounded the leader of the Öugés, who died while being brought off to the *Undaunted.*

A large body of Öngés had spread themselves in the water over the bar of the creek while Mr. Homfray, who was inside, was trying to come out, and beckoned to him in a friendly manner, but Mr. Homfray paid no attention to them and kept his boat straight for the entrance. It was lucky he had distrusted them, as they had treacherously dragged their bows and arrows through the water by their toes, and were intending to fight.

General Stewart noted on this visit:—

"It is very clear that the system of making hurried visits of a few hours at long and uncertain intervals does little good, and that much time and patience will be needed if we are ever to make friends of these savages.

"The actual occupation of the Little Andaman is at present out of the question, but the permanent presence of a Station Steamer will enable us to devote more time to our dealings with the inhabitants, as it is not very creditable to us that we should have held these Islands for so many years without doing something more than has yet been done towards ensuring the safety of persons who may] have the misfortune to be wrecked on these coasts."

In spite of the above remark, nothing more was done, General Stewart having left the Andamans, and the Öngés were left to themselves until February, 1880, when Colonel Cadell on his way to the Car Nicobar stopped for a few hours at the Little Andaman and left some presents on the shore but did not see any of the aborigines.

In the meanwhile, however, the Öngés had paid one of their periodic visits to the Cinque Islands, and, as related in the previous Chapter, their canoes had been found in October, 1878, on the coast of MacPherson's Straits, and in November, they were seen on the Cinque Islands, and were not molested.

On another occasion also, one of their canoes had been seen in Portman Harbour.

At this time it was thought that the people on the Cinque Islands were Jàrawas from Rutland Island, and though an idea was entertained by some that they might be Öngés who had come up from the Little Andaman, nothing definite was known in the matter.

In March, 1880, Colonel Cadell and I paid a longer visit to the Little Andaman.

After exploring a creek on the northern coast, called "Kúāī Échékwada," and leaving presents for the Öngés in an empty canoe we found on the bank, we went on to Jackson Creek and examined it. There was a nasty sand-bar, with a slight surf beating on it, at the mouth, and about a quarter of a mile up was a small cleared patch of swamp, with three canoes lying on the mud, and a broad road leading into the jungle; we did not see any of the aborigines.

The next day we went along the west coast to see if we could obtain a landing, but the surf being too high we returned to Jackson Creek.

We found that the presents we had left in the canoes on the previous day had been taken away, and that one of the canoes had been brought down from the clearing to the mouth of the creek.

Just as we were leaving it about thirty Ongés came out from the jungle to the water's edge, shouting and firing arrows at us.

We stopped our boat, waved some pieces of coloured cloth, and beckoned to them, and they tucked their bows and arrows between their legs, and, wading into the water, waved to us to come closer to the shore. We did not move, so they brought a canoe to come off and meet us; several of them were lying down on the bottom of the canoe with bows and arrows in their hands.

We pulled the boat round to meet them, but they suspected us of some treachery and went back to the shore, yelling at us. None of us were hit by their arrows, which fell round the boat like hail, and we did not return their fire.

I noticed that the Ongés, whom I now saw for the first time, resembled the aborigines of the North Sentinel, were smeared with yellow clay, had their hair clipped, but not shaven, and had bows, arrows, and canoes exactly like those I had seen on the North Sentinel in the previous month.

On our way back to Port Blair,—for after this inhospitable reception we did not remain any longer at the Little Andaman,—we examined the South Brother Island, and found on it huts like those on the North Sentinel, so concluded that the Ongés came across to the Island, a distance of about six miles, from the Little Andaman.

Owing to the nature of its shores, and the surf that beats on them, there is no anchorage for vessels, nor are there convenient landing places, except during the calm months of the year, so no further visits were paid to the Little Andaman until September, 1880, when I visited Hut Bay in the hope that I might find the people there more friendly.

When I arrived no one was to be seen, but after a time a few of the people peeped out of the jungle. I left presents at different spots, rowing along the shore and looking for a safe place to land.

On a point (Bálámé Óbángitōī) were some women catching fish, who, on seeing my boat, ran round the corner. I followed and found myself in a little bay, (Dāōgulé Bay), on the shore of which were many large huts, from which, on my approach, the aborigines swarmed. The surf was very high and prevented me from landing and leaving any presents for them.

I also landed on the South Brother and left presents there, having an idea of making that island my head quarters on some future occasion, and waiting in camp there till some Ongés, not knowing I was about, should come across from the Little Andaman.

In October another visit was paid, regarding which the following report was submitted —:

"On the 26th of October, 1880, the Chief Commissioner, I, and a large party of Andamanese started for the Little Andaman in the I. G. S. *Kwang Tung.*

" On the morning of the 27th we landed on the South Brother Island, and explored it. There were traces of a number of people having recently been on the Island, and from the amount of tortoise-shell about I should imagine their reason for coming to be to procure turtle, in the same way as the Andamanese living in Port Mouat go to Termugli Island.

" Leaving this, we went down to Jackson Creek, and seeing some aborigines at a hut to the north of the mouth, we rowed close to the shore, and sent some Andamanese to land a few coconuts. They swam close to the Öngés, and after much shouting and gesticulating a few of the latter came into the water, dragging their bows and arrows, which they never lost hold of, by their toes.

" The meeting was seemingly friendly, but, shortly after, one of the savages fired off an arrow which hit a Police constable who was pulling stroke in the boat, and gaping with his mouth wide open, in the mouth. We did not return the fire, but left the place and proceeded up the creek. Many canoes were seen there, and we were attacked at the mouth by about 80 Òngés, but, as we got off all right, we did not fire at them."

(The arrow was extracted from the left side of the Policeman's lower jaw, which it had pierced and splintered, after entering his open mouth, and no ill effects ensued. He bore the operation with wonderful pluck, never moving or uttering a sound, though he nearly fainted when it was finished.)

" We then went to the Car Nicobar, returning to the east coast of the Little Andaman on the morning of the 29th. We rowed opposite a large hut which was in course of construction, and a few Öngés came out from the jungle and appeared to be exceedingly friendly.

" We floated presents to the shore, which they took, and then some more men and some women came out. As the presence of the latter is a sign of friendship I sent some of my Andamanese on shore a little higher up the coast with presents. The Öngés, dropping their bows and arrows went up to them, and a most friendly meeting ensued, both parties putting their arms round each other's necks and dancing and shouting. We did not land for fear of alarming them, and after watching the scene for about an hour recalled our Andamanese and went off to the ship for breakfast.

" It seemed as though we had really made an impression upon these people at last, and on coming back to the hut at about 11 A.M., they renewed their demonstrations of friendliness, and I decided to land on a sandy beach about half a mile off, where there was no surf.

" A short time after doing so I saw the men leave the hut and come towards me, so sending on three men loaded with presents to meet them at the mouth of a creek, I waited for them to approach.

"Colonel Cadell, who was in another boat, had said he would remain near me and act as a covering party in case I was attacked, but as soon as I had landed he rowed away up the coast and left me.

" The Öngés had halted at the corner by the creek, owing to the high shingle bank of which I was unable to see them, and the next thing I saw was my three Andamanese running towards Colonel Cadell's boat followed by a shower of arrows.

" All the savages, in number about forty, ran towards me, and as soon as they got close commenced firing, whilst another party who had crept round in the jungle without our noticing them, surprised me from behind. As, however, I had not entirely trusted them, but had placed scouts along the belt of jungle, the alarm was given in time and we managed to get off without anyone being hit. In order however to frighten them away, the Chief Commissioner (who on seeing the attack had returned) ordered Lieutenant H. H. Dobbie, who accompanied the party, to fire on them with small shot; no one was hurt."

Among the presents I had brought them was a young pig, and I think this distracted their attention, for though they were close upon us the second party did not fire until after the boat had got away out of range. The moment they saw them rush out my Andamanese who were unarmed ran to the boat, and got their oars ready to pull, so that by the time I got to the boat with my Andamanese and convict orderlies, they rowed away as we scrambled in: indeed, my convict orderly did not get in, but hung on the side of the boat, and was dragged through the water for some distance till we helped him; good pullers as the Andamanese are, I have never, before or since, seen them row as they did on this occasion.

On the results of this trip I noted :—

"From what I have seen of these people on the various trips I have made to their country, I am convinced that by such mild measures as we have pursued very little can be done. Most probably the impression we have left in their minds is that we are afraid of them, and from the above example of their extreme treachery it becomes evident that a vessel in distress would meet with cruel treatment at their hands.

"By lying in wait at the South Brother Island for a turtling party; by establishing a small Settlement on the Little Andaman itself, or else by surrounding one of their huts at night, capturing the inhabitants (the surrounding party being thoroughly armed, and instructed to resist with force any attack on the part of the savages), and to keep those we captured long enough with us at Port Blair for them to appreciate our kindness, and for us to learn their language, appears to me to be the only methods by which the establishment of friendly relations with the Little Andamanese can be effected.

"How necessary these relations are may be seen from the facts that no vessel, however much in want of water, or in however great distress, dare touch at this Island; and it is certain that if (as has occurred before) a country trader making for the Car Nicobar should by accident arrive at the Little Andaman, or if any vessel not knowing the nature of the people should be driven there in a gale of wind, and receiving encouragement from the seeming friendliness of the natives (as instanced above), should attempt to land her crew and passengers, however large a party might go on shore, would assuredly be massacred. The Little Andamanese, although resembling the other Andamanese in all other particulars, are not so afraid of firearms, and in an attack are known to behave with great pluck and bravery."

In April, 1881, traces of the Öngés were found on the Sisters Islands, but no further visits were paid to the Little Andaman until September, 1882, when Major Protheroe and Mr. Godwin-Austen went down there and anchored in Hut Bay. The Öngés behaved as usual, taking the presents, trying to entice the people in the boat on shore by a show of pretended friendship, and then firing on the party.

Mr. Godwin-Austen notes on the visit:—

"In my opinion, leaving presents and avoiding a collision are the only means of bringing the Little Andamanese in at all, as the size of the Island, and the scarcity of landing places, would not be the only serious difficulty to be overcome should force have to be tried, and it would have to be remembered that, whenever presents are left there, that we ourselves are the aggressors by landing and not the natives who fire on us, and that we should at all risks avoid collision with them than which nothing is easier. It would be well if the Station Steamer whenever under weigh, either passing round the Islands or visiting the Nicobars, were to call in, leave presents of rope, cocoa-nuts, glass beads, etc., but stringent orders would have to be issued forbidding any one to land on any pretence except for the purpose of placing the presents on shore, and then returning at once to the boat, and the success of the whole scheme depends entirely on this."

Subsequent experience with the Öngés has shown us that this

scheme would only have been successful if such visits of conciliation had been paid about every fortnight, and even then years might have elapsed before they became really friendly. The Andamanese can only be ruled by fear (which need not mean tyranny), not by love, which they do not understand and ascribe either to weakness or treachery, and the sharp lesson we taught the Öngés in 1885 has been shown to be the simplest and most effective method of taming them.

Mr. Man visited the Little Andaman in September, 1883. He left presents for the Öngés, which were taken after a time in their usual distrustful way and no more was seen of them.

Mr. Man writes of this visit:—

"Their (the Öngés') conduct reminds me very much of that displayed towards us seven or eight years ago by the Yerewas (North Andamanese) during my first visits to Port Cornwallis and Stewart's Sound, and there can I think be little doubt that—as in the case of the Yerewas—frequent visits conducted after the manner suggested by Mr. Godwin-Austen, women being taken to show our friendliness, will before long tend to overcome the feeling of distrust which this isolated tribe has hitherto so persistently manifested towards us. This distrust appears due to a suspicion that the object of our solicitude to make their acquaintance is a desire to kidnap them into slavery, if nothing worse, for the two or three members of their tribe who in recent years have been carried away wounded or captive, died before we could restore them to their friends, who doubtless attribute the circumstances of their non-return to our supposed hostile sentiments towards their tribe."

Mr. Man appeared to have forgotten that with the tribes in the North Andaman we had a means of communication through interpreters, and that reports of us and our doings had filtered up to them through the different tribes, thus paving the way for our success there, but with the Öngés there was no such means of communication, nor could they have heard anything of us.

The next visit to the Little Andaman was paid on the 18th of April 1884, when Colonel Cadell accompanied by Captain Hobday of the

Survey of India, Lieutenant Burton, and myself with 38 Andamanese went there. On our way down we visited the North and South Brother Islands, where we found many traces of the aborigines though none of them were on the Islands at the time. Huts of recent construction capable of holding thirty people were found, with neat charpoys of bamboos which I had not observed before. Both of these Islands are low and have in the centre a depression which in the rains becomes filled with water. Quantities of pigeons of various kinds are to be found there, also duck and snipe.

After leaving the Brothers we proceeded up Kúāī Échékwada Creek, leaving a boat to guard the mouth. Traces of the aborigines were here seen, and a few came timidly out of the jungles and took the presents we left on the shore. We then visited the South Sentinel Island. No traces of the aborigines were here. The island is composed of coral, and abounds in lizards and land crabs. Turtle are also to be got in great numbers, for, being undisturbed here, it appears to be one of their favourite breeding places. *Birgus Latro*, the large robber crab, is also found on this Island.

We then visited the west coast of the Little Andaman, seeing huts and aborigines at places on the shore. We rowed up Jackson Creek leaving a guard boat at the mouth; a few Andamanese were seen on the coast to the north of the creek, and presents were left in various places. Steaming round the south of the island we anchored in Hut Bay on the evening of the 21st. Here the natives mustered in great force. A few of our Andamanese landed with presents which the Öngés took. Captain Hobday got into a canoe with the Goanese fiddler of the *Kwang Tung*, and paddled up and down in front of the hut where the Öngés were collected, while the Goanese played to them. Possibly the noise of the surf spoilt the effect of the music, but it was an amusing sight to us; probably the savages thought we were mad.

After waiting here till mid-day on the 22nd, we went on to the north-western creek, which was also explored. The aborigines were seen, and presents were left for them, which were taken.

We then returned to Port Blair. On our way up we landed on the Sisters and Passage Islands, and found traces of the Öngés, this Tribe being always easily identified by the shape of their bows, and their ornaments.

With regard to this visit I noted in my report:—

"This trip has been most satisfactory in every way. It is the first time on record that a lengthened visit has been paid to the Little Andaman without our coming into collision with the inhabitants. Although three large creeks were explored, one of which has never been before entered without a fight, the party was never once fired on. A series of such visits at short intervals would probably do great good. Further, it is an interesting fact to have traced the Little Andamanese to as far north as Passage Island. Referring to Mr. Man's report for the month of October, 1878, it will be found that two canoes, by their make unmistakeably Little Andamanese, were found in a small creek in Rutland Island. In February, 1879, a party of Jàrawas with canoes was seen on the Cinque Islands. It is quite possible that these were Little Andamanese who were returning from Rutland Island to their own country, and if so it would be possible to open relations with the Little Andamanese through the Rutland Island Jàrawas."

In this conjecture I was wrong, for I have since taken the Öngés over Rutland Island and they know nothing of the Jàrawas there.

In November, 1884, an expedition which had been sent to Rutland Island to look for the Jàrawas there observed smoke rising from the jungle in the Cinque Islands, but owing to the bad weather my party was unable to cross over there in their canoes. The Ougés were then on the Cinque Islands, and, as will be seen, this visit of theirs was the turning point in our policy, and from it dates our friendly relations with them.

In January, 1885, Colonel Cadell and I again visited the Little Andaman. We arrived off the mouth of Jackson Creek on the morning of the 13th, and Colonel Cadell with Lieutenant Black the Chief Officer of the *Kwang Tung*, and Mr. Jessop of the Port Blair Commission, went up the creek in a cutter, followed by Lieutenant Smith Fourth Officer of the *Kwang Tung* and Mr. Jackson, Apothecary, in a jolly-boat. After proceeding about $1\frac{1}{4}$ mile they landed, and going along a well-trodden path for about 600 yards came upon a large hut which was empty.

(One of our Andamanese had, however, stolen on in front, and throwing himself on a bed in the hut pretended to cry, as if rejoiced at meeting his friends. Lieutenant Black, taking him for an Ongé, rushed in and seized him, whereupon the Andamanese were much amused.)

Presents were left in the hut, and the party returned to the mouth of the creek where they found that 42 of the Öngés had collected on the sand spits on either side of the mouth, which were bare, it being low water. As there was only a passage of 30 or 40 yards in width for the boats to pass through (though it would have been easy to clear the spits with a few rifle shots), Colonel Cadell wishing to avoid bloodshed, instead of forcing the boats on, waited in the broad part of the creek for the tide to rise. Colonel Cadell writes:—

"Apparently mistaking our action for surrender, four natives put off in one canoe, and two in another, and coming alongside our boat they disdainfully refused the presents which we offered, and by very peremptory gestures and shouts ordered us ashore. The canoe with the four men made fast to the jolly-boat, and the savages commenced cutting away the lanyards and fenders, and by gestures ordered the rifles and compass box to be given up."

Colonel Cadell ordered the Officer in the jolly-boat to shove the canoe off, and on his doing so, one of the Öngés, snatching up his bow and arrows from the bottom of the canoe, sent an arrow through the helmet of Mr. Jackson, inflicting a slight scalp wound on his head " On this several shots were fired by our party, which appeared to take effect as the savages threw up their arms and fell into the water as if dead. One of them fell over the bow of the canoe and appeared to be hanging there, but we found that he had taken the painter of the canoe in his mouth and was towing it on shore. The other five supposed dead men were also seen presently to emerge from the water and enter the mangrove jungle, all, except one who had been hit in the calf by an arrow fired by one of our Andamanese, being unhurt."

By Colonel Cadell's order the man who was towing the canoe on shore was seized and brought into the boat, where we found that he was unwounded. Not being watched very carefully, owing to the general excitement, he attempted to escape and was again caught by our Andamanese while swimming to the shore, and as the tide had now risen and the sand spits become covered with water, the Öngés retired and the boats rowed off to the *Kwang Tung* without further molestation; the two canoes from which the party had been attacked were broken up by us as a mark of our displeasure.

During this day I had left with a party of Andamanese in a cutter and gone to a hut on the coast to the south of the creek's mouth. I sent some Andamanese ashore to leave presents, and after their doing so about 30 Öngés appeared, some of whom left their bows and arrows and came out in the water towards us. My people swam to meet them and succeeded in persuading one boy, aged about fourteen, to come into my boat. He did not seem at all frightened, and after keeping him about ten minutes I sent him ashore with a lot of presents. We waited for some time, but finding no others came off went to the mouth of the creek where we anchored. As soon as all the Andamanese had collected on the sand spits as related above, I sent presents ashore to them. The women, however, who were with them at the hut, had not accompanied them, and they seemed from their manner to be hostile as they threatened my Andamanese who were in the water near them, and when one of them, a man named Ría Chána, swam off and gave an Öngé a coconut, wrapped in a long strip of red cloth for convenience of carriage in the water, the Öngé turned and smote him on the head with it, to his anger and astonishment.

Our captive, whose name we long afterwards discovered to be Tálémé, was a fine well-built young man of about 22 years of age; he appeared healthy and not very frightened.

We remained at Jackson Creek (so-called from the above mentioned fight in which Mr. Jackson was wounded) all night and went on shore there again in the next morning leaving presents at various places, after doing which we proceeded to Hut Bay, on the east coast, and anchored there for that night. Presents were placed on the shore and a number of Öngés came and took them.

We again left presents there on the morning of the 15th, when the

Ongés fired on us, one arrow striking the awning of the Chief Commissioner's boat and passing close to his head. We fired one shot in return which passed over the heads of the Ongés. On the previous evening women had come out on the shore and no arrows were fired, while on this morning no women were to be seen.

Leaving here we landed at an empty hut on the east coast and left presents in it, and anchored off the south-west corner of the South Brother for the night. There were traces of natives on this island, but none very recent.

On the 16th we proceeded to the Sisters and landed there, leaving presents in some recently constructed huts; to Passage Island where recent traces of people were seen; and anchored for the night on the south-west of the North Cinque Island. A party of Malays who were collecting edible birds' nests were here in a boat, and said they were afraid to land as they had seen some Jàrawas on the beach the previous day.

We landed, and on searching through the North Cinque Island found fires and recent footmarks, but no Jàrawas. While there we saw smoke issuing from the jungle at the north end of the Great Cinque Island. This was from the camp of the people who had been here since the time they were seen in the previous November.

Early in the morning of the 17th Colonel Cadell, Lieutenant Black, and I landed on the Great Cinque, and on going a little way into the jungle found a camp of the savages and three of their canoes, but no Jàrawas. We sent some of our Andamanese into the jungle to look for them, and after about half an hour they returned with an old Jàrawa man with white hair. (At this time it must be remembered we thought that these people were Jàrawas who had come across to the Cinque Islands from Rutland Island.)

We took the old man on board the *Kwang Tung*, showed him several novelties, including a looking-glass which seemed to surprise him, and introduced him to our Little Andaman captive, with whom we found he could converse.

He was in a very bad temper, so I gave him a quantity of presents.

and took him on shore again, when he spat in my face and made himself generally disagreeable.

It was of great importance that we should ascertain if these people were Little Andamanese or Jàrawas, and being unable to postpone our return to Port Blair the three canoes which we had found were taken on board the *Kwang Tung*, to prevent the escape of the aborigines from the Cinque Islands, and we left.

On the 19th I returned to the Great Cinque Island bringing with me 49 Andamanese, 14 convicts, and seven Police, and camped at the north end. Mr. Oldham of the Geological Survey, being anxious to examine the island, accompanied me.

On the morning of the 20th an expedition was sent out which beat through the jungle from the north to the south end of the Island. Here the Jàrawas were found, engaged in making new canoes, and a fight naturally ensued. In addition to our Andamanese with their bows and arrows, the convict Petty Officers with the party were armed with revolvers, yet the Jàrawas fought most pluckily, only retreating on to a rock some little distance from the shore, and endeavouring to protect their women and children, until all their arrows were exhausted. I sent my boat with some police down to the rock, Mr. Oldham kindly volunteering to go in charge of it, and a rush being made, the whole party of Jàrawas, consisting of 24 men, women, and children, were captured and brought in to my camp.

Four of the Jàrawas were found to be wounded, and on our side convict Jhandu, No. 26,125 was hit with an arrow in the left side, and being brought into camp died the next morning. One of our Andamanese, a man named Bía Mulwa (an old and experienced hunter of runaway convicts and Jàrawas), was hit in the hand by an arrow.

The people caught were 8 men, 6 women, and 10 children; after studying them for a day I released 15 out of the 24 captives; *viz.*, 2 men, 4 women, and 9 children, giving them back their canoes, and returned to Port Blair on the 22nd with 4 unmarried men, 2 married men with their two wives, and one child.

The married couples I sent to the Andaman Home at Haddo, keeping in my own house the four unmarried men, the child, and the Little

Andaman captive, as I thought I was more likely to influence these by getting them alone and away from the others.

I found that Ápi, the little boy of the western tribe of Jàrawas, who had been caught in the previous year, could talk to the others a little, and he used to interpret to me what they said, although very shy of speaking to them; his doing so, indeed, to any great extent, would not be in accordance with Andamanese etiquette. After some days, as is always the case with aborigines who come from the distant islands to Port Blair, they all began to sicken from the change of diet, shock, etc., and were sent to Haddo hospital: the Little Andaman man having an attack of pneumonia from which he died on the 8th of February, and the nine Jàrawas having fever and bronchitis. One of the married men died of pneumonia in March.

The remaining Jàrawas recovered, and once they became acclimatised and accustomed to the new diet, etc., began to put on flesh and became very cheerful and happy.

They were of course very kindly treated, and while endeavouring to learn something of their language I also encouraged my Andamanese to mix with them and teach them Hindustani which I considered to be the most useful language for a means of general communication with all comers.

While I thought that our captives were from the Little Andaman, Colonel Cadell was of opinion that they had come from Rutland Island, the Jàrawas of which Island, he writes, have hitherto given us no trouble, but have steadily declined our overtures of friendship.

From whatever tribe they might subsequently prove to have come, it was evident that our capture was of the highest importance, as the people could converse with the Little Andamanese, as well as with Ápi, thus affording us a possible means of communication with all the Jàrawa tribes, and certainly with the people on the Little Andaman who were the most important.

The unmarried men had settled down again in my house after their attack of sickness, and began to get on fairly well with my Andamanese, so in February I sent them to spend a few days at the Andaman Home at Táracháng, and then took the whole party to Stewart's Sound in order to let them see that there were other tribes of Andamanese, and that we were on friendly terms with, and well received by, the savages whom we met on distant islands.

Of these people, two men named respectively Tómiti and Tálāī, a youth named Kógio Kāī, and the child named Eketi, showed special intelligence and friendliness. After a few weeks Tómiti became much attached to me, used to sleep in my dressing-room, and followed me about everywhere like a dog. The child Eketi, who was full of mischief and wickedness, became great friends with the Jàrawa boy, Ápi, and learnt a good deal of Hindustani. He used to lie in wait behind the hedge of my compound with a small bow and some arrows he had made, and shoot the Government bullocks as they passed in the carts, and when cuffed for doing this by the other Öngés, or by my Andamanese, used to bite and kick them. About 4 o'clock one morning when he and Ápi were supposed to be sleeping in the verandah outside my bedroom, and I was lying awake, I heard him rouse Ápi, saying "*Ápi Chini*" and then the little couple trotted off to my larder to steal sugar, at which amusement I surprised them.

In May 1885 I took all the Öngés on a long trip up the east coast, after hunting some runaway Burmese convicts as related in Chapter XVII, and we landed on the Table Islands where they helped me collect shells, and Tómiti acted as an orderly to me. I joined Colonel Cadell in the *Kwang Tung* near Landfall Island, and we then went down to the South Brother.

We found that the Öngés were quite familiar with it and clamoured to be put on shore at Kúāī Échékwada Creek, so on the 4th we landed two men, Tugaro Tekene, and Ótáni Wátói, and two women, China Tói and Nátudé Tótálikögé.

They went off into the jungle, and though presents were left for them they did not come back to take them as Colonel Cadell seemed to expect. He waited a whole day to see if they would come, but considering they had first to find their friends who might be anywhere in the interior, or even at the south end of the Island, and then to have the regulation dance and gossip over all that had taken place during their absence, it was not to be expected that they would trouble to come back. At one time it was thought the Ongés had come to take the presents, but they turned out to be a party of our own Andamanese from my boat, who were walking through the jungle and pretending to be the enemy.

We decided not to visit Jackson Creek where so much hostility had been shown on former occasions, but went along the north and east coasts. At Titāījé the Ongés came out on the shore and took presents from us, but would not let our Andamanese touch them. Our captives who (though I did not know it at the time) lived in the next village, Támbe Ébui, talked from the boat to the Ongés on the shore and were most anxious to join them. Tómiti wanted to take me ashore with him, as he assured me the Ongés would not touch me, but Colonel Cadell would not allow me to land. We went on to Hut Bay for the night, but the people here seemed to be very timid and would not come out to take their presents while we were near the shore.

We then went to Tōī Bálöwé, a bay further to the south, where there was a large hut (the biggest in the island), which was deserted; Tálāī, our captive, walked about round it, and seemed to know the place well. We returned to Hut Bay, and the next morning proceeded to the north examining the Sisters and Cinque Islands which our captives seemed to know well. They called the Little Andaman Égö-Bélong, and also gave names to all the small islands, but though they called Rutland Island "Gátinákói" they said they did not know it, or MacPherson's Straits, or any of the country to the north.

It was thus established that the captives were Ongés from the Little Andaman, who had come up to the Cinque Islands, and not Jàrawas from Rutland Island, and it was hoped that by their agency little difficulty would be experienced in making friends with the aborigines of the Little Andaman.

The four Ongés still with me, Tómiti, Tálāī, Kógio Kāī, and Eketi, remained at my house until the following November, when Colonel Cadell landed them on the shore of Bumila Creek

(Kwátinyáwé), on the north of the Little Andaman, under the following circumstances :—

"The *Kwang Tung* left Port Blair on the morning of the 12th of November and anchored near the Cinque Islands. No aborigines were found on them, and the four Jàrawas who had been captured there last January made eager signs to be taken to Égó-Bélong, the name they have for the north-west portion of the Little Andaman.

"On the following morning the ship steamed over to the north-west creek of Little Andaman, where two of our Jàrawas, Tómiti and Tálāī, were landed. Many presents were given them, and they were promised many more if they returned, but this they failed to do. The weather being threatening the *Kwang Tung* proceeded to West Creek Bay, and anchored there for the night.

"On the 15th, the other two Jàrawas, Kógio Kāī and Eketi, the latter a small boy, were given opportunities of landing, but they did not appear anxious to do so. Their delight was great when they were taken back on the following day to the north-western creek and put on shore.

"They explained by unmistakeable signs that they would come back for the canoe and other things which had been presented to them, and they promised to bring with them the Jàrawas who had been let go near the same spot in May last, as well as the two who had been landed two days previously. The ship stayed there all that day and the next, but they did not make their appearance again. We then felt much disappointed."

The *Kwang Tung* then left the Island.

As we have since learnt, the people whom we had in captivity are not very friendly with those at Jackson Creek and the country on the south-west of the Little Andaman, and of course would not land there.

They were given quantities of presents, in addition to all the property they had acquired during their stay in Port Blair and had taken with them. They were much attached to me, and it remained to be seen whether they had sufficient influence with their fellow-tribesmen to bring about a better understanding between us.

Had Colonel Cadell only understood it, the behaviour of the Öngés was perfectly natural, and there was nothing to be disappointed about.

They, of course, first went to see their friends, to find whom would take time, and the dances, talk, etc., would delay them; also, the Andamanese have no idea of time, punctuality, or accuracy.

They were scarcely likely to abandon their friends as soon as they met them, and rush back to the people who had taken them away and kept them in captivity for several months; and the one European with whom they were really intimate, myself, was not present, Colonel Cadell not having taken me with him when he released them.

In December 1885, I visited Bumila Creek and left a quantity of presents on the bank, but did not see any one. I then went on to Penang, and on my return journey again visited the creek and found that all the presents, except some rice and some South Andaman bows, had been taken, so left some more. None of the Öngés were seen.

I have since found that the Öngés between Jackson Creek and Ingo Tijálu are the most treacherous and hostile in the Island, and they seem to be avoided by the others. They have huts on the shore, but owing to the extremely heavy surf and dangerous landing are more or less Éremtágas. The country is divided into Septs, and these divisions appear to be jealously adhered to, so that it is rare to find a man of one Sept in the village of another, except as an occasional visitor.

All the coast people on the north and east coast appear to visit each other freely, and be on friendly terms, but they unite in abusing the people of the west coast.

The island is thickly populated, and I have reason to think that aborigines live in the interior as well as on the coast, as indeed might be expected on an Island 27 miles long and 15 miles wide.

In January 1886, Colonel Cadell again visited Bumila Creek and left presents for the Öngés which, on the withdrawal of his boat, were shyly taken.

No doubt, by this time, the accounts given by Tómiti and the others of their stay in Port Blair had been related to all the Òngés, and, while unable to shake off their old hostility entirely, they were in a state of mingled timidity and distrust. Anxious to secure the presents we brought them, yet they were not quite sure of our attitude, or our reasons for coming amongst them, nor could they overcome that greed for iron and other valuables which led them to massacre visitors, and break up their boats.

From November 1885 to March 1886, may, therefore, be called a time of neutrality in Little Andaman politics, the people being neither for, nor against, us.

With regard to their greed for iron and their habit of looting, I have heard much said to the detriment of the character of these savages; but, as iron is to them, so is gold to us, and how much better would a mob of the European lower classes behave if turned loose in a wild country, and met by an unoffending and unarmed people covered with golden and jewelled ornaments, and having golden utensils?

Further, how *did* the Spaniards (at that time one of the most highly civilised nations in Europe) behave in Mexico and Peru when they first conquered those countries?

CHAPTER XX.

Mr. Portman visits the Little Andaman in the *Ross*—Friendly relations established at Bumila Creek—Report on the visit—North end of the Little Andaman surveyed—Little Andaman visited in July 1886—Mr. Portman resides on the Little Andaman for two and a half months—Correspondence relating to this—Report on the work—Friendly relations established—Coast line of the Island surveyed—Öngés taken to the North Sentinel—Review of the past policy—Further visit to the Island—South end surveyed—Mr. Murray attacked by an Öngé, who was arrested and punished—Colonel Cadell's report—Two visits paid by Mr. Metcalfe to the Little Andaman—Öngés found to have constitutional syphilis—Öngés brought to Port Blair—Island frequently visited—Öngés come to the Cinque Islands, and assist the edible birds' nest collectors—Öngés taken to Calcutta—Our future policy towards the Öngés—Recent visits.

In March, 1886, the steamer *Ross* having arrived from Calcutta for the Settlement, Colonel Cadell directed me to proceed in her to the Little Andaman, and endeavour to make friends with the aborigines there.

Accompanied by Andamanese, Police, and convicts I left on the 4th March, arriving at the Little Andaman on the same day, and anchoring just south of the entrance to Bumila Creek.

On the 5th I left presents on the shore of a small bay a little further to the south, which I called "Eketi Bay," and these were taken by the Öngés.

On the 6th 20 Öngés appeared on the shore there, and presents were left on the sand which they took. They were all armed, and whilst leaving more presents for them they made a rush at me, but did not fire, and I shoved off my boat and got out of shot. They appeared too fierce for me to land and go amongst them, so I kept leaving presents at places out of their range, which they came and took.

Though I was not aware of it, I had commenced operations with the Pálalánkwé Sept, who were not on very friendly terms with any of my acquaintances except the child Eketi, and who would not, therefore, have been much influenced by what they might have heard from them. In the afternoon I went into Bumila Creek on the north coast, and anchored there.

This creek is the best shelter for a small vessel in the Island, but the entrance is difficult to find, being a winding channel through a coral reef, the smallest water in which at low water is only one fathom.

I wandered about, rowed along the coast, and left bundles of presents at different places, with flags of red cloth tied to the adjacent trees to attract the attention of the Óngés.

On the 7th and 8th no one was seen, but on the morning of the 9th three Óngés appeared on the north bank of the Creek. On going near them I found them to be the three who had lived during the previous year in my house, and were released here in November, 1885. (Tómiti, Tálāī, and Kógio Kāī.) They were quite friendly though clamourous for presents, and after my giving them some they induced others who were with them, twelve in number, but who were timid and had hid, to come out opposite the steamer without their arms.

I went ashore amongst them alone, in order not to alarm them, and took quantities of presents including two big turtles we had caught. They asked for water and I took them to a small well I had had dug in the jungle, where they soon became very friendly, and after staying all day by the steamer went home with their presents promising to return for more.

On the 10th no one was seen.

On the 11th 18 Óngés appeared on the north bank, among whom were our former acquaintances. While I was engaged in giving them presents, 12 men appeared on the south bank, who were armed, but after interchanging shouts with our friends, put their bows by. I went off to them in my boat, and gave them presents, and was kept going between the parties, distributing food and other articles in large quantities for about two hours.

I then steamed out of the creek and returned to Eketi Bay where our friends of the south bank joined me. They were the same people who behaved so inimically on the 6th, but were now quite friendly and took their presents eagerly.

On the 12th and 13th no Óngés came near me, and I returned to Port Blair to report progress to Colonel Cadell and obtain a fresh supply of presents.

It was on this occasion that we christened "Kwátinyáwé" Bumila Creek, from "Bumila-da" the Áka-*Béa*-da word for "a fly," the place being, after the Andamanese had camped there for a day or two, infested with myriads of these insects. Owing to its formation probably there are unusually large numbers of flies to be met with in the dry weather in all parts of the Little Andaman.

My Andamanese promptly made a pun on the word, and whereas the Áka-*Béa*-da name for the Little Andaman had formerly been "Wílima-Tára," "The land of casuarinas and sand," from the sandy beaches, and clumps of casuarinas growing there, which are hardly ever seen in the Great Andaman, they now called it "Bumila-Tára" "The land of flies and sand."

On the 17th I returned to the Little Andaman, anchoring this time off the mouth of the north-east creek, where there was shallow water and a heavy swell. The same evening, while trying to drop the steamer up into the creek in order to obtain a better anchorage, she grounded on the sand, and I shored her up, also putting out kedge anchors, and fastening a hawser from the ship to a tree on the shore.

On the morning of the 18th 17 Öngés appeared, without their arms, and I went on shore amongst them, giving them presents. They were all new to me with the exception of Tugaro Tekene, (who was most useful, ordering the others about, and assisted me materially,) and were perfectly friendly, not attempting to interfere with the steamer or do any mischief, though we were high and dry at low water.

I, with some of my Andamanese, spent most of the day on shore with them, dancing, singing, and playing about. They returned home in the evening, and, getting the ship afloat on the night's tide, I proceeded on the 19th to Jackson Creek, anchoring a short distance to the north of the entrance. We left presents at different places on the shore, and on the 20th at about 3 A.M., 17 Öngés came out opposite the ship. These people were also new to me and appeared friendly though timid. They were unarmed. After giving them a large number of presents I left in the afternoon and steamed down the west coast. Though we saw huts and smoke it was impossible to land owing to the surf on the reefs. On arriving in a bay about six miles north of the south-west corner of the island, I saw a large hut and some people on the beach so stood in and anchored. There was a very heavy surf, but as it only beat on sand I sent some Andamanese to swim on shore with presents.

The Ongés made no sign till about 5 P.M. when we saw them make a rush out of the jungle where they had been concealed and seize the presents. They were armed. On their collecting on the beach and shouting to us I sent a number of Andamanese ashore with presents, including a large turtle, which they took through the surf with much difficulty, and which, as I knew it would, delighted the Öngés more than anything else. They found there 23 people, chiefly women and children, who were timid but friendly and took all that was given to them. They had laid their bows and arrows down on the sand at some distance. After giving them everything we had I returned on board, and at dusk saw a number of men join them from the jungle.

On the 21st I steamed on round the south and east coasts, but was unable to effect a landing or obtain an anchorage anywhere, owing to the wind, sea, and heavy surf, so went along the north coast and anchored in Bumila Creek for the night.

On the 22nd we saw some Öngé women in the distance on the south reef, but could not get near them.

On the 23rd 14 Öngés came on the south bank, from their hut about three miles to the southward. They were unarmed and we had watched them when coming. They appeared to have left their bows and arrows in their hut, and simply came with a number of baskets to carry away the presents they expected. They remained on the bank till about 3 P.M., and I went ashore with a few Andamanese and remained with them. They were very delighted with their presents, and we all had a dance together. They were quite ready to do anything we told them, and helped to clean a canoe of ours, but we were unable to persuade any of them, or any of the other Öngés we had met, to come on board the steamer, or even to come and sit in the boat.

No others were seen and I returned to Port Blair on the 25th.

On this visit I noted in my Report:—

"Our present success at the Little Andaman is, in my opinion owing to our having captured those Little Andamanese at the Cinque Islands in February 1885, and having kept them for nine months in my house, where they were well treated and became quite friendly. No doubt the event of their visit to us was talked of throughout the Little Andaman on their return there in November last, and on my again appearing there word was passed amongst the aborigines not to be afraid nor to fire on us, but to come and receive the presents we had doubtless brought.

"Moreover presents had been left at the Little Andaman at intervals of a fortnight ever since November last.

"As I had the little Jàrawa boy Ápi with me on the second trip I was able to make out a good deal of what the Öngés said, and got on very well with them. At present they are of course very timid, and very little would provoke them, but by constantly visiting them and distributing presents in large quantities, taking particular care in all cases to conciliate the older men, and by avoiding all actions which might annoy or alarm them, such as landing near, or attempting to visit their huts, or trying against their will to persuade them on board boats or ships, we shall I think in a short time have them in quite as amicable relations as are the North Andamanese.

"The only presents which are now of any use to them are, iron of all kinds, files, turtles, pigs, red cloth, plantains, coconuts, and yams. These should always be given in large quantities."

From this visit dates the establishment of our friendly relations with the Little Andamanese, which, with the single exception of a murderous assault made by an Öngé on Mr. Murray in March 1887, (to be described presently), have never been interrupted.

The basis of our success has of course been our attack upon, capture, and subsequent taming of, the Öngés met on the Cinque Islands in January 1885, and we owe a great deal to the goodwill and intelligence of Tómiti, Tálāī, and Kógio Kāī.

When I met them at Bumila Creek on the 9th of March, this being our first meeting since their release on the Little Andaman in the previous November, I was uncertain whether they intended to be friendly, or to revenge themselves on me for their captivity, and I had taken precautions to defend the *Ross* should they attempt to try and board her in their canoes while she was at anchor in the creek, especially during the night.

Also, when I landed amongst them on their calling to me and showing that they had no weapons, I remembered former similar tactics at Jackson Creek, and would not allow any one to land with me in case the Öngés should object to my Andamanese, or the convicts, or Police, or perhaps take fright.

I ordered the boat's crew to keep their oars out and be ready at a moment's notice to take me on board and pull away, but my friends were to be trusted. I relied most on Tómiti, and he has never yet played me false.

The Öngés have a rather alarming way of rushing at a boat and shouting wildly, but we soon got used to this, as it is only inspired by their greed for presents and means nothing.

It was satisfactory to have got on friendly terms with the inhabitants of the Little Andaman after all that had gone before, and considering the bad character they bore; indeed, in the previous year, the Secretary to the Government of India in the Home Department had remarked to me, while he was in Port Blair on an official visit, that he did not believe that the Little Andamanese would ever be tamed.

Colonel Cadell now considered it safe for me to take a Surveyor down to the north end of the Island in order that he might fix the position of it, and connect it by triangulation with the Great Andaman Group, so on the 7th of April, 1886, I proceeded with Mr. Keatinge and his survey party to Bumila Creek.

No Öngés were seen till the 10th when a party of surveyors who were measuring Bumila Creek met with Kógio Kāī and a few boys.

On the 11th a dozen Öngés came on the north bank of the creek and were given presents, and I went on to Kúāī Échékwada. In the afternoon I met seven men on the bank of this creek, who were my friends the Pálalánkwés from Eketi Bay. They had come all that distance after the steamer and were delighted at finding us. I stayed on shore with them for about an hour, sending the boat off to the *Ross* for presents and on its return helped the Öngés to carry what I had given them for some distance down the coast. We parted on the best of terms.

The next morning I left Ápi, the little Jàrawa boy, with Kógio Kāi who was very anxious to have him. They had lived together in my house for some time, and Ápi seemed pleased to remain. He died of bronchitis a few months afterwards. He was quiet, gentle, and a rather stupid child.

Nothing more was seen of the Öngés, and as Mr. Keatinge had finished his work we returned on the 13th to Port Blair.

On the 24th July 1885, Colonel Cadell and I visited the Little Andaman in the R.I.M.S. *Nancowry*, anchoring in Bumila Creek.

The Öngés were found to be very friendly, the people from the south bank coming opposite the ship almost as soon as we anchored; quantities of presents were given to them as usual. The north coast people did not appear till the 26th, when Kógio Kāi came with a few men. He was induced to come on board, and the others seeing this, I had no difficulty in persuading the south bank people to do the same. It soon became only necessary to send the boat ashore when they crowded into it, the women and children on the south bank did not, however, come off. On the 27th, the north coast people again appeared and after receiving their presents returned, accompanied by Colonel Cadell and Lieutenant Deane, the Commander of the *Nancowry*, to their hut, which was some distance off in the interior. No Öngés were seen there.

We returned to Port Blair on the 29th.

The following incident showed how timid the Öngés still were, and how they distrusted us.

On the 27th, Colonel Cadell and Lieutenent Deane landed among the Pálalánkwés on the south bank, and Colonel Cadell, to amuse them, fired off his revolver in the air. All the savages slunk away into the jungle, and I had to go off to their hut with presents, and spend the afternoon in pacifying them. Colonel Cadell subsequently redeemed his character in their eyes by dancing a Highland reel to them on the beach.

With regard to this trip I noted—

" This visit has shown that the friendly relations established by me in March last remain, and it will only be necessary to visit the Island occasionally, distributing quantities of presents on each visit, in order to keep the people friendly.

" I am of opinion that we should not, as yet, attempt to visit their huts, show too great a curiosity as to their proceedings, use fire-arms in their presence, or show them any novelties likely to frighten them; but should content ourselves with receiving them whenever they choose to come for presents, and try to gain some knowledge of their language."

My health had failed during the year 1886, and a year's furlough to Europe had been granted to me from November, but on the 2nd of September I wrote to Colonel Cadell that, as I understood he wanted the survey of the Little Andaman Island to be completed during the coming dry season, as this was the last year the party from the Survey of India would be working at the Andamans, I would cancel the year's furlough which had been granted to me, make a preliminary survey of the Island myself, and finish taming the aborigines.

As my health was very bad and I was in urgent need of a change, I hoped that I might be allowed to go on leave as soon as the work was done.

I also submitted the following proposals regarding the work :—:

I requested that the steamer *Ross* should be placed at my disposal, also one large and seaworthy boat; the crew of the *Ross* being supplied with two months' rations. She was to be fitted with a new double awning, and new side curtains, extending completely round the ship.

I hoped that all her fittings would be carefully overhauled, and that such necessaries as spare shackle pins, etc., would be furnished;

also that the engine driver would be supplied with all necessary tools and extra appliances, and such spare gear as might be requisite.

I would take two servants, two convicts of the Andamanese department, two convict boatmen, 21 Andamanese men and six women, also two Andamanese canoes, tents for the party to live in on shore, and axes for jungle cutting, but I did not think it necessary to take a Police Guard, as they generally gave a great deal of trouble, frightened the Öngés, and were of little use.

I also decided to take a large lighter, in which extra water tanks and all the rations and stores were to be placed. (This was most useful, and was kept anchored in Bumila Creek.)

I proposed to remain at first in Bumila Creek, moving amongst those tribes with whom we were already on good terms, until I had acquired some knowledge of their language, after which I would gradually work round the coast as the sea and weather permitted.

Landing is very difficult almost all round the island, owing to which the work would necessarily progress but slowly, until the calm weather set in.

I also suggested that Major Strahan, who had succeeded Captain Hobday in charge of the survey party, should point out to me the tracks he wanted cut, and the hill tops he wanted cleared, but this was not done, and no survey has yet been made of the interior of the island.

Colonell Cadell wrote to me, in reply to my letter :—

"I consider it of great importance that you should remain here during the ensuing dry season in order that you may complete the establishment of friendly relations with the inhabitants of the Little Andaman, before the survey of the Island is recommenced in March next.

"I have, therefore, applied to the Government of India for your leave to be granted in March next. I have no doubt that it will be granted to you when the work is finished.

"I am much obliged to you for volunteering to postpone your leave."

He also wrote to the Government of India on the 3rd of September 1886, asking that my leave might be postponed from the 1st of November to the 1st of the following March. He detailed the considerable improvement that had been made in our relations with the Ougés during the past year, and added that he considered the entire pacification of this Trib , having regard to the position of their Island in the midst of a trade route, to be of great importance A portion of the north part of the island had been surveyed during the previous April, and that survey might now be completed. To ensure the safety of the survey party, however, it was necessary that I should spend most of the ensuing cold season at the Little Andaman in the *Ross*.

I proceeded to the Little Andaman on the 27th of October, and Colonel Cadell, a few days afterwards, left for England on $3\frac{1}{2}$ months' leave, Major R. J. Wimberley, the Deputy Superintendent, officiating as Chief Commissioner.

At the conclusion of my work, on the 21st of January, 1887, I submitted the following report to the Chief Commissioner, and it will be found to embody most occurrences of interest in connection with my stay on the Little Andaman.

"Sir,—

"I have now the honour to submit for your information a detailed account of the work I have done at the Little Andaman Island during the time I have been posted there.

2. In accordance with your instructions I left Port Blair in the steamer *Ross* on the 27th October 1886, having No. 1 Lighter and a ten-oared boat in tow. Six convicts and twenty-seven Andamanese accompanied me, and I had rations for three months for the entire party.

3. I arrived at the Little Andaman Island on the 28th of October, and anchored in Bumila Creek. For the next three days we were engaged in making a small clearing on the east bank of the creek and housing the party. The Ongés from the neighbouring huts came down

daily to visit me and were very friendly. I heard with regret that the little boy Ápi I had left with the Ékudi Sept in April 1886, was dead, but the remainder of those people who had lived with me in Port Blair all came to my camp.

4. Women and children came fearlessly to visit us, and the first difficulty I met with was that of preventing the savages from looting my camp of everything they fancied. By making an example of one of the first cases that occurred, and treating the delinquents somewhat roughly, I soon got them to understand that they were only to have what we gave them, not all they saw, and from that time, with two exceptions, to which I shall refer later, I have had no trouble. I have been very lavish of presents to all the people.

(It was of no use mincing matters with the Öngés, and as their thefts became intolerable I gave one man a beating and gave the others orders that he was never to be allowed near the camp again. This frightened them, and they behaved much better afterwards. I subsequently met the man in a village in the interior; he seemed quiet and shy, and crept away into the jungle.)

5. I had taken advantage of the break of calm weather which generally occurs in October, at the change of the monsoon, to go down to the Island, and very stormy weather began soon after, the north-east monsoon setting in; I, therefore, confined my work to going about amongst the neighbouring villages, endeavouring to gain influence over these people, and learning the language.

The Andamanese I had brought with me were occupied in turtling canoe-cutting, etc., and I encouraged the Öngés to go amongst them and associate with them. They soon took to swimming off on board the steamer, or coming in their canoes to visit me, and occasionally brought me baskets of dried fish as presents.

On the 3rd November three men whom I afterwards found belonged to the south coast of the Island paid me a visit, and were very pleasant.

(The drying and storing of small fish is a custom peculiar to the Öngés, and was probably learnt from that outside influence with which they *must* have been in contact at some previous period.)

The arrival of the three men was very interesting, as their conduct appeared to me to resemble that shown in the Great Andaman by men who come from one tribe to visit another. They were evidently on their best behaviour, were rather shy and quiet, and acted as if they were in a foreign territory, for when I afterwards met them on the south coast they were boisterous and noisy, whereas my friends, Tómiti, and the others, were in their turn then quiet and subdued.

Their meeting with Tómiti, who was helping my people cut a canoe, was:—'After a moment's silence on both sides the stranger sat on Tómiti's lap, they each hugged the other, patted each other's backs down the spine with a number of light blows, shed a few tears silently, (unlike the demonstrative howl of the Great Andaman people,) and after a few minutes both parties got up and began to talk and laugh.'

6. On the 12th of November I tried to go down the coast in the *Ross* and also to cross to the South Sentinel Island, but the weather was so bad that I was obliged to put back. The Little Andamanese with me gave me the name of the South Sentinel Island, Kilágá-Góāī, but said they had never been there.

On the 13th I coasted down to Tókyui and saw all the people there. They received me in an unconcerned way and appeared to take little interest even in the presents we had brought. I learnt that the man we had captured at Jackson Creek in January, 1885, who afterwards died in Port Blair, was from the Tókyui village, and that his name was Tálémé.

7. On the 14th very heavy rain commenced to fall, and on the 15th a cyclone set in, which lasted till the 20th. With the exception of the loss of her side curtains the *Ross* sustained no damage. I had both anchors down and hawsers passed outside all. Until the 18th I was unable to get ashore even on the banks of Bumila Creek, where we were anchored, and the convicts and Andamanese suffered very much. The clearing was eighteen inches under water, and the people were living on raised *Machans* they had made. All the Andamanese huts had been blown down, but the tents, being more sheltered, had stood. It would have been dangerous to have gone further into the

jungle owing to the falling branches of trees, and on the sand one could not stand up to the wind, but had to crawl along. Much damage was done in the forest, quantities of dead fish were washed up on the coast, and many birds and bats seem to have been killed. The Öngés suffered much from the cold and want of food, and several sick, whom I had seen at Tókyui on the 13th, had died.

As soon as the cyclone was over many of them came to me for food. The rain was so heavy during the storm that the creek was running with fresh water down to the mouth. After this storm the place seemed to become unhealthy, and from that time onward there was a great deal of sickness among the Andamanese and convicts. I did not suffer much until January.

8. Owing to the heavy sea outside I was unable to go anywhere until the 24th, and my Andamanese continued cutting boats and catching turtle. On the 24th I visited Jackson Creek. The landing here was very difficult owing to the surf, and our boat was swamped. It was impossible to enter the creek as the sand had now silted up so much, and I landed on the north side of it. Several Öugés met us and were given presents. I walked along the shore with them for some distance, and visited some sandstone caves in which were the grass variety of edible birds' nests. All the water here contains much lime, and stalactites are formed in the caves.

9. On the 28th I was visited by H. M. I. M. S. *Kwang Tung*, the Commander very kindly supplying me with such provisions, etc., as I required.

On the 29th I worked down the coast from Jackson Creek to Ápi Island, and went some way into the interior. The people received us in a friendly manner, but were very greedy for presents, taking everything they saw, not only out of the boats, but even from the persons of my Andamanese, and seizing many articles which could be of no possible use to them, (including my umbrella which they had to return). This behaviour I checked with the help of the interpreters I had brought down from Bumila Creek, and the people soon began to obey my directions, though a very little opposition, or an increase in their numbers would, I think, have led to a row.

(My Bumila Creek friends did not approve of my coming to see these people, abusing them, and saying that they would kill me.)

10. There being much sickness now among my party I came up to Port Blair with the worst cases on the 1st of December. There was a very heavy sea on and the *Ross* had a good opportunity of showing what a fine sea-boat she is. Two Óngés from the Ékudi village accompanied me, one of whom, Kógio Kāī, had been in Port Blair before as a captive in 1885. The other, a lad, named Óitá-Dángábé was woefully sea-sick until we got under the shelter of the Cinque Islands. I was interested in watching the two lads here, as Kógio Kāī was evidently describing to the other the fight which had occurred there in January, 1885, and he used to point to me and to my Andamanese, and abuse us, and then grin.

On the 4th of December I returned to the Little Andaman, (arriving there on the 5th) with some fresh convicts and Andamanese. The weather on the way back was even worse than what we had had coming up. My absence, leaving a small party of convicts and Andamanese on the Island, had been a good test of the work done, and I found on my return that the Ongés had been living with them in my camp, in the most friendly manner.

11. I was kept in the creek by bad weather until the 12th of December, during which time the crew of the *Ross* were employed in cutting and stacking firewood in order to save our coal, and the convicts and Andamanese went about with me, inland and along the coast to the different villages.

I also commenced a coast-line survey of the island with a prismatic compass and chain and made a map of the entrance to Bumila Creek. The Little Andamanese, or Öngés, as we found they called themselves, were constantly in camp and began to pick up a little Hindustani.

12. On the 13th and 14th I worked along the west coast surveying down to Tóchángédu, where my work was stopped by the heavy surf, so I began on the 15th to work east and south from the north point of the Island. A curious incident occurred on the 17th, which will illustrate the influence I have acquired over the neighbouring

people. Kógio Kāī told me that a man of his own Sept had stolen some knives belonging to us : I sent for the man, admonished him, and forbade him to come to the camp; Tálai, who was also of his Sept then escorted him to Támbe Ébui, and he has not since been allowed to visit us.

The Ékudi people on another occasion behaved in a similar manner to the Pálalánkwés (whom however they dislike), who had stolen some turtle spears, refusing to allow them to land near the clearing or visit us for several days : the turtle spears were returned to me.

13. By the 19th of December I had surveyed to as far as Titāījé meeting many people of all sizes and sexes, who were very pleasant and friendly, and I then returned to Bumila Creek, beached the *Ross* and cleaned and painted her. H. M. I. M. S. *Nancowry* called on the 21st, and on the 22nd I proceeded to Port Blair with the sick from the camp and with nine Ongés picked from the following Septs :—Ékudi, Pálalánkwé, Tókyui, Támbe Ébui, and Titāījé.

14. I remained in Port Blair until the 27th when I crossed with my party to the North Sentinel Island. The Ongés gave me their name for it, Chió-tá-kwó-kwé, and appeared to be well acquainted with it. They walked fearlessly about in the jungle, but on approaching some of the inhabitants on the evening of the 27th Tómiti said that they talked an entirely different language, and he did not understand them. None of the Sentinelese were caught, but the Ougés said that, though they also were Ongés, still they were a distinct tribe.

On the 28th I visited Port Mouat and the Labyrinth Islands, returning to Port Blair on the 29th; and on the 2nd of January I returned to the Little Andaman.

15. During their stay in Port Blair the greatest care was taken that the Ougés should not suffer in health, and they were shown everything I thought would interest them, including the athletic sports and the Military Parade on the 1st of January, and were also given quantities of presents, being allowed to have almost everything they fancied; they appeared so delighted with their visit that on the way back they said they would come up to Port Blair in their own canoes in the fine weather.

16. On the 3rd of January I started down the east coast, surveying. In addition to my party I was accompanied by Tómiti, Tálá, and Kógio Kāi, who were of the greatest assistance. People came out to meet us at each village, and everyone was quite friendly and pleasant. I found that Téyāi Creek, on the east coast, was blocked by a bar of shingle across the mouth, but we hauled a canoe over this and then went up the creek, which runs for a long distance inland. The country was swampy, but the forest had a slightly different appearance from that in the swamps of the Great Andaman. At one place was a sort of ferry with a small raft and a rope of canes across the creek. We did not see any of the aborigines in the interior.

On the 4th I anchored in Dāōgulé Bay, having been accompanied by nearly fifty people along the coast. They were inquisitive, and did not understand my proceedings when surveying, but became happier when I told some of them off to haul the measuring chains along the sand. On the 5th I met, at Tōī Bálöwé, Nátudé Tótáli Kögé, one of the women who was captured on the Cinque Islands in 1885. On the 6th I met, at Íngōie, on the south coast, the three men who had visited me at Bumila Creek on the 3rd of November last. I completed the survey on the 7th, closing on Ápi Island, and then returned to Bumila Creek.

When surveying along the south coast the Öugés came in great numbers, and gave some trouble. On one occasion I had just set up my prismatic compass, and adjusted it, when one of them knocked it over and grinned at me. I grinned back at him and hit him over the head with the stand of the compass, after which many of the Òngés left and I was not so much annoyed. There is a very heavy surf on the south-west and south-east corners of the Island, and it is only a little less along the whole of the south coast, so it was easy to appreciate the difficulties and dangers met with by the members of Lieutenant Much's expedition in 1867.

The only safe landing place is at Íngōie, a little to the east of the rock where the crew of the *Assam Valley* landed and were murdered; (now called Cadell Rock,) but of this landing place Lieutenant Much had, of course, no knowledge. I tried to find out from the Òngés whether they remembered anything of that expedition, but they either could not, or would not, understand me.

17. The weather now got stormy again and I began to suffer in health. The survey being finished, I having visited all the villages round the Island, and being on the best terms with all the people, and our stores being nearly exhausted, I considered that the work I had been sent to do had been accomplished; so I returned to Port Blair on the 19th of January with the entire party. I think we were on as friendly terms with the Öngés as we were with the inhabitants of the North Andaman in 1880.

18. From what I can learn I am of opinion that, while the whole of the Little Andaman Island is peopled by one race, calling themselves Ongés, these people are subdivided into Septs, who adhere more or less to their own country, and who appear to quarrel and fight among themselves. What little I have learnt of their language I have embodied in my work on the languages of the Andamanese, written at the request of the Chief Commissioner, but the amount is small. It differs almost entirely from any language with which I am acquainted, except that of the Jàrawa tribes.

The Öugés appear healthy, their principal diseases being chest complaints, coughs and colds, fever, itch, and scurvy; and in physique they compare favourably with the inhabitants of the Great Andaman. (At this time I was not aware that they had hereditary syphilis.)

Their manners and customs differ somewhat from those of the aborigines of the Great Andaman, the principal differences I have noticed being the following:—

The large circular huts built by them, some of which would accommodate sixty people.

The raised charpoys on which they sleep.

Their habit of cooking, drying, and storing in baskets, a small fish similar to a sprat.

The difference in the shape of their canoes at the bow and stern.

The difference in their ornaments, and the absence of necklaces of human and other bones, and broad, taselled belts.

The women wear a tassel of yellow fibre in the place of the leaf worn in the Great Andaman.

The difference in the shape of the bow, which is of the European pattern, but flatter.

The arrows used for shooting fish frequently have four heads of different lengths fitted into one shaft similar to those found on the North Sentinel.

The Öngés are by no means expert in the use of a canoe in rough water, and are unable to harpoon turtle. They paint their hair only with red earth, and do not paint their bodies with it; they do not allow their hair to grow long: the women do not keep their heads clean shaven.

Their staple food appears to be the seed of the mangrove, boiled, as that article of diet is always to be seen in their huts, supplemented of course by whatever else they can get.

I may here mention that, after close and continued observation of their habits, I entirely disbelieve the legend that they were formerly in the habit of visiting the Car Nicobar Island; how indeed, having regard to the apparent difficulties of such a journey in their canoes, this legend could have been seriously entertained, I cannot imagine.

It was very pleasant to see the numbers of healthy children of both sexes in the various villages; the Öngés seem to marry later in life than do the Great Andaman Tribes, but the same system of monogamy prevails.

The music of their songs is different from that of the Great Andaman people, is more pleasing, and is not accompanied by the clapping of hands, or the striking of a sounding board.

Their dance is peculiar and unlike that of the other Andamanese, being apparently an imitation of the act of coition. The Jàrawa tribe of the Great Andaman has a similar dance.

So far as I know they have no religion of any kind, and I have learnt nothing of their traditions or superstitions, from which they seem even freer than are our people.

In conclusion I may say that the Öngés are by no means fierce, being, if anything, of a milder disposition than are our Andamanese, and I became much attached to them, which attachment is, I think, returned. They are easily silenced or frightened, and are in great dread of a gun.

19. The survey of the Island made by me has been accepted by Major Strahan, and issued by the Survey Department, having been altered and adapted to observations taken at the north and south ends of the Island.

The Little Andaman, at the north end, consists of mangrove swamps and low belts of sandy soil on which the aborigines live. On the west and south-west coasts the land rises into low hills of a coarse sandstone, running more or less north and south. The timber appears to be much the same as that of the South Andaman, and the rocks are chiefly limestone and sandstone, with a good deal of actual coral rock on the east and south coasts. In one place, on the point south of Dāōgulé Bay, I noticed an outcrop of igneous rock. I did not see any minerals.

The products of the sea appear to be the same as at the Great Andaman, but the *Tubiporine* family of coral particularly *Tubipora Musica*, occurs in profusion. Dugong and turtle abound in the sea, and I captured two of the former, (one being a remarkably fine specimen, nine feet in length, and five feet in circumference) and many of the latter.

The Òngés are very fond of turtle, which they are unable to get with the facility with which our Andamanese catch them, as they are ignorant of the use of the harpoon, and turtle always formed a great part of my presents to them.

In rough weather landing is almost impossible on the coast, and in calm weather there are heavy ground swells and tide rips.

The following are the best anchorages for small vessels, near which are suitable landing places. Even these can only be used in calm weather:—

"Bumila Creek. (Only a very small vessel can enter this.)

Just north of Náchugé Point, opposite the entrance to Jackson Creek, a landing place being near the point, as well as in the Creek.

Íngo Tijálu.

Opposite Íngŏie, about half a mile from the shore.

Hut Bay,

Óbáté, opposite the mouth of the North-East Creek.

Landing is difficult in most places, and I always used an Andamanese canoe.

21. It may be interesting to give here a summary of our relations with the Little Andamanese.

Our first meeting with the inhabitants of the Little Andaman was the punitive expedition in 1867 under Lieutenant Much, which increased the savages' hatred of foreigners without increasing their respect for them.

General Stewart paid a conciliatory visit to the island in 1873, and after leaving presents was attacked. A skirmish ensued in which an Öngé was wounded and died while being taken on board the ship. Then followed the punitive expedition under Captain Wimberley, the effect of which must have been to largely increase the hatred and dread of the savages towards us, and at the same time have taught them to fear a gun.

After this the island remained unvisited till 1880 when attempts were again made to enter on friendly relations with the people by Colonel Cadell and myself. We frequently went there, and, though fired at, only once was the fire returned. In 1880, on one occasion, some of our Andamanese were able to land, touch the Öngés, and give presents into their hands, but on the same day they attempted to cut me off when ashore, and seize my boat.

This policy of visiting the Island and leaving presents was continued at intervals until the 13th of January, 1885, when, after rowing up Jackson Creek Colonel Cadell's boat was attacked by the Öngés, and after a skirmish one unwounded man, Tálémé, was captured. He subsequently died in Port Blair. From here we went to Hut Bay, where a slight skirmish also took place. While returning to Port Blair from this expedition a number of Jàrawas were found on the Cinque Islands, and I was despatched with a party of convicts and Andamanese to capture them. I returned to Port Blair with nine people, of whom one died in hospital, and two men and two women were released on the Little Andaman in May, 1885, having passed most of the intervening period in my house, where I endeavoured to conciliate them and gain their affection. Three men and a boy remained with me at my house until November, 1885, being treated well, I succeeded in attaching them to me, and it is in my opinion entirely owing to the affection borne me by these people, and by their agency, that I have at last been able to establish friendly relations with the inhabitants of the Little Andaman. Their names are Tómiti, Tálāī, and Eketi, residing at Támbe Ébui village, and Kógio Kāī residing at Ékudi village.

After their release on the Little Andaman in November, 1885, the Island was visited at intervals and presents were left, but none of the Óugés were met with until, in March, 1886, Colonel Cadell despatched me alone in the steamer *Ross* to endeavour to meet with them and conciliate them. At Eketi Bay where I first went I was threatened, but after spending a few days in Bumila Creek, the three men, Tómiti, Tálāi, and Kógio Kāī came out on the shore with about a dozen others and asked for presents, assuring me that they would not fire on me. I at once went on shore alone amongst them and gave them presents, and from that time to the present we have not come into any collision with the Little Andamanese, nor has a single shot been fired on either side. I remained at the Island nearly the whole of March, and my influence extended sufficiently to enable the Survey Party in April to map from Titāījé to Pálalánkwé. In July, 1885, when Colonel Cadell and I visited the island in the *Nancowry*, the Ongés were induced to come on board for their presents, and Colonel Cadell was able to visit their hut at some distance in the interior. The next visit was the one from which I have just returned.

22. With regard to their behaviour to shipwrecked crews, I am of opinion that the crew of any native vessel wrecked there would still be liable to be massacred, and though a European, if wrecked on the north coast might be well treated, I should not like to guarantee his safety. Shipwrecked sailors are rarely diplomats, and would be extremely likely to resent the looting of their ships or persons in a manner which would certainly lead to their being shot. This looting cannot

be prevented, the temptation being too great for any savage however tame, and the general education of the Öngés will take some years. It is, however, quite safe for any Settlement Official to visit the Island, and land. I would advise him first to land at Bumila Creek and take on board either Kógio Kāī, Tómiti, or Tálāi, or else one of the following:—

Wána Löégé (since dead) of the Ékudi tribe; or Kógio Kókélé (since dead,) of the Pálalánkwé tribe, who would act as interpreters at any other part of the island where he wished to land.

The presents which the Öngés most appreciate are, hoop iron, rod iron, files, sleeping mats, coconuts, plantains, and specimens of the articles used by our Andamanese, also turtle, which can easily be got at the South Sentinel Island. The Öngés are, I believe, quite willing to come to Port Blair in their canoes in the fine weather, but great care should be taken that they do not contract any disease, if they do come up. They will take to smoking kindly, but I have not encouraged this, as my aim is to keep them in their healthy primitive state, and I believe this can be done, and they can still be brought to obey our orders and remain on friendly terms with outsiders. We require very little of them, and a close intercourse with these savages means death to them.

* * * * * *

Colonel Cadell returned from leave in February, 1887, and being naturally anxious to see what had been done at the Little Andaman decided to go there early in March. Major Strahan agreed to come up from the Nicobars and meet him there, and while at the Island arranged to take the necessary observations for Latitude at the North and South ends. This visit unfortunately resulted in the one check we have received at the Little Andaman, *viz.*, the murderous attack made upon Mr. Murray, the Chief Engineer of the *Kwang Tung*, on the beach at Íngo Tíjálu, by an Öngé named Kóbédá Köté.

Mr. Murray had been stationed at the Andamans more than once, and had been present on board the *Undaunted* during Captain Wimberley's expedition to the Little Andaman in 1874, and had also been on the *Kwang Tung* during the recent operations there. He had, however, never landed on the Island, and, as he was about to retire from the Service, Captain Pryce, Commander of the *Kwang Tung*, and I, persuaded him to come for a walk on the shore, assuring him that the Ongés were perfectly friendly. We had reason to regret our importunity.

I submitted the following report on the visit:—

"2. On the 4th of March, 1887, Colonel Cadell, the Chief Commissioner of the Andamans, accompanied by Lieutenant-Colonel Roberts, 7th Regiment Madras Native Infantry, Mr. Portman, on special duty at the Little Andaman, Mr. Metcalfe, Officer in charge of the Andamanese, and a number of Andamanese, left Port Blair in the steamer *Ross* at 6 A.M., arriving in Bumila Creek, North end of the Little Andaman, at 2 P.M. Some of the Ongés visited us at once, and our old friends Tómiti, Tálāī, Wána Löégé, and Kógio Kókélé, were taken on board as interpreters.

"3. On the 5th we proceeded along the North coast, taking on board Kógio Kāī off Kúāī-Échékwada Creek After inspecting the Ariel Ledge we anchored at 10·30 A.M. off the mouth of the Téyāī Creek on the East coast. Several Ongés of both sexes were on the shore, and we landed amongst them, giving them presents. They were quite friendly, and we visited their hut at Titāījé. In the evening we rowed up the Téyāī Creek, which is one of the most beautiful in this Group of Islands. All our Andamanese remained on shore for the night with the Ongés, and had a feast of turtle.

"4. On the 6th none of the Ongés were seen, although we landed at two places, and we anchored for the night in Hut Bay on the East coast.

On the morning of the 7th two men appeared and were given presents, and we then went on to Tōī Bálöwé, a large hut on the southeast corner of the Island, measuring 60 feet in diameter and about 55 feet in height. Shortly after we landed a number of Öngés arrived and were given presents. I walked to a village of about 14 lean-to huts a little way in the interior, and my party were there regaled with pig and honey. As usual amongst these people there were a few ill-tempered, conservative old men, who refused to be pleased with us. Our interpreters decided to walk on round the coast and I brought on board two new men, sending them ashore again when we reached Íngōīe that afternoon. There is a good landing place here, the reef being broken in one place just opposite the hut; the best anchorage is in 8 fathoms, about half a mile from the shore.

In the evening we visited the rock where Lieutenant Much's expedition landed in 1867, and the Öngés pretended to have some remembrance of it.

"6. My Andamanese slept on shore, as usual, with the Öugés, a number of whom had followed us round.

On the 8th, H.M.I.M.S. "*Kwang Tung*" arrived with Lieutenant-Colonel Strahan and his Survey Party, and Mr. Man, the Officer in charge of the Nicobars. The Survey work was at once commenced; the Öngés were rather troublesome, trying to steal the metal of the instruments, but no fraças took place, and with the presents we had given them they were quite pleased.

"7. On the 9th, the Chief Commissioner, with Lieutenant-Colonel Strahan, Mr. Man, and Mr. Metcalfe went to the North end of the Island for the day in the "*Ross*" where Colonel Strahan observed for Latitude, and Lieutenant-Colonel Roberts and I remained behind in the *Kwang Tung*. Mr. Senior, Assistant Surveyor, and his party, landed at 8-30 A.M., at Íngōīe, and attended by the Andamanese, our Ongé interpreters, and two canoes with presents, proceeded to survey the coast round to Íngo Tijálu on the South-West corner. The canoes with the presents were swamped in the surf, and one canoe and all the presents were lost. The Öngés however, beyond being greedy for such metal as they saw, gave no trouble, and Mr. Senior having completed his work, came off at 4 P.M. to the *Kwang Tung*, which vessel, after looking for the shoal marked on the chart as being 4 miles South-west of the South-west end of the Island, and not finding it, had anchored off Íngo Tijálu. (The shoal was afterwards found by the R.I.M.S. *Investigator*)

Mr. Eldridge, 2nd Officer of the *Kwang Tung*, and Mr Baynes, a passenger, had been ashore bathing from a Nicobarese canoe, and some

Ongé women had joined them in the water, and seemed to be quite friendly.

"8. At 5 p.m. I landed with Captain Pryce, R.I.M., Lieutenant-Colonel Roberts, and Mr Murray, Chief Engineer of the *Kwang Tung*. I had with me as an interpreter Kógio Kāī, also two of our Andamanese, Riala and Lokala. Unfortunately I had no presents, they having been lost in the canoes. We were received on the shore by about 25 people, among whom were many women and children, and they were all unarmed except two men who had adzes. They were very greedy for presents and tried to loot the boat, but were prevented from doing so by Kógio Kāī and myself; Mr. Murray however gave them an iron bucket, which they had previously taken and I had recovered from them. They embraced Kógio Kāī, and we all walked along the shore together, taking two Khalassies from the boat's crew.

After we had proceeded about 200 yards Captain Pryce drew our attention to some fish on the beach, and he, with Lieutenant-Colonel Roberts and Mr. Murray stopped to look at them. I was a few paces behind talking to the Ongés by whom we were surrounded, when suddenly I heard a thud, and Mr. Murray cried out, "I am killed." I turned and saw him on his knees on the sand, the blood streaming from a wound on the back of his hand, and a tall Ongé standing just behind him with a large adze in his hand.

The attack was quite an unprovoked one, and from the fact that the women and children were present and none of the other Ongés were armed, I consider it to have been unpremeditated and without the approval of the others, who immediately began to retire.

Kógio Kāī called to me to shoot the Ongé but none of us had any arms, and we all went off to the boat, Captain Pryce and a Khalassie supporting Mr. Murray, and Lieutenant-Colonel Roberts waiting in the rear to see if the man was going to attack us again. He did not attempt to do so, and the Ongés all went to the landing place and sat down there. We returned to the *Kwang Tung* and I asked Captain Pryce to arm all the Europeans and place them at my disposal, which he did, and ordered away two boats. I also took with me Tómiti, Tálāī, and Kógio Kāī. On nearing the shore I sent Tómiti and Tálāī to see if the man who hit Mr. Murray was still there, Colonel Roberts, who kindly consented to take charge of the armed party, covered them from the boat.

They talked to the women for a minute, and then called out to me that the man had run away. I, however, saw a man with an adze in his hand sitting on the right, away from the others, and I asked Kógio Kāī if this was the man. He said it was, and called out to Tómiti, who, with Tálāī, seized the man and dragged him into the boat, having first snatched the adze out of his hand. None of the other Öngés attempted to rescue him, or to offer any resistance. Our prisoner was secured and taken on board the "*Kwang Tung*."

The Chief Commissioner, who had in the meantime returned in the "*Ross*," directed me to have the man tied up to to a gun and given twenty four stripes, which was accordingly done. He was then secured and taken to the "*Ross*," and Mr. Murray under the care of Mr Jackson, Apothecary of the "*Kwang Tung*," was also taken there for the purpose of being conveyed to Port Blair for medical treatment, his wound being a serious one. The "*Kwang Tung*" returned to the Nicobars.

9.—On the following morning six Öngés appeared on the beach, and I sent Tómiti and Tálāī ashore with some presents for them, and they explained what had been done to the prisoner, and that we intended to take him to Port Blair.

We then proceeded to Jackson Creek on the West coast, where the Chief Commissioner and Mr. Metcalfe landed and gave some presents to the Öngés, and we then went on into Bumila Creek where we anchored for the night. Our interpreters were landed here and loaded with presents, and on the 11th we returned to Port Blair, bringing with us the prisoner, whose name proved to be Kóbédá-Köté, an inhabitant of Gööjégé, a village on the West coast.

Until the interpreters left he did not seem to realise his position, but during the night of the 10th, after they had gone, he twice managed to get his hands free from the handcuffs, and once, although his feet were manacled together, slipped overboard and tried to swim on shore, but was caught by one of our Andamanese.

On arrival in Port Blair he was kept under the Chief Commissioner's house, guarded by Andamanese, and seemed fairly well, though he suffered from the wounds caused by the flogging he had received. (He died at his village in 1897.)

"10.—Dr. Dalgairns, Officiating Senior Medical Officer, reported that, though Mr. Murray's wound was a serious one, he was in no danger, and he eventually recovered.

"11.—I would draw attention to the behaviour of Tómiti and Tálāi, in arresting their own countryman and supporting our authority. Their conduct throughout the expedition had been excellent, and shows the influence we have over them."

When forwarding the above Report to the Government of India, Colonel Cadell wrote the following Letter, No. 1742, dated 23rd March 1887, to the Secretary to the Government of India in the Home Department.

"I have the honor to submit, for the information of the Government of India, a copy of a letter of the 12th instant from Mr. Portman giving an account of a visit to the Little Andaman in the beginning of this month.

"2. Before proceeding on privilege leave in November last, I placed Mr. Portman on special duty with a view to his cultivating friendly relations with the natives of the Little Andaman. An account of his operations was submitted in his report which was published in the Monthly Proceedings for December last.

"Mr. Portman, after enduring many hardships, visited all the natives living on the coasts of the Island, and made a survey of the whole coast line. He deserves much credit for the success with which he accomplished his arduous work.

"3. As it is inadvisable that there should be any break in the continuity of our proceedings with the Islanders, and as Mr Portman is about to avail himself of the furlough which he gave up in order to carry out the operations mentioned in the preceding paragraph, I proceeded with him to the Island immediately on my return from leave.

"It will be seen from his detailed report that we were peaceably received by the natives wherever we met them, except on one occasion, when an elderly savage attacked and severely wounded Mr. Murray, the Chief Engineer of the *Kwang Tung*; the reason for the assault being probably the man's disappointment at not having received any presents. The assailant was seized by his own countrymen.

"4. It would have been preposterous to deal with such a savage, and one whose language no one could understand, in accordance with the prescribed forms of procedure, so as soon as he was brought on board the *Kwang Tung*, he was tied up to a gun by my orders, and received two dozen stripes. He was then taken to Port Blair, and will be liberated in a few months."

In April Mr. Metcalfe went down to the Little Andaman with Mr. Keatinge of the Survey, who did some work on both the North and South coasts.

All the Öngés were friendly, and on the return of the party to Port Blair Colonel Cadell and Mr. Metcalfe went again to the Island, taking with them Kóhédá Koté, who had been for nearly two months in imprisonment.

He was released at Íngo Tijálu, and Colonel Cadell writes:—

"As a lengthened detention in Port Blair would in all probability have resulted in the captive's death, an event which might have endangered the friendly relations which have been with so much difficulty established with the Little Andamanese, and as another opportunity of visiting the Little Andaman was not likely to offer till after the monsoon, he was taken back to his home and released after about two months' detention. It is hoped that this act of clemency will have a good effect on the Islanders."

Colonel Cadell went round the Island and was well received everywhere.

In January, 1888, he and Mr. Metcalfe visited the Island, going round it, and landing wherever they could. Our friends were as usual taken from Bumila Creek, the first place stopped at, as interpreters, and all the Ongés were friendly except some at Jackson Creek, who behaved in a timid and semi-hostile manner.

The people here, and further to the south, have always been treacherous and hostile, and owing to the impossibility of landing at their villages, they can only be approached by a march of some miles through the jungle, which, unless very judiciously conducted, would probably end in a fight.

In March, on returning from England and resuming charge of the Andamanese, I visited the Little Andaman. All the Ongés were very friendly, and I brought some up to Port Blair for a short visit. Chína Tói, one of the women caught on the Cinque Islands in 1885 had died, also " Kógio Kokélé," my Pálalánkwé interpreter. Tálāī and Tómiti were married.

In July 1888 I took Íké, a Jàrawa we had captured on the coast of the South Andaman, to Bumila Creek, and as he seemed to attach himself to the Ongés, particularly to Kógio Kāī, I brought the latter with some others away with me. They remained for a few weeks in Port Blair, but did not seem to understand Íké very well.

In December, 1888, I visited the Little Andaman in the R.I.M.S. *Investigator*. I had noticed, in 1886, very curious sores on the bodies of the Öngés, and while on this visit saw one boy with sores at the corners of his mouth, whom I brought up to Port Blair for treatment.

Both Dr. Alcock of the *Investigator* and Dr. Gupta at Haddo, pronounced the sores to be those of constitutional syphilis, and they readily yielded to the treatment for this disease. Dr. Gupta, in diagnosing the case, drew my attention to the irregular and discoloured teeth of the Öngés. This has been before noticed; nearly all this tribe have exceedingly irregular and black teeth, with sharp edges, so different from the inhabitants of the Great Andaman who have pearly-white even teeth. Judging from the age of the boy brought up (about 15), and the general condition of all the Öngés, whatever their age might be, I am of opinion that this tribe have had constitutional syphilis for some very considerable period, though for how long, and in what manner it originated, I can offer no conjecture.

I have since seen a case of elephantiasis at the Little Andaman, and no doubt there is a good deal of scurvy there. Indeed there is some great difference between the Ougés and the other Andamanese, even the Jàrawas, which may result from the difference of food, and water, or of climate, or from some intermixture with the Malays, Chinese, or some other outside race.

Short visits were paid by Lieutenant-Colonel L. H. E. Tucker, Officiating Chief Commissioner, and Mr. Man, to the Little Andaman in February, and March, 1889, and Mr. Man again visited the Island in April on his way from the Nicobars to Port Blair. The Ôngés were friendly where seen, and presents were given to them. At Bumila Creek they helped to collect wood for the *Nancowry*, and when Mr. Man stopped there in June 1890, he noticed how anxious they were to show hospitality to us, and how, when some of our Andamanese wanted some fruit, an old woman abused the other Öngés because they were not sharp enough in climbing the tree and getting what was wanted.

Unfortunately some of the visitors began to loot their ornaments, etc., from the Ongés, who resented this but kept quiet, and I had to bring the matter to notice and request that such practices might be forbidden.

Colonel Cadell visited the Little Andaman in the *Nancowry* in November, 1889, landing on the 8th at Hut Bay and Chétamálé, and stopping off Tōī Bálówé and Titāījé. The Ougés were most friendly, and several came off on board the steamer.

On the 9th he visited Bumila Creek bringing off some men, and then steamed to the Sisters where he had been told several people had collected.

Two boatloads of Öngés (about 28 people), were there, and were much delighted at seeing him, and some small boys came on board the ship.

Presents were distributed at all these places, and the Öngés were most anxious to be allowed to come to Port Blair. Eighteen were brought up, and the following list shows their names, and those of the villages to which they belong.

Kógio Kāī. Dántudé-tótáli-bāī. Chéné-kwölé-kóchui. Tákwátó. All of Kwaudálé village.

Eketi. Dátobá-chui. Of Támbe Ébui village.

Íkwá-chui. Tuwedé-wautélōī. Of Óbáté village.

Wauténé. Of Tauté-kwau-mói village.

Kwé-loi. Ébau-koi. Of Bédé-ábdálu village.

Tuki-chédá kōi. Dauwetau-ti-tétálé-tángé. Chéó-káché. Of Chétámálé village.

Íkálá-sówé. Édá-kétá-bálöwe. Yóká-móté. Of Kwáté-tu-kwágó village.

Dáto-chui. Of Tōī-bálöwé village.

These people remained at my house till the 30th, and were on that date sent back to the Little Andaman. They had been given a quantity of presents, and were pleased with their visit, but owing to the change of the monsoon many of them had suffered much from bronchitis.

In December, 1889, the edible birds nests collectors were finishing the cleaning of the caves, which had been delayed by previous bad weather, when they were overtaken by a cyclone on the 21st while returning from Passage Island to Port Blair, and were driven on shore on the south end of the Great Cinque Island. Their boat was smashed to pieces on the rocks by the surf, but most of the articles in it, including the box of edible birds nest refuse, were saved.

A party of Öngés happened to be on the Little Cinque Island, and four of the men came down to the assistance of the convicts. The wind having moderated, the Öngés lent the four Andamanese, who were with the party as a guard, one of their canoes, and leaving the Cinque Islands on the 24th these men reached Chiriya Tápu on the 26th and walked up to the Settlement.

On hearing of the occurrence I went down to the Cinque Islands in the *Ross*, leaving at 2 A.M. on the 27th, and reaching the Islands at daylight.

The birds-nesters and their baggage were embarked after considerable trouble, there being a heavy surf, and I went to the Little Cinque Island, picked up the four Öngés who had helped the convicts, and brought all the people back to Port Blair.

On the 29th these four Öngés returned by the *Ross* to the Cinque Islands, their canoe being also brought back from Chiriya Tápu and restored to them. As they had behaved remarkably well they were allowed to choose whatever articles they fancied in Port Blair, and took back several canoe-loads of presents. I would contrast their behaviour on this occasion with that which we might have expected from them, had a similar mishap occurred even such a short time ago as 1885.

They were all from Támbe Ébui (Tómiti's village), and had been visited by the Chief Commissioner when at the Sisters in the previous month.

In March, 1890, I visited the Little Andaman and brought up some Öngés, who stopped with me for a few days.

In October, 1890, I again visited the Island and found the people where I landed very friendly, but there was too much sea on for me to go round. I brought back several Öngés to Port Blair, returning most of them to their homes the following week, but keeping a few for a month in order that they might learn a little Hindustani.

In February, 1891, Mr. Man called at the Little Andaman on his way from the Nicobars to Port Blair, and brought away eight Öngés who stopped with me for a while; and in March I went down there and brought up two sickly Öngés, whom I was able to cure and fatten, so that they returned to their friends in excellent condition shortly afterwards.

In November I called at Bumila Creek after the cyclone, and found all well; and in January 1892, I took Tómiti, Tálāī, Eketi, and Tálāī-Tudinomé to Calcutta as related in Chapter XVII.

This visit had a great effect on them and did much good.

Whenever I visit the Little Andaman the Öngés crowd into my boat, and after taking all the presents I have brought offer to come on board the steamer, and are willing to come to Port Blair, even demanding to be taken up there, and refusing to go ashore again when told to do so.

In March, 1893, Mr. Man and I took Monsieur Lapicque, a French Anthropologist, to the Little Andaman, to see " les vrais sauvages " as he described them.

We stopped in Bumila Creek and gave him every opportunity of observing the Ougés. On leaving I brought away with me Tómiti, Tálāī, Tálāī-Tudinömé, and two small boys.

In April, as I wished to ascertain how my Andamanese, by themselves, would be received by the Ougés at the Little Andaman, I sent the three above mentioned men back to the Little Andaman on the 4th in a canoe manned by a selected party of Andamanese, and the two small boys were kept by me for a few days longer, when, becoming sick, they also were sent back in the *Nancowry*.

My Andamanese returned after a long delay in May. They were indeed so long away that I had been anxious about them, and the *Nancowry* had been sent out to look for them.

They stated that they had landed at Ékudi, and saw a number of new Òngés, who were members of the inland tribe and had long straight bows like those the Jàrawas of the South Andaman use. These people talked the same language as the coast tribe, but were not well disposed towards our people. Indeed, because one of our men, (Wóloga), would not give up to them a file he was using, they threatened to shoot him, and were only prevented from doing so by the boy Eketi, who had apparently learnt wisdom when in Calcutta with me in February, 1892.

After leaving the Little Andaman our people were detained on the South Brother Island for ten days, being ill with fever, and unable to move, and they reached here in very poor condition.

On such a tale it is impossible to form any decided opinion, and until I have seen this inland tribe and their bows I cannot say whether they so closely resemble those of the Jàrawas as is stated. If they do, (which is not impossible), then what has been already suspected, *viz.*, that the South Andaman Jàrawas are merely Ongé Éremtágas, who have been left behind in the South Andaman when the Ár-*yaūto* Sept retreated to the Little Andaman before the advancing Áka-*Béa*-da, will be confirmed. The point is one of interest.

In March, 1894, I went round the Little Andaman, landing at the principal villages and finding the Ongés everywhere friendly.

I brought up 52 with me to Port Blair, where they remained for a month. While at my house they gave a good deal of trouble by stealing things, and Kógio Kāī, who was with them, had to interfere. One of the men got fever, and while delirious wandered away during the night and was never seen again. He is believed to have drowned himself, but Kógio Kāī declared that he had gone back to the Little Andaman by himself, (which was impossible).

The others were returned to their homes, and when I met Kógio Kāī on the Cinque Islands in the following year he declared that the missing man *had* got back to the Little Andaman!

In November, 1894, Moung Yu, the edible birds nest collector, met a number of Öngés on the Cinque Islands, and reported their being there to me. I went down to see them and found our old friends. I brought up eight men, five women, and seven children and they remained a week at my house and then went down to Chiriya Tápu, with a selected party of Andamanese, to cut some canoes they wanted. I also sent convicts to assist them, and told our people to watch them and study their ways.

They went on to Rutland Island, collecting honey there, and then returned to the Cinque Island in January. I then took four to Calcutta. (Tómiti, Tálāī, Kógio Kāī, and Eketi).

On their return from this visit, the details of which are given in Chapter XVII, they, with some others from the Cinque Islands, were taken to the North Sentinel Island, as I had heard that one of them, an old man, was a Sentinelese who had some years before left the Sentinel in a canoe and come across, *via* Rutland Island and the Cinque Islands, to the Little Andaman.

In February, 1896, I again visited the Little Andaman, going all round it, and finding the Önges friendly. We however saw very few (it being the honey season when they are all in the interior), until we anchored in Hut Bay, when about forty people came out on the shore, having followed us up from the southward.

I gave them presents, took three intelligent looking young men on board, and then went on to the north. At Óbáté I saw Tómiti and Eketi, and took two more lads, bringing the five up to my house.

Their names were Íjá-té-bó-bāi-í, Wói-égi, Télé-kóyé, Dámbui, and Tén-dédé-bāi-í.

There was no news at the Little Andaman; all my friends were alive and well, and no wrecks, fights, or casualties had occurred.

Assistant-Surgeon Chitts of the *Elphinstone* noticed one case of Condylomata among the Öngés, and is of opinion that hereditary syphilis is common among them, and that the disease must have been introduced at some remote period, long before our occupation of these Islands in 1858, so that, in this instance, at least, we have nothing with which to reproach ourselves. Whether the disease is to be traced to Malay pirates, or, through the Jàrawa tribe near the Settlement of 1790, *et seq*, will probably never be ascertained.

Both this and other circumstances have assured me that the Öngés have, at some remote period, had communication with the outside world, and have been influenced by some outside race. Possibly a close study of their language, habits, and legends, may enlighten us on this point. Individual Chinese or Malays may have been captured by them, have had their lives spared, and have lived with them.

All those we have seen are, in spite of the syphilis, large and well formed, and breed freely.

Of course the fact of syphilis being among them has to a certain extent modified our policy towards this tribe. Formerly our one object, after friendly relations had been established with them, was to prevent them from mixing with the convicts and other Andamanese, and contracting the disease, but now there is no objection to their going about the Great Andaman with the other tribes, and there will be no objection to our keeping parties of them up here all the year round.

The use to which I propose to put them at present is, to search for the Jàrawas and endeavour to establish friendly relations with them; for, if that is ever done, it will, I think, be done by the Öngés.

As regards our conduct towards the Öngés in the future there is little to be said.

The Little Andaman Island will probably never be occupied, as there is nothing on it to tempt a settler, and there are no harbours, so beyond visiting the people in order to keep in touch with them, and prevent them from massacring the crew of shipwrecked vessels, we have no duties there. Ongés should, whenever practicable, be brought up to Port Blair and encouraged to roam about the South Andaman jungles with the other Andamanese, care being of course taken that they do not contract any disease. Should they catch any infectious disease they should be kept in the Settlement at all hazards until danger of communicating the infection to their fellow-tribesmen is past: their death in Port Blair is to be preferred to allowing them to take back any infection to the Little Andaman, and it should be remembered that the other Ougés care little for the death of one of their tribe, especially if he be an unmarried man, for with the Andamanese it is "every man for himself," and such an occurrence would not affect our friendly relations with them.

In time they will, of their own accord, come up to Port Blair from the Cinque Islands, but at present I have not been able to persuade them to come further than the latter place. (Since writing the above several parties of Ongés have come up to Port Blair of their own accord; they are beginning to occupy Rutland Island permanently; and have already been of assistance to us there in catching runaway convicts.)

The most useful language they can learn is Hindustani, and it is more important that they should learn that tongue than that we should learn their language.

There is a great field for scientific research among the Öngé Group of Tribes, and the ground has scarcely been broken at present.

When in Port Blair, and indeed on their own Island, the Öngés should always be shown that we are the strongest race, and are to be obeyed. On this point no doubt should be permitted, and obedience must be enforced and all wrong-doing sternly punished, for the Andamanese are a forgetful race, and this discipline is necessary in the interests of shipwrecked persons.

In the event of the Öngés misbehaving in the future the best punishment for them is, to bring away all the people of the offending village to Port Blair, and keep them on the Great Andaman for about a year, teaching and training them to better ways at the same time.

The five Öngés above-mentioned were taken back to the Little Andaman by me on the 15th of April, when I stopped in Bumila Creek until the 19th. A number of people came to see me and were very friendly.

I especially noticed that, owing to their contact with us, the Öngés have commenced to make bows like those of the South Andaman Group of Tribes, discarding their own pattern which is probably the oldest of all, but the new bow is more rounded in shape, and is not ornamented with the criss-cross and dog-tooth incisions used in the Great Andaman.

Also their canoes are now being made with prows like those in the Great Andaman.

These changes should be borne in mind by future observers, otherwise erroneous conclusions will be arrived at.

Very curious types of faces were to be seen among the Öngés; some entirely Negroid; others Mongoloid; others Malayan; a special type which I have called the Öngé type; some like aborigines in the Great Andaman; and others like North American Indians. Nothing strikes observers of the Andamanese more than the number of types of face to be seen among them.

Tómiti told me that, some time before, an Éremtága tribe of Öngés with long hair, living at Àntigöi near the head of Téyai Creek, had attacked him and burnt down his village; they had also attacked and killed the people at Íngöie. In revenge Tómiti and his party had killed several of them.

This is exactly what might be expected on so large an Island, and no doubt much of interest will be discovered there in the future.

CHAPTER XXI.

Efforts made to improve the Andamanese—Orphanage and School established—Church Mission letter - Mr. Homfray's report—Mr. Man's report—General Stewart's report—Mrs. Hilton's report—Annual Report for 1873-74—Mistakes in the management of the Orphanage—Further management—Report for 1880-81—Report for 1882-83—Report for 1883-84—Mr. Chard's views—Colonel Cadell's note—Details of certain boys—Annual Report for 1887-88—Note on Joseph—Annual Report for 1889-90—Home for Children established by Mr. Portman—Annual Report for 1891-92—Phulla and Bira's case—Remarks about the Andamanese boys—Cases which have occurred—Annual Report for 1892-93—Mr. Portman's Home a success, and approved by the Government of India—Annual Report for 1893-94—Remarks on Ruth—Conduct of certain persons towards the Andamanese—Order by Major Temple—Note on the abilities of the Andamanese—Reasons for the extinction of the race.

In conclusion I will relate the efforts that have been made to improve the mental and moral status of the Andamanese, efforts which, though not as entirely successful as their promoters expected them to be, have yet done good.

Too much was expected in the first instance from the Andamanese, whose wandering careless nature, immature intellect, incapacity for grasping anything outside the ordinary practical wants of their every day life, and especially anything abstract, and general childishness, prevented them from understanding what they were taught or profiting much by it. From the beginning, the great mistake of placing them under the orders of, and in close association with convicts was made; and from them, and from the lower class of free residents, they learnt nothing but evil which they were only too ready to grasp and appreciate, which evil more than outweighed the good done.

Mr. Corbyn attempted to teach the Andamanese and bring them under some sort of discipline, and Mr. Homfray was most anxious to benefit and improve them, contributing largely from his own purse to anything that he thought likely to do good.

He at first, as in the case of the two boys taken away by Captain Anderson in 1868-69, (as related in Chapter XV), hoped that by sending some to India they might be educated there, and being kindly treated would return and influence the others, (having as an example the case of the three Andamanese sent to Major Tickell in Moulmein), but this proved to be a mistaken policy, and it was then determined that anything which was taught to the Andamanese, should be taught in Port Blair itself.

No one but those who have to do with the Andamanese can appreciate the difficulties which were met with in trying to isolate a number of children from their parents and associates, keep them under a restraint to which they were unaccustomed, and which they disliked, and teach them a new learning which required a steady and continued application on their behalf which was foreign to their natures, the results from which neither they nor the adult Andamanese could appreciate.

As related in Chapter XIV, Colonel Man took an interest in the education of the Andamanese, and wrote strongly on the subject of their improvement; and on the 27th of May 1869, Captain Laughton, the Executive Commissariat Officer in Port Blair, wrote to Mr. Homfray suggesting that an Orphanage and School should be established on Ross Island. Colonel Man approved of this proposal, and a Committee was formed in January 1870, of which Captain Laughton and Mr. Homfray were Members, and Mr. E. H. Man was Secretary.

In the early part of 1869 a few Andamanese boys were brought to Ross, and afterwards a few girls were procured. These were taught at Mr. Homfray's expense in the Asiatic School on Ross by a native scripture reader named Lazarus, who also exercised a general supervision out of school hours.

By September 1869, three young girls had joined the Orphanage, which then contained seven girls and four boys, and more were expected. Mr. Homfray wrote:—

"Great hopes are entertained regarding the future of this institution as regards the regeneration of the race."

The Orphanage remained in this state until October, when there were twelve boys and ten girls in it, and a matron took charge of it.

The expense being heavy and there being no support from Government, in January, 1870, subscriptions were invited from the general public and readily responded to, when the whole affair was put in the hands of the Committee above mentioned.

On the 21st of January, 1870, the Committee of the Port Blair Church Mission wrote that they wished to have a Mission to the Andamanese at the Settlement.

They asked the Government to give the Missionary quarters, and a convict crew, till he could man a boat with Andamanese ; that the Andaman Home should be put under his charge ; and, with reference to the establishment by Government of an Orphanage and School on Ross Island far removed from the aborigines, they added that one of the principal objects of the mission was, that schools should be opened in connection with it, in order that mutual assistance might be secured by this combination. They said :—

" It is a matter of regret if operations which ought to go hand in hand, should be so divided ; it is unadvisable to sever the children from their tribes, and thus render them unsuitable for future usefulness among their own people."

This proposal, with other matters, was submitted to the Government of India, and on the 13th of August, 1870, and grant of Rs. 100 per mensem to the Andaman Orphanage was sanctioned from the 1st of April, 1870. The proposals of the Mission Committee did not meet with the approval of the Government.

This was the first of many attempts on the part of Church Missions to get the Andaman Homes into their own hands, and to have the entire charge of the Andamanese, but the Government preferred to keep this race under the control of their officers, and it would appear wisely, as will be seen from certain cases detailed below.

In Mr. Homfray's Annual Report on the Andaman Homes for 1869-70 we find:—

"Two young lady governesses manage the Orphanage now. A death occurred there of an orphan girl of the Middle Strait tribes, aged 11, and as she had no friends here, she was buried in the jungles without ceremony.

"Moriarty's son, named Jerry, is the youngest boy in the school. He is liked the best, and is the first and only child born in the Home on Ross (on the 20th of February, 1866), and still living. Several have been born since, but have died. Jerry's mother is dead, and Moriarty has married again to a young girl by whom he has another son. The child is petted and carried about by the others. Another lad named Lambert is smart and lively, and he and Jerry are playmates and act as monitors (1) to the rest of the children.

(Jerry was employed by Mr. J. G. Apcar in Calcutta for a time in 1879, and afterwards was employed by Captain Eustace, R.A., in 1882 at Ambala, where he died in 1883. He was a confirmed drunkard, a thief, and a general bad lot. Lambert was a clever lad, but was led astray by the convicts, becoming very bad tempered and evil natured. He died of syphilis in 1880.)

"To make the Orphanage a success, the adults must be kept contented, the children must be well fed, the boys must be separated from the girls (a mistake—*M. V. P.*), they must always be well clad, (?), only children of six years of age and under must be admitted, (a mistake—*M. V. P.*), classes according to the abilities of the pupils must be formed, English must be the medium of communication, (Hindustani would have been better—*M. V. P.*), they must be taught handicrafts, too many must not be got, as it is difficult to look after large numbers.

"The relatives must visit the children occasionally. The children are better brought up in the Settlement than sent away to be taught in India, as the parents would object to the latter, and it would cause much sorrow and ill-feeling. The two lads sent to Calcutta in October, 1867, for tuition, at the application of Captain Anderson, died; I have not mentioned this to the Andamanese as they will feel it very much, though in time they may forget them.

"The children in the Orphanage are principally from the Port Blair and Port Mouat Tribes, and a few from the Middle Straits. The Andamanese are much pleased to see the children getting on so well, and so well cared for, and several additions have lately been made of their own accord. The alphabet, words of one syllable, numeration and addition are almost mastered."

It was necessary to bribe the parents to allow their children to come to the so-called "Orphanage", and Mr. Homfray was very liberal with his presents to them.

On the 2nd of May, 1871, Mr. E. H. Man submitted the first Annual Report on the Orphanage. The Government of India noted on it, that it was very interesting and contained a very satis-factory account of the progress made in the work of educating the Andamanese children.

The following extracts from this report are given :—

"In May, 1869, it was proposed by a few members of the community of Port Blair to open an Orphanage for Andamanese children, commencing with a few whom Mr. Homfray had tried to benefit by placing them under the charge of a native catechist on Ross. The old church was granted as a building.

"After some delay, a young Scotch widow offered to come as Matron if she might keep her two young children with her. This offer was accepted, as it was hoped that her children would mix with the Andamanese and do them good.

"She arrived on the 8th of December, 1869, and all appeared to go well.

"The adult Andamanese, seeing how well their children were cared for readily brought others, and at the end of the year the Orphanage consisted of twelve girls and ten boys, ageing from three to thirteen years.

" They were taught to be neat and clean, needlework, alphabet, and numeration. It was soon apparent that they possessed much intelligence, owing to which, and their remarkable docility and obedience, they readily mastered their simple lessons, all of both sexes shewing a great aptitude for needlework.

" This was upset however by the Matron receiving an offer of marriage from the Colour-Serjeant of the European Detachment which induced her to resign. The Orphanage was thus checked. Temporary arrangements were made, first with the wife of an Overseer, and when her health failed, with the wife of an Inspector of Police, and these did their best.

" In June, 1870, the Revd. Mr. Mitchell, who was with the Bishop on his visitation tour, and saw the Andamanese, got two ladies, Miss Bell and Miss Leadbeater of the Kidderpore Asylum, to take charge of the Orphanage on the same monthly salary of Rs. 50 that had been formerly paid to one matron.

" Their work continues to be satisfactory, and there are now 22 boys and 15 girls in the orphanage.

" The children make up their own clothing, and are very good at basket making. By this work they have already realised upwards of Rs. 100, also small sums have been added by the sale of needlework and fancy articles made by the girls.

" Nearly all the boys receive instruction every afternoon at the Superintendent's house from the gardener, dhobi, darzi, and carpenter.

" They are intelligent and willing.

" A net made from pineapple fibre, and a specimen basket and fancy mat made in their play hours are sent to Calcutta.

" They do not however readily learn English. They read a little and understand. They quickly pick up Urdu from their native surroundings. Four have been baptised. All attend church on Sunday.

"One boy and one girl have died since the Orphanage was opened.

" We hope soon to relieve Mr. Homfray of the charges he has borne, he at present supporting the Orphanage. We hope to obtain Rs. 50 or 60 per month from the residents."

General Stewart writes in his Annual Report for 1871-72, as regards the Orphanage :—

"The ladies who presided over the Orphanage intend to leave in July, and it will then be a matter of difficulty to get some one to take charge.

"Having so far civilised these little Andamanese, and introduced new habits among them, we cannot well break up the present arrangement. Most of the children have been two years here, and it would be almost certain death, especially to some of the younger ones, to send them back to the jungles. (?)

"Five of these little ones have been baptised, and so adopted by us, which entails a still greater necessity for our looking after their welfare."

(The work of doing so, however, when the baptised Andamanese turned out unsatisfactorily, devolved upon the Officer in charge of the Andamanese, who looked after them in common with the rest of the race; but their spiritual and religious supposed guardians did nothing for them.)

"The appointment of a married man to take charge of the orphanage, whose wife could look after the girls and younger children, while he instructed the boys in some useful handicraft or calling, such as carpentering, gardening, basket and net making, fishing or boating, is desirable.

"In this way the children would be taught to earn a livelihood for themselves, and be useful to others at the same time.

"Though, under the present system, they have certainly made some progress, yet it does not appear that the little reading and writing they may attain to can ever be of any use to them eventually. They would learn much more willingly and readily those things which by their natural habits they are more fitted for, and which would prove far more useful to them in after life than a superficial knowledge of English.

"They could, when a little older, be sent amongst their less civilised relations, and so in their turn teach them what they had themselves learnt."

The policy enunciated in this last paragraph has been proved by time to be the correct one, and has been pursued.

During the year 1872-73, Mrs. Hilton was in charge of the Orphanage for a short time. She states :—

" The girls can now make and mend their own clothes, and are quite perfect in The Lord's Prayer, Grace before and after meals, the three first answers of the Church Catechism, and the first lesson in the Bible."

She had tried to teach them sums in addition, but without much success, though they were perfect in the Multiplication Table to as far as six times six. "Martha" is described as being a very neat fancy worker in wools, but it is doubtful if this would be of much use to her in after life. (She married Bía Bōī, the Chief of Kyd Island, and settled down with him there until her death in 1888.)

"The girls are certainly more tidy and cleanly in their appearance and more intelligent and modest in their behaviour than they used to be. Three of the girls are marriageable and might be married and kept employed in or near one of our stations.

" The boys do not improve much, except in manners.

" They seem happy and contented but do not take any interest in any kind of work. They read English tolerably well, and write it well, but they do not understand the meaning of what they read and write.

" They are unable to express themselves in English, but always use Hindustani.

" School time over, they are at once longing to go off fishing, and are allowed to go.

" An attempt was made to teach them gardening, but without success.

" The Orphanage had 18 boys and 5 girls, and the general health is good."

It will be seen that already the girls were leaving the school, and their numbers were decreasing, while the number of boys there had increased. The Report itself shows that the system of education pursued was not successful or adapted to the requirements of the Andamanese, or their capacity.

Subsequent events showed that they were really learning much evil at this time from the convicts with whom they were far too closely associated, and sufficient supervision was not kept over them.

The Annual Report for 1873-74 shows that four girls were removed from the Orphanage during the year, three of whom were married to Andamanese and lived in the buildings appropriated to the married people on Viper Island. Three other girls, removed from the Orphanage during the previous year, had also married and were doing well.

A nursery for small children had been established on Viper Island, and in it were four girls and one boy; the former averaged about five years of age and attended the native school there.

This nursery was eventually closed, not proving a success.

In establishing the Orphanage the mistakes made at the outset were many. The natural customs of the Andamanese, *viz.*, free love before marriage and chastity afterwards, were ignored.

The system of education pursued was a wrong one.

The children should not have been kept on Ross Island, but rather at one of the stations on the mainland, and should not have been allowed to associate with convicts.

The ages of the children admitted should have been altered. Boys from 8 to 16 should have been taken, and girls from 5 to 10. These would have grown up together, could eventually have married, and the married couples would have remained in the Orphanage, with occasional leave to the jungle, and would have been perfectly happy.

Children whose nature was such as to utterly unfit them for the Orphanage life should not have been kept there by force, as was done, for they made the others discontented, or led them into mischief.

In 1874 the institution was moved from Ross to Viper Island, when 11 of the boys ran away into the jungle but were brought back by Moriarty. This was only what might have been expected, and such an occurrence should not have affected the move, which was a good one, but for fear of losing all the boys the Orphanage was re-transferred to Ross, with 20 boys only, and put under the charge of the Chaplain.

From this time little interest seems to have been taken in it except by the Chaplain, the Reverend Mr. Warneford, and the numbers in it dwindled, the institution not proving a success.

Mr. and Mrs. Wallis, (the Headmaster of the Government Schools in the Andamans, and his wife) instructed the Andamanese or supervised their education and the conduct of the Orphanage, until they left the Settlement in 1880, and appear to have done fairly well, keeping the boys to a certain extent away from the convicts.

Some of the boys, as they became too old for the school, went back to the jungle, and a few children were brought in to fill their places, but little attention or supervision was given them, and they were left almost entirely in the hands of convicts.

When Colonel Cadell became Chief Commissioner of the Andamans in 1879 he tried to revive an interest in the Orphanage, and in his Annual Report for 1880-81 he writes :—

" The Orphanage was in June, 1880, placed under the charge of Mr. Homfray who has always taken a great interest in the Andamanese, and through whose instrumentality friendly relations with them were originally formed. (?) The boys, 14 in number, attend school, and some of them are taught carpentering, and other useful trades.

" Nothing can exceed the care Mr. Homfray bestows on them.

" The number of children in the Orphanage having declined, the Government allowance has been reduced from Rs. 100 per mensem, to Rs. 70."

In his Annual Report for 1882-83 Major Protheroe wrote—

" The Orphanage remained under the charge of Mr. Homfray until his death in 1883, when it was handed over to Mr. M. V. Portman. At the commencement of the year there were 17 boys on the books, 3 lads were admitted, 2 were taken to Rangoon to be educated, and one returned to the jungle

"The number on the rolls at the close of the year was therefore also 17.

"They have been well fed and cared for, provided with suitable clothing, and a flannel shirt apiece, are taught English reading and writing, Urdu translation, and elementary arithmetic. They have made fair progress.

"The boys employed as domestic servants give satisfaction."

Of the two boys taken to Rangoon by Father LeRouvreur, one died, and the other, after being trained for a time in the Catholic School, was returned to Port Blair. He seems to have learnt little, and was a boy of bad character and not very intelligent.

In the Annual Report for 1883-84 Colonel Cadell writes—

"*Orphanage.*—Mr. Portman made over charge of the Orphanage to the Reverend Mr. Chard, the Chaplain of Port Blair, on the 15th of February, 1884. There were 17 boys in the Orphanage at the beginning of the year, 6 were admitted, and 16 were allowed to go back to the jungle by Major Protheroe, the Officiating Chief Commissioner, who ruled that no boys should be detained who were not orphans, or who were in the institution without the consent of their parents.

"Seven boys remained at the close of the year."

Mr. Chard was of opinion that the instruction given in the school was of little value, and was not assimilated.

He made the boys use their Andamanese names, and did not want to de-Andamanese them. He also thought that a loin-cloth was sufficient clothing for them. He writes—

"It would seem that an Andamanese boy's thoughts of earthly bliss all revolve round ' pig.' To get from the Officer in charge the indent upon the Commissariat Department for a pig, and to go to the mainland, fetch it home in triumph, and kill and eat it, is the one great happiness of our Andamanese boys. But to hunt it in the jungle with all the wild excitement of the chase, is to them, I believe a vision of happiness only to be realised in dreams. In illustration the following incident is given. On the 12th July the Parawala reported to me that all the Orphanage boys except two had run away. Two boys from Aberdeen had come over to Ross about 5-30 in the evening; during the temporary absence of the Parawala they had won over the Orphanage boys to a project to have a good time of it in the jungle. Our boys had been provided with a Nicobarese canoe with which to amuse themselves on the sea, fishing etc., the paddles being kept in the Parsonage. The boys, who freely circulate about the Parsonage whenever they like, went off with the paddles without any suspicion of their intention being aroused, and starting immediately, rowed without stopping 25 miles to the northward till they found themselves among friends somewhere in the Middle Straits. They remained away till the 4th of August, when they were brought back by adult Andamanese from the Home, who had been despatched after them. On returning the only explanation they offered of their flight was the one magic syllable 'pig.'

" This incident also probably serves to show what little success has attended the project of cultivating in Andamanese boys during their childhoods spent in the Orphanage a taste for settled life, for a livelihood gained by handicraft, farming, cultivation, or domestic service.

" These are the hopes which have hitherto been entertained about these lads—hopes which to a large extent have been disappointed.

" My predecessor whose knowledge of the Andamanese character and disposition, as you are aware, is most intimate, says in his last Annual Report that, when the boys have grown up, it is almost useless to keep them in the orphanage as they have a craving for the jungle life which necessitates their being sent back to their own people."

Colonel Cadell adds:

" Mr. Chard also thinks that the anxiety that this Administration has shown for years to wean these lads from a wild life is almost certain to meet with disappointment. They are by instinctive habit hunters, and the labours and routine of a civilised existence, seem irksome in comparison with the freedom of the jungle, added to which is the serious consideration that the attempt to train up Andamanese girls '*pari passu*' with the Orphanage for boys having practically failed, the lads, as growing up, have to look to the jungle for brides. It would probably be well to resign these hopes, and in future whilst offering them, as at present, an opening to a settled life, if they care to avail themselves of it, base their training upon the anticipation of their mostly reverting to the jungle on leaving the Orphanage. The object should be (religious instruction of a very rudimentary sort being taken for granted) first of all to train them in habits of cleanliness.

"I understand that the nomadic life of the Andamanese is not only due to their habits as hunters, but also to their want of regard for sanitary and cleanly ways which makes a frequent change of encampment necessary.

"Mr. Chard wishes to benefit the lads in their jungle life by teaching them things likely to make that life more pleasant, therefore he believes in sanitary lessons, building them up physically by good feeding, and just imparting enough instruction to enable them to communicate with us regarding the simple wants of their lives. Also to teach them such simple mechanical arts as will be useful to them in the jungle.

"The five hours now spent in schooling should be spent in a workshop.

"In fact a missionary for the Andamanese who is practical and will go to the jungle with them is required."

This missionary was eventually procured but found to be a failure in every way, and having been dismissed, the charge of the Orphanage was placed in the hands of Mr. M. V. Solomon, a Catechist, an earnest and intelligent man, under the supervision of the Chaplain, and was removed to Haddo. It had however become a very small establishment by this time, only nine boys being in it and no girls, and Nicobarese boys being gradually introduced the Andamanese have now been entirely withdrawn, and Mr. Solomon, with the boys, has been moved to the Car Nicobar.

There can be no doubt that Mr. Chard's views regarding the management of the Orphanage were correct, and he, Mr. Warneford, and, for a short time, Mr. Briscoe, were the only Chaplains who have taken a real interest in the boys, have worked for their welfare, and are gratefully remembered by them.

The education received by the boys in the early days of the Orphanage, and the discipline to which they were subjected, improved them mentally, and some of the cleverest and best Andamanese I have had under me have been educated there.

In February, 1880, a child named Joseph, who had been in the Orphanage, and for a short time in the service of Dr. Reid and of Mr. De-Roepstorff in Port Blair, was given by Colonel Cadell to Deputy Surgeon-General Joseph, who adopted him and took him away. He was a youth of bad character, and nothing was heard of him for some years.

Mr. Chard reports on the Orphanage for the year 1886-87:—

> "One boy died, one ran away, two were given to Mr. Metcalfe as servants, and five remained in the Orphanage.
>
> The boys are treated easier with fewer lessons, and are allowed to go about in the jungle with the Catechist."

Mr. Chard thought that two of the boys were specially good, and hoped to baptise them, for which end he was having them specially instructed. One was Wologa, a particularly bright and intelligent boy, who showed promise of becoming very useful from his greater aptitude for a settled life.

Wologa was led into bad practices by the convicts, but having been removed by me to the Home at my house, is now one of the most intelligent boys I have, though not intellectually capable of doing all that Mr. Chard hoped.

Luke, another boy, who was given at this time to Mr. Metcalfe, is the best behaved, most intelligent, and most refined of any of the Andamanese. His gentle quiet nature, obedience, and pleasant manner, greatly endeared him both to Mr. Metcalfe and myself.

Of all the men, however, who have been trained in the Orphanage, none have compared with Bulubu-la, commonly called Robert, or more generally "The Cat." He is a man of real ability, and has greatly assisted me by his advice in my management of the Andamanese, during the whole time I have had charge of them; so superior is he considered even by the other Andamanese, that now, when as I write I fear that he is on his death-bed, they admit that there is no one capable of filling his place and conducting his duties. (He died on the 26th April, 1896, aged about 40 years.)

In the Annual Report for 1887-88, Mr. Chard states that there are still only five Andamanese boys in the Orphanage, and hopes for more.

These ran away occasionally, but came back, and were well behaved on the whole, and amusing. Mr. Chard admitted that with the rapidly decreasing race he cannot hope for more boys. He wisely wished that Mr. Solomon had been with them from the first, instead of the convict Parawalas from whom they learnt so much evil.

The Orphanage was almost entirely given up to the Nicobarese by this time.

In the Annual Report for 1888.89 Mr. Chard writes that, of these five boys, two were made over to Mr. Portman as being too big for the school, two small boys being given in exchange, and one, a boy named George, was given to Mr. Man as a servant.

He then writes the following excellent history of "Joseph":—

"About the same time (November 1888), there came back to the Settlement a notable character named 'Joseph,' whose career is somewhat remarkable, and whilst for the Christian mind distressing, is at the same time interesting, as affording conclusive proof of the possibility of at least the intellectual and social development of this degraded race. That it should be incapable of moral and spiritual development as well, is unreasonable and indeed impossible to believe.

"Joseph was adopted when about eight years old by Deputy Surgeon-General Joseph, on the occasion of an official visit to Port Blair. (Dr. Joseph was struck at the time by the coincidence of the boy offered to him having the same name as himself.—*M. V. P.*)

"This gentleman placed him in school at Rangoon and afterwards at Bangalore. He acquired a thoroughly good colloquial and a rough literary knowledge of English. His patron in addition gave him a good grounding in the art of compounding medicines. I cannot discover whether the boy received systematic religious instruction. What it was, was probably given by Roman Catholic teachers, for I remember discovering him in the course of his varied career in a back slum of Rangoon, where I found him living with a Brahmin, and on expressing to him the hope that he was leading a sober life. ' Oh yes,' said he with great readiness, ' I wear the scapular.' After his patron's death he seems to have led a wandering life in South India in the companionship of Tamils and Telugus : his knowledge of these languages, especially of Tamil, is said by natives of education to be remarkable for its purity. His natural amiability, which is a pleasing characteristic of the Andamanese race, and his genius for being generally useful, no doubt afforded him a welcome in many a native bazaar, whilst his Negrito physiognomy rendered him such an object of interest to a South Indian Rajah (Vizianagram) on one occasion, as to lead to an offer for his services in His Highness' Brass Band.

"He at length found himself at Madras, and we have afterwards fleeting visions of him as cabin servant and under-steward on board B. I. S. N. Co.'s Liners, Compounder in the Rangoon General Hospital, in service on board a British Gunboat, whence he disappears from view for a short while on a short sentence within the walls of Bassein Jail.

"Subsequently being on the streets in Rangoon, the Bishop sent him across to the Orphanage with the hope that in his native land he might find useful employment. But it was too late. He was now certainly 20 years of age, probably older ; for years past he had been an *'enfant perdu'* in the lowest quarters of various native cities and had acquired the habit of drunkenness, and (to a phenomenal extent) of lying."

He was recovered by me, and for some months before his arrival I had been writing all over Burma trying to get hold of him, for I had heard of his abandoned and neglected state. The Clergy who should have done all for him, did nothing, and Dr. Joseph made no arrangements for his future, at his death, as he should have done.

When he arrived here I asked the Chief Commissioner to let me have charge of him from the first, but he was put in the hands of Mr. Chard, who was too kind to deal satisfactorily with such a scoundrel, and after he had forged Mr. Chard's name in the Bazaar on Ross Island for liquor, and had been locked up more than once for being drunk, he was made over to me as incorrigible. I tried to keep him in my house, but found that of no use, so sent him away to the jungles and have kept him there. He married an Andamanese girl, settled down, and is now doing fairly well.

In the Annual Report for 1889-90 I write :—

"The boy Joseph who was sent back to the jungle in the previous year, after having resided for ten years in India and Burmah, is doing very well. He is healthy and strong, gets on very well in the jungle, has become entirely an Andamanese, and will I hope, in time, forget the vices which civilisation and the outside world have taught him. He was shot in the leg by the Jarawas in February last."

Though he improved slightly, and being in the jungle is unable to obtain intoxicants, he remains, and I fear always will remain, a blackguard.

With a view to keeping the remnant of the Andamanese race alive as long as possible, I, at that time, established a Home for them at my house. I had noticed that, when Andamanese women were confined in the Homes, the children usually died, whereas if confined in the jungle the child had a better chance of living. Also, up to the age of 6 or 7 years, children throve better in the jungle than in the Homes, after that age there was a high death rate.

I therefore got such boys as were between the ages of 8 and 18 and kept them with a few married people with me. The girls I kept in a separate party in the jungle near the Settlement where they do very well, and as both parties grow up they marry and settle down either at my house, in the other Homes, or in the jungle.

I remark when writing of the epidemic of Russian Influenza which occurred in the year 1890 :—

"From the fact that though they all suffered from it none of the boys living at my house died of Russian Influenza, it would seem that my system of keeping them under my direct care is the only one which is likely to keep the people alive, and I propose during the next few months to bring in from the jungle all the children and unmarried young men and to keep them with me. By this plan they will be kept in health and good discipline, will learn the jungles round the Settlement, and so will be very useful hereafter in runaway hunting when the men at present in the Home are dead."

In the Annual Report for 1891-92 I write :—

"In March 1892 Convict Phulla, No. 3363 B, was awarded 18 stripes and 2 years chain gang for committing unnatural crime with an Andámanese lád named Bira. The convict was Manji of the Chaplain's boat, and Bira, with another Andamanese boy named Wóloga, were in the service of the Chaplain. These two boys were formerly in the Andaman Orphanage, which is under the charge of the Chaplain, and becoming too old for school, were taken by the Chaplain into his service. I protested against this at the time, both to the Superintendent and to the Chaplain, knowing from past experience with other boys that it was not desirable to keep Andamanese on Ross Island ; I also pointed out on more than one occasion that great care and supervision should be exercised, or the boys would be sure to fall into vicious ways. The record of the case under report shows that the boy Bira used to drink, and committed unnatural crime with the convict on several occasions extending over a long period of time. I have since learned that the other boy, Wóloga, was addicted to similar vices. Both boys are now at my house where they are well looked after, but the taste for drink can, I fear, never be eradicated.'

"The Home for Andamanese boys at my house has been extended and improved during the year, and the number of boys is now 57, of all ages, between 26 and 5 years. Two of these are married and their wives are living with them in huts in my compound. So far this Home has been a great success. The boys being examined daily by a Compounder and the greatest care being taken about their diet, exercise, and clothing, they are all in excellent health and no deaths have occurred during the year. They have been trained to work for a short time daily at some one of the following duties ; gardening, waiting at table, pulling a boat, drawing a Jinricksha, engine and dynamo driving, assistants in photographic work, and are made to practise daily in the gymnasium. This Home, however, entails constant vigilance both on my part and on the part of my servants, and an amount of attention and supervision which I do not think anyone else would be likely to give to it.

" Seeing these boys at my house, and not understanding the work necessary to keep them in order and prevent their falling into vicious habits, many people ask for them as servants, but as in the majority of instances in which such requests have been complied with in former times the results have been bad, I have not allowed any to go out into service. At present two girls are in the service of two of the Subordinates in Port Blair, and as these girls have been with them for many years, have completely forgotten their own language, and have no wish to rejoin the Andamanese, I have no intention of interfering with them. Mr. Man, who was formerly in charge of the Andamanese, has two boys in his employ, and there are no others out in service, nor do I think it advisable that any others should be allowed to go. Major Wimberley took an Andamanese girl with him to New Zealand in 1882. She was sickly, and with a diseased constitution, and though she did well in the climate of her new home, she seems to have broken down from overwork, and got some spinal disease. Great care was then taken of her, she was encased in plaster of Paris, and was brought back to Port Blair where she died.

" With the above-mentioned girls in the service of the subordinates, so long as they remain in Port Blair, no great trouble will be experienced, but should the girls be taken away to India when these subordinates retire from the service, (which in my opinion should not be permitted) the same difficulty will arise as in the case of Joseph.

"Among those who have thus been in the service of private individuals the following cases have occurred :—

"When the Orphanage was on Ross Island, under the charge of Mr. Homfray, various scandals occurred, and one evening in 1882 a row took place at the Settlement Mess-house between a convict and an Andamanese serving there. The reason for this row was an attempt on the part of the convict to commit unnatural crime with the Andamanese.

"As it was found impossible to keep the Andamanese separated from the convicts so long as the Orphanage was on Ross Island, it was removed to Haddo.

'Jerry,' an Andamanese boy, was allowed to go to India, in the service of Captain Eustace, R. A., in 1882. Jerry was then known as a confirmed drunkard, having learnt the vice in the Orphanage on Ross Island, and he soon after died at Amballa.

"'Joseph' was allowed to enter the service of Surgeon-General Joseph in 1880, and on the death of the latter was turned loose on the streets in Madras. He appears to have wandered about in Madras and Burmah, living from hand to mouth, and to have learnt every vice he was capable of understanding. Nominally a Roman Catholic, the only kindness he received was from the Catholic priests. On my return from England in 1888 I heard about him, and after considerable trouble succeeded in getting him back here. He now lives entirely in the jungle with his own people as I am unable to allow him in the Settlement on account of his bad habits.

"'Ruth,' an Andamanese woman, was for many years in the service of Mr. Homfray. During this period she was fairly well looked after, though her moral character was not all that could be wished. Since Mr. Homfray died she has been in the service of several people, all of whom declined to keep her for long. She formed *liaisons* with the servants in the different houses, and had more than one child. Though a Christian, and nominally under the charge of the Chaplain, she is now living in the Haddo Hospital, and has a child by one of the Native hospital officials, to whom she is attached.

(Also, since writing the above report, one of the Andamanese girls in service in Port Blair, by name Topsy, has had two children by Natives of India.)

"Pleasant as the Andamanese appear to casual observers, their attractiveness is more owing to the absence of vice in their composition, through ignorance, than to the actual possession of virtues. They appear to me to have the natures of English school boys of the lower classes, with, in the cases of the older ones, the passions of the mature savage. Of merry and happy natures, they are still passionate and cruel; though affectionate to each other, and particularly to children, they have short memories and no idea of gratitude. Discipline is foreign to them (each going his own way), and they stick to nothing for long. Having no moral code they at once adopt all the pleasant vices of civilization they can understand, but are not intellectually capable of deriving any advantages from their intercourse with strangers. I do every thing in my power to prevent their association with the convicts from whom they learn nothing but harm, and my aim is to keep them healthy, employ them on light useful work, which will gradually raise them intellectually, teach them what little I can by conversation only, and this without making their lives unhappy.

"I pursue the English public school system of mixing boys of all ages, and making the elder exercise an influence for good, and a check, over the younger. As savages to be tamed, improved, and kept in health, the work is worth doing; but I deprecate their being taken by people in Port Blair as ornamental pages, pets, and play-things while the humour lasts, without any real care or supervision being exercised; and then discarded when their master is tired of them, or leaves the Settlement.

(Of the other people who have had Andamanese servants, Mr. Godwin-Austen had some so long as he remained in Port Blair, who were treated very well by him, and were happy and contented. One of these, a boy called the "Tarbaby," was of a specially pleasant and intelligent nature.

Mr. Metcalfe also had Andamanese servants whom he treated very kindly and who were much attached to him; and Mr. J. G. Apcar, after parting with Jerry, was sent two other boys for a year, whom he treated well and who came to no harm by their stay in Calcutta.

Other officials in Port Blair have for short periods been permitted to have Andamanese servants, but these either refused to remain with them, being overworked, or else were neglected, learnt bad habits, and had to be withdrawn.)

In my Annual Report for 1892-93 I write :—

"The Home of Andamanese at my house has been maintained during the year and the results have been most satisfactory. At the close of the year the Home contained 66 people, from all parts of the Islands, of whom the majority are children from 7 to 16 years of age. There are six married couples, and of the children, two are boys of about seven from the Little Andaman.

"The health of the people in this Home has been excellent during the year, no deaths having occurred. The expense of their food is borne by the Home funds, but all other expenses, such as costly tonics, and medicines, luxuries, and presents of all kinds, are defrayed by me.

"Even people who have had no experience of the Andamanese have noticed the superior physique and intelligence of men who have been long in this Home, and I am able to persuade them as they grow up, to marry and remain with me. Some few are either unsuited to the restrictions and discipline, or persistently object to them, and these I have allowed to return to their country, as I do not wish the Andamanese to consider they are kept under compulsion; but those who have gone are now employed either on the Trepang fishery, or are posted at important places where they have been instructed to collect news, and bring it in to me, thus making use of their superior intelligence and training.

"Among other things, I have supplied the boys at this Home with three bicycles, to which they took a great fancy when in Calcutta. They learnt to ride in a few days, and are now constantly out on them. I use them as orderlies when wishing to send an urgent letter.

"The man Joseph has much improved, and I am now able to allow him to live in the Haddo Home, as he wishes to do. During the stay of the French Yacht *Semiramis* in Port Blair, I attached him to Mr. Lapicque as an orderly, and he has been of great use, nor have I had any complaints about his conduct.

"The two boys, formerly in the service of the Chaplain, whose case was mentioned in my last Annual Report, have been with me during the year. Their behaviour has been good, and I hope they have forgotten the vices taught them by the convicts on Ross Island.

"The woman 'Ruth' is still living at Haddo with her half-breed child, which she takes very good care of. As she declines to return to the Andamanese, there seems nothing for it but to permit her to marry the convict for whom she has an affection. Her children will be interesting scientifically."

She has not, however, been allowed to marry the convict. The child strongly resembles a Papuan, and it may be that the Papuans are a hybrid race of Negrito-Polynesians, the latter race eventually exterminating the former.

In 1893-94, I write:—

"The Home of Andamanese at my house has been maintained during the year, and there are now 81 people in it, including 11 married couples

"Three boys died of influenza in January, but the general health of the remainder has been good, and they compare in physique very favourably with the other Andamanese. Several of them have been away for a month or so at a time in their native jungles, and thus they do not lose their jungle accomplishments and knowledge.

Codliver Oil, Chemical Food, Port Wine, and other tonics have been supplied to the delicate children with excellent results.

"The people at this Home have been given a small sailing boat which some of them have learnt how to use, and also such illustrated books as Wood's Natural History, which they appreciate and understand.

"The difference both in physique and in intelligence between the Andamanese in this Home and those in the jungle is very marked and is noticed at once even by casual visitors to Port Blair.

"'Ruth' the Andamanese woman of bad character who has been mentioned in former reports is now living in a small house in my compound. She is encouraged to associate as much as possible with the Andamanese, and to employ her usefully, she has been appointed sewing-mistress in the Aberdeen School, where, as she is really clever both at plain and fancy sewing, and understands the use of a sewing machine, she is doing good work. Her attainments in this line are far superior to those of the other sewing mistresses in the Settlement Schools.

"Of her character perhaps the less said the better, but a strict watch is kept over her movements, and her best trait is her affection for, and the attention she gives to, her half-breed child."

This Home has continued up to the present time with an average of about 80 people in it, many of whom are married, and has been a great success. Many of the elderly Andamanese come to it during the rains, and thus the youngsters associate with their relations and are happy and contented. They are well fed on a varied diet, and as they are often allowed to go to the jungle for a fortnight or so, to hunt etc., they do not lose any of their jungle accomplishments.

The only ancient Andamanese custom which appears to have entirely died out, owing to the diminished numbers of the people, is that of catching turtle and large fish in nets.

"Ruth" and her child are still with me. Owing to misconduct she has been dismissed from the Sewing-Mistress-ship of the Aberdeen

School, and she is now employed in making and repairing the clothes of the Andamanese at the Home. Her child is being taught English and Hindustani, also to sew; she has picked up more than one Andamanese dialect, and may in time marry one of the boys at the Home.

Topsy, and her two half-breed children are also living in the same house with Ruth, in my compound. Her employer, after the birth of her second child, being himself a married man with children, found it impossible to keep her. He had always treated her kindly, but the ineradicable savage element was too much for him.

One of the difficulties which those who were anxious to guard the Andamanese from learning vicious habits have had to contend with, has been the conduct of temporary residents in, and of visitors to, Port Blair, towards the aborigines.

In spite of frequent protests on the part of the Officer in charge of the Andamanese, money was given to them, or they were induced to sell their bows, etc., for some ridiculously small sum, (and it must be admitted that they were only too willing to do this), and with this money liquor was purchased in the bazaar.

This evil was to a certain extent stopped by the Chief Commissioner making it a penal offence to sell intoxicants to the Andamanese, but even then liquor was given to them by officials who should have known better. On one occasion, in 1883, Bia Mulwa was given two bottles of rum, which he took to the Haddo Home.

Several cases have occurred of persons having connexion with the Andamanese women, and it has been such a common amusement for a few people on Ross Island to make the Andamanese boys drunk, that I have had to prohibit the Andamanese from visiting that Island.

My personal remonstrances having no effect on people who appeared to think it amusing to degrade the aborigines to their own level, Major Temple, the present Chief Commissioner of the Andamans, issued the following Settlement Order on the 14th of May, 1895 :—

"All residents in Port Blair are reminded that it is strictly contrary to the wishes of the Government of India that the Andamanese should in any way be supplied with intoxicating liquor by any person not in responsible charge of them.

" It must be remembered that they are still savages, without self-control, and quick-tempered, and liable to commit, when under the influence of drink, acts of violence which might bring very serious trouble upon any person who might on enquiry be found to have supplied it."

As to whether the Andamanese race are capable, were they not becoming extinct, of any great rise intellectually and in their habits, I think I may answer that they are capable of considerable development, as regards matters of fact. Abstract speculations, and learning which has no tangible or visible result, are distasteful to them, and they are incapable of grasping or entering into such studies: their memories, also, are too defective for them to retain such learning.

In answer to Chapter XXII, Psychology, in " Notes and Queries on Anthropology", I would state :—

The inaccuracy of the Andamanese in relating to another the abstract ideas they have obtained, and their limited capability of forming such abstract ideas for themselves, or of realising the meaning of such when told to them, is a bar to their mental development.

Their attention is easily wearied, and, except when it affects the wants of their daily life, they do not continue an occupation for long; they are restless and fond of novelty and change.

Their memory is soon dulled by lapse of time, though they take notice of occurrences and details which one would not consider likely to impress a savage.

Of periods of time they have, of course, no accurate idea.

They are fairly good colloquial linguists, but not so good as might be expected judging from other aboriginal tribes.

The novelties they see in the Settlement of Port Blair, or in India, unless explained to them, are either dismissed as something belonging to the " Sahibs," and not understood, or else compared with their own utensils, customs, etc. They judge of the motives and actions of others entirely by comparison with their own, (and in this perhaps are not unlike members of higher races), and are unable to appreciate an action done with regard to probabilities in the distant future; with them such action would have reference to an occurrence in the past, or something immediately pressing.

The children are, as regards their quickness in learning, perhaps slightly in advance of the ordinary stupid English country school children, but are nothing like as precocious as the children of the Natives of India. Their ability for absorbing abstract and school learning appears to cease at about 18 years of age, though they do not always forget what they have learnt, and are often improved mentally by their education; but even the most intelligent, after attaining about 35 years of age, appear to lose their acquired intelligence and sink to the level of the other savages (who, however, are by no means fools).

In no single study can they be compared favourably with Europeans; science, religion, and trade being probably their worst points.

They are fairly honest, amongst each other, but consider the property of persons not Andamanese as a fair prey. Their truthfulness is on a par with their honesty. If not influenced by fear, and their minds not prejudiced by leading questions, they will generally tell the truth about what they know, but if asked about things of which they are ignorant, they will at first answer that they do not know, and then, if further pressed, will give such answer as they think the questioner would like. This latter mode of untruthfulness they have probably learnt from the convicts, at least to a greater extent than they used it before our advent.

They are, on the whole, an affectionate race, though that affection is short-lived, and with them absence certainly does not make the heart grow fonder. They are such creatures of impulse, and so free from any legal or moral restraint, that they are accustomed to act on their impulses, and the least thing will turn their affection for a person into anger against him.

Though individuals are plucky, courage is not a strong point of the Andamanese character.

They are unable to reason outside their own experience, and have little power of generalisation.

Education makes little impression on the men, and they are at all times willing and anxious to return to their savage state, but the women, when educated and brought up in European families, prefer that life, and do not care to return to the jungle, assimilating in habits and ideas with the Natives of India.

In the construction of their weapons, utensils, etc., they act according to the precedents established by their forefathers, and even when obvious improvements on their own methods are pointed out to them, they are slow to adopt them although their own personal comfort is affected. They have, at least, taken kindly to our medicines and treatment in hospital, and no doubt, were it possible to educate generation after generation, they would considerably alter for the better in time. They have strong will power, every man being a law unto himself, and are very loth to fall in with the ideas of others; they are not very highly imaginative, generally repeating with alterations ideas which have been handed down to them, and they have little originality.

The Öngés appear to be the least conservative of the Groups of Tribes, being apparently ready to exchange their own customs for anything which they find to be better.

Their speech is voluble, and they are emotional and easily excited; while slightly affected by dreams, in the truth of which they partially believe, they are not subject to mental or other illusions, and are very seldom somnambulists.

I have been frequently asked, "Why are the Andamanese race dying out?" The reason has generally been supposed to be, "On account of the syphilis introduced among them by the convicts," but I do not entirely agree with this.

Syphilis by itself would not have exterminated the race, for we find that it has been introduced at some remote period in the Little Andaman, and the aborigines there are numerous and fertile, and the children survive their birth; but there have been no Settlements on the Little Andaman, nor have the Öngés made any alterations in their modes of living or their foods.

The epidemics of measles and Russian influenza killed off many of the race in the Great Andaman, and weakened the constitutions of others, but without these epidemics the race was becoming extinct and they only hastened its end.

The Andamanese have had no fresh blood for many centuries, and continued in-breeding has weakened their constitutions. The savage, far from being, as people often suppose, a robust man, is generally very delicate. He can do certain surprising feats in the water or on land because he is accustomed to do them, but he cannot compare with a European in his endurance of new hardships and altered circumstances. Had the Andamanese been left entirely alone, no doubt they would have continued to exist for many centuries in the same state, and it is possible that the Öngés of the Little Andaman, if so left alone, may do so, and as we require nothing from them except that they should be friendly, and help instead of massacring the crews of shipwrecked vessels, care should be taken that this tribe is not interfered with more than is absolutely necessary ; but with the aborigines of the Great Andaman circumstances were different.

It was found necessary, on our occupation of the Islands in 1858 to prevent the Andamanese from opposing the development of the Settlement, from murdering the convicts, and, later on, from plundering.

They were then utilised in capturing runaway convicts, and to compensate them for the annexation of their country, and to cement and continue the friendly relations established with them, Homes for them to which they were encouraged to resort, were established with the best intentions. These Homes, however, were most deleterious, in them the Andamanese learnt to smoke, contracted new diseases, and were given new foods to which they were unaccustomed. Their customs and modes of life were also altered ; several well-meaning but mistaken persons were anxious that they should change their mode of life entirely, and should settle down to agriculture.

They were even to be forced to do this, in short to be fitted to a bed of Procrustes, regardless of the results.

In their own jungles they were well sheltered from the cold winds and storms by the forest, in the depths of which little wind can penetrate; we dragged them out of these and made them live in open clearings at all times of the year.

The Ár-*yáuto*, being more accustomed to exposure, have survived the longest, but the Éremtága Septs at once succumbed to chest diseases, and inflammatory ailments caused by chills. Further, the change of diet, etc., appears to have rendered the men sterile, and syphilis aiding, in the few instances in which children are born, they do not survive.

There is an old and well-known chemical experiment in which a warm concentrated solution of sulphate of soda is boiled in a glass tube drawn out at one end. While ebullition is proceeding freely, the tube is hermetically sealed, and by this means is exhausted of air. The solution when left to itself cools without the solid being precipitated, although the liquid is *supersaturated*. But if the end of the tube be broken off and air allowed to enter, crystallisation immediately commences at the surface, and is quickly propagated through the whole length of the tube.

The Andamanese race are like this solution. So long as they were left to themselves and not in any way interfered with by outside influences, or their customs, food, etc., altered, they would continue to live; but when we came amongst them and admitted the air of the outside world, with consequent changes, to suit our necessities, not theirs, they lost their vitality, which was wholly dependent on being untouched, and the end of the race came.

CPSIA information can be obtained
at www.ICGtesting.com
Printed in the USA
LVHW081213060119
602919LV00009B/155/P